IMMIGRATION, EMIGRATION, AND MIGRATION

NOMOS

LVII

NOMOS

Harvard University Press
I   *Authority* 1958, reissued in 1982 by Greenwood Press

The Liberal Arts Press
II   *Community* 1959
III   *Responsibility* 1960

Atherton Press
IV   *Liberty* 1962
V   *The Public Interest* 1962
VI   *Justice* 1963, reissued in 1974
VII   *Rational Decision* 1964
VIII   *Revolution* 1966
IX   *Equality* 1967
X   *Representation* 1968
XI   *Voluntary Associations* 1969
XII   *Political and Legal Obligation* 1970
XIII   *Privacy* 1971

Aldine-Atherton Press
XIV   *Coercion* 1972

Lieber-Atherton Press
XV   *The Limits of Law* 1974
XVI   *Participation in Politics* 1975

New York University Press
XVII   *Human Nature in Politics* 1977
XVIII   *Due Process* 1977
XIX   *Anarchism* 1978
XX   *Constitutionalism* 1979
XXI   *Compromise in Ethics, Law, and Politics* 1979
XXII   *Property* 1980
XXIII   *Human Rights* 1981

NOMOS LVII

Yearbook of the American Society for Political and Legal Philosophy

IMMIGRATION, EMIGRATION, AND MIGRATION

Edited by

Jack Knight

NEW YORK UNIVERSITY PRESS • *New York*

NEW YORK UNIVERSITY PRESS
New York
www.nyupress.org

References to Internet websites (URLs) were accurate at the time of writing. Neither the author nor New York University Press is responsible for URLs that may have expired or changed since the manuscript was prepared.

ISBN: 978-1-4798-6095-1

For Library of Congress Cataloging-in-Publication data, please contact the Library of Congress.

New York University Press books are printed on acid-free paper, and their binding materials are chosen for strength and durability. We strive to use environmentally responsible suppliers and materials to the greatest extent possible in publishing our books.

Manufactured in the United States of America

10 9 8 7 6 5 4 3 2 1

Also available as an ebook

CONTENTS

PART III. IMMIGRATION AND LEGITIMATE INTERNATIONAL INSTITUTIONS

PREFACE

JACK KNIGHT

This volume of NOMOS—the fifty-seventh in the series—emerged from papers and commentaries given at the annual meeting of the American Society for Political and Legal Philosophy in New Orleans, Louisiana, on January 4, 2013, held in conjunction with the annual meeting of the American Association of Law Schools. Our topic, "Immigration, Emigration, and Migration" was selected by the Society's membership.

The conference consisted of three panels, corresponding to the three parts of this volume: (1) "Why Do States Have the Right to Control Immigration?," (2) "Law's Migrations, Mobilities, and Borders," and (3) "Immigration and Legitimate International Institutions." The volume includes revised versions of the principal papers delivered at that conference by Sarah Song, Judith Resnik, and Thomas Christiano. It also includes essays that developed out of the original commentaries on those papers by Adam B. Cox, Michael Blake, James Bohman, Jennifer Hochschild, and Cristina M. Rodríguez. I am grateful to all these authors for their insightful contributions.

Thanks are also due to the editors and production team at New York University Press, and particularly to Caelyn Cobb. On behalf of the Society, I wish to express gratitude for the Press's ongoing support for the series and the tradition of interdisciplinary scholarship that it represents.

Finally, thanks to Andrew Rehfeld of Washington University in St. Louis for organizing the original conference with me and to Samuel Bagg of Duke University for providing expert assistance during the editorial and production phases of this volume.

CONTRIBUTORS

MICHAEL BLAKE
Professor of Philosophy and Public Affairs, University of Washington

JAMES BOHMAN
Danforth Professor of Philosophy, St. Louis University

THOMAS CHRISTIANO
Professor of Philosophy, University of Arizona

ADAM B. COX
Robert A. Kindler Professor of Law, New York University

JENNIFER L. HOCHSCHILD
Henry LaBarre Jayne Professor of Government and Professor of African and African American Studies, Harvard University

JUDITH RESNIK
Arthur Liman Professor of Law, Yale University

CRISTINA M. RODRÍGUEZ
Leighton Homer Surbeck Professor of Law, Yale University

SARAH SONG
Professor of Law and Political Science, University of California, Berkeley

PART I

WHY DO STATES HAVE THE RIGHT TO CONTROL IMMIGRATION?

1

WHY DOES THE STATE HAVE THE RIGHT TO CONTROL IMMIGRATION?

SARAH SONG

Public debate about immigration proceeds on the assumption that each country has the right to control its own borders. The right to control immigration is broadly assumed to flow from state sovereignty. This view is reflected in early American immigration jurisprudence. In establishing the national government's power over immigration, the U.S. Supreme Court declared, "Every nation has the power, as inherent in sovereignty, and essential to self-preservation, to forbid the entrance of foreigners within its dominion, or to admit them only in such cases and upon such conditions as it may see fit to prescribe."[1] The power to control immigration has been qualified in certain respects by international law, such as in the case of diplomats whose privileges are well-defined in law and over whom the host state's discretion is limited. However, when it comes to the question of the right to exclude foreigners, international law accords enormous discretion to states. While there are constitutional limits in some countries on how noncitizens already inside the territory can be treated, when it comes to foreigners outside the territory, states may act solely on the basis of considerations of advantage or convenience. As Linda Bosniak has observed, this "hard on the outside and soft on the inside" approach is reflected not only in law but also in many normative theories of migration and citizenship: an ethic of inclusion applies to noncitizens inside the territorial boundaries of the state, while an ethic of exclusion applies to those outside.[2]

But what, if anything, justifies the modern state's power over borders? Why, if at all, does the state have the right to control immigration? Many scholars of immigration and citizenship take this question for granted, focusing instead on questions about the substantive content and procedures of immigration law and policy. The reason for this is partly pragmatic. After all, states exist, and they exercise power over borders, whether or not there is a good justification for such exercise. In addition, scholars of migration and citizenship understandably focus their attention on more pressing questions about the substance and procedures of immigration policy. But I also think that many immigration scholars really believe that the state has the right to control its own borders, even if they have not developed the normative grounds of their view.

How, if at all, might the state's right to control immigration be justified? This chapter provides an answer in three sections. First, I examine the earliest immigration law cases in U.S. history in order to uncover the underlying assumptions about sovereignty and immigration control that make up the normative foundations of U.S. immigration law. These cases rely on dominant principles of international law of the day, especially the work of Emer de Vattel. I argue that while these cases make clear the great extent of the state's power over immigration, the leading theorist they rely on falls short of providing adequate normative justification of the state's right to control immigration. In the second section, I turn to contemporary political theory and philosophy for justifications of the right to control immigration. I critically assess three leading arguments, based on (1) cultural and national identity, (2) freedom of association, and (3) property. In the third and final section, I offer an alternative argument based on the idea of democratic self-determination.

I. SOVEREIGNTY AND IMMIGRATION CONTROL IN U.S. IMMIGRATION LAW

The U.S. government's power over immigration—its "plenary power"—was established by the U.S. Supreme Court's decision in the *Chinese Exclusion Case* (1889).[3] This case is a good place to begin our analysis of the normative foundations of the modern state's right to control immigration because it contains the American nation's very first assertion of national sovereignty over immigration. It marked, in Rogers Smith's words, a "significantly novel" and "momentous" shift toward viewing immigration regulations as acts of relatively unbridled national sovereignty, not exercises of the police powers of state governments or the federal commerce power as was the case for much of the nineteenth century.[4] What normative principles ground this assertion of state sovereignty and the power to control immigration?

Chae Chan Ping, a Chinese laborer, came to the United States in 1876, in a period when the Burlingame Treaty of 1868 seemed to permit unrestricted immigration from China. The United States had negotiated the treaty with an eye toward recruiting Chinese laborers and improving trade with China, but racist and nativist sentiments against the Chinese became widespread in California and nationally. In 1882, Congress suspended immigration of Chinese laborers for ten years. Those already in the United States who wished to leave and return were required to obtain certificates to show they had come before November 1880. Chae obtained a certificate in 1887 and returned to his native China. The following year, while he was still abroad, Congress barred the return of Chinese laborers, regardless of whether they had certificates.

Aboard a ship in San Francisco Bay, Chae challenged the 1888 statute in a petition for habeas corpus on two grounds. First, he argued that the statute violated the 1880 treaty provision that Chinese laborers already in the United States could leave and return. Writing for the majority, Justice Field acknowledged the conflict between the treaty and statute but found that although they were on an equal footing, the statute prevailed because it was enacted later in time. Chae's second challenge was that, as a constitutional matter, the 1888 statute was "beyond the competency of Congress to pass it."[5] This case provided the Court with its first opportunity to address directly the question of the federal government's power to exclude foreigners.[6] In setting out the conceptual framework for immigration law, the Court's main concern was to establish the federal government's immigration power under the Constitution, not to question whether the rights of individual aliens might constrain Congress's immigration power.[7]

Justice Field held that the federal government has the power to regulate immigration and that the political branches could exercise this power without being subject to judicial review:

> The power of exclusion of foreigners being an incident of sovereignty belonging to the government of the United States, as part of those sovereign powers delegated by the Constitution, the right to its exercise at any time when, in the judgment of the government, the interests of the country require it, cannot be granted away or restrained on behalf of any one. . . . Whatever license, therefore, Chinese laborers may have obtained, previous to the act of October 1, 1888, to return to the United States after their departure, is held at the will of the government, revocable at any time, at its pleasure. (609)[8]

The principles upon which the Court established Congress's power to control immigration were maxims of international law dominant at the time, which viewed the right to exclude as essential to sovereignty:

> That the government of the United States, through the action of the legislative department, can exclude aliens from its territory is a proposition which we do not think open to controversy. Jurisdiction over its own territory to that extent is an incident of every independent nation. It is a part of its independence. If it could not exclude aliens it would be to that extent subject to the control of another power.[9]

The Court goes on to affirm a virtually unlimited right to exclude, including the exclusion of "foreigners of a different race . . . who will not assimilate with us" and are thereby "dangerous to [the] peace and security" of the nation.[10]

Two years later, in *Nishimura Ekiu v. United States* (1892), the Court expanded the plenary power doctrine in two ways.[11] First, it broadened the plenary power doctrine by applying it to Congress's procedures in the enforcement of immigration laws and not just its substantive rules for admission and exclusion as in the *Chinese Exclusion Case*. Second, it rejected a challenge based on a claim of individual constitutional right. An administrative officer declared that Nishimura was likely to become a public charge, which in turn made her excludable under the statute. She argued that due process required a judicial proceeding.[12] As in the *Chinese Exclusion Case*, the Court invoked principles of international law to establish that the immigration power belonged to the federal government and the political branches in particular:

> It is an accepted maxim of international law, that every sovereign nation has the power, as inherent in sovereignty, and essential to self-preservation, to forbid the entrance of foreigners within its dominions, or to admit them only in such cases and upon such conditions as it may see fit to prescribe. . . . It belongs to the political department of the government.[13]

In establishing the government's immigration power, the Court cites the Swiss author Emer de Vattel, whose *Les droit des gens* (*The Law of Nations*, 1758) was the most important book on international law in the eighteenth century. Vattel was "the favorite authority in American theory of international law" in the first decades after the American founding, and his influence in the United States extended through the nineteenth century.[14] The passages of Vattel cited by the Court in *Nishimura* focus on the right of sovereign nations to refuse entry to foreigners:

> The sovereign may forbid the entrance of his territory either to foreigners in general, or in particular cases, or to certain persons, or for certain particular purposes, according as they may think it advantageous to the state. There is nothing in all this, that does not flow from the rights of domain and sovereignty.[15]

After this passage cited by the Court, Vattel goes on to discuss the example of the Chinese government, which "fearing lest the intercourse of strangers should corrupt the manners of the nation, and impair the maxims of a wise but singular government, forbade all people entering the empire." Such a prohibition was "not at all inconsistent with justice, provided they did not refuse humane assistance to those whom tempest or necessity obliged to approach their frontiers. It was salutary to the nation, without violating the rights of any individual, or even the duties of humanity, which

permit us, in case of competition, to prefer ourselves to others"
(II.94).

Vattel's references to "justice" and "humane assistance" hint at
moral constraints on state sovereignty. He claimed to be following the German author Christian Wolff, whose *Ius gentium method
scientifica pertractatum* (*The Law of Nations Treated According to Scientific Method*, 1749) Vattel expressly sought to develop and extend.
Wolff derived the duty to mutual aid by way of an analogy between
the law of nature among individuals and the law of nature among
states. Wolff's naturalism was influenced by Aristotle and has ante-
cedents in Aquinas, Grotius, and Leibniz. In this tradition, nature
exhibits an order and teleology to which the faculty of reason gives
human beings privileged access.[16] The "law of nations" was simply
the law of nature of *individuals* in the state of nature as applied
to *states*. Vattel adopted this analogy, clinging to the language of
naturalism but limiting its role to the support of individual rights
in a liberal society. Like Wolff, Vattel viewed "a political society"
as "a moral person" with "an understanding and a will of which
it makes use for the conduct of its affairs." When a people con-
fer sovereignty on any one person, they thereby "invest him with
their understanding and will, and make over to him their obligations and rights, so far as relates to the administration of the
state, and to the exercise of the public authority" (I.40).[17] As in
the case of persons, the primary duties of states are (1) to preserve and perfect themselves, and (2) to assist each other in fulfilling those duties each state owed to itself. States should "cultivate
human society," primarily through trade so long as the pursuit of
commerce did not conflict with their primary duties to themselves.
Yet states, like persons, should remain free and independent, constrained by the rules necessary for their common society but otherwise autonomous (I.23). Vattel optimistically suggested that states,
acting upon the principles of natural law alone, would ultimately
form a universal republic: "A real friendship will be seen to reign
among them; and this happy state consists in a mutual affection"
(II.12).

Vattel's optimism was counterbalanced and ultimately out-
weighed by his realism. He acknowledged "most nations aim
only to strengthen and enrich themselves at the expense of others" (II.16). Self-interest prevents states from adhering to the

principle of mutual aid in foreign affairs. Instead, he suggests that states should rely on a morally less appealing but more workable vision of a world order based on a balance of power. In doing so, he repudiated Wolff's idea of a *civitas maxima* as the foundation of the voluntary law of nations in favor of a system of sovereign states based on a balance of power.[18] Vattel emphasized that while nations, like individuals, have a general duty of assistance to others, this duty was limited by the perfect right of a state to its own self-preservation and self-perfection.[19] The duty of mutual aid is a contingent obligation, extending only insofar as a nation's liberty and well-being permit. Vattel derives moral obligation not from an external source but from what he viewed as man's most basic motive: self-love and a desire for the happiness of a perfect soul.[20] He applied this very same motive to nations: a nation's duty of self-preservation and self-perfection could be derived only from its basic self-interest and its desire to attain the highest level of national happiness. Like individuals, nations could attain collective happiness only by developing more enlightened forms of self-interest, forms that take into account the well-being of other nations but that make the national interest primary.[21]

Wolff and Vattel were the first to provide an explicit articulation of the principle of nonintervention, the key element of Westphalian sovereignty. The fundamental norm of Westphalian sovereignty is that "states exist in specific territories, within which domestic political authorities are the sole arbiters of legitimate behavior."[22] Vattel argued that no state had the right to intervene in the domestic affairs of other states. Although he adopts an argument made earlier by Pufendorf, Vattel is frequently credited with giving the principle of the equality of sovereign states the prominence it has had in international law ever since. Reasoning by analogy, he claimed that just as men are equal in the state of nature, states are also equal, regardless of whether they are small republics or large kingdoms. Vattel was, of course, aware that states are actually vastly unequal in resources and power, but his point about equality—understood as a normative principle—was that all nations are equally independent, equal in dignity, and equal in the rights and duties they have under natural law.[23]

Vattel's theory of sovereignty has had important implications for the legal regulation of the movement of goods and people across borders. A state's duty to self-preservation and self-perfection is "perfect": it outweighs the obligation to assist other states in their efforts to preserve and perfect themselves. The state's duty to other states is "imperfect": it does not create an obligation to do anything in particular, and no other state can claim to have been injured by an alleged violation of it. So, for example, while a state ought to enter into mutually advantageous trade relations with other states and sell its products at a "fair price," considerations of self-preservation allow it to limit trade or even reject commerce with other states altogether.

Vattel's realist perspective also has implications for immigration policy. As in the case of trade, a state could decide to close off its borders entirely to strangers, including those seeking a right of passage to "escape from imminent danger" or "procur[e] the means of subsistence," if it proved contrary to the interests of the nation.[24] In considering whether the "exiled or banished" have a "right to dwell somewhere on earth," Vattel erred on the side of asserting a state's right to exclude:

> Every nation has a right to refuse admitting a foreigner into her territory, when he cannot enter it without exposing the nation to evident danger, or doing her a manifest injury. What she owes to herself, the care of her own safety, gives her this right; and in virtue of her natural liberty, it belongs to the nation to judge, whether her circumstances will or will not justify the admission of that foreigner. (I.230)

> Thus also it has a right to send [asylees] elsewhere, if it has just cause to fear that they will corrupt the manners of the citizens, that they will create religious disturbances, or occasion any other disorder, contrary to the public safety. In a word, it has a right, and is even obliged, to follow, in this respect, the suggestions of prudence. (I.231)

These two passages were cited in their entirety by the U.S. Supreme Court in *Fong Yue Ting v. United States* (1893) to expand the U.S. government's power over immigration.[25] In this case, the Court expanded plenary power beyond the *exclusion* of foreigners outside the territory to *deportation* of resident aliens already inside the U.S. territory. An 1892 statute had extended the ban on Chinese immigration for ten years. Those already residing in the United States could stay only if they could get a white witness to testify to their pre-1892 residency. Fong and two other Chinese laborers claimed pre-1892 residency but were unable to produce white witnesses.

Writing for the majority, Justice Gray rejected Fong's constitutional challenge to the white witness rule, finding no meaningful distinction between the power to exclude a noncitizen outside the territory and the power to deport a noncitizen already present in the territory: "The power to exclude aliens and the power to expel them rest upon one foundation, are derived from one source, are supported by the same reasons, and are in truth but parts of one and the same power."[26] Relying on both the *Chinese Exclusion Case* and *Nishimura,* Justice Gray concluded that the political branches could continue to regulate immigration immune from judicial review. In a subsequent case, *Yamataya v. Fisher* (1903), the Court suggested that a noncitizen already inside the U.S. territory who objected to deportation procedures might have some success.[27] While leaving the plenary power doctrine untouched, the Court refused to permit Yamataya's deportation on two grounds: (1) aliens inside the United States can invoke more constitutional safeguards than aliens outside the territory, and (2) courts reviewing deportation orders should examine procedural due process questions more closely than substantive immigration rules.[28]

Taken together, these four foundational immigration law cases suggested constitutional objections by foreigners *outside* the United States would not be successful, but foreigners *inside* the United States might have some success in challenging deportation orders.[29] We have seen how the Court, drawing on Vattel, established the federal government's immigration power by declaring it to be "inherent in sovereignty." The right to exclude foreigners was simply assumed to be crucial to the self-preservation of states. Yet, neither the Court nor the key theorist cited by the Court provides a compelling justification for the state's right to control immigration.

Vattel himself viewed territorial sovereignty as analogous to private property, but what he says is more metaphorical than adequate to the task of justifying territorial sovereignty. While he distinguishes between the concepts of sovereign rule (*empire*) and ownership (*domain*) of the national territory, he tends to emphasize their interrelatedness. He defines the concepts in the following way:

1. The *domain*, by virtue of which the nation alone may use this country for the supply of its necessities, may dispose of it as it thinks proper, and derive from it every advantage it is capable of yielding.
2. The *empire*, or the right of sovereign command, by which the nation directs and regulates at its pleasure every thing that passes in the country. (I.204)

Vattel also emphasizes the connection between ownership and sovereignty in discussing how a nation comes to acquire sovereignty: "When a nation takes possession of a country to which no prior owner can lay claim, it is considered as acquiring the *empire* or sovereignty of it, at the same time with the *domain* . . . . The whole space over which a nation extends its government, becomes the seat of its jurisdiction, and is called its *territory*" (I.205). A nation may acquire sovereignty by another route: "a number of free families" who were "previously in possession of the domain" may "unite for the purpose of forming a nation or state" and thereby "acquire the sovereignty over the whole country they inhabit" (I.206). Thereafter, although different types of property (private, common, joint) may be legally established within the national territory, the nation continues to enjoy a kind of ownership not only over the land but also over everything within its territory that is "susceptible of ownership," including goods to which private individuals hold legal title (I.235).

Vattel's blurring of ownership and sovereignty must be understood in historical context. While political rule and property ownership were distinguished for some purposes by the Roman law terms *imperium* and *dominium*, the latter term also connoted rule, especially in medieval usage, that was retained in the English word "dominions" and the technical use of *dominium* in jurisprudence to denote the territorial dimension of sovereignty. While property came to be thought of as private and thus devoid of public authority, ownership of certain property carried with it the franchise until modern times. And because the state's sovereign authority extended not only over people but also over land, conceptions of sovereignty continued to include attributes of ownership in addition to jurisdiction and legislation. As Whelan observes, in the seventeenth and eighteenth centuries, although the two terms are distinguished, there is a substantial amount of conceptual overlap, usually to the advantage of absolutist and patrimonial theories, which in one way or another portray the ruler as not only the sovereign but also the owner of his country.[30]

How, then, might we understand Vattel's emphasis on the connection between sovereignty and "public ownership of a country" if not for the reason of defending absolutist and patrimonial theories, which he explicitly rejected? One reason for emphasizing the connection is that sovereign power includes some specific powers that appear to be derived from the nation's collective ownership of the goods in its territory (e.g., the power of eminent domain and the power of taxation). Second, it supports Vattel's derivation of the state's *right to exclude* aliens from the state's *right of ownership* of the country:

> Since the lord of the territory may, whenever he thinks proper, forbid its being entered, he has no doubt a power to annex what conditions he pleased to the permission to enter. This . . . is a consequence of the right of domain. Can it be necessary to add, that the owner of the territory ought in this instance to respect the duties of humanity? The case is the same with all rights whatever: the proprietor may use them at his discretion.[31]

Vattel's derivation proceeds by way of analogy: just as a property owner can exclude others from his property, the sovereign state can exclude foreigners from its territory. As I will argue later, while metaphorically alluring, the property argument for a state's right to exclude falls short as a convincing justification of the state's right to control borders. I turn now to take up the question to which Vattel and early American immigration jurisprudence do not provide a satisfactory answer: What, if anything, justifies the modern state's right to control immigration?

II. CONTEMPORARY JUSTIFICATIONS OF A STATE'S RIGHT TO CONTROL IMMIGRATION

This section examines three leading normative justifications of a state's right to control immigration, based on three distinct grounds (1) cultural and national identity, (2) freedom of association, and (3) property. I discuss the limits of these arguments with the aim of setting the stage for an alternative justification in the final section of the chapter.

A. Cultural and National Identity

In his well-known discussion of the idea of membership, Michael Walzer offers a defense of the state's right to control immigration based on the value of *distinctive cultures and groups*:

> The distinctiveness of cultures and groups depends upon closure and, without it, cannot be conceived as a stable feature of human life. If this distinctiveness is a value, as most people . . . seem to believe, then closure must be permitted somewhere. At some level of political organization, something like the sovereign state must take shape and claim the authority to make its own admissions policy, to control and sometimes restrain the flow of immigrants.[32]

Walzer's argument here assumes that a central purpose of states is the protection of distinctive cultures and groups. Combined with the empirical premise that protection of distinctive cultures "depends upon closure," he concludes that "something like the sovereign state" must form and claim the authority to make its own admissions policy.

Walzer echoes Vattel in suggesting the right to control immigration flows from state sovereignty and then moves to offer a justification of this right in terms of cultural preservation:

> Admission and exclusion are at the core of communal independence. They suggest the deepest meaning of self-determination. Without them, there could not be *communities of character*, historically stable, ongoing associations of men and women with some special commitment to one another and some special sense of their common life.[33]

For Walzer, the normative ground for a state's right to control immigration is the preservation of a distinctive communal identity. As for the extent of this right, Walzer recognizes that self-determination is "not absolute": it is subject "both to internal decisions by the members themselves" and to "the external principle of mutual aid."[34] If we look at Walzer's discussion of particular examples, the constraints on the state's right to exclude appear to be quite weak. The right of nations to cultural self-determination is taken to be consistent with the "White Australia" policy in which the Australian government imposed racial restrictions in its immigration policy.[35] It is not surprising that an account of state sovereignty based on preserving the "distinctiveness of cultures and groups" would include racial exclusion in light of the historical salience of race to national identity.

Political theorist David Miller has developed the cultural argument for a state's right to control borders in more explicitly *nationalist* terms focusing on language and what he calls "public culture." Miller views the right to control immigration as part of a more general theory of a state's territorial rights, which includes control over the land itself, resources on the land, and the movement of people and things across territorial borders. Miller takes the following as his starting premises:

1. The public culture of many societies is worth preserving.
2. Citizens of these societies have an interest in controlling "the way that their nation develops, including the values that are contained in the public culture."[36]

He points to the example of Québec. The French language is a vital part of Québécois culture and identity. Québécois citizens have good reason to "differentiate sharply among prospective immigrants between those who speak the national language and those who don't." Miller leaves open how restrictive an immigration policy has to be in order to maintain "cultural continuity"; it will depend on "the empirical question of how easy or difficult it is to create a symbiosis between the existing public culture and the new cultural values of the immigrants."[37]

On the nationalist account, a state's right to control immigration is the collective right of nations with deep ties to the territory.

There are at least two ways that proponents of such a view have conceived of the relationship between the nation and territory. The first is an argument about *national identity.* Territory is taken to be central to the development of national identity. On Miller's account, there is a two-way interaction between a state's territory and the culture of the people who live on it. On the one hand, the culture adapts to the territory: whether the climate is hot or cold or whether the territory landlocked or open to the sea will encourage the development of certain customs and discourage others. On the other hand, the territory itself will be shaped and reshaped according to the "cultural priorities" of the people as they make their lives upon the land. Their "transformation" of the land may not be intentional or coordinated, but it nonetheless reflects their "cultural values." Through living on and shaping the land, the people endow it "with meaning by virtue of significant events that have occurred there, monuments that have been built, poems, novels, and paintings that capture particular places or types of landscape"; the inhabitants of a land come to attach value to living in a place that is rich in historical meaning.[38] The philosopher Chaim Gans makes a similar claim: the fact that a territory is "of primary importance in forming the historical identity of the group" is considered "a strong enough reason for the purposes of determining sovereignty over it."[39]

A second way that proponents of the nationalist account of territorial rights have connected nations and territory is a quasi-Lockean argument about *labor.* It is not only in virtue of mixing my labor with the land but also in virtue of my adding value by laboring on a piece of land that I come to have a legitimate claim of ownership over it. In Locke's well-known formulation:

> The *labor* of his body, and the *work* of his hands, we may say, are properly his. Whatsoever then he removes out of the state that nature hath provided, and left it in, he hath mixed his *labor* with, and joined to it something that is his own, and thereby makes it his *property* . . . . [I]t is *labor* indeed that *puts the difference of value* on every thing.[40]

On Locke's account, labor is the ground for private property rights. Building on Locke's labor theory of value, Tamar Meisels has developed a nationalist theory of territorial rights based on the concept of "settlement." Settlement refers not only to the physical presence of individuals on a piece of land but also to "the existence of a permanent physical infrastructure," which members of the nation have constructed. Sometimes such settlements are built in a conscious, premeditated manner, but more often than not they "simply evolve over time" as individuals or members of particular groups settle in a given place.[41] Similarly, Miller argues that as the members of the nation "transform" the land, thereby adding value to it, "the nation as a whole has a legitimate claim to the enhanced value that the territory now has."[42]

It is important to note that Meisels's and Miller's arguments are *quasi*-Lockean. While they are inspired by Locke's labor theory of value, their appeal to Lockean principles is more metaphorical than literal.[43] What is crucial to the nationalist justification is the *expressive* element reflected in claims of "settlement" (Meisels) or "transformation" (Miller). Acts of settlement/transformation express a particular national identity. By working the land, members of a nation are not simply adding value to it; they are, as Meisels puts it, "shaping the territory so as to coincide with a particular way of life." For example, nations must "choose between various modes of architecture and forms of agriculture," as well as "whether to industrialize, and, if so, to what extent and in what fields" and "whether to build churches or synagogues or mosques."[44] The enhanced value cannot be separated from the territory itself. Because the value added by the labor of the nation is, in Miller's words, "*embodied* in cultivated fields, buildings, roads, waterways, and all the rest," there is no way for the nation to retain that enhanced value without also retaining the territory. Thus, the case for a nation's right over the relevant territory is "straightforward": such a right "gives members of the nation continuing access to places that are especially significant to them, and it allows choices to be made over how these sites are to be protected and managed."[45]

Nationalist arguments for a state's right to control immigration suffer from at least four problems. First, they fail to account for the right of *collective* ownership, which is crucial for the nationalist account to go through. The labor of "settlement" and the work of "transformation" of the land are performed by *individuals*, not by "the nation." So why should the collective entity of "the nation" gain property rights over the territory and not the particular individuals who actually performed the labor?

Second, why is settlement alone a morally sufficient ground for private property rights and rights of territorial jurisdiction? The Lockean view is that productive use of land is what generates legitimate entitlements to land. Locke himself famously suggested that "nine tenths . . . nay . . . ninety-nine hundredths" of the value of "the products of the earth useful to the life of man" is the result of human labor, and value-enhancing labor upon previously unowned land grounds a legitimate entitlement to it.[46] Miller and Meisels adopt this Lockean view in suggesting that members of the nation enhance the value of the land they work and build upon. But why should such acts entitle one to exclusive ownership of the land and not simply partial ownership proportional to the value one has added? The more basic question is why productive use of the land and other resources should be the sole or primary basis for generating rights to property and territorial jurisdiction.

A related third weakness of the quasi-Lockean "settlement" argument is its suggestion that *any group* that transforms the land is entitled to territorial control, including over territory that an existing state already claims territorial rights over. For example, if Korean immigrants in Los Angeles construct houses, restaurants, and monuments expressing their particular culture and call it Little Korea, do they thereby acquire territorial rights over that piece of Los Angeles? Many of us would say that while Korean Americans have a legitimate claim to private property rights over the fruits of their labor, they do not have territorial rights over the parts of Los Angeles they have worked. The nationalist might respond that immigrants reside and labor in the national territory with the existing nation's consent, and under the terms of that contract, their labor grounds a claim to some property rights but not territorial rights over the land they work. To make this response, however, nationalists would have to prioritize consent over the role of value-enhancing labor in establishing a claim to territorial control.

Finally, Meisels and Miller do not explain why labor confers rights of *territorial jurisdiction* over an entire territory rather than simply rights of *private property*. Imagine that a group of people settle in an uninhabited part of Oregon and build houses, schools, and places of worship as well as till fields and plant crops. Could they then declare that they have rights of territorial jurisdiction over Oregon? We tend not to think of unoccupied land within the borders of an existing state as *terra nullius*. Accounts based on current settlement would permit these occupiers to stay and even give them exclusive rights to determine the political destiny of the land they've occupied. As Anna Stilz has argued, if the only rationale for the acquisition of jurisdictional rights is that land has been labored upon, the state cannot have jurisdiction over undeveloped areas.[47]

We need a way to distinguish *property rights in the strict sense* (the right to control, use, and benefit from a particular resource) and *rights of jurisdiction* (the right to make first-order rules that define property rights and other rights and to interpret and enforce those rules, as well as second-order rules about who holds jurisdiction over what persons and resources). As Allen Buchanan has argued, a compelling theory of territorial rights and boundaries must distinguish between (1) jurisdictional authority (the right to make, adjudicate, and enforce legal rules within a domain), (2) metajurisdictional authority (the right to create and alter jurisdictions, including geographic jurisdictions), and (3) property rights of individuals and groups within jurisdictions.[48] I will return to the property rights versus jurisdictional rights distinction later in examining attempts to ground the state's right to control immigration in more literal interpretations of Locke's theory of property.

B. Freedom of Association

Some have defended the state's right to control immigration by appealing to the value of freedom of association. Christopher Heath Wellman makes such a case, beginning with the premise:

1. Legitimate states are entitled to political self-determination.

While he does not provide a defense of the principle of political self-determination, he emphasizes that the right of self-determination is owed to a group of people not merely in virtue of their standing as autonomous individuals but also in virtue of their special group role or standing. For example, it would be wrong for Sweden to forcibly annex Norway not only because doing so fails to respect the individual autonomy of Norwegians but also because it fails to respect their special standing as Norwegian citizens: "their collective achievement of maintaining a political institution that adequately protects the human rights of all Norwegians."[49] I will return to the importance of self-determination for a defense of the state's right to control borders in the final section of the chapter.

Wellman's defense of a state's right to control borders rests on two additional premises:

2. Freedom of association is an integral component of self-determination.
3. Freedom of association includes not only the right to associate but also the right to dissociate.

The premise that freedom of association is a key part of self-determination is reflected in "the widespread conviction that each of us enjoys a privileged position of moral dominion over our self-regarding affairs, a position which entitles us to freedom of association."[50] Wellman argues that freedom of association includes both the right to *include* and the right to *exclude* potential associates, quoting Stuart White's discussion of freedom of association: "With the freedom to associate, however, there comes the freedom to refuse association. When a group of people gets together to form an association of some kind (e.g., a religious association, a trade union, a sports club), they will frequently wish to exclude some people from joining their association. What makes it *their* association, serving their purposes, is that they can exercise this 'right to exclude.'"[51] White's discussion centers on intimate and religious associations within one political society.

Wellman's innovation is to extend the value of freedom of association to the state itself, arguing by way of analogy with small-scale associations. We would vehemently object if a government agency were to force an individual to marry another against her will. Similarly, we would object if a golf club were forced to admit members against its will. He concludes:

> Just as an individual may permissibly choose whom (if anyone) to marry, and a golf club may choose whom (if anyone) to admit as

new members, a group of fellow citizens is entitled to determine whom (if anyone) to admit into their country.[52]

For the very same reason an individual can reject a suitor, citizens of a legitimate state can reject foreigners who seek to enter. Citizens have the presumptive right, Wellman argues, to "close doors to all potential immigrants, even refugees desperately seeking asylum from incompetent or corrupt political regimes that are either unable or unwilling to protect their citizens' basic moral rights."[53]

Insofar as Wellman's argument relies on an analogy with marriage, religious groups, and golf clubs, it is unconvincing. First, his analogy runs together crucial differences between these associations and the political community. The latter is not an intimate or small-scale association. I do not share a home, a place of worship, or a sports club with all my compatriots. A political community is typically large enough that I need not have intimate or regular contact with citizens I do not know. Wellman acknowledges that our interest in not being forced into association with others applies most clearly in the case of intimate associations, but he maintains that this objection does not defeat the presumptive right of free association of large-scale associations, such as the state. To make his case, Wellman draws on White's discussion of intimate and religious associations, but on closer inspection, we see that what is at stake for intimate and religious associations is unique to those associations and does not apply to the political community:

> If the formation of a specific association is essential to the individual's ability to exercise properly his/her *liberties of conscience and expression*, or to his/her ability to *form intimate attachments*, then exclusion rules which are genuinely necessary to protect the association's primary purposes have an especially strong presumption of legitimacy.[54]

The case for freedom of association rests in part on the nature of the association's *purpose*. We respect freedom of association in the marital context because of the intimate purpose of such associations, and we respect freedom of association in the religious context on account of the expressive purpose of such associations. But

the liberal state is not an intimate association, nor is it straightfor-
wardly an expressive association. As Sarah Fine has argued, while
the liberal state is committed to certain values (e.g., toleration,
equality before the law, and individual liberty), there is reasonable disagreement about the basic list and ranking of such values.[55]
Even if there were consensus on a list and ranking, adherence to
such values is not sufficient to suggest that the state is an expressive
association of the kind religious associations are—namely, associations committed to and expressive of comprehensive religious and
moral doctrines.

Wellman acknowledges that freedom of association for groups
that are "intimate or related to liberty of conscience and expression" is especially valuable, but he argues that freedom of association should not be restricted to these contexts. To make his case,
he offers another analogy, this time between the golf club and the
state:

> If no one doubts that golf clubs have a presumptive right to exclude
> others, then there seems no reason to suspect that a group of citi-
> zens cannot also have the right to freedom of association, even if
> control over membership in a country is not nearly as significant as
> control regarding one's spouse.[56]

But the political community is distinct from a golf club in at least
two morally important respects. First, the state is not a voluntary
association. Most of us live and die in the countries we are born citizens of. This lack of voluntariness to political membership raises
the stakes of membership. Exclusion from a particular state can
be hugely consequential in a way that exclusion from a golf club
typically is not.[57] Outsiders have significant interests in becoming members, and exclusion brings high costs (and not just costs
associated with expressive or intimate purposes) to nonmembers.
Another reason that a state is different from a golf club is that
states don't exist in a competitive environment conducive to market entrants. If a golf club refuses to admit me, I can form my own
or join another. If a state refuses to admit me, I can neither form
my own nor easily join another.

In light of these crucial disanalogies between the state and
small-scale associations such as marriage, religious groups, and

golf clubs, the burden rests on proponents of the free association argument to elaborate why freedom of association remains so fundamental for states even if citizens will typically never have anything approaching face-to-face relations with the vast majority of her compatriots. Wellman suggests two reasons. First, the *sheer size* of the group dramatically shapes the experience of being a member. For example, as a private golf club increases its membership, there will be more wear and tear on the golf course. Similarly, as a political state increases the number of new members, citizens' lives will be affected by population density. This concern about "wear and tear" associated with increased membership depends on empirical considerations, and it does not deliver a principled justification for a state's right to control its own borders.

A second reason has to do with the power to shape the association's future. Control over rules of admission and membership are significant in part because new members will subsequently have a say in how the association is organized. Members have a say not only in determining future membership but also in determining the future course of the association more generally, including decisions about "the host state's cultural make-up, the way its economy functions, and/or how its political system operates." Wellman emphasizes that it is this connection between a group's membership and its future direction that underscores why freedom of association is "such an integral component of self-determination."[58] Wellman's point about the state's "cultural make-up" brings him remarkably close to Walzer's and Miller's views, which I find unpersuasive for reasons discussed earlier. Wellman is on to something when he raises the future direction of how the political system operates, but I think developing this point requires elaborating the connection between self-determination and democracy. A democratic association is a distinctive type of association, and I believe a more compelling case for the state's right to control borders can be found by examining the conditions of democratic association.

A second major weakness of Wellman's argument is the absence of any explicit justification for the state's jurisdictional rights over its territory of which the right to control immigration is a part. He blurs together the right to exclude those who want to be admitted to *citizenship* or *political membership* and the right to exclude those who want to be admitted to the state's *territory*. But there are distinctive considerations that apply to justifying the state's right to control the movement of people into and within its territory. Consider again the case of golf clubs. Assuming a golf club has the right of ownership over a parcel of land, club members have not only the presumptive right to exclude outsiders from admission to club membership but also the right to exclude outsiders from entering and using the club's property. Club members, as joint owners of the club, have the right to control club property. Wellman implies a similar ownership-based account of territorial rights of the political community when he says: "My right to freedom of movement does not entitle me to enter your house without your permission . . . so why think this right gives me a valid claim to enter a foreign country without that country's permission?"[59] Just as an individual property owner is entitled to exclude outsiders from his house, members of a country are entitled to exclude outsiders from entering the country. Wellman's analogy runs together two types of rights that need to be distinguished, private property rights and rights of territorial jurisdiction.[60] Territorial rights are distinctive to states, and analogies with private property rights do not get us very far.

C. Property

Another defense of the state's right to control immigration appeals to the concept of property. These arguments draw literally rather than metaphorically upon Locke's theory of property and political authority. We can distinguish individualist and collectivist Lockean theories of territorial rights.

Consider first the *individualist* Lockean account. According to Locke's well-known theory of property, the right to private property is viewed as a natural, prepolitical right. Locke begins from the theological premise that God gave the earth to humankind in common and argues that individuals come to hold private property rights in particular parcels of land in virtue of mixing their labor with and adding value to that land.[61] How does he move from a group of individuals with a natural right of private property over parcels of land to the collective entity of the state with territorial rights over land and people? The answer is Locke's theory of the social contract: individual property owners make a voluntary agreement with one another in order to form a state with territorial jurisdiction. It is on the basis of voluntary consent that individual property owners give up their rights of jurisdiction over their property to the state. It is worth quoting Locke at length here:

> Every man, when he at first incorporates himself into any commonwealth, he, by uniting himself thereunto, annexed also, and submits to the community, those possessions, which he has, or shall acquire, that do not already belong to any other government: for it would be a direct contradiction, for any one to enter into society with others for the securing and regulating of property; and yet to suppose his land, whose property is to be regulated by the laws of the society, should be exempt from the jurisdiction of that government, to which he himself, the proprietor of the land, is a subject. By the same act therefore, whereby any one unites his person, which was before free, to any commonwealth, by the same he unites his possessions, which were before free, to it also; and *they become, both of them, person and possession, subject to the government and dominion of that common-wealth*, as long as it hath a being.[62]

Individual property owners not only enter into an agreement about the control and use of their respective bundles of property but also enter into a contract to transfer to the state *jurisdictional rights* contained in their bundle of property rights, including rights of lawmaking, enforcement, and adjudication of disputes. On Locke's account, the state's jurisdictional rights are derived from individuals' prepolitical property rights by way of their free consent.

There are several problems with the individualistic Lockean account.[63] First, on the Lockean account, a piece of land can become subject to the state's authority only via the consent of individual property owners, but some individuals occupying a state's territory have not consented to its authority. There will be pockets of anarchists who have actively refused consent to the state's authority, yet continuity of territorial jurisdiction is necessary for the uniform application of the law, which in turn is necessary for government to fulfill its aims.

The way Lockeans have dealt with this problem is to assume either that jurisdiction is already continuous or that there are strong incentives for anarchists to submit to the state's authority. Robert Nozick famously adopted the second move, a move that is ultimately unpersuasive:

> We have discharged our task of explaining how a state would arise from a state of nature without anyone's rights being violated. The moral objections of the individualist anarchist to the minimal state are overcome. It is not an unjust imposition of a monopoly; the *de facto* monopoly grows by an invisible-hand process and by morally permissible means, without anyone's rights being violated and without any claims being made to a special right that others do not possess.[64]

How exactly does this work? The anarchist's objection is that the state's claim to a monopoly on the use of force within the state's territory violates her rights not only because the state claims to be the exclusive holder of the right to punish and exact reparations but also because it forces her to pay for protection that she would rather provide herself. Nozick maintains that anarchists (whom he also calls "independents") can be compelled to join the state voluntarily in exchange for adequate compensation for the loss of utility they experience by having to join. Adopting the concept of compensation from welfare economics, he argues that taking autonomy away from the independents is justified by giving security to those who voluntarily joined the state. The appropriate price of compensation is the amount that would return independents' utility to what it was before they were compelled to join, but rather than asking independents to determine the price themselves, the state would determine a fair price by some other process, based on interpersonal comparisons and trade-offs between the needs of independents and the needs of everyone else.[65] But this move is vulnerable to the very objection Nozick makes against utilitarianism: it fails to take the rights of each and every individual seriously. Nozick's claim that individuals who initially refuse to give their consent to the state can be compelled to join the state for some adequate state-determined compensation fails to respect the rights of the independents.

A second problem with individualistic Lockean accounts of a state's territorial rights is that they assume a piece of land, once subjected to the state's authority, is *perpetually* subjected. Individuals give up not only their *jurisdictional* authority (the right to make, enforce, and adjudicate legal rules within a domain) but also their *metajurisdictional* authority (the right to create or alter jurisdictions, including geographic jurisdictions). While it is the original parties to the social contract who give up both types of rights, the agreement is taken to be binding on all future generations. But this assumption is at odds with Locke's own claim that individuals are by nature "all equal and independent."[66]

Hillel Steiner has taken Locke's "all equal and independent" claim very seriously, arguing that individuals do indeed retain metajurisdictional authority and thereby have the right to exit the state with their property whenever they wish. As he puts it, "Precisely because a nation's territory is legitimately composed of the real estate of its members, the decision of any of them to resign that membership and, as it were, to take their real estate with them is a decision that must be respected."[67] The problem, of course, is that Steiner's solution requires us to abandon any conception of territorial rights as securing stable borders within which a state has a legitimate monopoly on the use of force and the right to establish justice.[68] One might reject Steiner's approach and instead interpret Locke as saying that a social contract that does not bind future generations would fail to live up to the primary purpose for which the political community was created: "for their comfortable, safe, and peaceable living one amongst another, in a secure enjoyment of their properties."[69] If each new member of every generation could secede if she wanted to, the political community could not last. Yet, if we take seriously Locke's insistence on the equal freedom of each individual, it is hard not to conclude that the (individualist) Lockean account of territorial rights fails to provide convincing reasons for believing a state's rights of jurisdiction trump an individual's right to equal freedom.

These difficulties with individualist Lockean accounts get at a deeper problem. In attempting to derive a state's territorial rights from individual property rights, they conflate private property rights with jurisdictional rights. Like the quasi-Lockean nationalist theories, individualist Lockean theories jump from the rights generally conferred by property ownership to the much wider set of jurisdictional and metajurisdictional rights claimed by states.

Take the example of my backyard. Because I own my backyard, I can exclude people from entering it, but my property ownership is insufficient to determine who has the right to make the rules governing my backyard as well as yours.

Does a *collectivist* Lockean theory of territorial rights fare better? While the Lockean argument for territorial rights has typically been understood as an argument about private property rights, Cara Nine argues that there is no reason that a more direct Lockean argument for territorial rights cannot also be made. Her strategy is to argue by analogy between an individual's property rights and a state's territorial rights: the state acquires territorial rights in the same way that individuals acquire property rights. The theory is "collectivist" because it claims that the collective entity of the state can directly acquire rights to land without prior reference to property rights or individual consent. On Nine's account, an agent has a right to land if (1) it is capable of changing the land, thereby creating a relationship with it, and (2) the relationship is morally valuable in terms of the Lockean principles of liberty, desert, and efficiency. The relevant agent in her account of territorial rights is the state, not individual citizens or the nation.

Not just any act upon the land will do; only morally valuable acts upon the land generate a legitimate right to it. Nine emphasizes the state's morally valuable role in making, interpreting, and enforcing property law, which is integral to determining how land is developed, and its role in establishing and maintaining markets, which create value in land and products deriving from the land. The state's territorial rights are justified for the same reason a person's property rights are: "because, on Lockean arguments, they help to realize the values of liberty, desert and efficiency."[70] First, a system of state territorial rights is "the best way to protect and promote liberty," since individual liberty requires "a physical space where the people's values can be brought to bear." The state also has a moral claim to the land based on the principle of desert because the state is "a unique and significant author of the land's value." Finally, a state system of territorial rights can make most efficient use of the land.[71]

Ryan Pevnick also adopts a collectivist Lockean approach with an explicit focus on the issue of immigration. In contrast to Nine's argument by direct analogy, Pevnick adopts a very broad conception of property that he takes as encompassing both private property rights and territorial rights. He begins with the idea of self-determination, arguing that the right of a group to be self-determining can be justified by reference to "the group's *ownership* of goods produced through the labor and contribution of members." He calls this the "associative ownership" view. Pevnick takes the basic Lockean intuition—that we are entitled to the fruits of our labor so long as it does not harm others—to explain why we would allow a voluntary association to make its own decision about its future. Members of the association have produced something that would not have existed but for their labor, and this justifies members' claim to make decisions about the future of the association, including whom to admit as future members.[72]

By adopting a broad conception of property, Pevnick seeks to show that the Lockean intuition underlying an individual's or a voluntary association's claims to ownership can be extended to *states*, even though the latter are nonvoluntary, intergenerational associations. People are born into particular states and simply find themselves subject to the coercive power of the state in whose territory they happen to reside. Pevnick, nonetheless, maintains the plausibility of viewing citizens as "joint owners" of state institutions, analogous to owners of the family farm:

> Like the family farm, the construction of state institutions is a historical project that extends across generations and into which individuals are born. Just as the value of a farm very largely comes from the improvements made on it, so too *the value of membership in a state is very largely a result of the labor and investment of the community.* The citizenry raises resources through taxation and invests those resources in valuable public goods: basic infrastructure, defense, the establishment and maintenance of an effective market, a system of education, and the like . . . these are goods that only exist as a result of the labor and investment of community members.[73]

In contrast to Nine, Pevnick argues it is the labor of *individuals in their role as citizens*, not simply "the state," that grounds the claim of joint ownership over public institutions. Like Miller and Meisels, Pevnick invokes Locke's labor theory of value to ground a state's territorial rights, but he differs from them in steering clear of the idea of the nation in favor of individual citizens. In virtue of their aggregate labor, individual citizens help to create and maintain public goods and institutions, thereby gaining a right of joint ownership. Pevnick takes this ownership claim as grounding a claim to "at least some discretion in making future decisions about how those resources will be used," including whether and to whom the good of membership will be given in the future.[74]

Anticipating the objection that his "associative ownership" view of a state's right to control immigration blurs together rights of territorial jurisdiction and rights of private property, Pevnick acknowledges that we cannot understand the state's territorial jurisdiction as a kind of private property strictly construed. He defines "jurisdiction" as the authority to administer a system of rights, including private property rights, within a given territory, yet he maintains that jurisdiction can still be understood as a claim about *property writ large*. Following Jeremy Waldron, he defines "property" or "ownership" as a general term for "rules that govern people's access to and control of things," such as land, natural resources, the means of production, and manufactured goods, as well as (for some) ideas, inventions, and other intellectual products. So when he calls someone an "owner" of a resource, he is simply saying that she has some bundle of rights over it, and the task is to elaborate the nature of those rights. Pevnick concludes that we should view *jurisdiction* as a kind of *collective property*: "The community as a whole determines how important resources are to be used. These determinations are made on the basis of the social interest through mechanisms of collective decision-making—anything from a leisurely debate among the elders of a tribe to the forming and implementing of a Soviet-style 'Five-Year Plan.'"[75]

There are several major difficulties with Pevnick's and Nine's collectivist Lockean accounts. First, they blur together private property rights and jurisdictional rights, a point I have already belabored. The second problem has to do with the relationship between the collective entity of "the state" and individual members or "owners." Why should the collective entity of the state gain jurisdictional rights over the territory and not the particular individuals who actually performed the labor as agents of the state? How do we get from an aggregation of individual property owners to the collective entity with jurisdictional rights, if not by requiring the consent of individual members or by making certain meta-physical assumptions about the nature of the state? For example, in considering the implications of "associative ownership" for long-term unauthorized migrants, Pevnick implicitly relies on the role of consent. A person's contributions to the maintenance of public institutions are not enough; the consent of existing members seems to be necessary. As he puts it, "In the case of illegal immigrants, by entering the country illicitly such individuals took their place in their community without the consent of the citizenry." While he acknowledges that unauthorized migrants make contributions through working and paying taxes, he contends that citizens have no obligation "to pass ownership of their institutions to illegal immigrants" because the migrants have "put themselves in this situation without the consent of the citizenry."[76] Pevnick's reliance on consent in the treatment of unauthorized migrants reveals that there is more to the claim about self-determination than simply claims about ownership through value-enhancing labor and fair exchange. By viewing claims of jurisdiction as a kind of property claim, Pevnick's account obfuscates what is distinctive about territorial jurisdiction.

Third, Pevnick does well to draw on the idea of self-determination, but his ownership account leaves unanswered important questions about the nature of self-determination. He views the right to self-determination as the right to *democratic* self-determination: the right of individual members to have an *equal* say in the making of the laws to which they are subject. Pevnick relies on an analogy between the state and voluntary associations, but voluntary associations rely on a range of decision-making procedures. For example, a student group or the Rotary Club may make decisions democratically, but a religious organization or a business may concentrate decision-making power in the hands of one or a few. This suggests that collective ownership claims of members support a right to self-determination that is consistent with a range of decision-making procedures, only some of which may be democratic. Another way of putting it is this: the fact of collective ownership alone cannot entail a right to democratic self-determination.[77] Our intuitions about collective ownership suggest that owners are entitled to *some* say in decisions regarding their collective property, but not necessarily an *equal* say.

How, then, do the collective ownership claims of citizens generate a specific right to *democratic* self-determination? Pevnick might reply that the ownership claims of citizens over public institutions they have built are special and thus give citizens a right of democratic self-determination, but this begs the question of how that right is to be justified.

III. THE VALUE OF SELF-DETERMINATION AND A DEMOCRATIC JUSTIFICATION

Another way to justify the state's right to control immigration is as part of a more general right of democratic self-determination of a people. The idea of self-determination stands for the proposition that members of a collective have a *pro tanto* right to make their own decisions about the policies promulgated in their name. Self-determination is a claim about self-rule. I briefly examine different accounts of the idea of self-determination to set the stage for a democratic justification of a state's right to control immigration.

First, on a *holistic* account of self-determination, states are said to have the right of self-determination because states, like persons, are moral entities with the capacity to realize their nature in the pursuit of ends. As discussed earlier, this view is reflected in Wolff and Vattel's arguments for the nonintervention principle in international law, which is based on an analogy between individuals and nations:

> Nations are regarded as individual free persons living in a state of nature. . . . Since by nature all nations are equal, since moreover all men are equal in a moral sense whose rights and obligations are the same; the rights and obligations of all nations are also by nature the same.[78]

The problem here is that states qua states do not think or act in pursuit of ends. Only individual people (or perhaps all sentient beings) think or act, either alone or in groups.[79] Much more needs to be said about the idea of the state as a moral entity before this view can be persuasive.

A second way of approaching a state's right to self-determination is in terms of *individual consent.* As Walzer suggests, "The rights of states rest on the consent of their members. . . . [G]iven a genuine 'contract' it makes sense to say that the territorial integrity and political sovereignty can be defended in exactly the same way as individual life and liberty."[80] If one adopts a contractarian approach, the state's right to self-determination comes to rest on the autonomy of individuals—in particular, the freedom to associate with others in the pursuit of collective ends. As Charles Beitz puts it, "The liberty of states is a consequence of the liberty of persons to associate."[81] As we saw in discussing Wellman's defense of the state's right to control immigration, the familiar problem is that there are few, if any, governments that are genuinely free associations, constituted by the actual consent of all citizens. Indeed, only a small subset of citizens, including immigrants who become naturalized citizens, have actually given their consent. As numerous critics have argued, territorial states are not voluntary associations. People do not freely create, join, and exit them. Most of the world's people (roughly 97 percent) live out their lives in the countries they happened to be born citizens of. One might respond by acknowledging that states are not free associations while also maintaining that state institutions derive their legitimacy from periodic affirmation via elections or acts of "tacit consent." Drawing on Locke, one might argue that by not exiting the territory of the state into which I was born or by not participating in political dissent, I tacitly consent to the state's authority. The problem with this response is that state institutions define the processes through which consent can be expressed, and it is these very institutions—to which we have not consented—that stand in need of justification.

A third way of understanding self-determination is as derivative of more fundamental principles, such as principles of justice. Beitz calls this the idea of a "hypothetical contract": a government is legitimate if it *would* be consented to by rational persons subject to its rule.[82] The argument for respecting a state's right to self-determination is that interference with this right would violate principles of justice that *ideal*, not actual, citizens *would* endorse regarding the terms of their association. On this account, we should respect a state's sovereignty and refrain from interfering in its affairs because the state's institutions are just, on some conception of justice. Intervention is justified only if the state is unjust and interference would promote the development of just domestic institutions.

Yet, one troubling feature of this third approach is that it views self-determination as a mere means to justice, failing to capture something intuitively important about self-determination. Consider an example provided by Beitz:

> Country A is an imperial country, and area B, a territorially distinct area with generally accepted boundaries, is A's colony. Since A is the most benevolent of all possible imperial countries, there is no reason to think that granting independence to B will decrease the amount of social injustice in B; indeed, the opposite seems more likely because of various political and economic complications inside B which we don't need to explain. Nonetheless, the residents of B, in a fair and free election, overwhelmingly indicate their preference for national independence.[83]

On Beitz's account of self-determination, which views self-determination as derivatively important in terms of its contributions to justice, country A should resist the results of the election and refuse to grant area B independence. Beitz responds that "intuitively, this seems implausible," and yet he ultimately concludes that this response is "weaker than it may seem" because it "simply does not apply to many real world cases."[84] But what if it did? If a benevolent imperial power like country A could do a better job ensuring substantively just outcomes, we would have to oppose B's move for independence on Beitz's view. We need to account for the independent value of self-determination, even while recognizing that it may serve as an important component of justice.

I want to suggest that self-determination is not only an element of justice; it is also a part of an ideal of *democracy*. The democratic principle of self-determination stands for the proposition that a group of people has the right to make its own decisions about policies made in its name. Self-determination is a claim about self-rule. In international law, the right of self-determination is understood as the right of a people to determine its collective political destiny through democratic means.[85] The first article of the UN Charter, signed in 1945, declares self-determination to be a fundamental right of all peoples.[86] The idea of a universal right of self-determination is further enunciated in the International Covenant on Civil and Political Rights, which states, "All peoples have the right of self-determination. By virtue of that right they freely determine their political status and freely pursue their economic, social and cultural development."[87]

We can build on the idea of self-determination to develop an alternative, democratic justification for a state's right to control immigration. My argument consists of the following claims:

1. A people/demos has the right of self-determination.
2. The right of self-determination includes the right to control admission and membership.
3. The demos should be bounded by the territorial boundaries of the state.
4. Citizens of a territorial state, in virtue of their role as members of the (territorially defined) demos, have the right to control admission and membership.

I briefly elaborate each of these claims in the following.

A. A People/Demos Has the Right of Self-Determination

This is the idea of popular sovereignty: that a group of people (the demos) ought to have independent political control over significant aspects of its common life. As a concept in international law, self-determination was seen to apply only to specific territories (first, the defeated European powers; later, the overseas trust territories and colonies) and was understood primarily as a right of secession. It has evolved to be understood as a right of all peoples to participate in democratic processes of governance.[88] The claim of self-determination need not be understood solely as a claim for full political independence or autonomy; it is a claim for some independent political control over significant aspects of its common life. Self-determination implies an independent domain of political control, but it leaves open the domain of control (what sorts of activities and institutions the group controls), the extent of its control over various items in the domain, and the particular political institutions by which the group exercises control over its domain.[89]

What is the content of the right of self-determination? We can begin by looking to the principles and practices of international law. Thomas Franck suggests three components to the normative entitlement to democracy in international law, which already enjoy "a high degree of legitimacy in international law": the right to participate in political processes, the right of free political expression, and the right to take part in "periodic and genuine elections which shall be taken by universal and equal suffrage and shall be held by secret vote or by equivalent free voting procedures." Together these elements aim at "creating the opportunity for all persons to assume responsibility for shaping the kind of civil society in which they live and work."[90]

Turning to moral and political theory, a more minimalist interpretation of the right of self-determination says it is a right to *some* say in the making of the policies to which one is subject. For example, one might focus on accountability rather than equal rights of participation, identifying, as Buchanan does, three features that make up a more minimal conception of democracy: (1) representative majoritarian institutions for making most general laws "such that no competent individual is excluded from participation," (2) the highest government officials are accountable to the people by being subject to removal from office, and (3) there are institutionally secured freedoms of speech, association, and assembly, which are required for reasonably free deliberation.[91] On a more demanding interpretation of self-determination, what is required are *equal* rights of participation in the governing processes. For example, Thomas Christiano defends the idea of each citizen having "an equal say" in determining the most fundamental public rules.[92] This more demanding interpretation is required for an account of self-determination to count as democratic self-determination.

What are the grounds of the right of democratic self-determination? To anticipate the objection that democratic self-determination is inherently incompatible with respecting individual human rights, it is important to see that self-determination can be derived from the premise that all persons qua persons should be treated with equal concern and respect (the moral equality principle). There are different views about what it is about persons that is to receive equal respect (e.g., whether it is the well-being/good of persons or the autonomy of persons that is the proper object of equal consideration), which we need not settle here. The moral equality principle is the most common justification offered for basic human rights, rights whose violation poses the most serious threat to the individual's chances of living a decent human life. The familiar list of basic human rights includes the right to life, the right to security of the person, the right against enslavement and torture, and the right to resources for subsistence, among others. More controversially, the case can be made that respecting the moral equality of persons also requires recognition of the right to democratic governance. Equal consideration requires that all persons be regarded as equal participants in significant political decisions to which they are subject. The right to democracy is an important element of the institutional recognition of the equality of persons.

Even if one rejects the idea of a human right to democratic governance, there are instrumental reasons for recognizing the right to democracy as a legal aspiration in international law. Democratic governance is of such great instrumental value for the protection of human rights that it ought to be required for any government to be considered legitimate. Evidence in support of this argument is Amartya Sen's work showing famines are much less likely in democracies, as well as the "democratic peace" literature that suggests democracy is the most reliable form of government for securing peace, which should lessen the violation of human rights.[93] These arguments support the case for understanding the right of self-determination as a right to *democratic* governance.

B. *The Right of Self-Determination Includes the Right to Control Admission and Membership*

The right of self-determination of a people is the right to independent political control over significant aspects of its common life. As Frederick Whelan puts it, "The admission of new members into the democratic group . . . would appear to be such a matter, one that could not only affect various private interests of the current members, but that could also, in the aggregate, affect the quality of their public life and the character of their community."[94] Walzer goes even further: "Admission and exclusion are at the core of communal independence. They suggest the deepest meaning of self-determination."[95] I agree with the basic claim made here by Whelan and Walzer but part ways with Walzer on the grounds for self-determination. In my view, the right of self-determination derives not out of a concern to preserve a distinctive cultural identity as discussed earlier, but rather from respecting the right of individuals to be regarded as equal participants in significant political decisions to which they are bound.

C. The Demos Should Be Bounded by the Territorial Boundaries of the State

This is a controversial claim, which I have defended in another essay and which I can only briefly summarize here.[96] I begin with the normative requirements of democracy. A settled conviction about democracy is that it is rule by the people who regard one another as equals. What is required to meet this demand of equal regard? The idea of equality might enter a theory of democracy at different levels: at the level of normative justification and at the level of institutional design.[97] A more complex view of democracy differentiates between normative justification and the institutional requirements of democracy. As a matter of justification, the idea of equality places limits on the sorts of reasons that may be given to explain why we should accept one rather than another conception of fair terms of democratic participation. It is the role of a theory of *political equality* to connect the normative justification with the institutional requirements of democracy. Political equality is a constitutive condition of democracy. Political equality requires protecting certain equal rights and liberties, as well as ensuring the equal worth of these rights and liberties by providing equal opportunities for political influence.

The realization of political equality depends on the existence of a stable bounded demos. The modern state demarcates such a stable demos. The boundaries of the demos are already demarcated according to the boundaries of state membership, but my argument is not that we should accept the state system because it is the status quo. My point is that we have reasons internal to democracy for bounding the demos according to the territorial boundaries of states. What are these democratic reasons?

First, it is a historically contingent but morally relevant fact that the modern state is the primary instrument for securing *the substantive rights and freedoms constitutive of democracy*. Without the state, individuals will disagree about what rights they have and when rights are violated. Even if individuals agree on what rights they have, some people may not respect those rights without a common third-party enforcer. A state system of public law establishes a common view of the rights of individuals, and it has the coercive means to enforce that view. The state also provides institutions for adjudicating conflicts among individuals. In short, the institutions of the modern state serve legislative, executive, and judicial functions necessary for the creation and maintenance of the system of rights, including rights of participation.[98]

A second reason for bounding the demos according to the boundaries of the territorial state has to do with *solidarity*. The state is not simply an instrument of decision making or a means to securing rights; it is also a key site of solidarity, trust, and participation. Democratic participation happens not in a vacuum but in relation to a rich network of institutions. Trust plays an indispensable role here. As Charles Tilly has argued, trust "consists of placing valued outcomes at risk of others' malfeasance, mistakes, or failures." Trust relationships are those in which people regularly take such risks. Trust is more likely among a group of people who come together repeatedly within a stable infrastructure of institutions and who share a sense of solidarity rooted in a shared political culture. To the degree that individuals integrate their trust networks into political institutions, the greater the stake people have in the successful functioning of those institutions. As Tilly puts its, individuals "acquire an unbreakable interest in the performance of government. The political stakes matter."[99] A shared political culture based on common citizenship is crucial for fostering trust and solidarity, which in turn enables democratic participation.

A third reason for bounding the demos according to the territorial boundaries of states focuses on the connection between citizens and their *political representatives*. Democratic representatives must be accountable to a specified demos. As Seyla Benhabib has argued, "Democratic laws require closure precisely because democratic representation must be accountable to a specific people."[100] A system of territorial representation ensures that political representatives know in advance *to whom* they are accountable. Territorial representatives know they are acting on behalf of the citizens of their state, and the solidarity based on a common political culture within a state is likely to make representatives more attentive to their constituents than if the constituents were all of humanity constituting a global demos or episodic demoi defined by the "all subjected" or "all affected" principles of democratic legitimacy.[101]

In sum, the demos should be bounded by state boundaries because the state (1) is the primary instrument for securing the conditions of democracy, (2) serves as the primary site of solidarity conducive to democratic participation, and (3) establishes clear lines of accountability between representatives and their constituents.

Among the many objections one might raise is that democratic theory, properly understood, presupposes an *unbounded demos.* Focusing directly on the issue of border control, Arash Abizadeh has argued that the democratic theory of popular sovereignty is incompatible with "the state sovereignty view," which says immigration control should be under the unilateral discretion of the state itself. Abizadeh comes to this conclusion by way of two premises: (1) that the demos is, in principle, unbounded, and (2) that democratic justification for a state's regime of border control is owed to all those subject to the border regime's coercive power. He defends the first premise by arguing that the contrary thesis (that the demos is inherently bounded) is incoherent. The incoherence is said to stem partly from the "boundary problem" in democracy theory: that democracy "cannot be brought to bear on the logically prior matter of the constitution of the group itself, the existence of which it presupposes."[102] As I have argued elsewhere, the claim that democratic theory cannot answer the boundary problem rests on a narrow, proceduralist conception of democracy.[103] If we instead view democracy as a broader set of substantive values and principles, including the principle of political equality, we have reasons internal to democracy for bounding the demos according to the territorial boundaries of the state.

Abizadeh argues that the incoherence of attempts to bound the demos also stems from an externality problem: state action, including its border policies, always involves exercising coercive power over members and nonmembers, and such power must be justified to all subjected to coercion. This point connects to Abizadeh's second major premise that interprets the idea of democratic legitimacy as requiring all those subject to a state's coercive power to have an *equal* say in the exercise of that power.[104] While I agree with Abizadeh that justification is owed to all those subject to the coercive power of the state, I disagree with the conclusion that justification must take the form of equal enfranchisement of all members and nonmembers in state policy making. It is plausible to think the demand for justification can be met in other ways that are compatible with democratic principles, such as supporting policies that respect the basic human rights of all those subjected to the policy and supporting the development of democratic institutions in the home states of nonmembers.

One reason for thinking that it may be compatible with democratic principles to have different responses for members and nonmembers arises from distinguishing coercion and authority in theorizing democratic legitimacy. Abizadeh interprets the principle of democratic legitimacy as requiring justification to all those who are subject to a state's *coercive power*. Another way of approaching democratic legitimacy is more attentive to, in Joshua Cohen's words, "democracy's institutional character": democratic legitimacy "arises from the discussions and decisions of members, as made within and expressed through social and political institutions designed to acknowledge their *collective authority*." We can recognize that democracy comes in many forms, but "more determinate conceptions of it depend on an account of membership in the people, and correspondingly, what it takes for a decision to be *collective*—made by citizens 'as a body.'"[105] The demos is not an aggregation of individuals coerced by the same power but rather an enduring collective that makes decisions with binding authority.

D. Citizens of a Territorial State, in Virtue of Their Role as Members of the (Territorially Defined) Demos, Have the Right to Control Admission and Membership

If claims 1 to 3 are plausible, then it is citizens of a territorial state, in virtue of their role as members of the territorially defined demos, who have the right to control borders and membership. Citizens are both the ultimate beneficiaries and the ultimate authors of the exercise of jurisdictional authority, through democratic processes of participation and representation.

In contrast to the property justification, the state's right to control immigration is neither an instance of nor derived from private property rights; it is a jurisdictional right. In contrast to the cultural and nationalist accounts, the state's right to control immigration is not grounded on a claim about the importance of preserving a distinctive culture or national identity; it rests on the right of members of the territorially defined demos to be self-governing as political equals. Self-governance includes not only control over current collective decision making and the future direction of the political system but also the right to regulate admission into the territory and into full membership. In contrast to the freedom of association argument, the state's right to control immigration does not rest on analogies with marriage, religious associations, and golf clubs, and it does not elide property rights over golf clubs with jurisdictional rights over a state's territory. The state is importantly disanalogous from other associations not only because state membership is typically nonvoluntary but also because of the state's indispensable role in meeting the constitutive and instrumental conditions of democratic participation and representation.

IV. CONCLUSION

It is important to clarify the ways in which the arguments presented here are limited. In pursuing the question of why the modern state has the right to control immigration, I have not provided an answer to the important question, How should the state's claim to control immigration be weighed against the migrant's claim to enter? To answer this question, we need to consider not only the perspective of the political community but also the perspective of migrants. More than twenty-five years ago, Joseph Carens famously made the case for open borders, concluding "there is little justification for restricting immigration."[106] Although Carens did not grapple seriously with the idea of self-determination and the normative requirements of democracy, his essay is a powerful reminder that consideration of what migrants are owed should be central to any debate about the ethics of migration. In this chapter, I have argued that the state has a *pro tanto* right to control immigration based on the normative requirements of democracy. This is *not* to say that this right is an absolute constraint that "trumps" all other considerations. *Pro tanto* reasons for action are typically contrasted with conclusory reasons for action; the latter require us to act, regardless of other considerations in play. *Pro tanto* reasons are reactions for action, but they may be overridden by competing reasons.[107] The next step is to develop a broader normative framework for considering the claims of migrants alongside the claims of political community.

In addition, I want to clarify that the democratic argument for the state's right to control immigration is *not* an argument for "closed borders" or "exclusion." The democratic argument offered here speaks to the question of *who* has the right to control, not how open or closed borders should be. I believe democratic political communities have strong reasons, arising from the values and principles of liberal democracy, for supporting more porous border policies than most countries have pursued in practice. Exploring these reasons and their implications for contemporary immigration policy is a task I leave for another day. The point of this chapter has been to take seriously the idea of the democratic right of self-determination and its implications for who has the right to control immigration.

Notes

I am grateful to the participants of the 2013 conference of the American Society of Political and Legal Philosophy and the Vanderbilt Social and Political Theory Workshop for helpful comments and discussion. Special thanks to Michael Blake, Adam Cox, Marilyn Friedman, Paul Gowder, and Emily McGill-Rutherford for their comments, and to Jack Knight for his guidance as Editor of NOMOS.

1. *Nishimura Ekiu v. United States*, 142 U.S. 651, 659 (1892), citing Emer de Vattel, *Les droit des gens* [*The Law of Nations*] (1758), ed. Béla Kapossy and Richard Whatmore (Indianapolis: Liberty Fund, 2008), II.94, II.100.

2. Linda Bosniak, *The Citizen and the Alien: Dilemmas of Contemporary Membership* (Princeton, NJ: Princeton University Press, 2006), 99. Bosniak interprets Michael Walzer as an exemplar of such a "separation" approach. He accepts the right of political communities to control "first ad-

missions" (immigration), but once persons are admitted to the national territory, "second admissions" (naturalization) into full membership "are subject only to certain constraints of time and qualification, never to the ultimate constraint of closure" (Michael Walzer, *Spheres of Justice* [New York: Basic Books, 1983], 61). I examine Walzer's view in greater detail later in the chapter. For discussion of the feasibility and desirability of making this distinction, see Bosniak, *The Citizen and the Alien*, and Adam B. Cox, "Immigration Law's Organizing Principles," *University of Pennsylvania Law Review* 157 (2008): 341–93.

3. *Chae Chan Ping v. United States*, 130 U.S. 581 (1889).

4. Rogers M. Smith, "Beyond Sovereignty and Uniformity: The Challenges for Equal Citizenship in the Twenty-First Century," *Harvard Law Review* 122 (2009): 919. For other interpretations of these canonical immigration law cases as novel assertions of strong state sovereignty, see Stephen H. Legomsky, *Immigration and the Judiciary: Law and Politics in Britain and America* (Oxford: Oxford University Press, 1987), 177–222; Louis Henkin, "The Constitution and United States Sovereignty: A Century of Chinese Exclusion and Its Progeny," *Harvard Law Review* 100 (1987): 862–63; Bosniak, *The Citizen and the Alien*, 51.

5. *Chae Chan Ping*, 130 U.S. at 603.

6. The Constitution explicitly mentions the power to "establish an uniform Rule of Naturalization" (Art. I, § 8, cl. 4), but it is silent on the power over admission and exclusion of foreigners outside the territory.

7. As Hiroshi Motomura observes, this was an earlier era of constitutional law when equal protection was on its way toward "separate but equal" and judicial recognition of the substantive and procedural rights of individuals was "far beyond the constitutional horizon" ("Immigration Law after a Century of Plenary Power," *Yale Law Journal* 100 [1990]: 551).

8. *Chae Chan Ping*, 130 U.S. at 609.

9. *Chae Chang Ping*, 130 U.S. at 603–4.

10. *Chae Chan Ping*, 130 U.S. at 606.

11. *Nishimura Ekiu v. United States*, 142 U.S. 651 (1892).

12. Motomura, "Immigration Law after a Century of Plenary Power," 552.

13. *Nishimura Ekiu v. United States*, 142 U.S. at 659.

14. The U.S. Supreme Court cited Vattel as its prime authority for international law cases into the late nineteenth century. Arthur Nussbaum notes that in the history of the law of nations, Vattel's book attained a circulation second only to Grotius's *De jure belli ac paci* (*On the Law of War and Peace*, 1623–24). He attributes Vattel's influence to several factors: the need for a systematic reference book on international law at a time when there was a rapid increase in international legal problems; the outdat-

edness of Grotius's seventeenth-century work; "the ambiguity of Vattel's propositions—indeed, the ambiguity of an oracle" that made it an easy reference in diplomatic correspondence; and the fact that "the spirit of the work" was "well in accord with the principles of the Declaration of Independence." See Nussbaum, *A Concise History of the Law of Nations* (New York: Macmillan, 1954), 160–61.

15. Vattel, *The Law of Nations*, II.94, cited in *Nishimura Ekiu v. United States*, at 659.

16. Nicholas Greenwood Onuf contends Wolff was the last systematic thinker to give this teleological vision unqualified support ("*Civitas Maxima*: Wolff, Vattel and the Fate of Republicanism," *American Journal of International Law* 88 [1994]: 283).

17. See also Frederick G. Whelan, "Vattel's Doctrine of State," *History of Political Thought* 9 (1988): 76–81.

18. Nussbaum, *Concise History of the Law of Nations*, 150–51; Onuf, "*Civitas Maxima*," 297–301.

19. Vattel, *The Law of Nations*, I.13–14. After World War I, Vattel was interpreted as an unconditional supporter of reason of state who "disguised his evil intentions through words of sublime charity" (Béla Kapossy and Richard Whatmore, "Introduction," in Vattel, *The Law of Nations*, xiv–xvi). By contrast, other interpreters of Vattel maintain that his approach is "more humanitarian, more cosmopolitan, and, in a measure, even democratic" (Nussbaum, *Concise History of the Law of Nations*, 157).

20. Emer de Vattel, *Essay on the Foundation of Natural Law and on the First Principle of the Obligation Men Find Themselves under to Observe Laws*, in *The Law of Nations*, 752.

21. Kapossy and Whatmore, "Introduction," xvii; Whelan, "Vattel's Doctrine of State," 83.

22. Stephen D. Krasner, *Sovereignty: Organized Hypocrisy* (Princeton, NJ: Princeton University Press, 1999), 20.

23. Whelan, "Vattel's Doctrine of State," 80. This emphasis on the equality of sovereign states is reflected in the Preamble to the UN Charter (1945), which speaks of the "equal rights . . . of nations large and small."

24. Vattel, *The Law of Nations*, II.123.

25. *Fong Yue Ting v. United States*, 149 U.S. 698 (1893) at 707–8.

26. Ibid. at 713. Justice Gray also rejected the claim that deportation constitutes punishment: "The order of deportation is not a punishment for crime. It is not a banishment, in the sense in which that word is often applied to the expulsion of a citizen from his country by way of punishment" (730).

27. *Yamataya v. Fisher*, 189 U.S. 86 (1903). The government had arrested and tried to deport Yamataya four days after she had landed in the United States.

28. Motomura, "Immigration Law after a Century of Plenary Power," 554.

29. However, in a series of cases in the twentieth century, rather than softening the plenary power doctrine's harshest aspects in regard to the treatment of noncitizens present in the U.S. territory, the Court has upheld the U.S. government's power to exclude such noncitizens. See, e.g., *United States* ex rel. *Knauff v. Shaughnessy*, 163 U.S. 537 (1896); *Shaughnessy v. United States* ex rel. *Mezei*, 345 U.S. 206 (1953); *Harisiades v. Shaughnessy*, 342 U.S. 580 (1952).

30. Whelan, "Vattel's Doctrine of State," 74.

31. Vattel, *The Law of Nations*, II.100; cf. II.94. For further discussion, see Whelan, "Vattel's Doctrine of State," 73–75.

32. Walzer, *Spheres of Justice*, 39.

33. Ibid., 62 (emphasis in original).

34. Ibid.

35. He proposes that Australians, given their racial preferences in the early twentieth century, faced one of two choices: they could discharge the duty of mutual aid to "necessitous men and women, clamoring for entry," either by admitting them or by yielding some of their land for the needy strangers to establish a separate community, thereby preserving a "white Australia" (Walzer, *Spheres of Justice*, 46–47).

36. David Miller, "Immigration: The Case for Limits," in Andrew I. Cohen and Christopher Health Wellman, eds., *Contemporary Debates in Applied Ethics* (Oxford: Blackwell, 2005), 200.

37. Ibid., 200–201.

38. David Miller, *National Responsibility and Global Justice* (Oxford: Oxford University Press, 2007), 218.

39. Chaim Gans, *The Limits of Nationalism* (Cambridge: Cambridge University Press, 2003), 100.

40. John Locke, *Second Treatise of Government*, ed. C. B. MacPherson (Indianapolis: Hackett, 1980), § 27, 40.

41. Tamar Meisels, *Territorial Rights*, 2nd ed. (New York: Springer, 2009), 118.

42. Miller, *National Responsibility and Global Justice*, 218.

43. As Meisels puts it, "For all the references to property argumentation and to Locke himself throughout this book, none of its arguments entails the straightforward and unequivocal application of Lockean property arguments—or any other theory of property for that matter—to the national case" (*Territorial Rights*, 8).

44. Ibid., 126–27.

45. Miller, *National Responsibility and Global Justice*, 218–19 (emphasis in original).

46. Locke, *Second Treatise of Government*, § 40.

47. Anna Stilz, "Nations, States, and Territory," *Ethics* 121 (2011): 577.

48. Allen Buchanan, "Boundaries: What Liberalism Has to Say," in Allen Buchanan and Margaret Moore, eds., *States, Nations, and Borders: The Ethics of Making Boundaries* (Cambridge: Cambridge University Press, 2003), 233.

49. Christopher Heath Wellman, "In Defense of the Right to Exclude," in Christopher Heath Wellman and Phillip Cole, *Debating the Ethics of Immigration: Is There a Right to Exclude?* (Oxford: Oxford University Press, 2011), 25.

50. Ibid., 31.

51. Stuart White, "Freedom of Association and the Right to Exclude," *Journal of Political Philosophy* 5 (1997): 360–61.

52. Wellman, "In Defense of the Right to Exclude," 37.

53. Christopher Heath Wellman, "Immigration and Freedom of Association," *Ethics* 119 (2008): 109.

54. White, "Freedom of Association," 381, cited in Wellman, "In Defense of the Right to Exclude," 32 (emphasis added).

55. Sarah Fine, "Freedom of Association Is Not the Answer," *Ethics* 120 (2010), 349–50.

56. Wellman, "Immigration and Freedom of Association," 114.

57. This is not to deny that in some contexts, exclusion from a golf club or other voluntary associations, such as the Jaycees or Boy Scouts, can result in significant harms to those excluded. Context-sensitive judgments are necessary to determine whether the harms are significant such as to require constraints on the association's right to exclude.

58. Wellman, "In Defense of the Right to Exclude," 39–40.

59. Wellman, "Immigration and Freedom of Association," 135.

60. Wellman does suggest a territorial requirement of sorts: that states must be "sufficiently territorially contiguous" to fulfill their functional purposes. In his work on secession, he suggests the territorial contiguity requirement justifies state coercion of all inhabitants within a state's territory. However, while this requirement might support the state's claim to coerce those individuals already inside its borders, the requirement has no bearing on the state's right to exclude foreigners outside its territory who wish to enter. See Wellman, "Immigration and Freedom of Association," 131; Christopher Wellman, *A Theory of Secession* (Cambridge: Cambridge University Press, 2012), 16–17; Fine, "Freedom of Association Is Not the Answer," 355.

61. Locke, *Second Treatise of Government*, chap. 5.

62. Ibid., 8, § 120, p. 64 (emphasis added).

63. My discussion of the first two problems with individualistic Lockean accounts is indebted to Anna Stilz, "Why Do States Have Territorial Rights?," *International Theory* 1 (2009): 185–213.

64. Robert Nozick, *Anarchy, State, Utopia* (New York: Basic Books, 1974), 114–15.

65. Ibid., chaps. 4–5.

66. Locke, *Second Treatise of Government*, chap. 2, §6, p. 9.

67. Hillel Steiner, "Territorial Justice," in Simon Caney, David George, and Peter Jones, eds., *National Rights, International Obligations* (Boulder, CO: Westview Press, 1996), 144.

68. Cara Nine, "A Lockean Theory of Territory," *Political Studies* 56 (2008): 150–54.

69. Locke, *Second Treatise of Government*, chap. 8, § 95, p. 52. Locke himself did not directly address the aspect of territorial rights pertaining to control over the movement of people and goods across borders. It is interesting to note that Locke has been a source for property-based defenses of a state's right to control immigration, as well as a source for contemporary libertarian arguments in favor of open borders.

70. Nine, "A Lockean Theory of Territory," 155–56 (emphasis added).

71. Ibid., 157–61.

72. Ryan Pevnick, *Immigration and the Constraints of Justice* (Cambridge: Cambridge University Press, 2011), 33–34.

73. Ibid., 38.

74. Ibid., 44.

75. Pevnick, *Immigration and the Constraints of Justice*, 43–44. See also Jeremy Waldron, "Property and Ownership," *Stanford Encyclopedia of Philosophy* (2004).

76. Pevnick, *Immigration and the Constraints of Justice*, 164, 165.

77. For elaboration of this point, see Shelley Wilcox's review of Pevnick's book (*Ethics* 122 [2012]: 617–22).

78. Christian Wolff, *Jus gentium method scientifica pertractatum* [1749], sec. 2, pp. 9, 16.

79. See Charles Beitz, *Political Theory and International Relations* (Princeton, NJ: Princeton University Press, 1979), 76.

80. Michael Walzer, *Just and Unjust Wars: A Moral Argument with Historical Illustrations* (New York: Basic Books, 1977), 54.

81. Beitz, *Political Theory and International Relations*, 77.

82. Ibid., 69, 80.

83. Ibid., 103.

84. Ibid.

85. Thomas M. Franck, "The Emerging Right to Democratic Governance," *American Journal of International Law* 86 (1992): 52.

86. Charter of the United Nations, Article 1, June 26, 1945.

87. International Covenant on Civil and Political Rights, December 16, 1966.

88. Franck, "Emerging Right to Democratic Governance," 54–5. James Anaya's distinction between "constitutive self-determination" (when a group makes a fundamental choice concerning its political status) and "ongoing self-determination" (self-government, though not necessarily full independence) captures two important dimensions of self-determination.

89. Another way of putting it is that the right of self-determination is a moral right, which could take a range of legal forms and may sometimes be overridden by competing moral values. As some theorists of international law have emphasized, "the right of self-determination" is a moral right that encompasses a diverse bundle of legal rights, which needs to be disaggregated and includes not only the right of secession but also forms of intra-state autonomy, such as federalism. See Buchanan, *Justice, Legitimacy, and Self-Determination: Moral Foundations for International Law* (Oxford: Oxford University Press, 2004), 333, 343.

90. Franck, "Emerging Right to Democratic Governance," 91, 63 (quoting from the Universal Declaration of Human Rights, Article 21), 79.

91. Buchanan, *Justice, Legitimacy, and Self-Determination,* 146.

92. Thomas Christiano, *The Constitution of Equality: Democratic Authority and Its Limits* (Oxford: Oxford University Press, 2008). See also Joshua Cohen, "Deliberation and Democratic Legitimacy," in Alan Hamlin and Philip Pettit, eds., *The Good Polity: Normative Analysis of the State* (Oxford: Basil Blackwell, 1989), 17–34.

93. Amartya Sen, "Democracy as a Universal Value," *Journal of Democracy* 10 (1999): 3–17; Bruce Russett, *Grasping the Democratic Peace: Principles for a Post–Cold War World* (Princeton, NJ: Princeton University Press, 1993). For more discussion of moral egalitarian and instrumental arguments for a human right to democracy, see Buchanan, *Justice, Legitimacy, and Self-Determination,* 142–44.

94. Frederick G. Whelan, "Citizenship and Freedom of Movement," in Mark Gibney, ed., *Open Borders? Closed Societies? The Ethical and Political Issues* (Westport, CT: Greenwood Press, 1988), 28.

95. Walzer, *Spheres of Justice,* 62.

96. Sarah Song, "The Boundary Problem in Democratic Theory: Why the Demos Should Be Bounded by the State," *International Theory* 4 (2012): 39–68.

97. Charles Beitz, *Political Equality: An Essay in Democratic Theory* (Princeton, NJ: Princeton University Press, 1989), 17–19.

98. Thomas Christiano has argued for the necessity of justice for democracy and the indispensable role played by the state in establishing *justice* and, from these premises, has developed a democratic theory of terri-

tory. See Christiano, "A Democratic Theory of Territory and Some Puzzles about Global Democracy," *Journal of Social Philosophy* 37 (2006): 81–107. My argument views *democracy* as an independent ideal and asks what substantive rights and goods are required by the ideal, although I think what I am saying here is consistent with an account, such as Christiano's, that links the demands of justice with the demands of democracy.

99. Charles Tilly, *Democracy* (Cambridge: Cambridge University Press, 2007), 74.

100. Seyla Benhabib, *The Rights of Others: Aliens, Residents, and Citizens* (Cambridge: Cambridge University Press, 2004), 219.

101. On the limits of empathy and the difference that size makes, see Robert A. Dahl, *On Political Equality* (New Haven, CT: Yale University Press, 2006), 42–44, 59–63. See also Rousseau, *On the Social Contract, in The Basic Political Writings*, trans. Donald A. Cress (Indianapolis, IN: Hackett Publishing, 1987), 2:9.

102. Arash Abizadeh, "Democratic Theory and Border Coercion: No Right to Unilaterally Control Your Own Borders," *Political Theory* 36 (2008): 46, quoting Frederick G. Whelan, "Prologue: Democratic Theory and the Boundary Problem," in J. Roland Pennock and John Chapman, eds., *NOMOS XXV: Liberal Democracy* (New York: NYU Press, 1983), 40.

103. Song, "The Boundary Problem in Democratic Theory."

104. Abizadeh develops his democratic version of the coercion principle ("the democratic justification thesis"), building on the work of Joseph Raz and Michael Blake. Blake argues that a state's coercive practices trigger a demand for moral justification to all persons subject to coercion if we are to take seriously the individual autonomy of persons. It is worth noting that Blake seems to assume that the boundaries of state coercion coincide with the state's territorial boundaries. See Joseph Raz, *The Morality of Freedom* (Oxford: Oxford University Press, 1986), and Michael Blake, "Distributive Justice, State Coercion, and Autonomy," *Philosophy and Public Affairs* 30 (2001): 257–96.

105. Joshua Cohen, "Procedure and Substance in Deliberative Democracy," in *Democracy and Difference: Contesting the Boundaries of the Political* (Princeton, NJ: Princeton University Press, 1996), 407.

106. Joseph Carens's essay remains the leading defense of the claim that all persons have the right of freedom of movement across national borders, premised on the moral equality of all human beings and considered from libertarian, utilitarian, and Rawlsian principles (Carens, "Aliens and Citizens: The Case for Open Borders," *Review of Politics* 49 [1987]: 251–73).

107. On this distinction, see Charles R. Beitz, *The Idea of Human Rights* (Oxford: Oxford University Press, 2009), 116–17.

2

THREE MISTAKES IN OPEN BORDERS DEBATES

ADAM B. COX

What might justify laws that restrict the free movement of people across international borders? In this chapter I hope to correct three common mistakes made by those who try to answer this question.

First, I argue that debates about open borders often conflate three quite distinct questions—about whether border restrictions are ever permissible, about when they are permissible, and about who gets to decide which are permissible. Keeping these questions separate, as well as understanding the analytic relationship among them, is crucial to making progress on philosophical issues related to international migration.

Second, I want to draw attention to a historical mistake that often lurks in the background of open borders debates. Early American immigration jurisprudence often features prominently in discussions by both legal scholars and political philosophers. This is because the canonical cases from the period of Chinese exclusion are widely seen as the moment when the U.S. Supreme Court definitely rejected open borders claims and laid out the legal justification for state-imposed restrictions on migration. As I will show, however, this view is mistaken. These canonical cases were not about open borders arguments, and as a result they have little or nothing to say about what might justify restrictions on migration.

Third, and perhaps most ambitiously, I want to suggest that it will be very difficult to make a persuasive argument in favor of border restrictions without *simultaneously* tackling the question of what principles of equality require for those who are admitted into a state's territory. These twin questions are typically segregated in philosophical work on immigration, but I believe they are tied together in ways that are too often overlooked.

I will make these three points not in the abstract but instead in response to Sarah Song's provocative essay "Why Does the State Have the Right to Control Immigration?," which is included in this same volume. Song's essay is an exemplar of the best work being done on open borders questions today. As I will explain, she shows persuasively why many other approaches to the question posed by her title are doomed to fail, and why her approach is among the most likely to succeed. While I use her essay at a few points to highlight my concerns about open borders arguments, it is only because some aspects of her approach share much in common with others participating in the same conversation.

I. Three Questions about Open Borders

The philosophical literature on open borders often conflates three conceptually distinct questions. Pulling these questions apart helps clarify the stakes of the debate. It also helps us see that the analytic relationship between the three questions depends very much on our approach to answering any one of them. Understanding these relationships is crucial to making progress on them.

The first question is the one that is perhaps most foundational: Are open borders morally obligatory? In other words, is it always wrong to restrict freedom of movement across international borders? Second, if it is not always wrong to restrict movement across borders, is it ever wrong? That is, if exclusion is sometimes justified, what principles limit exclusion?[1] Third, if it is not always wrong to restrict migration, who gets to decide when such restrictions are permissible? Here the focus is on who applies the relevant principles in concrete situations; the question is one of institutional choice.[2]

Teasing apart questions about the existence, limits, and location of authority is in many ways familiar terrain for political philosophers. Locke, for example, thought that both in the state of nature and in political society everyone had the same basic rights, but at the same time he thought that in political society the state gets to judge violations, and individuals do not.[3] But all too often these distinctions get papered over when open borders are debated. Often this is not because the distinctions go unrecognized; instead, it is because these conceptually distinct questions are thought to be interrelated in ways that would make pulling them apart irrelevant.

Consider the second and third questions. From time to time it is suggested that if there are limits on exclusion, then the receiving state cannot be the institution in charge of deciding whom to exclude; conversely, one might think that if the receiving state wields the power to exclude, there can be no limits on that power. In other words, our answer to question 2 might dictate our answer to question 3, or our answer to question 3 might dictate our answer to question 2.

Michael Walzer, who defends the state's right to decide whom to admit, is sometimes (mis)read as suggesting such a relationship between the second and third questions—as arguing that if the state has the authority to pick new members, there can be no limits on its selection criteria. Song suggests something similar in her discussion of Emir Vattel and early American immigration law. Vattel emphasized that "every nation has a right to refuse admitting a foreigner into her territory, when he cannot enter it without exposing the nation to evident danger, or doing manifest injury," reasoning on which the Supreme Court relied to conclude that "every sovereign nation has the power . . . to forbid the entrance of foreigners."[4] Song suggests that this logic of authority inherent in sovereignty entails the claim that the U.S. government must have virtually unrestricted power over immigration—power largely immune from constitutional constraint, judicial oversight, or even moral objection.[5]

But to say that the nation-state must be the one to judge whether to admit a person does not dictate that there can be no moral constraints on that judgment. There are plenty of situations where we believe that a person or an institution has the power to make a decision, and yet simultaneously believe that there are limits on that decision. For example, we might think that the state—and not private parties, or some foreign government—has the authority to decide on the structure of the state-run public school system. But that does not mean the state has unrestricted power to pick any structure it prefers. It might not be permissible, for instance, for the state to establish racially segregated schools. Note that even Vattel can be seen as acknowledging that the presence of authority does not entail the absence of constraint. In the preceding quote, he emphasized the state's right to make the exclusion decision—to judge whether the circumstances are such that an immigrant's admission will do injury to the state. But saying this acknowledges the possibility that it would be wrong for the state to exclude a person if it concluded that the person's admission would not in fact injure the state in any way.

Thus, it is crucial to keep separate the question of a state's authority to control migration from the question whether there are limits on its exercise of that authority. The fact that these questions are often conflated can be traced, I suspect, to a long-standing puzzle about the nature of "public law." Public law is addressed in some sense to the government itself. But this produces a puzzle: How can law bind the state when there is no external enforcement agent?[6] Constitutional law is supposed to control the state and limit its decisional freedom, but any limits embodied in constitutional law can be enforced only by the state itself.[7] If legal constraints are seen as binding only to the extent that there is an external enforcement agent—or, worse, if a command cannot actually *be* law unless it is backed by external enforcement—then constitutional law will appear to be either unenforceable or perhaps not law at all.[8] On this reasoning, if the state has the power to decide whom to admit, then there can be no limits on that power because there is no agent external to the state who could enforce those limits.

But this is a mistaken way of thinking, as should be plain from the preceding examples. The concept of law does not require an agent of enforcement entirely external to the system. Moreover, if the concern is enforcement (rather than obligation, which is the usual focus in the philosophical literature on migration restrictions), it turns out that there is a rich set of mechanisms that, in practice, promote significant levels of compliance with public law.[9]

In short, therefore, open borders debates are really about three questions, not just one. This does not mean, of course, that the questions are entirely unrelated. Whether they are related turns on the form of argument being pursued. Song's approach highlights this fact. Her chapter is entitled "Why Does the State Have the Right to Control Immigration?" As this title indicates, she seeks to justify closure by reference to rights held by "the state." Because it is the state's rights claim that itself justifies departures from open borders, the question whether it is ever permissible to restrict freedom of movement across borders cannot be answered without reference to the question of which institution should control the border. On other accounts, however, these two questions need not be related in the way they are for Song. Consider a welfarist approach. An argument that border closure was morally permissible on welfarist grounds might, depending on its form, tell us little or nothing about which institution should control migration decisions.

II. The Irrelevance of Early American Immigration Jurisprudence

Many who defend restrictions on migration do so by reference to the rights of "the state," "the nation," or related concepts. Given this common approach, it is unsurprising that legal theorists and political philosophers often seek out justifications for these rights claims in the canonical American immigration cases decided in the late nineteenth century. These cases are widely understood as the historical moment when the Supreme Court squarely rejected arguments in favor of open borders and stridently defended the right of states to exclude noncitizens. This makes the cases signal events in the history of American immigration law, as well as in the intellectual tradition of the open borders argument.

Song follows this well-trodden path. Her essay opens with the case of Chae Chan Ping, a Chinese laborer residing in California who was excluded from the United States when he returned from a trip abroad. He challenged the statute under which he was excluded as "beyond the competency of Congress to pass it,"[10] language that is often understood to be nothing less than a facial challenge to the federal government's power to restrict migration. For this reason, many, including Song, see *Chae Chan Ping v. United States* as "provid[ing] the Court with its first opportunity to address directly the question of the federal government's power to exclude foreigners."[11] The Court's reasoning that such a power is inherent in sovereignty is taken as a rejection of Chae Chan Ping's claim that no such power existed—that is, as a rejection of an argument in favor of open borders. Reading the case through this lens, Song ultimately finds the Court's justifications for the power to restrict migration thin and unpersuasive.

This common understanding of the most famous case in American immigration law is mistaken. *Chae Chan Ping* has little to nothing to do with open borders questions. The central reason is that Chae Chan Ping's lawyers conceded that the government had the authority to restrict immigration—or even to close the nation's borders entirely. In their opening brief to the Supreme Court, Ping's lawyer George Hoadly began by acknowledging that Congress had authority to abrogate the treaty with China that formed the basis of some of Ping's claims. Hoadly continued:

> Neither do we dispute the power of Congress to adopt the system, which the Chinese themselves have abandoned, of excluding intercourse with foreigners. . . . We do not deny the plenary power of Congress over the treaty and over its own legislation so as to forbid the future immigration of Chinese laborers.[12]

A subsequent brief filed by Hoadly's cocounsel, James Carter, emphasized the same point: "The inherent right of a sovereign power to prohibit, even in a time of peace, the entry into its territories of the subjects of a foreign state will not be denied."[13]

There are no iconoclastic open borders claims here. Instead, it turns out that the argument made by Hoadly and Carter on behalf of Chae Chan Ping was one quite commonly made, in all sorts of contexts, by nineteenth-century constitutional lawyers: it was an argument about vested rights, or what were often called "private rights" during this period. Ping argued that the treaty with China, along with subsequent implementing legislation conferred on him "rights, of which he cannot be deprived by subsequent legislation."[14] Analogizing to other private rights contexts, Ping contended that the legislatively conferred right to return was no different than rights in real property, or the right of residence (an aspect of "liberty") accorded citizens. Property rights were perhaps *the* classic private right, even when held by noncitizens: once conferred by treaty, property rights were vested and could not be abrogated by the subsequent repeal or withdrawal from the treaty. Similarly, citizens could not be stripped of their right of residence by mere legislation.[15] Thus, on the basis of these twin private rights analogies, Ping argued that he had acquired "a vested right to return, which could not have been taken away from him by any exercise of mere legislative power."

The limited nature of Chae Chan Ping's claims was not lost on the Court itself: "Here the objection made is, that the act of 1888 impairs a right vested under the treaty of 1880, as a law of the United States, and the statutes of 1882 and 1884 passed in execution of it."[16] Ultimately, of course, the Court rejected this argument. The opinion concludes by holding that "whatever license, therefore, Chinese laborers may have obtained, previous to the act of October 1, 1888, to return to the United States after their departure, is held at the will of the government, revocable at any time, at its pleasure."[17]

Chae Chan Ping is not, therefore, a canonical case about the rejection of open borders arguments. It should not be surprising, therefore, if the case does not provide a satisfactory justification for a state's right to control its own borders. None was called for by the posture of the case. It is true, of course, that the Court writes that the power to exclude is "incident of sovereignty belonging to the government of the United States, as part of those sovereign powers delegated by the Constitution."[18] But these passage appear largely because there was lingering uncertainty about whether the power to exclude was possessed by individual states or, instead, by the federal government. This question of institutional choice was hotly contested during the period of Chinese exclusion.[19] But the existence of the power itself appears to have been widely accepted. Indeed, not a single federal court decision published between 1875 and 1889—that is, from the passage of the first federal exclusion law up to *Chae Chan Ping*—contains evidence that litigants ever questioned the basic power of a sovereign state to exclude noncitizens.

Thus, the *Chinese Exclusion Case* is not, as is often assumed, a case about open borders. Nonetheless, the basis for this frequent confusion about a nineteenth-century immigration case provides a window into contemporary debates in political philosophy about open borders. In part it confirms the long-standing truth of Song's comment that "public debate about immigration proceeds on the assumption that each country has the right to control its own borders." For this reason, the history of American immigration jurisprudence is unlikely to be a fruitful source of arguments about whether it is ever permissible to restrict the movement of people across international borders. It has much to say about that power's limits and institutional location (though even here many misunderstand the significance of these canonical early immigration cases) but little to say about the foundational question that is typically the focus of philosophical work on migration.

III. EXCLUSION AND NONDISCRIMINATION

A group of people, governed by a particular set of institutions, reside in a territorially defined state. What justifies their right (or the state's right) to keep new people out of this territory and out of the institutions set up within the territory? This is the question Song sets out to answer. As she shows convincingly, answering it requires explaining and justifying in some way the connections between three concepts: the people (or "nation"), the public institutions (or "state"), and the physical space within which the people live and the institutions govern (or "territory"). But I want to suggest that a persuasive answer must also grapple with what is often thought to be an entirely distinct question: What does equality demand for those people whom the state does choose to admit to the territory? In other words, questions about border control are deeply intertwined with questions about the fair treatment of those who are present within a state's borders.

A. *Looking to the Past or to the Future*

To set the stage, it is helpful first to show why Song's approach to justifying state control over immigration is among a class of approaches most likely to succeed—even though I believe it ultimately comes up short. Song surveys a variety of potential justifications for state border controls that are unified by the common goal of linking in some fashion nation, state, and territory. In my view, all these approaches (and I suspect all approaches we can imagine that focus on the relationship between these three ideas) fall into two broad categories. The first is backward looking, and the second is forward looking.

Backward-looking approaches all basically boil down to creation stories. Each account tries to figure out how *this particular* group of people acquired the right to control *this particular* piece of land and keep others off of it. The theories inevitably draw on ideas of settlement, transformation, and the investment of labor—on some past act that gives the existing group of people a claim to control territorial access. As Song notes, these accounts are Lockean, or at least quasi-Lockean. This is true of Tamar Meisels's theory of settlement, David Miller's account of the way a nation's public culture transforms its territory, Cara Nine's argument that the state acquires territorial ownership (and the right to exclude) by investing in the land in ways that change it in morally valuable ways, and Ryan Pevnick's account of how the labor on the land of individual owners creates a claim of joint ownership over the territory and public institutions.[20] These approaches do differ in their details: some focus more on the inputs, others on the way in which those inputs transform the territory; some ground the entitlement in the acts of individuals, others in the acts of a group (the nation), and still others in the acts of the public institutions of the state. Yet the common thread is that the entitlement is traced back to a set of valuable actions that took place in the past. Before those acts took place, no such entitlement existed.

It is easy to understand the appeal of this approach: the focus on the past helps block certain troubling possibilities, such as the one that often plagues utilitarian accounts of territorial control—that on the right empirical premises the theory might make colonialism appear perfectly permissible or even morally obligatory. Moreover, this first approach connects people to a *particular physical territory*. This is why ideas of settlement and investment are so important. They are what ties the people to a particular geographic place and gives them a claim against others over that space—a claim akin to the collective ownership of private property that is accompanied by a right to exclude.

Nonetheless, it seems to me that these backward-looking accounts are destined to be plagued by the same sort of problems that have plagued Lockean theory for centuries. The problem is that the system that is being justified is already up and running, that people who live under it were mostly born into it and thus cannot be considered "voluntary" members, and that these people are not the same people who settled the land or made the investments that are being invoked to justify the claim of ownership. These common criticisms of Lockean approaches have been picked up on by Anna Stilz and others, and they are laid out persuasively in Song's essay.[21] The objections are also familiar in constitutional theory, where they frequently crop up in the dead-hand complaints theorists raise about certain versions of constitutionalism—particularly originalist approaches.[22]

The second approach to justifying a state's right to exclude is forward looking: it takes states and the citizens who currently populate them as basic social facts—that is, as not themselves in need of justification—and then tries to figure out whether these geographically circumscribed polities and institutions should be required to leave their borders open to all comers. Forward-looking theories all share same basic syllogistic structure. They claim (1) that there is something valuable about (or being produced by) the existing state and its people, however the state and its people came to be; (2) that the valuable attribute or good will be threatened if the territory is open to all comers; and therefore (3) that it is necessary to exclude at least some new people in order to preserve the attribute or good.

The second approach ties people to a set of territorially circumscribed institutions under which they happen to live. But because it is not backward looking, this approach cannot explain why we have the particular combinations of nation-state-territory that we happen to find ourselves with. Why exactly does France have the right to control the French Riviera? Or, more radically, why should France control the territory France happens to control, rather than the territory currently controlled by Spain or by Ghana?[23] This is precisely the sort of failing that theories of settlement and investment are designed to overcome. Those theories look to past acts to explain why France controls France and not some other place. But my view is that this is a failing about which we should not fret because, for the reasons noted earlier, the Lockean promise of answering that question is illusory.

A second problem for the forward-looking approach is not so much conceptual as normative: the theory depends on the idea that the existing state and its people generate something valuable that is worth preserving. What is this good? There are many possibilities raised in the literature. Territorially bounded states and the people who live within them might solve certain public goods problems in ways that provide justice to the people who live under those institutions (Beitz); they might protect large-scale systems of redistribution; they might generate and sustain a national identity (Walzer) or a public culture (Miller, Song) that is either good for its own sake or because the solidarity and civic motivation fostered by the culture motivates insiders to behave in ways that produce some other valuable end; or they might provide a mechanism for securing self-determination, freedom of association, self-governance, or the collective decision-making power of the existing polity (Wellman, Song). Exploring this last possibility is really the core of Song's essay, part of a larger project she has been working on to explain the relationship between migration and self-governance.

Each of these theories about the value generated by particular combinations of nation, state, and territory is open to a few different sorts of objections. For one thing, we might simply doubt the purported value of the collective good. Some theorists argue, for example, that "national identity" is not a valuable good worth preserving. Second, these forward-looking claims might be thought to be problematic because they are to some extent contingent. Perhaps another configuration of institutions and people could also solve thorny collective action problems—maybe even better than the existing set of nation-states. And perhaps the shuffling of institutions and peoples would give rise to a different but equally valuable national identity or public culture. Thus, there is often a temptation to combine these theories with some backward-looking element to try to avoid such problems, as David Miller's account of public culture ultimately does. But if we put aside temptation, then these accounts, of which Song's is one, do provide a promising path for identifying what might justify exclusion.

B. Self-Selection and Sorting

So far so good. We can see that there are powerful (if not neces-sarily decisive) arguments in favor of the syllogism's first premise, even if each of us might disagree about which goods precisely are most valuable. But that is not enough. The logic of the forward-looking accounts is (1) that there is something valuable produced by the existing state and its people, (2) that inclusion might threaten that valuable good, and thus (3) that preserving that good requires excluding at least some outsiders from the terri-tory. What if the second premise is incorrect in at least some cases? Exclusion might not be needed to protect some goods.

To see that there is no necessary connection between the pres-ervation of a valuable good and exclusion *of any kind*, consider Song's concept of self-governance. American states (as well as member states in the European Union) may not restrict freedom of movement across their borders. Nonetheless, we typically think of them as having well-functioning democracies—as being to some extent self-governing—despite the fact that they cannot restrict entry into their territories.[24] In fact, for American states it is not just the power to exclude from the territory that is denied: they are also prohibited, as a matter of constitutional law, from excluding newcomers from participating in politics. Thus, it is not obvious that protecting self-determination requires exclusion from either the territory or the polity.

Song attempts to resist this reality, and foreclose the possibility that there can be self-determination-without-exclusion, by arguing the following:

A. The "ideal of democracy" entails self-determination.[25]
B. "The right of self-determination includes the right to control admission and membership."
C. Control of admission and membership derives "from re-specting the right of individuals to be regarded as equal par-ticipants in significant political decisions to which they are bound."[26]

But together these propositions lead in three directions that undermine their force. First, the syllogistic logic of propositions A and B would force us to conclude that American states and European Union member states are not democracies because they cannot control admission to their territories. Second, the categorical claim that self-determination requires that the existing demos control the shape of the future demos has implications that I suspect Song would not embrace. On this account it would appear to be within the power of the existing polity to deny membership to the future children of existing citizens, or even to strip current members of citizenship.

Third, and perhaps most important, the idea that insiders must control access to the territory in order to satisfy the moral equality of persons—that is, in order to respect "the right of individuals to be regarded as equal participants in significant political decisions by which they are bound"—seems to fail on its own terms. After all, every person excluded by immigration restrictions is excluded by virtue of a significant political decision by which that person is bound. Thus, by its own terms, proposition C provides an argument in favor of giving those excluded a say in a state's exclusion decisions, precisely the point that Song wants to deny.

This dilemma is not an artifact of anything peculiar about Song's approach. Instead, it is an applied example of a general problem in democratic theory on which Song has done interesting work—a problem often labeled the "boundary problem." This problem has eluded a satisfactory solution for generations. The fact that the problem plaguing many theories of territorial exclusion turns out to be equivalent to the boundary problem in democratic theory leaves me pessimistic that the dilemma will be solved in the migration context.

C. Not All Exclusion Is Spatial

Putting aside this conundrum, however, perhaps there are other reasons why at least some exclusion is necessary to preserve one of the valuable goods proposed by the forward-looking theories. Certainly many people have the intuition that the syllogism's second premise is sometimes correct. Even if this is true, however, it only entails the conclusion that some form of exclusion is necessary. It does not necessarily justify territorial exclusion.

Freedom of movement across international borders is often not sufficient, in itself, to threaten the valuable goods defended by the forward-looking theories. Instead, for most of the valuable goods described earlier, two conditions are necessary to create a risk of undermining the good: freedom of movement *plus* nondiscrimination against newcomers. To protect the welfare state, for example, a state could exclude those who might place great demands on it. Alternatively, the state could permit them to enter but restrict their access to public assistance. (In fact, the United States and other countries do precisely this.) To protect the institutions of democracy from "dilution" by outsiders, one could exclude outsiders from the territory. Or one could simply deny them the access to the franchise for some period of time. (Again, this is what the United States and other nations do.) To be sure, there are some goods, like public culture, that might be deeply affected by the entrance of outsiders regardless of the treatment (or even sometimes precisely because of the treatment) of those newcomers. Nonetheless, the fact that not all exclusion need be territorial—that newcomers can often be excluded from valuable institutions or goods without being physically excluded from a territory—means that any theory attempting to justify territorial exclusion must explain why discrimination against newcomers is not an acceptable substitute for territorial exclusion.

Scores of theorists writing since Michael Walzer penned *Spheres of Justice* have assumed that newcomers must be treated like existing citizens.[27] Although Song is not always explicit about her view on equality for immigrants, her argument that "the demos should be bounded by the territorial boundaries of the state" might be understood as an implicit argument in favor of what we might call simple territorial equality—the idea that every person physically present within a state must be treated alike. This approach requires that those admitted to the territory be treated like citizens and formally integrated into the demos. On the other hand, there is also language in Song's essay that points toward a different view. Defending a state's right to exclude people who were not themselves given a chance to participate in the formulation of the exclusion policy, she argues that not all people subject to the state's coercive authority need to be treated like citizens: "The demos is not an aggregation of individuals coerced by the same power but rather an enduring collective that makes decisions with binding authority."[28] In other words, political equality need extend only to *members*, and not everyone who is coerced by the state must be accorded membership. The structure of this argument at least implies that it might be permissible to admit migrants to the territory without also welcoming them as full members who are entitled to political equality and a say in the state's future policies. If this is correct, then protecting self-determination (as defined by Song) will not in all cases require that a state have the right to exclude people from its physical territory.

Ultimately, my goal is not to argue that either of these possible views is correct—though, as Adam Hosein and I have argued elsewhere, it is far from clear that principles of *equality* require that a principle of *equal treatment* be afforded to new arrivals.[29] Instead, my position is simply that these questions about what equality requires should be central in open borders debates. Even if territorially defined states produce valuable moral or social goods, and even if these goods would be threatened in the absence of exclusion, not all exclusion is territorial. Defending territorial exclusion requires, therefore, explaining why other forms of exclusion cannot or should not serve as substitutes.

IV. Conclusion

Migrants and the legal institutions that regulate them are necessarily complex. Yet the philosophical conversation about open borders tends to flatten these complexities. Open borders debates tend to elevate the status of a single question concerning migration—whether it is ever permissible to restrict freedom of movement across borders—as analytically prior and morally more important than all others. Doing so trivializes questions that are far richer historically and more significant politically—questions about when, and under what conditions, a particular migrant may be excluded; about how that migrant must be treated after entry; and about who should make and enforce those rules. Those questions are at the core of centuries of political conflict over immigration law, both in the United States and elsewhere. But the reason to focus on them is not only because they are more historically and politically salient. It is also because, as I hope I have shown in this chapter, giving more attention to them will also help us produce persuasive accounts of the rights and obligations related to migration.

NOTES

1. One common way of thinking about this question is by asking whether a decision to exclude a person violates her rights. Michael Walzer, for example, argues that states have an obligation to admit refugees even though exclusion is generally permissible. See Michael Walzer, *Spheres of Justice* (New York: Basic Books, 1984). Interestingly, arguments of this sort often run together two quite different conceptions of rights. One conception is that rights are trumps—entitlements held by individuals that override some government action or create a corresponding duty on the part of the government. This view is reflected in the claim, made by Michael Walzer and others, that states have an obligation to admit refugees even though exclusion is generally permissible. The idea is that some people are so badly off that they must be permitted to enter. But rights need not be conceptualized in this way. They also can be seen as prohibitions on the government's acting for certain impermissible reasons. On this account, it might be wrong for a state to exclude a person because of her race or religion. But excluding even refugees might be permissible so long as the reason for the state's action is permissible—if, say, the state has already accepted many refugees and concludes that its system of social services would be overwhelmed by accepting more. On the distinction between these two conceptions of rights, see Richard H. Pildes, "Why Rights Are Not Trumps: Social Meanings, Expressive Harms, and Constitutionalism," *Journal of Legal Studies* 27 (1998): 725–63; Matt Adler, "Rights against Rules," *Michigan Law Review* 97 (1999): 1–173.

2. The institutional options are in theory vast and could include the state into which the person wants to enter, the state from which the person is leaving, some international body, private parties living in either the sending or the receiving state, and so on. In the philosophical literature, the fight is typically over whether a receiving state should have unilateral authority to make such decisions. In practice, it is interesting to note that a broad array of persons and institutions have been empowered to make immigration screening decisions. See Adam B. Cox and Eric A. Posner, "Delegation in Immigration Law," *University of Chicago Law Review* 79 (2012): 1285–349.

3. Many thanks to Adam Hosein for this point.

4. See Emer de Vattel, *Les droit des gens* [*The Law of Nations*] (1758); *Chae Chan Ping v. United States*, 130 U.S. 581 (1889).

5. Sarah Song, chapter 1, section I, this volume.

6. For a recent restatement of this view, see Daryl J. Levinson, "Parchment and Politics: The Positive Puzzle of Constitutional Commitment," *Harvard Law Review* 124 (2011): 657–746.

7. Democracy is sometimes seen to pose a similar puzzle.

8. Something like this was Hobbes's view.

9. For a nice discussion of the issue and some potential mechanisms of stability and compliance, see Paul Pierson, *Politics in Time: History, Institutions, and Social Analysis* (Princeton, NJ: Princeton University Press, 2004).

10. *Chae Chan Ping v. United States, 130 U.S. 581 (1889).*

11. See Song, chapter 1. See also Hiroshi Motomura, "Immigration Law after a Century of Plenary Power: Phantom Constitutional Norms and Statutory Interpretation," *Yale Law Journal* 100 (1990): 545–613, 551 ("Justice Field's opinion *established* that the federal government has the power to regulate immigration, and it further suggested that the political branches could exercise this power without being subject to judicial review.").

12. Brief for Appellant by George Hoadly and James C. Carter at 16, 18, *Chae Chan Ping v. United States*, 130 U.S. 581 (1889) (the "Hoadly Brief").

13. Brief for Appellant by James C. Carter at 3, *Chae Chan Ping v. United States*, 130 U.S. 581 (1889) (the "Carter Brief"). Briefs filed by both the United States and the State of California emphasizes these concessions: "Indeed, the counsel for appellant . . . concede—1st. That Congress has the power to abrogate a treaty between the United States and a foreign power. 2d. That the Exclusion Act of October 1st, 1888, was intended to abrogate and does abrogate prior treaties with China, so far as Chinese laborers are concerned." Brief for Appellee on Behalf of the State of California at 2, *Chae Chan Ping v. United States*, 130, U.S. 581 (1889); Brief for Appellee United States at 14, *Chae Chan Ping v. United States*, 130, U.S. 581 (1889). Like Chae Chan Ping's briefs, the appellee briefs frame the case as about whether "certain valuable or vested rights have been acquired of which Chinese laborers cannot be deprived by legislation." California Brief at 2; United States Brief at 14.

14. Hoadly Brief at 17.

15. This is not to say that a citizen's right of residence, or other private rights for that matter, were absolute. Private rights could be taken from a person, but only in accordance with certain procedural forms. For example, a person's core right to liberty—to be free from physical restraint—could be taken only as punishment after a judicial trial. A citizen's right of residence was commonly viewed in the same light during this period: A citizen might be banished, but banishment could take place only following a judicial trial, as punishment for an offense that existed at the time the punished conduct was undertaken. See, e.g., In re Look Tin Sing, 21 F. 905 (C.C.D. Ca. 1884) ("no citizen can be excluded from this country except in punishment for crime"); *cf.* In re Yung Sing Hee, 36 F. 437 (C.C.D. Or. 1888). On

this understanding, Chae Chan Ping's exclusion would have been doubly problematic had it been treated legally like the banishment of a citizen: it would have been the result of a retroactive bill of attainder; and it also would have been imposed without a judicial trial. See Hoadley brief at p.71.

16. *Chae Chan Ping*, 130 U.S. at 603.

17. Ibid., 609.

18. Ibid., 606.

19. This debate is alluded to in Ping's briefing, which notes that there may well be a serious question whether the federal government or the states possess this sovereign power to exclude. See Carter Brief at 3.

20. See Tamar Meisels, *Territorial Rights*, 2nd ed. (New York: Springer, 2009); David Miller, *National Responsibility and Global Justice* (Oxford: Oxford University Press, 2007); Cara Nine, "A Lockean Theory of Territory," *Political Studies* 56 (2008): 150; Ryan Pevnick, *Immigration and the Constraints of Justice* (Cambridge: Cambridge University Press, 2011).

21. See Anna Stilz, "Why Do States Have Territorial Rights?," *International Theory* 1 (2009): 185–213.

22. See Adam M. Samaha, "Dead Hand Arguments and Constitutional Interpretation," *Columbia Law Review* 108 (2008): 606–80.

23. I suspect that these problems are related to a more general set of criticisms of group rights and so may not be unique to immigration or thinking about nations and states.

24. The idea that exclusion may not be necessary to preserve self-determination can be extended to other valuable goods as well. Consider cultural distinctiveness. Michael Walzer argued in *Spheres of Justice* that exclusion was justified in order to preserve such distinctiveness. But as Joseph Carens pointed out, there are plenty of communities that have "distinctive cultures and ways of life" despite having open borders. See Joseph Carens, "Aliens and Citizens," *Review of Politics* 49 (1987): 251–73, 266–67. Self-selection and sorting can be as powerful as, and sometimes more powerful than, formal restrictions on freedom of movement.

25. To be clear, Song's defense of self-determination is instrumental. She views self-determination "as derivative of more fundamental principles, such as principles of justice. . . . [W]e should respect a state's sovereignty and refrain from interfering with its affairs because the state's institutions are just." Song, chapter 1. In other words, self-determination is valuable only insofar as it produces a just set of institutions or outcomes.

26. See Song, chapter 1.

27. See Walzer, *Spheres of Justice*.

28. See Song, chapter 1.

29. See Adam Cox and Adam Hosein, "Immigration and Equality," NYU School of Law, Public Law Research Paper (2012).

3

JURISDICTION AND EXCLUSION

A RESPONSE TO SARAH SONG

MICHAEL BLAKE

It isn't much fun to comment on an essay with which one is fundamentally in agreement. Disagreement breeds argument, which is productive; agreement breeds congratulation, which is not. The worst temptation for the commentator is to focus on the increasingly small bits with which one disagrees. The sort of comment thereby produced often amounts to the statement: what's wrong with your view is that it isn't *quite* my view.

Rather than perform this sort of exercise, I am going to focus my commentary on a few questions that I think Song's view—and my own—will have to deal with. These questions aren't designed to show that the view is wrong; because I largely agree with it, I don't particularly want to show that. I want, instead, to show that there are some points at which the moral story about immigration will have to be supplemented. To do this, I will start first with the things about which Song and I agree. I will then give two arguments with which I think views like ours will have to deal. I will then give some brief notes about how it is that we would have to deal with them; at this point, I suspect, Song and I might begin to part company, although I would of course be entirely happy to discover that we continue in agreement.

So, to begin with, I think Song is entirely right to think that the right to exclude is a jurisdictional right.[1] Most defenses of the right spend too little time on what a state is, qua state—a political community, with a defined jurisdictional reach. It is right to place jurisdiction back at the center of our account of exclusion. I similarly agree with Song's dismissal of property-based and association-based accounts of exclusion. These accounts tends to ignore, in my view and on Song's, what is interesting and unique about the state—its jurisdictional reach and the morally significant relationships that emerge from presence within that jurisdiction. I agree, finally, with Song's rejection of culturally based defenses of the right to exclude. Indeed, I might go even further than she does here; these sorts of defenses seem to me to confuse the notion of a good with the notion of a right. Even if cultures were always good things, whose existence provided benefits for all those who inhabit them, we cannot thereby infer that we have a right to do whatever is needed to defend these cultures. While a particular good may provide a rationale for the use of our rights, it is an entirely separate matter to explain why that right exists; culturally based accounts of the right to exclude ignore this fact, to their detriment.

All this, then, we have in common. Again, there will be small points of disagreement; I believe, for example, that the right to exclude is based not on the needs of democracy but on the right to refuse to become the agents charged with the defense of someone's human rights, where those human rights are adequately protected elsewhere.[2] But instead of focusing on these differences, I am going to proceed to the two points on which I believe our views are in need of amplification.

The first of these looks to the issue of federalism and subsidiarity. The arguments Song gives for the benefits of democratic closure are, strictly speaking, insensitive to federal level; if solidarity and knowing who one represents are good things for democratic functioning, they are good things both within the sovereign state and within the federal subunit. This might be considered a problem, since now it appears that not only the United States but also the state of Louisiana, Orleans parish, and the city of New Orleans are all democratic spaces, and the argument for the right to exclude would seem to apply with equal strength to all of them. It makes democratic life easier within Louisiana, after all, if the state

representatives from Louisiana know who they represent; it similarly helps Louisiana be a democratic society when Louisianans
are able to rely upon the sorts of trust created by a common background and set of cultural institutions. But if these considerations
give the same rights regardless of where they are found, then they
might seem a bit problematic; while many of us would be happy to
defend the right of the United States to keep out unwanted immigrants, few of us would want the state of Louisiana to have the
equivalent right to keep out unwanted visitors from (say) Seattle or
Berkeley. Legally, moreover, the absence of such a right is uncon-
troversial; while states often tried to keep out unwanted paupers
from other states in the late eighteenth century—and some have
tried to do similar things more recently—they simply don't have
such a right under the U.S. Constitution, and they rarely pretend
they should.[3] But if Song's argument is right, then why should this
be so? The problem here, I think, is that the argument Song gives
strictly speaking only describes why the right to exclude is a good
thing for the democratic functioning of a set of political institutions. It doesn't tell us anything about how those political institutions relate to *other* political institutions, whether they are above or
below in a federal system. We have to add some account of federalism and subsidiarity before we can rest assured that the argument
in question, while it proves the right of the state to exclude, has
not proved entirely too much on the way to that conclusion.

The second point looks to the issue of interpersonal justification.
The worry is simply this: What can be said to the would-be immigrant at the border, who is seeking admission?[4] The justification
would have to be one that respects the moral equality of the would-
be immigrant and the current residents of the territorial jurisdiction to which that individual is seeking admission. I am not sure,
though, how the right to exclude as Song develops it can do this
job, without running into problems rather similar to those found
in nationalist defenses of the right to exclude. The reason for this
is simple: all the notions given by Song in her defense of the importance of border closure identify good things that emerge from the
border's being closed. Trust, solidarity, knowledge of who we are
and who we represent—these are all good things that help democratic self-government. Given the importance of self-government,
these good things are a special category of goods; we are not here

being told to justify the exclusion of a would-be immigrant with reference to the pleasant things we continue to have while we keep them out. They are, instead, things that are helpful to the establishment of democratic self-government, which we might think of as being a set of relationships that are of inherent moral importance. But these goods are, at most, things that are *helpful* in the creation of democratic self-rule; we can imagine, after all, flourishing democratic communities with less than fully maximal amounts of trust, or solidarity, or representative identity. (Indeed, all actual states, even the most well-ordered, have deeply imperfect scores on any of these values.) And that means that the justification we offer to the one who wants admission is not: sorry, you can't come in because your presence would make morally rightful relationships impossible. It is, instead: you can't come in because your presence would make morally rightful relationships slightly more *difficult.* And I am not sure, without some more argument, why we are able to say this to a would-be immigrant, while thinking that we are still entitled to call ourselves moral egalitarians. If the would-be immigrant would actually make a democratic society cease to exist by her presence, then that's a good enough reason to keep her out; democracy, like the constitution, is not a suicide pact. But if the justification for exclusion isn't imminent destruction but merely a suboptimal-but-possible set of circumstances for democratic self-rule, why do we think this is a sufficient rationale to deprive the would-be immigrant of the right to move across borders?

A hypothetical might help make this case. Imagine that aesthetic enjoyment of nature is a moral imperative; looking at pretty things is not just good but a rightful sort of relationship, incumbent upon all good people. So: I've got an obligation to be on a plot of beautiful land, staring at the trees. Now you wander onto the land. Your presence here won't make my rightful relationship with nature impossible; you're just a slight impediment to my maximally achieving the sorts of relationship I ought to try to cultivate. (You're not a tree, but neither are you so hideous you negate the value of staring at the trees.) Could I push you off the land, citing my need to enjoy nature? It's hard to say in the abstract, of course, but I think you could at least speak back to that right by saying—hey, I need to stare at nature too! If it's possible for both of us to stare at nature here, why shouldn't we both have the right to do so? Sure, your maximal nature-staring will be impeded by my presence, but it will be made only *less than perfect*—not wrongful, or somehow less than morality would require. I think the first inhabitant here is obligated to take the hit and accept a less than perfect ability to have a relationship with nature. To say otherwise would seem to be saying to someone at the border: yes, it would be possible for you to come in and enjoy the relationships that we think people ought to have, but we'd rather maximize the good things than let you be a part of them. And I'm not sure why this sort of justification is ever acceptable, when it's used as a justification for the sorts of coercion that exist at the border. When someone wants to cross into our country, and we say we'd rather have more of certain goods, even though we'd have *enough* when they come in, and then we use physical violence to exclude them when they try to come in anyhow—well, all this looks to me very much like the insistence that the freedom of others is legitimately trumped by the self-interest of others. If John Rawls was right that the problem with utilitarianism was its ignoring the separateness of persons, then the view defended here might come very close to committing the same sin against the persons of would-be immigrants at the border. Indeed, I'd say it's the same issue I find with the nationalist defense of exclusion: the fact that a given action would help produce a good does not, in itself, defend the existence of a right to do that action.

As I said at the beginning, I think answers exist to both of these problems. In both cases, though, I think getting clearer on these answers might provoke some interesting additions to the theory. The first one can be dealt with comparatively easily; if Louisiana doesn't have a right to exclude, it's likely because of something having to do with the self-conception of the United States. We could easily imagine a close possible United States that had allowed the states of the Union to run their own immigration systems; I wouldn't want to live there, but I don't think it's morally impermissible for something like it to exist. This means, though, that the right to exclude isn't inherent just in a democratic self-government but in a particular sort of democratic self-government—one that conceives of itself as having a particular sort of relationship to the federal units beneath (and, perhaps, above) its authority. I think getting clearer on what that might be would make Song's view more persuasive. And I believe something interesting might emerge when this account starts taking international institutions seriously. If novelty continues to emerge in international forms—if the neo-medieval view of international relations begins to accelerate—then we might arrive at some situations in which transnational institutions create a single democratic polis (whatever that means!) out of what once were sovereign states. Where this happens, the right to *some* forms of international migration might emerge from the same materials we use here to deny these rights. Europe, for example, has many of the attributes needed to understand itself as a single community of self-rule; it has a Parliament, certain rights to trump the legal rules made by federal subunits, a system for judicial review, and so on. This might mean that the right to mobility within Europe is required, for the same reasons it is required between Louisiana and California. I do not want to draw too much significance out of this; I only want to point out the small irony—that once Song's view is fully developed, it may end up defending the moral necessity of the right to move across national borders.

The second issue with the view is, I think, more philosophically vexing. The issue is what, precisely, can be said to the would-be immigrant that does not violate the notion of moral equality. One solution would be to simply say that Rawls was wrong, and that we are sometimes allowed to justify a restriction on freedom with reference to the maximization of a good—or, perhaps, that Rawls properly interpreted would not be offended by such a statement made at the border. I have to say I am not a fan of this strategy; what's appealing about the liberal project is that it insists upon moral equality, and to let this moral ideal be a merely local value is unduly dismissive of liberalism's potential. But I think we could start an alternative solution here by looking at what it is that individuals are truly entitled to, as part of the project of ensuring moral equality. We would have to focus, then, not simply on what makes political communities flourish but on what people are entitled to simply in virtue of being human. We might imagine, for example, that people are entitled to have *some* space within which they are guaranteed the rights of democratic self-government—but not that they are entitled to have those rights protected by the institutions that they would most prefer. (To borrow Robert Goodin's metaphor: we are entitled to a lifeguard at the beach, but no lifeguard may have to guard all beaches—and we are not necessarily entitled to select the lifeguard we most desire.)[5] Getting clear on how this would work would require us to shift attention away from the needs of the current inhabitants, to the moral rights of the would-be immigrant. This shift would have the benefit of making us look directly at the most morally central issue: whether or not these rights give rise to a claim on the part of that immigrant to entry. Song's story right now only gives us part of the answer: it provides an account on which the current members of the state have a reason to seek closed borders, given the benefits that closure would provide. But until we see why it is that the would-be immigrant does not have a right to entry, it seems that the answer is only partial. Justifying exclusion to outsiders would have to make an appeal to what they are owed, not simply what is useful for current insiders.

I would end by reiterating what I said at the beginning: I believe there are answers to these issues, and nothing I said here is intended to disprove Song's methods or her conclusions. Indeed, these methods and conclusions are both exactly what I would hope for; they focus on the right aspects of the situation, and they derive answers I think are both sensible and defensible. Song's view is at worst incomplete, and incompleteness is a much more venial sin than inaccuracy. I'm happy to be a fellow traveler on Song's road, and I hope to have been of some use in making that shared road more useful in future debates.

NOTES

1. I am focusing primarily on Song's arguments from political theory, not her analysis of legal history—although I would note, in passing, that I am not sure I agree with her linking of international relations realism and unilateral statism. Unilateral statism of the sort defended in early modern philosophy, after all, was compatible with the existence of genuine moral duties to strangers; as Song notes, Vattel defended the idea that the territorial state had duties to outsiders thrown against it by tempest and necessity. This sort of idea is incompatible with realism understood as a prescriptive account of state duties. On my view, unilateral statism can be a more moderate thesis about the rights of a political community; realism is a more extreme thesis of both these rights and the legitimate moral constraints on how they might be deployed.

2. I develop this account in "Immigration, Jurisdiction, and Exclusion," *Philosophy and Public Affairs* 41 (2013): 103–30.

3. The most important case on this subject is *Shapiro v. Thompson*, 394 U.S. 618 (1969), which struck down Connecticut's residency requirement for access to public benefits.

4. This question, obviously, is inspired by Arash Abizadeh, whose writings have given it more force in recent years. See "Democratic Theory and Border Coercion: No Right to Unilaterally Control Your Own Borders," *Political Theory* 36 (2008): 37–65.

5. Robert S. Goodin, "What Is So Special about Our Fellow Countrymen?," *Ethics* 98 (1988): 663–86.

PART II

LAW'S MIGRATIONS, MOBILITIES, AND BORDERS

4

BORDERING BY LAW

THE MIGRATION OF LAW, CRIMES, SOVEREIGNTY, AND THE MAIL

JUDITH RESNIK

Law in the United States is awash with efforts to delineate borders (alien/citizen, authorized/unauthorized migrant, federal/state) as justifications for legal rules controlling human movement. Yet the literature mapping the illegalization of the migration of peoples does not reference that many borders have become readily traversable, if not invisible, through interdependent government efforts resulting in the legalization and internationalization of subsidized mail services. And, while the politics of migration are much debated, the post is infrequently acknowledged as either a political or a legal site.

I bring together these domains not to equate the migration of persons and families with the movement of objects but rather to clarify how reliant governments are on border crossings and to underscore how political imagination reshapes sovereign practices. Two major shifts, both predicated on states forwarding their own national identities, have moved in opposite directions: one imagining the globe as a "single postal territory" and the other turning migration into a crime. In pursuit of both, governments expanded their role as providers of services—from creating a transnational currency in stamps for mail to patrolling borders and building detention centers.

Neither set of practices is secure. Spectacles of desperate migrants, seeking both physical safety and economic well-being and grounding claims of fair treatment in transnational human rights, have turned the border into a site of sovereign dysfunction—making plain that neither law nor land can readily be bordered. In contrast, while the cooperative sovereign negotiations entailed in the movement of mail have demonstrated governments' capacities to expand economic markets and their political influence while also promoting interpersonal relationships and political liberties, the universalist aspirations and redistributive utilities of these state-run services are now under pressure from private providers, able to selectively cream off segments of markets, and from illiberal forces, aiming to control and channel the content of exchanges.

Will either the punitive migration or the subsidized mail regime last? Answers turn on whether political will can be marshaled and constitutional law enlisted to undo the criminalization of migrants and to sustain states as central sources of collective identities aiming to protect liberty and to enhance equality. By tracing the criminalization of migration through state and federal initiatives in the United States during the last several decades and sketching the development of the Universal Postal Union, I aim to disrupt the sense of inevitability about either trajectory. My hope is to refocus migration debates on the normalcy, rationality, and legitimacy of human movement in search of better circumstances. New states risk more of their sovereignty by performing their incapacity to stem migrants than expressing their sovereign identities through supportive infrastructure services that facilitate the movement of persons seeking to cross boundaries. Political invention is thus required to turn such cooperation into a taken-for-granted government activity, akin to the state-subsidized interjurisdictional, cooperative postal system that has become so normal as to be unseen.

I. BORDERING

Opposition [to registration laws for aliens] was based upon charges that their requirements were at war with the fundamental principles of our free government, in that they would bring about unnecessary and irritating restrictions upon personal liberties of the individual, and would subject aliens to a system of indiscriminate questioning similar to the espionage systems existing in other lands.

> *Hines v. Davidowitz*, 312 U.S. 52, 71 (1941)
> (Justice Hugo Black, for the Court)

[A]ny investigatory detention . . . may become an "'unreasonable . . . seizur[e],'" . . . [but] I know of no reason why a protracted detention that does not violate the Fourth Amendment would contradict or conflict with any federal immigration law.

> *Arizona v. United States*, 132 S. Ct. 2492, 2516 (2012)
> (Justice Antonin Scalia, dissenting)

Signatories to this Treaty "form . . . a single postal territory for the reciprocal exchange of correspondence."

> Treaty of Berne, Article 1, 1874

A series of puzzles prompts this inquiry into the regulation of the movement of persons and objects. Above I quoted snippets from two U.S. Supreme Court immigration cases, one decided in 1941 and the other in 2012. They capture a shift in constitutional discourse from the aspirational assertion that harassing aliens was antithetical to American identity to the contemporary era, when stigmatization through surveillance, detention, deportation, and criminalization of unauthorized migrants has become an ordinary government practice at both state and federal levels. The excerpt from the 1874 Treaty of Berne brings transnational interactions into view through that ambitious effort to eliminate border-barriers so as to facilitate reciprocal commercial, political, and personal interactions through postal services.

Today, few people pause to marvel at the fact that placing a stamp on a letter in the United States and putting it in a blue box sends that piece of mail securely across national boundaries to arrive in a country thousands of miles away. But before the 1870s, posting a letter abroad was no ordinary act; given various land and sea routes, the transit was treacherous, prices varied, and charges were sometimes collected upon receipt. The founding in 1874 of what is now called the Universal Postal Union (UPU), identified as the second-ever government-based international organization,[1] aimed to overcome cumbersome interactions among individuals, countries, and commercial enterprises by imagining the world as a "single postal territory."[2]

That new orientation depended on interactions among sovereigns, expanding their capital markets and promoting their political ideologies. Those (often colonial) initiatives facilitated public and private exchanges that transformed individual and collective practices, as both national and international subsidies enabled diverse groups of people to gain new communicative capacities. These efforts produced the current commitments to universal, government-provided, uncensored mailing services. In the twenty-first century, however, fragile states, waning national support, private competitors, and new technologies challenge that infrastructure.

The movement of objects is, of course, not to be equated with the movement of people. But the invention of a universal postal union represents government choices to respond to the Westphalian development of sovereign borders by committing to their erasures for specific purposes. My argument is that it is likewise normatively desirable to promote the choices of individuals and families to move and that to do so requires both national commitments to the morality, legality, and utility of migration and new international institutions facilitating migration. My claim is that such an approach is not only useful for individuals, families, and communities bound up in cross-border networks but also essential for the viability of the nation-state in the twenty-first century.

Legalization, in the sense I advance it here, references both the recognition of the status of the estimated 11 million individuals residing in the United States who have crossed borders without permission and taken up long-term residency and the commitment to change the valence of movement so as to detach entry-without-permission from the punitive infrastructure that has been built during the last seventy years. Before 1929, in the United States, permission to enter was needed, but crossing a border was not a criminal act. Regulation need not rely on criminalization, just as citizenship need not be the only form of relationship that residents of a place have with a body politic.

Many commentators have addressed the import of democracy and of human rights for migration and the political and moral arguments for liberalizing entry for economic migrants as well as political refugees.[3] And, around the world, a few courts have addressed whether migration can be punished as a crime and the kind of sanctions that can follow unlawful entry.[4] In this chapter, I focus on the genealogy and breadth of U.S. legal sanction systems, so as to clarify the number of disheartening innovations over the last decades and the toll that punitive treatment of migrants takes on the rights of citizens, on the interpretation of U.S. constitutional law, and on American identity. My argument is that the criminalization of migration has turned the border into a vivid spectacle of national dysfunction, in which both state and federal governments perform their own incompetence, as they also undermine American constitutional commitments to equal treatment of all persons.

Normalizing migration through cooperation across borders may seem counterintuitive, given images of legions of migrants negotiating treacherous paths to transverse borders and anxieties about terrorism. Yet, even as migration has "increased almost sixfold" over ninety years when the population grew threefold,[5] most people do not leave their countries of origin. In 2012, the world's population was estimated to be 6.9 billion people, of whom 214 million—3 percent—were migrants, living outside their countries of origin.[6] By 2015, the number had risen slightly; 244 million people—some 3.3 percent of the world's population—were migrants.[7]

Numbers are, of course, only a part of the story. Attention is focused on immigration in the United States and in Europe because the movement of persons and things is neither symmetrical across borders nor uniform around the globe. In migration studies, the nomenclature of "sending" and "receiving" denotes that difference—raising concerns at one end that high migrant exit rates deplete sending countries' capacities and, at the other, that high entry rates overwhelm receiving countries' resources.[8] The United States is a receiving country.[9] Forty million people, or 13 percent of the country's population of more than 300 million, were born outside the country,[10] and millions more are children of those born abroad.[11]

More than that: America was born through migration, prompting U.S. Supreme Court Justice Anthony Kennedy to explain in

2012 in *Arizona v. United States* that "[i]mmigration policy shapes the destiny of the Nation."[12] His opinion for the Court in that case—bearing the name of a state in conflict with the national government—reflected that some parts of the United States receive more migrants than do others and have views hostile toward migration. The decision held that federal law precluded states from adding criminal sanctions on unauthorized migrants on top of those already imposed by federal statutes and implemented (or not) through executive branch prosecutions.

I juxtapose materials on the migration of persons and the movement of objects to reflect on the dynamic changes in U.S. law governing both so as to analyze the varying functions of and aspirations for sovereign borders. Until 1929, entering the United States without permission was not a violation of federal criminal law.[13] Moreover, in 1941, in *Hines v. Davidowitz*, the Supreme Court rejected Pennsylvania's public registration of aliens as antithetical to America's commitments to "personal liberties," a posture the Court contrasted with the licit "espionage systems in other lands."[14]

Yet, in the nineteenth century, the Court had countenanced Chinese exclusion laws,[15] and just four years after *Hines*, the Court upheld the internment of citizens of Japanese ancestry as a permissible response during World War II.[16] During the course of several decades, the constitutional law on liberty shifted, as state and federal laws imposed stigmatizing disabilities on migrants through constructing steel barricades, detention centers, and employment bans.

These decisions are the outgrowth of politics that, thus far, courts have not ruled constitutionally impermissible. Thus, a vast investment of resources, reliant on criminal and civil regulations and permitted under constitutional law, has worked to marginalize migrants. The shadows of these laws extend beyond the category of the alien and thereby make searches and oversight of citizens both plausible and legal. Criminalization has captured tens of thousands of individuals, resulting in an incarcerated population exceeding 2 million people. Technologies of oversight have expanded, such that the National Security Administration, using methods unimagined only short times ago, can skirt borders, governments' sovereignty, and citizenship status in pursuit of knowledge about both persons and objects.

The criminalization of migration took place during the last century; the reconfiguration of mail services occurred before then. Private entities once provided limited postal services that lacked uniform pricing, took circuitous routes, and reached only selected recipients. Further, mail was not a secure source of interpersonal or commercial exchange. Yet, during the last 150 years, mail gained protections, enshrined in many constitutions and reflecting the commercial and interpersonal utilities as well as commitments to individual autonomy, privacy, and free expression. In the twenty-first century, surveillance of electronic exchanges and cell phones makes mailed correspondence a relatively private form of communication.

How did migration become so entwined with the criminal law? How did mail come to move easily across borders? And what role does sovereignty play in both arenas? To understand the current construction of American border law requires knowing the building blocks. First, I detail how law and practices—not land—delineate borders for migrants in the United States. Second, given ongoing debates about the allocation of national and local power, I explore the respective roles of state and federal governments in shaping contemporary laws. An assertion of the hegemony of national law's authority to displace state law misses how much "the national" incorporates state-created approaches to alienage. Illustrative is the degree to which federal registration regulations came to resemble the Pennsylvania law that, in 1941 in *Hines,* the U.S. Supreme Court rebuffed as antithetical to American commitments.

Third, I elaborate the expansion of government surveillance authority over migrants through public and private sector actors working in the civil and criminal systems. As the law shifted to accommodate such regulation, constitutional law also tolerated oversight of citizens. Just as aliens can now be required to show documentation, citizen-recipients of federal benefits may be required to submit to home searches, citizen-prisoners to warrantless searches of their cells, citizen-schoolchildren to testing for drugs, and all persons to surveillance of their transnational phone communications.

Fourth, I turn to border erasure and state services in creating subsidized national and international postal services. Sovereigns once used mail to oversee information flows and to maintain control of their populations. But interests in empires, capital markets, global literacy, and nation-building intersected with social movements insistent on equality and with technologies facilitating the travel of both persons and things. Governments responded with major investments in networks enabling individuals to exchange largely uncensored information within and across borders.

Because what is now known as the Universal Postal Union came into being in 1874, "an individual can post a letter and expect it to be delivered safely to any designated place in the world within a relatively short span of time."[17] The UPU, the second-oldest international organization composed of state members, is a pioneer of geopolitical bureaucracies—traversing World Wars I and II and the birth and demise of the League of Nations, to land under the umbrella of the United Nations. Yet, akin to the small percentage of the world's population that moves across borders, mail generally circulated within national borders. In 2012, the number of letters and parcels in the mails was tallied to be close to 370 billion, of which some 5 billion (1.3 percent) went across a national border. In 2014, the number of letters and parcels in the mails was tallied at 327.4 billion items, down 2.6 percent from 2013, when some 3.46 billion letters and parcels crossed a national border.[18]

The history of postal services brings a fifth point into sharp relief, about the functionality and future of such state services— now under siege by another border erasure, encoded in nomenclatures of globalization and privatization.[19] Globalization helps to explain the inevitability of migration, the permeability of states' borders, and the anxiety about migration.[20] Amid disagreements about the novelty, import, utilities, and distributive impacts of privatization and globalization, commentators agree that state sovereignty, at least in the form it took in prior centuries, is under siege.[21]

Migration offers an opportunity to reconstruct the shape and to revitalize the commitments of nation-states to service provision, within and across borders. Social and political movements, using law, have produced many changes—the criminalization and illegalization of migrant movement; federalization of migrant law; globalization and privatization of government functions; and another, less familiar, effort, "postalization." That term comes from U.S. debates about whether telegraph services should follow the example of the post office and be operated and owned by the federal government.[22] That "postalization" is the outlier makes vivid the success of the other movements in turning equally awkward locutions into ordinary language.

I bring together these domains not to equate the migration of persons and families with the movement of objects but rather to clarify how reliant we are on both state identity and border crossings. The literature mapping the illegalization of the migration of peoples does not reference the legalization and internationalization of subsidized mail services, making many borders traversable, if not invisible. And, while the politics of migration are much debated, the post is infrequently acknowledged as a political and a legal site. Choices abound about what meaning to ascribe to delineations such as alien/citizen and federal/state. Assuming the naturalness of those divides deflects attention from the need for governments to create their identities through providing services to people residing in and seeking to affiliate with their legal regimes.

My purpose in bringing the mail into migration studies is to undo a sense of the normalcy about the borders that are now constructed. It is no more "normal" to place a person's act of crossing a border into the category of "crime" and to permit police to stop individuals to ask for identity documents than it is "normal" to put a letter in a box and assume state cooperation and subsidies will result in safe transit of that item hundreds or thousands of miles through systems aiming to provide universal services around the world.

Further, I hope to dislodge complacency about the "twilight of sovereignty," sometimes celebrated by cosmopolitans, arguing the unfairness of the nation-state as the unit by which rights and opportunities are allocated as well as citing the production of horrors that have been imposed in the name of sovereign states. In addition, the global scope of problems such as climate change and terrorism makes plain the limits of individual states—prompting some to call for recognition that this form of governance has reached its end.[23]

But the last century also witnessed states' capacity to generate new commitments to the equality and dignity of all persons and to freedom of movement. States invested in redistributive efforts that produced a host of services; the infrastructures of border controls, detention facilities, and post offices are the examples detailed here. Whatever the aspirations for "the global," rights, injuries, and services are made material in daily experiences in particular places governed by specific legal rules turned into practice.

Thus, it is the *eclipse* of sovereignty—of government and its services—that is my concern. Border surveillance and postal systems are both expressions of sovereign capacities; these institutions developed along with other government services, such as police, courts, prisons, education, and health care. The motivations for governments to take on such work are diverse. The nineteenth-century commitment to liberty of transit of pieces of paper and packages was produced by a mix of economic, political, imperial, colonial, humanitarian, and democratic agendas that prompted states to render their borders functional points of contact. The inventions of national mail services and of transnational cooperation via the Treaty of Berne in 1874 underscore the potential of sovereignty (democratic or not) to create new service institutions that reshape opportunities at both individual and aggregate levels. The question today is whether governments can join together to undo the stigmatization of migrants and to help people who want or need to move.

Of course, the relocation of individuals and families (even when labeled "human capital") poses many more complexities than does the transitory nature of the exchange of letters and objects, even as free movement of objects and open exchanges also have profound effects. But the need for action located at the level of the nation-state and yet engaging in transnational responses is parallel. Migration policy today is somewhat akin to mail practices in the 1860s, when various bilateral or multilateral treaties paved the way for some transnational transit but were profoundly incomplete. In addition to developing safe networks of transit for mail and deciding which entities counted as relevant actors, questions once abounded about resources, translated in that context in terms of whether to require payment on receipt or when sending, how to price mail and develop stamps as a new transnational currency, and what infrastructure to create for delivery services. More profoundly, new norms had to be developed about the free movement of ideas and the desirability of shifting sovereign authority to facilitate commercial and interpersonal interactions. The idea of mail as a subversive threat to the status quo may be hard for contemporary readers to imagine, unless put in the context of some countries' current efforts to limit access to Internet services.

The idea of compatible, reciprocal services for mail, which had to take into account enormous variations in state sovereign infrastructure capacities and political ideologies, ought to inform twenty-first-century migration policies, directed at the cyclical and the permanent movements of persons in receiving and sending countries. In closing, I discuss institutions such as the International Organization for Migration (IOM), which developed after World War II to respond to refugee emergencies, and which has since focused on migration management "for the benefit of all,"[24] the social and economic benefits of migration, and the "dignity and well-being of migrants."[25]

Yet the IOM, dealing mostly with populations in crisis, is only beginning to explore what "openness" to migration could mean and has not taken its agenda to be the full support of economic migrants and the complete decriminalization of the activity of migration.[26] The regulation of borders does not require that unauthorized entry be a crime. Were governments to want to organize and to support movement, they know how to invent transnational organizations, obligations, and the provision of site-specific resources and rules.

Mail and migration thus pose parallel, albeit distinct, questions about the roles played by governments working in concert to shape the norms and agendas around border crossings. One could couch the motivations of government to support both forms of movement in neoliberal terms. People embedded in capital markets rely on border exchange, border effacement, and border security for economic growth, and some argue the net effect is a reduction in social justice and an exacerbation of inequalities.[27] As Paul Jakob Marperger, an early eighteenth-century proponent of international mail, put it: the "friendly exchange of correspondence" between "the European powers," "the princes of Asia," and the "Barbarian States" was needed so that "Commerce and Engineering would flourish!"[28]

Migration is likewise linked to development, with evidence from empirical studies that migrants are not a "drain" on the public purse and may well be a net gain.[29] Under this analysis, self-serving public and private sector actors impose or relax limits on migration of people and on the movement of letters and parcels to forward their own economic well-being, and may do so without seeking to mitigate the exploitation of laborers, to protect the environment, to provide fair wages, or to ensure political participatory opportunities and free expression.

Yet, such a neoliberal analysis is incomplete, for it fails to acknowledge that capital and political expansion through global networks has also facilitated new imaginations about individual and collective rights and capabilities and about the state as a central provider of diverse goods and services. The capacity to exchange mail endowed individuals with communication opportunities that altered what they could read, learn, and do. Likewise, migration is an artifact not only of receiving countries' appetites for labor but also of individual's agency and of the networks and communities aiming to alter life opportunities through movement.

Aspiring and new entrants pose important and difficult questions for polities professing commitments to human dignity, liberty, and equality. Responses other than barriers are possible, as illustrated by the Refugee Convention after World War II and by the invention of new governance structures, including those supporting national and international mail services. These new institutions demonstrate governments' potential to provide redistributive and democratic services, as well as the inequalities and challenges that reside within such attempts. Seen together, mail and migration instruct on the centrality of governments and on the need both to detach political imagination from its "methodological nationalism," with nation-states as the unit of analysis, as well as to "bring the state back" to forge new norms and infrastructures.[30]

Major gaps in mail services are located in poorer countries with limited infrastructure and wobbly governments. Meanwhile, private global providers are competing with the UPU, and countries with more robust economies are privatizing their internal postal services. Globalization and privatization place in jeopardy the cross-subsidies that state regulation imposes on the distribution of postal services.[31] These developments raise questions about whether the norms of uncensored personal correspondence and universal service, to which 192 member states of the UPU formally subscribe, will be sustained. The question of migration raises parallel concerns—about how to generate new legal commitments to change from criminalization to subsidization of human movement, so as to recognize the needs both of migrants and of long-term residents of the receiving countries.

In short, over the course of two centuries, governments expanded their repertoires and capacities as sources of services—from crafting a shared symbolic and economic system for the exchange of mail to patrolling borders and building new detention facilities. This century's question is whether political will can be marshaled to sustain states as central providers of social ordering that generate cooperative, redistributive exchanges respectful of individual liberty and aiming to enhance equality. My aim is to invite attention to the utilities of government and to the project of shifting normalcies so as to probe whether states' coordination to decriminalize migration and to facilitate movements of persons seeking to cross boundaries could become a taken-for-granted government service, akin to state-subsidized interjurisdictional, cooperative postal systems, now at risk of becoming a relic of eras when governments were central.

II. Legalizing, Illegalizing, and Criminalizing Migration

A. *Disentangling Territory, People, and Law from Borders*

> The "power of a court to try a person for a crime is not impaired by the fact that he has been brought within the court's jurisdiction by reason of a 'forcible abduction.'"
>
> *Frisbie v. Collins*, 342 U.S. 519, 522 (1952)

Territory seems the obvious starting place for understanding the law of borders. As Justice Oliver Wendell Holmes explained in 1908, "boundary means sovereignty, since, in modern times, sovereignty is mainly territorial,"[32] and legal doctrines frame the reach of law in terms of when its "extraterritorial" application is permissible.[33] Further, the U.S. Constitution's Fourteenth Amendment commands states to accord any "person within its jurisdiction" equal protection of the law. But such formulations are incomplete because the "border" that constitutes the country's "jurisdiction" is not an artifact of tidewaters, rivers, and mountains alone. Law both specifies lines and at times redraws them, altering the import of a person's presence in material space.[34]

One form of extended jurisdiction is the deployment of public or private employees in other countries to police entry from afar. For example, in 1894, the United States authorized railroad screenings in Canada of individuals seeking to come to the United States.[35] By 1918, the United States had turned its consular offices into preliminary national borders by requiring prospective admittees to obtain visas.[36] Passing that screening made an applicant eligible for another inspection, either at the landmass of the United States or at other outposts. Beginning in the 1950s, "preinspection" became available at several airports, primarily in Canada.[37] The Illegal Immigration Reform and Immigrant Responsibility Act of 1996 (IIRIRA) authorized more airports as preinspection stations,[38] and in 2004, the Intelligence Reform and Terrorism Prevention Act added some two dozen additional offshore sites.[39]

Once past these checkpoints, the next inspection—and perhaps entry onto U.S. lands—comes by way of Customs and Border Protection (CBP), a part of the Department of Homeland Security (DHS), created in 2003 to replace the Immigration and Naturalization Service (INS).[40] Yet this border is also not always contiguous with the country's edges. The Immigration and Nationality Act of 1952 granted "any officer or employee of the Service authorized under regulations prescribed by the Attorney General [the] power without warrant" to "board and search" vessels "within a reasonable distance from any external boundary of the United States."[41] Since 1957, a Department of Justice regulation has defined reasonable to be "a distance of not exceeding 100 air miles from any external boundary of the United States."[42] Homeland Security has an "international footprint,"[43] as it develops a network of "border threat" efforts—sharing information, undertaking joint initiatives with northern and southern neighbors (one aptly named "Beyond the Border"), and entering into memoranda of understanding with various foreign countries.[44]

Moving to the country's interior adds other complexities. The INS established inland permanent checkpoints; one has operated since the early 1970s in San Clemente, California—66 miles from the land delineating the United States from Mexico.[45] Since the 1990s, individuals apprehended there, as well as within 100 miles of any exterior border, can be subjected to "expedited removal" if they are unable to establish continuous presence for two weeks.[46] The option of expedited removal results in returning an individual and, absent claims of asylum or claims of status as a refugee, legal permanent resident, or citizen, requires no judicial review of the immigration officer's assessment.[47] One consequence of expedited removal is inadmissibility for five years subsequent to that removal.[48] Thus, the use of expedited removal suggests either that due process applies but less process is due, or that entry without permission (as contrasted with overstaying visas) does not trigger due process protections. Border proximity also licenses the CBP to stop individuals and ask for a show of papers to verify status—a practice sufficiently common to make the phrase "papers please" a part of popular parlance. (Estimates are that about two-thirds of the U.S. population lives within 100 miles of land and coastal borders.)[49]

Another legal attenuation of physical boundaries comes from the United States' view of its authority to reach outside its own territory to kidnap individuals alleged to have violated its law. This jurisdiction-by-violence has been sanctioned by the U.S. Supreme Court under what is known as the "*Ker-Frisbie*" doctrine, named after a pair of cases rejecting defendants' claims that such a seizure violated their due process rights.[50] In 1952, the Supreme Court explained that the "power of a court to try a person for a crime is not impaired by the fact that he has been brought within the court's jurisdiction by reason of a 'forcible abduction.'"[51]

This approach was reaffirmed in 1992 in *United States v. Alvarez-Machain*,[52] in which a noncitizen argued that his abduction from Mexico violated the "law of nations," a concept dating from eighteenth-century traditions that are themselves border expanding. The premise is that certain acts may take place outside any sovereignty's borders (such as piracy on the high seas) and are so fundamentally wrong that they license any country's exercise of jurisdiction over the wrongdoers. One could call this "jurisdiction-by-outrage" and understand that it supports a form of what today is called "universal" jurisdiction."[53] The "law of nations" was woven into the U.S. Constitution, which authorizes Congress to "define and punish Piracies and Felonies committed on the high Seas, and Offences against the Law of Nations."[54] Congress promptly did so by creating a criminal offense as well as a civil right, offering its courts to aliens bringing tort actions for violation of the law of nations.[55]

As illustrated by the *Ker-Frisbie* defendants, the Constitution seems to create entitlements for persons in the United States. The text of the Fourteenth Amendment (incorporated through the Fifth Amendment to apply to the federal government) insists that no state shall "deprive any person of life, liberty, or property without due process of law," nor "deny to any person within its jurisdiction the equal protection of the laws."[56] One could interpret the exercise of power outside the country—to apprehend a person as contrasted to seeking extradition—as an exercise of the country's jurisdiction and therefore constrained by the Constitution. Yet the Court's ruling meant that constitutional protections applied once inside the United States but did not constrain the mode by which the government brings people in.

But the law is more complex, for another disjuncture between territorial boundaries and legal regulation comes from reading the Constitution as licensing the government to treat some individuals physically present in the United States as not entitled to all the legal rights derived from being "within its jurisdiction."[57] In other words, crossing the border is an important act of law production but does not yield uniform results.

One variable is how one enters. The Supreme Court has concluded that some constitutional protections apply to those who entered lawfully (by way of a visa, a valid passport, and a second inspection at or near the border) and subsequently overstayed their permitted entry. In a 1903 decision, the Court ruled that procedural protections had to be accorded before deportation to ensure the person was deportable.[58] But the government can admit an individual not entitled to entry and then legally treat that person as if such a person were outside and, hence, without due process rights. The conceit rests, in part, on solicitude for some of the "excludable" (now described as "removable"),[59] deemed to be better off on land than at sea or detained on ships awaiting decisions about entry.[60] Exemplars include a group of some 125,000 Cuban "Marielitos" (named because they traveled by boat from Mariel Harbor in 1980),[61] and a group of Haitian refugees who were held in the 1990s at Guantánamo Bay before it gained its current valence as the detention center for alleged terrorists.[62] This fiction of being absent is subject to the obvious critique that it renders some persons not "persons"; its poignant upside is that it lowers the pressure on the United States to keep people offshore.

Litigation over 9/11 detainees offers up yet more examples of the complex border threads interlacing the confinement of individuals, dominion over territory, and U.S. law. Over objections from the Bush administration, the Supreme Court insisted that American control over Guantánamo Bay through a long-term lease rendered aliens confined there by the United States eligible to invoke federal habeas corpus rights to contest their confinement.[63] Further, courts have concluded that citizens held under U.S. control in jails abroad may bring claims, but courts have refused to hear noncitizens held at U.S.-run facilities, such as in Bagram, Afghanistan.[64]

Other borders are erected by burdens imposed on migrants because immigration status can affect whether a person can get a job, a driver's license, government benefits, and an apartment. Some of these decisions are made at the national level, and others depend on state and municipal laws. Migrants thus bump into a myriad of micro-internal boundaries across the country, as their experiences—and rights—can vary depending on where they live.[65]

Another approach to border building comes by way of shifting the focus from government authority to that of individuals. As of 2015, more than 40 million people in the United States are "foreign born,"[66] and many more live with people born abroad. An estimated 11 million of those millions were present without the requisite documents, which is a substantial increase over the 2 to 4 million undocumented migrants in the United States in 1980.[67] Nine million people lived in "mixed-status" families in which some members lack legal authority to be in the country.[68]

Thus, just as the government moves its borders through the construction of off-site consular offices, inspection stations, and interior checkpoints and by kidnappings, people who cross also move the import of borders by reshaping social and political cultures, by creating the many hyphenated identities (denoted through terms such as "Italian-Americans" and "Japanese-Americans"), and by raising questions about obligations to individuals who are not citizens. The "DREAMERS" offer one example of vocal undocumented migrants, brought to the United States as children, evoking "the American dream" as they argue for their rights to remain and to have paths to citizenship.[69]

In addition, American constitutional law crisscrosses the citizen/noncitizen divide.[70] One analysis of U.S. migration calculated that as of 2011, 4 percent of the population and 8 percent of the labor force were not documented and that, as a result, those persons lacked "social, economic, and civil rights."[71] But the equation of a lack of rights with the undocumented is incomplete. More than 2 million people are incarcerated. Citizens who are imprisoned and those released, along with those who receive federal and state benefits, are often required to submit to government surveillance and given limited access to government services; some are also disenfranchised. Being a citizen of the United States can still result in being "outside" arenas of rights, opportunities, and forms of capital. The border of citizen/noncitizen shares the instabilities of the borders located on land.

Thus, a first proposition is that borders have no fixed meaning, let alone invariable materiality. Law and people's personal movements and relationships make and erase physical and constitutional borders. A second point, discussed below, is that the contemporary focus in U.S. law on the hierarchical relationship between federal and state law—federal law's supremacy and preemptive force—misses how porous the border is between state and federal law. The contemporary linkage of unlicensed migration to crime and stigma and the battles over relief from deportation depend on decades of state and federal governments interacting with migrant populations, whose modes of travel, countries of origins, and numbers have shifted in light of technologies of transport and of policies, both domestic and foreign. I turn therefore to sketch some of the legal history exemplifying that decisions to control borders are founded on the interdependence of state and federal law and need not, inevitably, result in decisions to criminalize crossings.

B. Jointly Producing the Criminalization of Migration: The Permeable Boundaries of State and Federal Law

It has never been the policy of the Government to punish criminally aliens who come here in contravention of our immigration laws.

Deportation has been the remedy. A reversal of that policy ought to be based on a clear legislative declaration, and not on judicial construction of statutes which leave the subject in such uncertainty and doubt as do the statutes here under consideration.

Flora v. Rustad, 8 F.2d 335, 337 (8th Cir. 1925)

Once here, aliens are required to register with the Federal Government and carry proof of status on their person. . . . Failure to do so is a federal misdemeanor.

Arizona v. United States, 132 S. Ct. 2492, 2499 (2012)

Gerald Neuman has warned against imagining U.S. borders in the nineteenth century as open; rather than unfettered hospitality, states limited movement through regulations, through laws on slavery, vagrancy, and poverty that applied to migrants, whether foreigners or not.[72] The warnings needed today are against overestimating the federal government's role in immigration, in terms of either the criminalization of migration or efforts at liberalization. The content of contemporary federal law reflects various state-based initiatives, from those promoting the illegalization of migration through registration, surveillance, employment and welfare barriers, and criminal penalties to new initiatives mitigating some of those harms. Thus, while some narratives track the pushes and pulls between liberalization and illiberalization in federal law,[73] my interest is the interdependency of developments in state and federal law shaping approaches to migration.

1. Federal Preemption of Pennsylvania's "Constant Harassment" of Aliens

State and local actions have long been prompts for federal initiatives. In 1906, a decision of the San Francisco School Board to separate Asian children in public schools sparked protests from the Japanese government. That "local" event produced a federal foreign policy problem. One result was the Immigration Act of 1907.[74] That legislation created the U.S. Immigration Commission (known as the Dillingham Commission) that, in 1924, prompted federal legislation imposing literacy tests for migrants, numerical restrictions, and limits on Asian immigration.[75]

The 1924 quota system was aimed, as a member of Congress commented in 1929, "principally at two peoples, the Italians and the Jews."[76] By the late 1920s, the focus was on other "others." Anti-Mexican sentiments permeated discussion in the House of Representatives, as proponents of making entry after deportation into a crime claimed that migrants brought with them poverty, disease, and drinking,[77] as well as competition in labor markets[78] and challenges to America's identity.[79] The arguments for criminalization were not only that border crossing was illicit and specific groups toxic to the body politic but also that many migrants were themselves already criminals ("bootlegging drugs and narcotics").[80] Members of Congress sought a new federal provision to stop them from "poisoning the American citizen."[81]

Yet, as sociologists of law have long insisted, a law on the books is not a law in action. Congress enacted a provision in 1929 making border crossing a crime,[82] but the conflation of criminal law and immigration—collapsing the autonomy of the two domains and producing the new shorthand of "crim-immigration" or "crim-imm"[83]—is an artifact of changing policies during several decades at both state and federal levels.[84]

To map those decades, however, through the lens of federal lawmaking with the major legislative landmarks of 1929, 1986, and 1996, is to miss that state legislatures were often ahead (in the sense of imposing punitive measures) and that, even when preempted by federal legislation, state laws became the basis of subsequent federal laws incorporating aspects of what states had pioneered. Likewise, if the focus shifts from hostility to liberalization and efforts aimed at incorporation of migrants, the exploration needs to see the interaction between state and federal initiatives.

The expansion of the punitive approach can be seen through comparing the Pennsylvania law of 1939, which was struck down by the Supreme Court in *Hines v. Davidowitz*,[85] with current federal law, which the Court held in 2012 precluded Arizona from adding additional criminal sanctions.[86] The 1939 Pennsylvania statute addressed aliens, eighteen or older, who had not filed a declaration of "intention to become a citizen . . . within three years."[87] The state required that they register and pay a fee annually, that they carry registration cards—to be produced if requested by police officers or if seeking a motor vehicle license.[88]

Violation of these provisions would subject the individual to a fine of no more than $100 and incarceration of no more than sixty days.[89] As a federal appellate judge in 1939 described the system, "the alien is thus placed under the constant surveillance of the police power of Pennsylvania, not as any other resident might be placed upon the commission of a crime or for the good of the Commonwealth, but simply because he is an alien."[90] In the language of contemporary political science, Pennsylvania was insistent on setting migrants apart to prevent them from being incorporated into the body politic.[91]

Lawyers challenged this system on behalf of two individuals who exemplified the "two peoples, the Italians and the Jews," [92] iconic in congressional immigration debates of the era. Bernard Davidowitz, a naturalized citizen, alleged that because of his "foreign appearance" [read Jewish][93] and a "strongly noticeable foreign accent,"[94] he would be harassed if the law went into effect. Vincenzo Travaglini[95] was born in 1893 in Abruzzia, Italy, moved to the United States in 1920, and resided in Philadelphia.[96] Both sought (long before the 1966 revisions to the federal class action rule) to proceed "on behalf of themselves and . . . all other residents or citizens or taxpayers who may lawfully join" them.[97] (Newspaper reports estimated that 300,000 to 400,000 aliens lived in Pennsylvania.)[98] Although the case bears Mr. Davidowitz's name, a three-judge court ruled in 1939 that because Mr. Davidowitz was a citizen, the act did not apply to him, and his claim was not justiciable.[99]

Reaching the merits for Travaglini, the lower court held that Pennsylvania was precluded from entering the field of immigration and that Pennsylvania had unreasonably deprived aliens, as "person[s]" protected by the text of the Fourteenth Amendment, of equal protection of the laws.[100] The court explained that while federal law then required five years of continuous residence to be eligible for citizenship, Pennsylvania's system imposed a shorter time frame—applied to those who had not declared their "intention to become a citizen within three years."[101] Moreover, Pennsylvania's extracting such statements of intent was noxious: "While naturalization of aliens residing within our borders is a matter to be encouraged, the desire of an applicant for citizenship should be inspired and engendered by his observation of and experience with the living example of true democracy. It must never be compelled by an act of oppression or tyranny."[102]

In 1940—before the case was decided by the Supreme Court—Congress enacted its own registration obligations,[103] mandating the fingerprinting of all "aliens fourteen years of age or older" who were in the United States for thirty days or more.[104] (This legislation, known as the Smith Act, was also aimed at the "subversive advocacy" of citizens.)[105] The federal provisions did not require aliens to be card-carrying. Rather, the fingerprints and the registration were to be kept "secret" and were not to be turned over to states without permission of both the Commissioner of Immigration and the Attorney General of the United States.[106] Further, violators of the obligation to register could be penalized only upon a showing of a "willful failure to register."[107]

When arguing the *Hines v. Davidowitz* case before the Supreme Court, the Solicitor General explained that this "complete and integrated" federal system was in service of the "deliberate purpose of Congress to protect the civil liberties of aliens."[108] In contrast, Pennsylvania law put aliens under "the constant threat of intrusive surveillance by the state police," who would have "the power . . . to subject aliens whom they may for any reason deem undesirable, to constant harassment."[109] The government argued that Congress had rejected such an approach because of the "widespread conviction that registration was closely akin to the systems of police surveillance of certain European countries, and that to subject aliens to such surveillance might lead to grave abuses in administration and engender disaffection and disloyalty."[110] Although the federal government did not press, as the lower court had, that the law violated the equal protection guarantees of the Fourteenth Amendment equal protection claim, the government did argue that the Pennsylvania statute violated the Civil Rights Act of 1870. That statute provided that all persons—aliens included—"shall have the same right . . . to make and enforce contracts . . . and to the full and equal benefit of all laws . . . as is enjoyed by white citizens, and shall be subject to like punishment, pains, penalties, taxes, licenses, and exactions of every kind, and to no other."[111]

Today, the Supreme Court's opinion in *Hines v. Davidowitz*, issued as World War II was under way, is cited for its holding that the federal government occupies much of the field of immigration and preempts state laws in conflict.[112] Justice Black's opinion for the Court articulated that proposition while insisting that American identity required limiting the power of governments (state and federal) to interfere with "personal liberties."[113] In Justice Black's words: "Opposition to laws permitting invasion of the personal liberties of law-abiding individuals, or singling out aliens as particularly dangerous and undesirable groups, is deep-seated in this country."[114] And, as I quoted at this chapter's outset, he asserted that requiring aliens to register and to display that status was "at war with the fundamental principles of our free government, in that they would bring about unnecessary and irritating restrictions upon personal liberties of the individual, and would subject aliens to a system of indiscriminate questioning similar to the espionage systems existing in other lands."[115] Pennsylvania's approach was "a departure from our traditional policy of not treating aliens as a thing apart," whereas the federal registration system would "protect the personal liberties of law-abiding aliens" while leaving them "free from the possibility of inquisitorial practices and police surveillance that might not only affect our international relations but might also generate the very disloyalty which the law was intended to guard against."[116]

The Court also made plain that its ruling looked outward, for not all foreign governments were careless about personal liberty or seeking converts. Rather, the United States was a party to treaties imposing transnational obligations of hospitality that "not only promised and guaranteed broad rights and privileges to aliens sojourning in our own territory, but secured reciprocal promises and guarantees for our citizens while in other lands."[117] The American identity of liberty was embedded in affiliation with "treaties and international practices . . . aimed at preventing injurious discriminations against aliens," especially those who were "perfectly law-abiding" and who had met "rigid requirements as to heath, education, integrity, character, and adaptability to our institutions."[118]

The reference to "law-abiding" aliens is important to understanding *Hines*, which was litigated on behalf of individuals who were not accused by either the state or federal government of unlawful entry. The decision's nonharassment principle was not articulated in today's terms of "illegal" or "legal," "authorized" or "unauthorized," "documented" or "undocumented" immigrants.

Moreover, the ruling came shortly before the United States entered World War II—heightening the concern about the geopolitical impact of the Pennsylvania statute, a state in which many German immigrants lived.[119] Nonetheless, during the early 1940s, in a world replete with frightful treatment of humans based on their identity, the U.S. Supreme Court spoke about protecting human liberty in general terms. While noting that Congress had the power to deport aliens found guilty of "conduct contrary to the rules and regulations laid down by Congress,"[120] the Court rejected making public stigmatization a facet of the government-alien relationship.

But of course those words have to be read against a backdrop of institutionalized discrimination against a host of aliens, albeit not organized against those of German descent. In 1882, Congress sought to exclude Chinese migrants by providing that "the coming of Chinese laborers to the United States be . . . suspended" and making it unlawful "for any Chinese laborer to come or, having so come . . . to remain within the United States."[121] Under the Geary Act of 1892, which continued that exclusion through 1902, Chinese laborers in the United States had to carry a "certificate of residence" or produce a "white witness" to attest they had arrived in the United States before the passage of the act.[122] Turning to the southern border, as Douglas Massey recounts, in the late 1920s the United States began a campaign of mass roundups and deportations of Mexicans.[123]

Moreover, not long after the 1941 *Hines* ruling, stigmatization became part of many citizens' lives, as well as those of aliens. World War II inspired curfews and the internment of Americans of Japanese ancestry; anticommunist laws required oath-taking for many state and federal positions. In 1945, Justice Black wrote the opinion in *Korematsu v. United States*, in which the Court infamously upheld a military order, addressing "all persons of Japanese ancestry, both alien and non-alien, from the Pacific Coast,"[124] and making criminal the refusal to report to an internment camp.[125] As Justice Jackson argued in his dissent, Fred Korematsu's "offense" was "being present in the state whereof he is a citizen, near the place where he was born, and where all his life he has lived."[126]

As this brief history underscores, the questions, then as now, are whether constitutional obligations constrain government surveillance, detention, and criminalization. The categories of law (state and federal) and of status ("citizen," "lawful alien," or otherwise) are interactive templates on which those answers are made and remade. Constraints on government require theories of the limits of sovereign power vis-à-vis persons. As the *Korematsu* decision and national toleration of racial segregation made plain, the category of citizen did not provide a safe harbor for all the many persons who fell within that definition.

2. Licensing Law Enforcement Oversight

In the decades after *Hines*, federal law took on aspects of Pennsylvania provisions that, in 1940, had been found to impose "unnecessary and irritating restrictions"[127] on noncitizens' liberties. By 2012, when the U.S. Supreme Court decided *Arizona v. United States*, federal law had come to require that "aliens carry proof of registration"[128] and to permit inquiries into individuals' migration status by federal officials, by employers,[129] and in some instances, by state law enforcement officials.[130]

Yet *Arizona v. United States* also marked a significant victory for migrants. The decision insisted that federal law limited states' authority to require alien registration and to criminalize immigration,[131] and that ruling became the basis on which lower courts have struck other state criminalization provisions.[132] Although the *Arizona* decision was no ode to liberty, the practical impact of federal preemption is to constrain the number of crimes for which migrants can be pursued; the number of law enforcement agents who can be dispatched; and therefore the number of times that individuals can be stopped, questioned, and detained.

Those constraints come from the different law enforcement capacities of the federal and state governments and from constitutional limitations on how federal authorities can enlist state police. In 2012, some 66,000 federal employees focused on border control; the total included 46,000 CBP agents and 20,000 employees of Immigration and Customs Enforcement (ICE).[133] State and localities employed more than ten times that number; 765,000 individuals were "sworn" law enforcement officers.[134] Further, in 1997, in *Printz v. United States*, the Court held that Congress cannot "commandeer" state law officials to participate in federal enforcement efforts—in that instance, to police access to guns.[135] When the rule of *Printz* is applied to migration, it limits what is often termed Congress's "plenary power" over immigration.

But while the Arizona decision counseled that states cannot unilaterally deploy their own police officers to augment immigration enforcement, federal law can invite them in. Congress encouraged state and local law enforcement officials to join "287(g) agreements" with the federal government so that designated state officers, trained by ICE, could undertake immigration law enforcement functions.[136] Even as that program was curtailed in 2012, another initiative, called Secure Communities, welcomed local law enforcement officials to provide the Federal Bureau of Investigation with fingerprints of individuals arrested; those data were then compared against federal databases to screen for immigration detainers.[137]

In 2012, the Department of Homeland Security described a 97 percent rate of "activated jurisdictions," which meant that law enforcement offices in most counties had the capacity to participate in Secure Communities,[138] and thereby to help identify potentially deportable individuals. Reportedly, such cooperative programs had, between 2008 and 2012, led to the removal of 159,409 individuals.[139] The department also explained that 180,000 "front-line law enforcement personnel" have been trained under another initiative, the Nationwide Suspicious Activity Reporting (SAR) effort.[140] As a consequence, just as Arizona's law could have been used to target individuals on the basis of their appearance, race, and presumed national origin, the concern has been that local law enforcement could do so through 287(g) agreements, Secure Communities, the SAR program, or, when these programs terminated, through other initiatives.[141]

How much the mix of *Arizona* and *Printz* protected migrants depended on the budget for federal law enforcement, federal politics and executive initiatives, decisions by local leaders, and court interpretations of constitutional obligations.[142] As Ingrid Eagly detailed, localities have different models of "noncitizen criminal justice."[143] For example, although the federal government had reported that, by 2014, nationwide "activation" of its data collection system was in place, several localities had no systemic engagement or declined to participate in the federal detention efforts[144]—reassured by court rulings affirming the voluntary nature of local involvement.[145] Further, a few states enacted laws (dubbed "TRUST") that directed their employees not to honor ICE detainers unless individuals have been convicted of serious crimes.[146] In addition, some localities were not interested in sustaining the expenses of detention or were concerned that ICE detainers alone did not support Fourth Amendment probable cause requirements for detention.[147] Thus, both judgments of local officials and rulings by judges narrowed the pipeline for deportation in some places.

Indeed, those states and cities were important to debates in Congress in 2013 about immigration reform and, when the national legislative effort faltered, to President Obama's decision in 2014 to shape a national policy of "deferred action" on deportation for an estimated 3.6 million unauthorized migrants living in the United States.[148] Thus, in 2014, the Secure Communities program was replaced with the Priority Enforcement Program, which continued to leave a good deal of the data-sharing provisions of the prior program in place but reflected the executive branch's efforts to constrain deportation somewhat.[149] One estimate was that, if implemented, the new approach could "reduce deportations from within the United States by about 25,000 cases annually."[150] But whether the president's 2014 initiatives will take effect is, as of this writing, pending before the courts.[151] Meanwhile, other localities continue to prime the pump for deportation by using their own criminal law as the basis (or, as critics feared, as the pretext) for stops and detention,[152] by enacting new provisions to exclude migrants from rental housing and from driver's licenses,[153] and by contesting the authority of the executive to organize a program for deferred deportation affecting millions of migrants.

My point is not to debate whether the Arizona ruling was, as many immigrant rights advocates believe, as "good" a judgment as one could expect given the Court's composition,[154] but rather to demonstrate that the decision is evidence of the acculturation to surveillance that has taken place in the years since *Hines*. Even as federal statutory preemption protected migrants from certain forms of harassment,[155] and even as the Court has repeatedly invoked backdrop principles of constitutional law (the Fourth Amendment, and the Equal Protection and Due Process Clauses) as restraints on government treatment of migrants, *Arizona v.*

United States rested on federal exclusivity rather than on liberty's imperatives.

To clarify the doctrinal limits of *Arizona* requires a few more details of the route the case took to the Court and the bases of the ruling. In 2010, a group of civil rights organizations sought to enjoin the Arizona law based on liberty claims—specifically, that it violated the Fourth Amendment, due process, equal protection, and the freedom to travel, as well as that the Arizona law was preempted by federal law.[156] The U.S. government brought an independent lawsuit—focused on the preemption, federal law-supremacy issue—which was decided first and which the Supreme Court agreed to hear.[157] That trajectory was not happenstance but the result of litigators and judges who thought that the preemption claim had a higher likelihood of success before the Court than the civil rights claims.

Nonetheless, when arguing the case in 2012, the government insisted—as it had sixty years earlier in *Hines*—that federal law protected immigrants from harassment. Indeed, the federal government characterized the Arizona law as posing a "more significant harassment problem" than had the Pennsylvania law invalidated in *Hines*; because "the policy applies to all stops and arrests whenever there is reasonable suspicion that the person is unlawfully present, it threatens to result in the unnecessary detention of lawfully present aliens, a consequence with significant foreign-policy consequences for the National Government."[158]

The five-person majority decision by Justice Kennedy agreed with the government that much of what Arizona had enacted was precluded. Yet the opinion is not laced with references to America's identity as a government committed to limiting government surveillance of individuals. And the global perspective—the treaties of reciprocal hospitality adverted to in *Hines*—appears in the Court's decision only as the need to have "one voice" in foreign affairs,[159] rather than as an obligation to participate in cooperative internationalism. Thus, even as the majority opinion spoke warmly about immigrants (the "history of the United States is in part made of the stories, talents, and lasting contributions of those who crossed oceans and deserts to come here"),[160] the focal point was federal authority. State registration requirements and additional criminal penalties were impermissible not because they breached American conventions on liberty and equality or international agreements about how to treat foreigners but because federal law provided "a full set of standards," and hence states had intruded on a field that Congress had left no "room for States to regulate."[161]

Specifically, the Court explained that federal law had made "the failure to carry registration papers" a misdemeanor that could be punished by imprisonment, probation, or a fine,[162] whereas Arizona law criminalized the same activity but did not include the lesser sanctions of probation or pardon.[163] Moreover, federal law had not made it criminal for an undocumented alien to seek work, whereas Arizona sought to do so. The Court also rejected Arizona's new grounds for arrests and detention without a warrant if an officer has "probable cause to believe" that a person was "removable" from the United States.[164] Federal law was less intrusive, for it provided instead that, as a general matter, such persons were to be given a Notice to Appear, which is a document that itself "does not authorize an arrest."[165]

One provision of Arizona's law survived the 2012 facial challenge. Section 2(B) (a "papers-please" provision) required state officers to make a "reasonable attempt to determine the immigration status" of any person who had been stopped, detained, or arrested for other reasons; further, if "reasonable suspicion exists that the person is an alien and is unlawfully present in the United States," an officer could keep that person under arrest until that person's "immigration status" was determined.[166] Moreover, if a person were stopped for a nonimmigration reason (not based on "race, color or national origin . . . except to the extent permitted by the United States [and] Arizona Constitution[s]") and if consistent with the "civil rights of all persons and respecting the privileges and immunities of United States citizens,"[167] the state could detain that person until obtaining citizenship status information. The Court concluded that, while not facially impermissible, consideration could be given on remand to whether those challenging the law could prove the "adverse" consequences of its operation to "federal law and its objectives."[168]

A version of *Hines*'s civil liberties concerns remained, for worries about "unnecessary harassment"[169] and detention can be found in the opinion. The majority commented that "[d]etaining people solely to verify their immigration status would raise constitutional concerns," just as a "seizure that is justified solely by the interest in issuing a warning ticket to the driver can become unlawful if it is prolonged beyond the time reasonably required to complete that mission."[170] As a 2012 decision focused on a South Carolina's migrant criminalization statute explained, the *Arizona* decision served as a reminder that while "status-checking provisions" were on their face permissible, states were not authorized to hold such persons in custody absent federal supervision.[171]

Yet, as the dissenters (Justices Scalia, Thomas, and Alito)[172] complained, the centerpiece of the majority decision was the doctrine of implied executive preemption[173]—or what may now be understood as "plenary power preemption."[174] For the majority, it was the executive's prosecutorial powers and control over matters that "touch on foreign relations"[175] that precluded state decision making; some aliens ("a veteran, college student, or someone assisting . . . a criminal investigation") whom federal officials had determined "should not be removed" could be swept up by state law officials, interfering with "the discretion of the Federal Government" that Congress had authorized.[176]

3. Surveillance, Security, and American Values

The details of the internal debate within the *Arizona* decision are in service of my argument that "American values" are constructed and reconstructed in many sites, including the law on the rights of "others." Comparing the interstices of the law of Arizona and of federal law shows how the systems of surveillance, disclosure, oversight, and detention of the two "sovereigns" look (as the dissenters in *Arizona* argued) more similar than not and, as I will later discuss, create the predicates for government oversight that have also been applied to citizens.

To focus solely on the Supreme Court's output, however, misses the other mechanisms by which the obligation imposed on migrants to make public their status became so ordinary that phrases like "papers please" entered common parlance. A return is therefore in order to the first half of the twentieth century, to underscore that American law was not as univocally welcoming as Justice Black had suggested in *Hines*. In 1941, Pennsylvania was no outlier. It was not the first state to require registration, nor were aliens the only targets. Rather, sixteen states had passed laws obliging all aliens to register with state authorities.[177] Thus both *Hines* and *Arizona* reflect underlying struggles over U.S. values, as both tolerance and intolerance have a long pedigree in the country's history.

Indeed, since the country's inception, Congress had "experimented with alien registration laws a number of times," famously targeting Chinese immigrants in the nineteenth century[178] and then shifting as the aliens in focus varied depending on the border proximate to the proponents of control and on images of who the foreigners were. During the 1930s, anxieties about communism mixed easily with hostility toward foreigners and interests in protecting domestic laborers.[179] On the West Coast, local enactments (such as laws disabling aliens from owning property or getting fishing licenses) were anti-Asian,[180] while East Coast efforts reflected anti-Semitism, anti-Catholicism, and anti-Irish sentiments, and the southern border states were anti-Mexican. The resulting chorus had refrains about "Asian Hordes," "the Yellow Peril," and the "Mexican Menace."

Before the 1940s, several bills seeking to require registration of aliens and of communists had been introduced both in the U.S. House of Representatives and in the Senate.[181] Proposals called for pre-visa fingerprinting[182] and for "[n]ation-wide official registration and fingerprint records of all aliens now in the United States."[183] Those debates sound familiar today, with proponents of registration linking aliens and criminality, and opponents disagreeing on the empirical claims, discussing the expense, and arguing that registration was antithetical to American values.[184]

In 1940, Congress enacted the federal provisions that Justice Black relied on to preempt Pennsylvania's statute in *Hines*. In 1952, Congress endorsed an anti-immigrant surveillance bill that President Truman unsuccessfully vetoed as violative of American values.[185] Thus, twelve years after the Court ruled in *Hines* that it was anti-American to expose aliens to the requirement that they carry identity cards, Congress imposed that mandate, which has remained on the books (albeit differently implemented) since 1952.[186] Moreover, Congress put citizens as well as aliens under surveillance by way of the Internal Security Act, which required registration by "communist organizations."[187]

Explanations of how "American values" came to find such policies lawful come, of course, from histories of segregation, Chinese exclusion laws, World War II, *Korematsu*, politics, the Cold War, racism, and the success of McCarthyism.[188] In 1952, the *Harvard Law Review* published an essay, "State Control of Subversion: A Problem in Federalism," explaining that "increasing international tension" had prompted "state and municipal governments, as well as Congress, . . . to erect a legislative bulwark to guard the security of this country against subversion."[189] Federal legislation targeted the immigration and naturalization of "subversive aliens,"[190] and state surveillance laws also proliferated.[191]

The legality of some of the state initiatives was, as in *Hines*, contested; preemption questions arose in the context of "loyalty oaths by teachers and other state employees," the exclusion of "subversive groups from recognition in political parties," and the withholding of "various state benefits from persons engaging in subversive activity."[192] Pennsylvania, for example, banned persons advocating the "overthrow of the government" from its public assistance—except if they were blind.[193]

The expansion of migrant oversight came in conjunction with changing demographics of migrant populations, as the focus moved from Europe and Asia to Mexico. Various ideologies and agendas—America as a land of migrants; cheap labor to supply growing agriculture and other industries; national labor movements aiming to protect domestic workers; racial and ethnic hostilities—produced different accommodations during the twentieth century. My focus is on the entrenchment of the criminal paradigm while, as Jennifer Hochschild documents in this volume, one could map instead the forms of inclusion of migrants that proliferated over the decades.[194]

During the last few decades, the southern border has been the flash point. As Douglas Massey explained the policy shifts, in 1942 the United States and Mexico entered into the Bracero Accord, which authorized temporary workers to come to the United States.[195] By the late 1950s, about 500,000 people legally entered yearly from Mexico; some 50,000 were permanent residents, and the rest were temporary workers, on whom the agricultural industries, especially in California, relied.[196] For many years, that "entirely legal" movement of large numbers of persons (augmented, as Kitty Calavita documented, by the entry of thousands of unauthorized migrants)[197] provided an accommodation that lasted until the 1960s.[198] Migrants coming from the Western Hemisphere—whether through the Bracero Accord or otherwise—were not subjected to numerical quotas.

In 1965, Congress terminated the Bracero Accord and amended the quota systems that had prohibited immigration from Asia and Africa. Instead, Congress imposed a new system of quotas of 20,000 immigrants per country in Europe, Africa, Asia, and the Pacific.[199] A decade later, countries in the Americas were likewise subjected to numerical caps, placed at 20,000.[200] Yet workers and employers continued to produce a flow of undocumented entrants.

Thereafter, legal migration increased as well; by 1978, 135,000 persons entered from Mexico, in part through family sponsorship from relatives with a permanent resident status or citizenship.[201] In Massey's account, the volume fluctuated with the economies of both countries and ran between 70,000 and 150,000 entrants a year, albeit "most . . . unauthorized"; generally, "arrivals were set off by departures."[202] Relying on figures from Homeland Security, Massey also tracked the rise in "apprehensions per officer" of unlawful migrants, which grew from 30,000 in 1965 to 464,000 in 1977.[203]

The Immigration Reform and Control Act (IRCA) of 1986 is an important, if ironic, marker of the punitive turn. IRCA's amnesty program resulted in the admission to lawful permanent residence of 2.7 million persons, subject to conditions about learning English and seeking citizenship.[204] The congressional enactment reflected a broader movement, in that Belgium, the Netherlands, France, Spain, and Australia also enacted forms of "regularization" and incorporation of migrants.[205]

Yet the U.S. initiative put the status of alien in high relief, by obliging employers to obtain documentation of their employees' status and imposing employer liability for hiring unauthorized workers.[206] State laws again provided models for these new federal restrictions aimed at the private sector.[207] A decade later, Congress expanded enforcement through providing civil sanctions of employers and employees and criminal penalties for employers.[208] Thus, by the end of the century, mandatory disclosures by employers cast shadows on both the individuals listed and the businesses

using this form of labor. Shaming became commonplace, exemplified by a local newspaper in New Haven, which ran a headline in
November 2012 that announced which businesses had been fined
for employing undocumented individuals.[209]

Massey argued that federal and state oversight of employers,
coupled with legislative initiatives against immigration, obscured
that migration was down; "the volume of undocumented entries
had . . . peaked in the late 1970s."[210] But the popular press instead
wrote of "the Latino threat,"[211] and federal budgets for borders
and barriers grew to support the "full scale militarization of the
busiest border sector in San Diego" through "Operation Gatekeeper."[212] Anti-immigration efforts, including the 1996 federal
legislation expanding the grounds for deportation, resulted in rising numbers of deportations, from 150,000 in the late 1990s to
more than 280,000 in 2009.[213]

By then, some 11.2 million people lacking the requisite documents (6.5 million of whom came from Mexico) were in the
United States.[214] Massey attributed the number of persons staying to the "war on migration," which imposed so many risks
that it turned a "circular flow of male Mexican workers going to
three states into a settled population of Mexican families living
in 50 states."[215] Moreover, federal policies—closing off entries
at El Paso and San Diego (by way of "steel walls, watch towers,
motion detectors, air surveillance, and additional Border Patrol
officers")—shifted the flow to Arizona, rendering it, in Massey's
words, "ground zero" and encouraging Mexican settlement elsewhere in the country.[216]

4. "Save Our State:" California's Prop. 187 and Federal Lawmaking

> Farewell then, Aeschylus, great and wise,
> Go, save our state by the maxims of thy noble thought.
>
> Aristophanes, *The Frogs*, circa 405 BCE

In 1850, the American Temperance Union discussed how laws limiting alcohol consumption could "save our State from the pollution which so recently threatened her destruction."[217] A century
later, opponents of constitutional revisions in Maryland also created a group called Save Our State,[218] as did environmentalists in

the 1980s.[219] Californians in the 1990s were thus not the first to wave this banner, but since then, this phrase has become standard fare for anti-immigration and antiforeign law legislation.[220]

In 1993, one such group promoted a ballot initiative known as Prop. 187, aiming "to establish a system of required notification by and between such agencies to prevent illegal aliens in the United States from receiving benefits or public services in the State of California."[221] The voters approved the measure,[222] and in 1996, Congress enacted its own provisions, incorporating many of the characteristics of Prop. 187. Thus, in 1997, a federal trial court held Prop. 187 preempted.[223] The federal Personal Responsibility and Work Opportunity Reconciliation Act of 1996 (PRWORA, generally called "welfare reform")[224] was one of three statutes that, as an ensemble, entrenched migrant illegalization. This legislation closed off access for certain lawful aliens to public benefit programs by drawing new status distinctions that linked authorized and unauthorized migrants and that temporarily barred some lawful residents from eligibility for food stamps and Supplemental Security Income (SSI); all nondocumented individuals became ineligible as well.[225] The Illegal Immigration Reform and Immigration Responsibility Act[226] mandated detention of migrants under certain circumstances[227] and created categories of offenses that triggered deportation, and the Anti-terrorism and Effective Death Penalty Act (AEDPA)[228] expanded the crimes of "moral turpitude" for which migrants could be deported.[229]

September 11, 2001, opened the twenty-first century with yet more fuel for antimigrant sentiments.[230] While the Immigration and Nationalization Service was not itself much of a "service," the title of a new amalgam—the Department of Homeland Security—laid no claim to that orientation.[231] The Homeland Security Act of 2002 formally dissolved another "service" entity—the Customs Service—which dated from 1789. Those functions became a part of the DHS under a new name—the aforementioned Customs and Border Protection.[232]

Funds for border protection steadily increased. In 1930, the federal government had employed about 1,200 people to patrol the northern and southern borders—or about one person per forty miles.[233] In contrast, CBP's 2004 allotment was $6 billion; in 2011, Congress authorized $11.4 billion to support a staff then numbering more than 58,000.[234] Homeland Security's 2013 budget overview explained it had "deployed unprecedented levels of personnel, technology, and resources to the Southwest Border."[235] In addition, in 2011, under a program called "Operation Stonegarden," DHS awarded some $55 million in grants to local law enforcement in border areas.[236] The CBP's website reported that, in 2012, it "processe[d]" 932,456 passengers and pedestrians a day, and that on one day, it had seized 13,717 pounds of drugs, apprehended 932 individuals, refused entry to 470, and arrested 61 people.[237]

Many commentators have raised concerns about the methods used by CBP—that its surveillance and questioning extend across citizens and migrants, both authorized and unauthorized.[238] And under the PATRIOT Act of 2001 (reauthorized repeatedly) as well as pursuant to the Foreign Intelligence Surveillance Act of 1978 (also amended after 9/11), surveillance authority expanded, reaching from migrants to citizens to libraries and human rights organizations.[239] In 2013, the Supreme Court rebuffed claims by several individuals and entities, alleging they were subject to surveillance, on the grounds that such concerns were too speculative.[240] Yet their fears were validated soon thereafter. Revelations by Edward Snowden detailed that the National Security Agency's Bulk Telephony Metadata Program involved collection and storage for several years in what one federal district judge described as a government collection "indiscriminately" reviewing "the metadata of hundreds of millions of other citizens without any particularized suspicion of wrongdoing."[241]

5. Disaggregating, Reaggregating, and Indexing the States

Even as the 2012 majority decision in *Arizona v. United States* placed migration policy under the rubric of "foreign affairs," states and localities experience migrants on a daily basis—as they run schools, streets, and community services. Migration is therefore also a "domestic affair," and the insistence on federal supremacy has not silenced state and local actors who, as I have detailed, are central to national as well as subnational lawmaking.[242]

Thus far, my discussion has focused on anti-immigrant measures in Pennsylvania, Arizona, and California. But states are neither univocal nor solo actors, and initiatives in these three states do not capture the diverse activities under way. Some states offer hospitality, welcoming noncitizens' participation and facilitating incorporation through inclusionary rules protecting employees,[243] providing in-state tuition, and offering identification cards for all city residents.[244] The City of New Haven, for example, provides residents, regardless of citizenship status, identification cards to welcome them as "active participants" in the community.[245] Moreover, state approaches are not static. California is illustrative. Despite its centrality in formulating the restrictive policies of the 1990s, California became the first state to permit migrants without documentation to become members of its bar.[246] Further, its recent initiatives related to health care, licensure, and education could be understood as protecting a form of state citizenship for migrants without documents.[247]

In short, various and sometimes conflicting agendas crisscross the states in a dense pattern of activities. One tally, by a proponent of using state law to "reduce illegal immigration," counted more than 1,500 bills introduced by 2007 and characterized the "vast majority" as "designed to discourage illegal immigration in one way or another."[248] A 2013 report on immigration legislation from the National Council of State Legislators (NCSL), which identifies pending legislation on a variety of topics, described an average of about 1,300 bills related to immigration and of about 200 laws enacted yearly since 2007.[249] That volume reflects both the politics of immigration and state-federal interactions. For example, during the first half of 2012, state lawmakers' proposals dropped by 40 percent, "from the peak of 1,592 in the first half of 2011,"[250] while in 2013, the NCSL tallied "a 64 percent increase from the 267 laws and resolutions enacted in 2012." The NCSL attributed the decline in 2012 to "state budget gaps and redistricting maps," as well as to developing law on preemption, putting into question "states' authority to enforce immigration laws" and making it wise "to postpone action."[251] The rise in 2013, in turn, was due to "a spike in resolutions, with 31 states adopting 253 resolutions, up from 111 in 2012."[252]

Statutory enactments are all the more relevant, as Arizona's S.B. 1070 illustrates. In 2011, five other states—Alabama, Georgia, Indiana, South Carolina, and Utah—adopted punitive provisions similar to Arizona's. Legislation after *Arizona v. United States* aimed to skirt federal preemption by imposing sanctions based on "state" law violations—such as failure to obtain a residency permit—rather than on immigration status. Even as federal courts invalidated some of the provisions,[253] these antimigration efforts drew a myriad of new internal boundaries to mark the citizen/noncitizen divide. Driver's licenses—issued by states under federal regulation via the 2005 REAL ID Act—became a focal point.[254] For example, Alabama classified obtaining a driver's license as a "business transaction" and made it a felony for an alien "not lawfully present" to enter into business transactions with the government.[255] Arizona's governor issued an executive order to bar "DREAMERS"—whom a federal executive order had made eligible for deferred action because of their arrival in the states as children[256]—from obtaining driver's licenses.[257] (That provision was enjoined by the federal courts, which concluded that state authority to impose such a classification on noncitizens was preempted by the federal government.)[258] In 2013, North Carolina proposed to put a pink strip (a color lighter than Nathaniel Hawthorne's scarlet *A*) on licenses issued to noncitizens.[259] Thereafter, some states imposed new restrictions by requiring more frequent renewals or requiring that a license of a noncitizen bear a marking that differentiated it from that of a citizen.

Thus far, I have taken states—and their laws—as the unit of analysis. Yet the continuities across borders make plain that joint and related efforts are under way. Earlier, I mapped the interaction between state initiatives and federal lawmaking—an axis described in federalism literature as vertical, as illustrated by the preemptive force of federal law in *Arizona v. United States.* Many state initiatives exemplify the impact of horizontal exchanges, spawned in part through private or special interest groups (often known as "PIGS" and "SIGS") pressing for liberal or illiberal immigration policies. The Chamber of Commerce and the agriculture industry have been active in supporting forms of entry through "side" and "back" doors."[260] Another relatively new voice aiming to affect migration policies is the private prison industry, supplying beds for detention and devices for surveillance.

Further, several translocal organizations of government actors shape policies; elsewhere, I offered the acronym "TOGAs" for such organizations, which are private entities whose members gain social and political capital from their shared commitments to the government structures for which they work.[261] These norm entre-preneurs are conduits, generating policy proposals in different states and localities that mirror each other.[262] Just as some states are hostile and others hospitable to migrants, cross-border orga-nizations also have differing policy agendas. State Legislators for Legal Immigration (SLLI), founded in 2007 by a Republican state representative from Pennsylvania, has criticized the failure of the federal government to protect the states from "invasion."[263] SLLI aimed to include legislators from all states and, as of 2012, had at least one member hailing from forty-one different states.[264] This organization overlaps with another effort, which has produced proposals in more than a dozen states to repeal the birthright citi-zenship provision of the Fourteenth Amendment.[265]

In contrast, several TOGAs, including the U.S. Conference of Mayors and the National League of Cities, have promoted reforms to facilitate entry and legalization for some migrants. The National League of Cities has sought recognition of the "human and civil rights" of both citizens and noncitizens and supports temporary worker programs and paths to legalization for millions of residents lacking documentation.[266] The U.S. Conference of Mayors sup-ported efforts to have children who are residents gain permanent status and championed legal access for agricultural workers as well as reexamination of various barriers to citizenship.[267] Moreover, in *Arizona v. United States*, neither organization took the expected position against federal preemption of state and local laws but instead argued against state law; as the National League of Cities explained, that Arizona's S.B. 1070 created an impermissible cli-mate of fear.[268]

Another window into state and local activity comes from two inventive professors who created the Immigrants' Climate Index (ICI), assessing state and local laws enacted between 2005 and 2009 to determine the degree to which a given place created posi-tive benefits for or enacted negative restrictions on migrants.[269] The professors tallied two-thirds of the laws enacted as "restric-tive" and rated a third "beneficial";[270] they concluded that state-level legislation was more likely to be positive for legal migrants than local-level enactments. States that ranked the highest on the 2009 positive metric were from various parts of the country, albeit not from the South.[271] This research identified growth in the number of undocumented immigrants as key to prompting restrictive laws and concluded that more laws were "restrictive" than welcoming of migrants.[272] Douglas Massey has trained our eyes to look at another variable, which is the movement of people within the United States. Massey argued that Arizona's anti-immigration laws were the product of two migrations—one from outside the United States and one from inside, as Phoenix's population skyrocketed when former residents of southern states moved west.[273]

The back-and-forths continue. Even as 2013 ushered in efforts to legalize "DREAMERS," federal immigration legislation seemed in the offing, and Maryland reinstated access to driver's licenses for unauthorized migrants.[274] Other states continued to delegitimate migrants by demanding more exacting forms of documentation to obtain driver's licenses and to rent apartments, and thereby creating new, contested frontiers in migration policies. That pattern continued in 2014 and 2015, as the president shaped a national program for deferring deportation, and Texas, joined by twenty-five other states, filed a lawsuit to enjoin its operation.[275]

6. Authorized Discrimination

Political developments have encumbered the movement of people and inscribed the negativity of the status of noncitizen. Despite many objections, the terms "illegal immigrant" and "unlawful aliens" have become fixtures that the alternatives—"undocumented immigrants,"[276] "irregular migrants,"[277] "unauthorized migrants,"[278] and "settled immigrants"—have yet to displace. Moreover, federal law has come to impose disabilities on lawfully admitted, legal permanent residents.

Neither the vocabulary of illegality nor hostility to migrants was inevitable; aliens did not have to come to be seen as "outlaws."[279] Given that during the twentieth century, federal law came to dominate migration and that economic developments created interest groups seeking to expand the labor pool, federalization could have had a different impact. If, as the *Hines* Court had proposed, federal law had been read to prohibit the "constant harassment" and surveillance of aliens, a broader swath of state practices would have been displaced through doctrines based on the liberty, dignity, and equality of all persons. Moreover, out of self-interest, the government could have aimed to forge links between aliens and the body politic by acknowledging their contributions as taxpayers and workers and by seeking to weave them into the identity of the state. Instead, federal law itself became a source of intrusiveness by bringing immigration status into focus for employment and for benefits and by enlisting state officials and private employers in monitoring compliance with federal oversight of aliens.

In the middle of the twentieth century, more constitutional shelter for aliens seemed to be in the offing. Building on the anti-stigmatization approach in *Hines*, the Supreme Court held that restrictions on aliens purchasing land, getting fishing licenses, and being admitted to the bar were impermissible forms of discrimination.[280] As part of its jurisprudence developed in response to the civil rights movement, the Court explained in 1970 that "[a]liens as a class are a prime example of a 'discrete and insular' minority . . . for whom such heightened judicial solicitude is appropriate," and therefore that "classifications based on alienage, like those based on nationality or race, are inherently suspect and subject to close judicial scrutiny."[281] In 1971, in a five-to-four ruling, the Court held that states cannot exclude undocumented children from public education. The Court rested its analysis of the Equal Protection mandate on an amalgam of the importance of education, the role of schools in preparing individuals for citizenship, and the innocence of children.[282]

Yet under current doctrine, both federal and state law can classify based on alienage and treat noncitizen residents, whether lawfully present or not, differently. Federal constitutional law thus enables state and federal governments to discriminate (within boundaries) on the basis of alienage. Vivid examples come from federal law, where legislation inscribing gender-based, racialized distinctions for access to citizenship by non-U.S. children of U.S. citizens has been deferentially reviewed under the rational basis test.[283] Further, in 1976, in *Mathews v. Diaz*, the Supreme Court upheld a congressional directive that prohibited permanent resident aliens from receiving Medicare benefits until after they had lived in the United States for five years. The Court predicated its ruling on the view of the line-drawing's rationality (that individuals who have lived for longer periods in the United States "may reasonably be presumed to have a greater affinity with the United

States than those who [have] not")[284] and that the "task" of categorizing belonged to Congress; "the responsibility for regulating the relationship between the United States and our alien visitors has been committed to the political branches of the Federal Government."[285]

Moreover, even as state laws aimed at noncitizen lawful residents are generally strictly scrutinized in light of equal protection concerns,[286] state limits on who can "participate in the processes of democratic decision making" have passed muster under a lower, rational-basis standard.[287] States cannot prevent lawful citizens from becoming lawyers,[288] from obtaining fishing licenses,[289] or from all competitive civil service positions.[290] But states can preclude aliens—including those lawfully resident in the United States—from specific forms of employment if a job falls within what the Court has styled a "political function" exception, involving "discretionary decision making, or execution of policy."[291] States had, the Court explained, "constitutional prerogatives" to assign only citizens to employment related to "the process of self-government."[292]

Under an expansive rubric of what work relates to "self-government," the Court upheld state exclusions of lawful resident noncitizens from public school teaching and from serving as police and probation officers.[293] Despite dissenting justices' criticism that the lines drawn between permissible and impermissible forms of state-based discrimination defied logic,[294] constitutional law permits states to limit opportunities for persons fully compliant with all requirements for entry and residence, and therefore to make, as well as to mark, divisions that are in tension with what *Hines* seemed to have promised.

Again, boundaries exist. Even as state laws discriminating against resident undocumented migrants are subjected to the forgiving rational basis analysis, some laws have been found to violate that standard. Illustrative was the 2014 invalidation as irrational of Arizona's effort to bar "DREAMERS"—but not all other undocumented migrant residents—from receiving driver's licenses.[295] And, thus far, federal law has not precluded states that want to do more—such as provide in-state tuition rates for migrants—from doing so.[296]

Yet, as exemplified by *Mathews v. Diaz*, the federal government has a lesser burden when treating aliens differently than it does citizens. While in *Hampton v. Mow Sun Wong*, the Supreme Court struck a complete ban imposed by the federal Civil Service Commission on aliens holding civil service jobs,[297] the Court assumed that, subject to due process constraints against arbitrariness, Congress or the president could impose alienage restrictions based on national interests the Court recognized as important.[298] The Civil Service's assertion of efficiency was an insufficient national interest to justify denying aliens "substantial opportunities for employment."[299]

In sum, relying on Congress's Article I powers to "establish a uniform Rule of Naturalization,"[300] the Court has generated a line of constitutional case law predicated on federal supremacy rather than on rights of personhood. Therefore, and counterintuitively from the perspective of equal protection theory, both the substance of equal protection rights and the kinds of scrutiny vary with the level of government imposing the disability. The result is a patchwork of decisions in which the Court oversees state laws affecting aliens and imposes important limits on state stigmatization of aliens. Yet, while creating a federal floor, the Court has both permitted states to draw employment lines based on alienage and tolerated many federal laws imposing disabilities.[301]

Many commentators have been critical of the results. As Michael Perry explained decades ago, "If it is unjust for a state to treat a person as inferior on the basis of a morally irrelevant trait, there is no conceivable basis for concluding that it is any less unjust for the federal government to do the same."[302] The Court has not, however, framed the question as one of justice. Rather, in this line of cases as in *Arizona v. United States*, federal authority—not equality or liberty—does the central work, leaving the federal government largely unconstrained in shaping policies making alienage the object of suspicion.

C. *"Crim-Imm"*

A brief reflection on the consolidation of the criminalization of migration is in order, again by placing it in the context of prior attitudes and practices. Despite social science data indicating that immigrants are "less likely to commit serious crimes" than "native-born,"[303] migration has become suffused with the aura of crime, and crime has become a reason to deport migrants. Further, the perceived legitimacy of state control of migrants works in tandem with the expansion of state oversight over citizens as well. The growth in the numbers incarcerated in the criminal system, in many parts of the world, reflects a broad punitive turn;[304] undocumented migration has provided a new justification for detention, and some migrants are detained for years because they have no country to which to return.[305]

1. The Production of Illegality

In the early part of the twentieth century, deportation, a "civil" penalty, was described by the jurist Learned Hand as a "dreadful punishment, abandoned by the common consent of all civilized peoples."[306] Further, as noted, in 1925, federal appellate judges were not willing to imply presidential powers to criminalize entry.[307] Even as 1929 marked the creation of the new crimes—the misdemeanor of unlawful entry and, after deportation, a felony upon a second unlawful entry[308]—a variety of impediments, including transportation costs, limited the government's interest in criminal sanctions and civil deportation.[309] While permitted by migration law, the practices were cushioned by an appreciation for its impact, reflected in Supreme Court admonitions to presume statutes protected the due process rights of the individuals involved.[310]

Yet by 2011, when litigating *Arizona v. United States*, the federal government proudly trumpeted that it had deported ("removed") almost 400,000 people that year.[311] Furthermore, the number of individuals in migration detention on a daily basis rose from 18,000 in 2004 to 34,000 in 2012.[312] Over the course of one year (2011), more than 400,000 were held (for varying lengths of time) in the immigration system.[313] Newspapers reported harsh conditions and that a small number of individuals were detained in solitary confinement.[314] By 2014, the focus had shifted to "unaccompanied minors"; an estimated 50,000 children sought refuge from lawlessness in countries in Central America.[315]

In addition to detention prior to deportation, federal prosecutions have become commonplace, adding to the spectacles produced by employer raids, "papers-please" inspections, and "civil" detention and deportation. The terms "crimmigration" and "crim-imm" entered the lexicon to capture that the criminal law and immigration systems, once formally discrete, are being conflated.[316] This linkage was underscored when, in 2010, the Supreme Court ruled that a criminal defendant, who was misinformed that his guilty plea would not result in deportation, had a constitutionally inadequate lawyer.[317]

Given the ease with which one becomes inured to what exists, the novelty of federal criminalization merits attention. One marker is a 1984 law review article, "Arrest without Warrant,"[318] complaining about low levels of federal action against migrants.[319] Unusual for its time in calling attention to migration law, the essay described the investigatory work by the INS to be, "by the standards of federal law enforcement," at "the high volume end."[320] The criticism was of a "de facto liberalization of immigration enforcement," which the author attributed to the limited resources available for investigation, detention, adjudication, and deportation, as well as to the procedural rights of the criminal system and "sensitivity to public criticism" when individuals with family ties were required to leave.[321]

Within twenty-five years, the picture looked very different. David Sklansky provided data through 2009 that tracked a dramatic rise in criminal indictments—from fewer than 10,000 prosecutions a year in 1996 to more than 90,000 in 2009.[322] Ingrid Eagly noted that "[n]ot since Prohibition has a single category of crime been prosecuted in such record numbers by the federal government."[323] In 2010, ICE memos set forth priorities for arrest, detention, and deportation—focused on national and public safety threats, those who had recently crossed the border, and noncitizens interfering with border control efforts.[324] As of 2013, immigration-related charges represented 25 percent of the federal prosecution caseload.[325]

Sanctions include both incarceration and deportation, and persons convicted of a crime of "moral turpitude" can be subjected to lifetime bars on reentry absent special permission.[326] Further, since 1996 and under the eerie term "removal,"[327] such sanctions have become more frequent. In 2005, some 40,000 persons were removed based on criminal convictions;[328] by 2009, the number was 393,000.[329] A 2014 report concluded that 4.5 million people, many of whom had "deep ties in the United States," had been deported since 1996.[330] Whether to think that approach efficacious depends on the baseline chosen. Estimates, as noted, are that about 11 million people reside without documentation in the United States.

The constraints preventing federal prosecutions and deportations from rising unendingly (and which make the preemption rule of *Arizona v. United States* protective of migrants) come from a mix of the relatively small size of the workforce composed of federal law enforcement officers, prosecutors, immigration judges, and Article III judges, and of political attitudes toward migrants. The caseload for immigration judges was, as of 2013, more than 1,200 cases per judge per year, as contrasted with some 300 to 500 cases per federal district judge per year.[331] Concerns about decision making in immigration come from various vectors, including judges both in immigration and in Article III courts, scholars, and the American Bar Association, which has documented the overload, the unevenness, and the unfairness.[332] The Obama administration's 2014 initiatives to defer deportation illustrate the other buffer, as segments of the body politic rebel against the ruptures of families and the threats of dislocation that haunt unauthorized migrants and their families.

Yet, despite complaints about resource challenges, one facet of the system—detention—has garnered substantial increases in funding. For fiscal year 2013, DHS sought almost $2 billion to provide detention at a cost of $120 to $164 per detainee per day.[333] Some states and localities are eager to receive some of those funds,[334] and so is the private prison industry (starting in the 1980s),[335] which is now a major source of housing for migrant detention. As of 2011, half of the immigrant detainees were housed by private providers,[336] whose lobbyists pressed for more detention[337] and fashioned mechanisms such as real estate investment trusts to hold detention properties. Thus, even as a 2011 shareholder report from a private prison corporation recorded concerns that state policies had reduced incarceration for those convicted of crimes, the company found solace that, at "the federal level, initiatives related to border enforcement . . . have continued to create demand for larger-scale, cost efficient facilities."[338]

2. Categories of Rights and Wrongs

On one account, purposeful migration without permission is a crime, constituted by the willful failure to respect the sovereignty of a polity by intruding on or by taking a form of its and its peoples' property and identity.[339] With crime as the model, incarceration and deportation are appropriate sanctions. A competing account is that unauthorized entry is akin to the civil tort of trespass,[340] to which the state may respond by ejecting the trespasser. Another possibility—at the core of my discussion—is that migration ought not to be seen as wrong in either sense, even if it can be subjected to regulation based on the concerns for the well-being of migrants and of the receiving community.[341] "Legalization" is typically used in reference to changing the status of those present in the country, but its deeper purchase would be to override the idea that border crossing without permission is illicit. Legal activities can, of course, be subjected to regulation, including penalties (such as civil fines or restitution) for noncompliance, rather than governed by regimes reliant on deportation and incarceration.

Much more could be and has been said about the morality of the border and appropriate modes of regulation, but instead of debating decriminalization and the aggressiveness of exile, the punitive approach is generally taken for granted. Questions that ought to be directed at exploring how to conceptualize unauthorized entry are funneled instead into discussions about how to label the law regulating immigration and whether enforcement is best understood in "civil" or "criminal" terms.

What "best" means depends on whether the goals are to be more (or less) protective of migrants; to be more (or less) careful when sorting individual claims of rights to remain; to be more (or less) enabling of deportations; to be more (or less) stigmatizing; and how to create safety and community life—all while being cost-effective.[342] For example, one could argue that categorizing immigration as criminal could help migrants by protecting them more because, under current law, criminal defendants—but not migrants—have rights to remain silent (protected by *Miranda v. Arizona*),[343] and, if facing prison terms, rights to counsel (protected by *Gideon v. Wainwright*).[344] But in practice, the erosion of *Miranda* on the criminal side or some efforts to use its protections as a voluntary matter on the civil side could reduce the salience of the criminal/civil distinction, just as the limited implementation of *Gideon* makes aspects of its promise illusory.[345] Moreover, efforts are under way to provide counsel for "civil" deportation.[346]

Keeping deportation as a "civil" sanction, in turn, also offers certain protections, including the potential for lessening the stigma of entry without authorization. Moreover, criminal defendants, once properly charged, can be held in detention prior to trial for long periods, while migrant detainees are not supposed to be subjected to indefinite detention.[347] But critics argue that "civil" detention is an oxymoron because the confinement is intrinsically punitive.[348] Other factors in choosing between the "criminal" or "civil" label include which system gives more discretion to the government,[349] whether the current link between criminal convictions and "civil" removal gives more or less power to prosecutors,[350] and the resulting implications for the expansion or shrinking of judicial discretion.[351]

Yet this very debate deflects attention from three problems. First, under current law, the federal government has both systems at its disposal, to mix and match to leverage its power against individuals. Second, federal law has recruited third parties—employers—as part of its apparatus of surveillance and oversight, and thus expands both the aegis of government and the negativity associated with migration. Third, the crim-imm options work to reframe the gravity of deportation of migrants ("the great expulsion")[352] as presumptively less harmful than imprisonment, positioned as the only alternative. The denouement is that the migrant has been repositioned from "alien," "irregular," and "undocumented" to "illegal" and "criminal alien," with a new term of art—"priority aliens"—emerging to flag those high up on the government deportation queue.[353]

At least thus far, constitutional law has not proved to be a robust constraint on the expanding state control. To undo this apparatus requires a mix of formulating substantive constitutional constraints on the criminalization of movement and the political will to revise not only law enforcement procedures, detention obligations, and deportation practices but also employment practices and limiting benefits and jobs based on alienage. Further, as the conflict over the 2014 Obama administration liberalization efforts reflects, to have such a shift succeed requires that decriminalization and destigmatization norms are grounded in state, as well as federal, law and politics.

That work has become all the more difficult because of cross-border developments sustaining the propriety of border barriers.

From "Fortress Europe" and the rapid growth in detention centers on- and offshore,[354] initiatives around the globe inscribe outsider entry as wrongful. In 2015, the few thousand who had trekked from Africa to Calais in hopes of reaching England were described as "swarms" rather than seen as terrified seekers of safety.

3. The Permeable Boundaries of the Fourth Amendment: Migrants, Citizens, Government Benefit Recipients, Students, and Detainees

Proponents of border enforcement argue that bright lines come with marking borders, entitling citizens to protection and legitimating the limited rights accorded noncitizens. Critics of the treatment of migrants also rely on citizen/migrant distinctions to argue that migrants should be accorded the same rights as citizens.[355] But reliance on the line between alien and citizen to insulate the citizen or to protect the alien is unwise, for the dynamic relationship of government to individuals is shaped through interactions with both citizens and noncitizens. What is needed instead are theories of liberty—rather than theories of citizenship—if state control is to be contained.

An example comes from the law of the Fourth Amendment—deciding when a search has taken place, whether it was reasonable, whether exemptions from the reasonableness requirement exist, and whether consent can be implied or required as a predicate to receipt of a government service.[356] In terms of migrants, current law authorizes searches at inspection sites—the borders—where the government gains a kind of immunity from its obligations under the Fourth Amendment. The law permits border searches of both citizens and aliens, explained as "a narrow exception to the Fourth Amendment prohibition against warrantless searches without probable cause . . . deemed reasonable simply by virtue of the fact that they occur at the border."[357]

Once past the border, another Fourth Amendment question is whether its protections embrace noncitizens. In a 1990 decision, Chief Justice Rehnquist read the Fourth Amendment to protect the "right of the people," dependent on a relationship between people and their government.[358] Therefore, a Mexican defendant—who had "no previous significant voluntary association with the United States"—could not suppress evidence seized from a search of his property in Mexico.[359] But the discussion also reflected that persons who "have otherwise developed sufficient connection with this country to be considered part of that community" could be protected.[360] Lower courts have since relied on a mixture of the Fourth Amendment and due process to suppress evidence obtained from aliens through "egregious searches."[361]

Once the Fourth Amendment applies, issues emerge about what constitutes a search or a seizure and about what circumstances license either without warrants. Physical appearance can be used as a factor in a search;[362] indeed, critics charge that there is a "Mexican exception to the Fourth Amendment,"[363] raising fears of racial profiling. As for seizures, lower court cases have—as discussed earlier—held that federal immigration detainers per se are not grounds for probable cause to arrest.

State surveillance of migrants expanded during the same decades in which state oversight of other categories of individuals also expanded. Illustrative is the treatment of recipients of federal and state benefit programs. In the 1950s and 1960s, when governments gave aid to families with dependent children, some localities initiated what were known as "midnight raids"—searching for a "man in the house" and therefore a reason to end state assistance because of his liability for child support.[364] The policy (like border practices) was racialized, with patterns of such inspections concentrated in certain areas of the South.[365]

In 1971, in *Wyman v. James*,[366] the Supreme Court addressed the question of whether benefits could be conditioned on government officials making "periodic" home visits. While noting the backdrop of the Fourth Amendment, the Supreme Court rejected its application on the grounds that the caseworker's entry into the home of the recipient was predicated on rehabilitative rather than investigative purposes, and hence was not a "search" for purposes of the Fourth Amendment.[367] Alternatively, the Court reasoned that, if subject to the Fourth Amendment, home visits/searches were not unreasonable in light of the government's interests in fiscal integrity.[368]

Wyman became the basis for household searches for evidence of ineligibility and fraud,[369] and, akin to the treatment of migrants, the focus was on "verification" of status. For example, in the 1990s, California officials in San Diego County launched "Project 100%," requiring all county aid applicants, as well as recipients, to agree to requests for searches. The officials authorized to search homes were not only social workers (as in *Wyman*) but also members of the county's Public Assistance Fraud Division inside its district attorney's office.[370] Parallel "home visits" programs were put into place in Los Angeles and Milwaukee. Despite the potential for criminal prosecutions, constitutional challenges to both programs were unsuccessful.[371] Judges justified the practices based on the idea that the expenditure of public funds produced "diminished privacy interests of those seeking public aid."[372]

Welfare applicants and recipients are not the only categories of citizens for whom special search rules developed. Probationers are often told that a condition of probation is "consent" to searches.[373] Other individuals, walking on the streets and in their own apartment complexes, have become targets, seeking protection based on arguments that such "stop and frisk" policies violate the Fourth Amendment.[374] Schoolchildren provide another example, as the Supreme Court has upheld random drug testing of students.[375] Thus, as a federal appellate judge protesting home searches of recipients of benefits put it, once the government provision of goods and services suffices as a license to search, the risks are "limitless, . . . eroding the Fourth Amendment rights of various groups of people in this country . . . [receiving] disability benefits, Medicare and Medicaid benefits, [and] veterans benefits."[376]

Detention is another basis for searches that are not bounded by distinctions based on citizenship. For example, when Russell Palmer claimed that correctional officials had violated the Fourth Amendment by destroying his personal property in a "shakedown" of his cell, the Supreme Court concluded that prisoners had no rights against unreasonable searches; a "recognition of private rights for prisoners cannot be reconciled with the concept of incarceration and the needs and objectives of penal institutions."[377] In 2011, the Court expanded the custodial authority to search in the context of a search of a woman arrested after the police noticed that neither she nor her children wore seat belts.[378] In 2012, the question was whether an individual stopped by a state trooper and detained could be subjected at a county jail to a "strip search" that included display of intimate parts of the body.[379] The Court's answer again was in the affirmative, given the need for "readily administrable rules" and the "risk of increased danger."[380] In short, when DHS explained in its 2013 budget request that it was working with "Federal, State, local and private sector partners to expand the Nationwide Suspicious Activity Reporting (SAR) Initiative," its approach to enlist and "train State and local law enforcement to recognize behaviors and indicators related to terrorism, crime and other threats"[381] fit inside the expanding array of justifications for searching, seizing, and detaining both citizens and aliens.

III. LIBERTY OF TRANSIT THROUGH A "SINGLE POSTAL TERRITORY"

As Donald Massey explained, the southern border of the United States was once readily traversed by individuals going back and forth between Mexico and various work sites in the United States. Today it is a hazardous crossing that, Massey argued, contributes to the growth of undocumented individuals residing permanently in the United States.[382] I turn now to explore the opposite trajectory, aimed at reducing barriers to movement rather than entrenching the illegality of transit. That contrast is provided by the fact that sending a letter across borders was once burdensome and in some instances hazardous for the carriers, who could be subjected to surveillance and targeted by thieves. Innovations of relatively recent vintage have rendered the activity banal, as a taken-for-granted, publicly provided, (almost) universal service.

To credit technology alone is to miss the remarkable amount of law and politics that created national systems of mail exchange, altered expectations of communication among persons distant from each other, and produced one of the first international state–based organizations—the UPU. Empires, colonization, the economy, technology, and theories of free expression have reframed the idea of what governments can and should do.

The development of transnational mail, imagining a "single postal territory," provides an exemplar of government interdependencies that migration politics should engage. Postal services based in governments reflect intergenerational commitments to producing and sharing economic and political ventures celebrating cross-border interactions that benefit individuals, businesses, and governments themselves. Of course, such services are freighted with complaints ranging from corruption to inefficiencies, but government postal services have generated expectations of supported communications across oceans that merits credit for political creativity located in sovereign-state cooperation.

A. *Inventing International Organizations: The Universal Postal Union*

> The right of transit is guaranteed throughout the entire territory of the Union.
>
> Convention of Berne, Article X, 1874

The law of migration has made familiar the refusal to permit strangers to enter. Messengers carrying letters and parcels into territories controlled by others once faced similar impediments—absent empires aiming to erase borders and separate identities.[383] When permitted entry, foreign postmen used special passports and operated through restricted routes.[384] Political will has revised these expectations, as parcels now travel more freely than persons.

The rise of the nation-state occasioned bilateral treaties permitting mail service. An English-French treaty providing a courier service in the seventeenth century is one example,[385] and a postal service developed by the Hanseatic League another. Over time, a European competition for routes and services developed,[386] complete with some countries subsidizing transport companies[387] and imposing obligations on times to delivery.[388] Competition did not, however, solve the problem of the lack of standardization. In 1850, Austria, Prussia, and all German-speaking states formed the German Postal Union that set a single tariff, reduced transit rates, distributed foreign mail for free, and simplified the process of settling accounts.[389] Another entity, based in London and called the "International and Colonial Postage Association," aimed to rationalize exchanges.[390]

But all such responses were partial; by 1873, Germany was a party to seventeen bilateral agreements that entailed various classifications and prices. Units of measurement likewise varied. The United States and Great Britain relied on the ounce; France, Belgium, and Italy on the gramme; and Germany and Austria on what they called a zolloth; some countries required mail to be prepaid, and prices varied not only by destination but also by route and by the number of sheets of paper used[391]—resulting in a "maze of rules and regulations bewildering to public and postal officials alike."[392]

Twenty-two countries met in Berne, Switzerland, in 1874 and, after fourteen sessions, created a General Postal Union—named thereafter the Universal Postal Union.[393] Within a few weeks, twenty-one countries agreed to become a "single unit for the exchange of postal correspondence, standardized and simplified postal rates and procedures, and created the second oldest international organization."[394] They decided on a "standard classification of correspondence," a "common tariff structure" independent of distance, and a "universal weight scale."[395] International mail thus would approximate the experience of domestic mail; affixing a stamp to a letter sent it to any member country.

To simplify accounting, the Treaty of Berne relied on the assumption that "since a letter generally brings forth a reply, the correspondence exchanged between any two countries is nearly enough equal to enable accounting to be dispensed with as between the countries of origin and destination"; the originating country collected and retained the post fee, with accounting for intermediate transport services thereafter.[396] The Treaty of Berne also imposed an obligation to forward the international mail by the same routes (the "most rapid") in use for domestic mail.[397] The exchange crafted a form of international currency, even as debate continued about whether the "intermediary" territory could impose transit fees,[398] and many decades later, in 1969, the method of pricing changed and terminal fees were added to adjust for disparities in sending and receiving—paralleling, to some extent, the asymmetry among countries as sending or as receiving migrants.

Implementation of the Treaty of Berne entailed creating what was then a novel institution and today is one of many examples of a "geopolitical bureaucracy."[399] As Leonard Woolf explained in 1916, conflicts over "national interests" were intense, and countries had regularly to compromise.[400] Almost a century later, another commentator detailed how the UPU "weld[ed] together the hugely diverse and initially mistrustful political and bureaucratic systems of Europe and North America"[401] that organized not only international mail transit but also an arbitration system to deal with accounting disputes, uniform colors for international stamps, exchange rates for currencies, and statistics providing metrics of utility.[402] Further, members reconvened every three years "with a view of perfecting the system of the Union."[403] What the twenty-two countries made became "the cradle of an emerging international political order," now associated with many other institutions that have much higher visibility.[404]

The 1874 UPU organized nation-states in cooperative ventures that worked (to borrow again from Leonard Woolf's 1916 description) a "revolution in the constitution of the society of nations" that, in the decades thereafter, enjoyed its own "placid obscurity."[405] And like its national analogue, the political prompts ranged from economics to interest in promoting literacy, exporting culture, and enhancing while controlling colonial functions.[406] An 1875 publication made the point: the UPU was "an intimate association of the civilized countries of four parts of the world," and its "boundaries will be no other than the very frontiers of civilization."[407]

The UPU represents commitments to border crossing as well as the triumph of sovereignty, its limits, the diverse impacts of joint ventures, and the uselessness of unilateralism. The goal is for all "users/customers [to] enjoy the right to a universal postal service . . . at all points in their territory, at affordable prices."[408] Like the international organizations that have followed, the UPU relies on states to implement the project of crossing their own boundaries.[409]

The history of the UPU offers up puzzles, that have since become familiar to international organizations, about the status of such entities and their import for the sovereignty of their members.[410] For example, when a few colonies were admitted with (briefly) equal voting status, a horrified 1933 commentator objected to giving colonies "international personality" that would "introduce in international law a precedent for abolishing the international effects of what is known as territorial sovereignty of states over their colonies and of establishing equality between them."[411] Territories posed yet other questions, since some but not all were members.

In 1948, after the UPU affiliated with the United Nations, the era of "open" membership ended. The UPU adopted a rule reflecting the Cold War; "sovereign" countries could be admitted only after securing an affirmative vote by two-thirds of the members.[412] Over the decades, country-to-country conflicts disrupted services, and individual countries sometimes blocked deliveries.[413] Further, as countries split (i.e., East and West Germany, North and South Vietnam or Korea, and the two Chinas), new versions of the issues of admittance and status emerged.[414] But exclusion is self-negating if the point is the "universal" movement of mail. Natural disasters, world wars, and terrorism have all altered the flow.[415]

Yet membership grew and services expanded to include special delivery, parcel post, free mail for prisoners,[416] insured letters, postal orders, and picture postcards, helping to democratize communications because the small amount of blank space welcomed less skilled writers.[417] By 1938, air had become the "normal means of conveying all first-class mail in Europe without any extra charge whatsoever to the general public."[418] In 1947, the "all-up" principle—that letters and postcards would be "dispatched by air transport"[419]—was put into place. In 1948, as noted, the UPU became a special agency of the United Nations—a status designed to leave the UPU's own "sovereignty . . . unimpaired."[420] The UPU opened its first building in Berne in 1953.[421]

Legal rights to private correspondence took shape during the second half of the twentieth century. Article 8 of the European Convention on Human Rights protects the privacy of a person's "home" and "correspondence."[422] Article 17 of the International Covenant on Civil and Political Rights also protects individuals' privacy, including in the "family home, or correspondence."[423] Much of the jurisprudence addresses prisoners' access to the mails (including some affirmative obligations to enable such exchanges),[424] and a few decisions insist on rights that mail be free from surveillance, absent national security justifications.[425]

By 2012, the UPU counted 192 countries as members and 660,000 post offices around the world when it celebrated its twenty-fifth Postal Congress in Doha, Qatar.[426] Paralleling the first Congress, the ambitions remained expansive. The UPU aimed for "the lasting development of efficient and accessible universal postal services of quality in order to facilitate communication between the world's inhabitants by guaranteeing the free circulation of postal items over a single postal territory composed of interconnected networks."[427]

By then, new issues were on the roster. The questions included how to be "green" in light of the "environmental awareness" of the carbon emissions created by air mail and how to be socially responsible,[428] a reference to the terrible working conditions of some postal employees. Other challenges were the problem of a lack of "interoperability" among postal networks because of disparate qualities and standards, including for "electronic postal services" that facilitated interaction through new information and communication technologies (ICTs), expanded e-commerce, and enabled participation in the digital economy.[429]

B. Governments, Services, Privatization, and Redistribution

Postal systems continue to serve as a marker of the interest in supporting the movement of objects through cross-border cooperation. But questions are emerging about the ambitions for such services and what role governments should play in subsidizing them. From the fifteenth through the twentieth centuries, the postal services moved from a private, fragmented system into a nationalized and international one, aiming for uniform and universal coverage. While some governments relied on postal services for revenue, others subsidized the post in pursuit of providing universal postal services through intergovernmental cooperation to individuals across the globe. That ambitious goal was a fixture during much of the last century, whatever its difficulties in practice. But during the last few decades, the critique of governments' redistributive, welfarist activities has prompted reconsideration of the kinds of services to be supported. Private entities have come to the fore, offering fee-for-service post to those who can afford their rates. This shift may return postal services to the fragmented model of earlier centuries.

What privatization means in this context is unclear. Several countries have made what were once parts of government into semiautonomous agencies or private companies, albeit with regulations that cabin some operational choices. For example, the United Kingdom's "Royal Mail," which dates from 1635 as a "public" entity, provided the government with revenues for much of its history. But in the last decades, revenues declined, prompting debates about remodeling its structure.[430] In the Postal Services

Act of 2011, the UK Parliament removed all restrictions on the transfer of shares from Royal Mail Holdings, which had been government owned,[431] and a public offering took place in 2013.[432] Yet public subsidies and regulation remained, as did government responsibility for previously committed pensions. Further, the law required the continued provision of a universal postal service—to maintain the public interest in universal access and affordable postage—through the obligation that one (or more) authorized mail service be a Universal Service Provider.[433] For those interested in political economy, the 2011 Postal Services Act could be understood as a mechanism to raise capital for the Royal Mail (designated as the Universal Service Provider) while aiming to continue the same services.[434]

A shift in the structure of the postal services has also taken place in the United States, which had, since the country's inception, given much greater economic support to the mail than has the United Kingdom. In the United States, the founding generation saw the mail—and especially newspapers—as a way to link commerce and to create a body politic. Federal government investments in transportation networks for mail were substantial, and after the Civil War, the federal government sought to generate a "federal presence" around the country, by building its own facilities. Congress authorized projects that brought both construction jobs and federal employment to localities around the country.[435] While in some localities, the government combined post offices and courthouses, the number of post office buildings outstripped courthouses and became the dominant federal space around the country. "At once public and private, anonymous and personal, the mail was a site of new and recognizably disruptive forms of social and commercial connection."[436]

The federal government thereby proved itself to be a local service agency. As the discussion of *Arizona v. United States* made plain, another common government-funded service—police—is located at state and local levels. Visiting the police station requires a special purpose; going to the post office could be a daily event. Further, once home delivery became commonplace,[437] state officials made regular visits to people's homes—not (per *Wyman v. James* as oversight of benefit recipients) in search of misbehavior but rather to provide personal mail delivery services.[438] Home delivery has produced encounters between individuals and the state that are neither freighted by surveillance nor appreciated as a form of social service assistance that they are. Subsidized mail could be understood as putting us all on the government "dole."

But this "civic mandate" of the post office is being overshadowed by a model focused on "postal accountability."[439] The U.S. Postal Service was once a government department; in 1970, Congress shifted its organization to create a semiautonomous entity, operating under mandates to provide universal mail but limited in the kinds of auxiliary services it can offer.[440] In addition, Congress required the Postal Service to pre-fund health care benefits of employees; that obligation has created a mountain of paper debt.[441] Even as the Postal Service was held by the Supreme Court to be inseparable from the United States for purposes of antitrust laws,[442] some commentators described it as in a "death spiral," caused by the development of electronic communication and competition from private providers.[443]

In 2009, 13,000 fewer post offices existed than in 1951, with more cutbacks under way.[444] While protests from rural communities and postal employees' unions stemmed some post office closings and cutbacks, the face of the government is fading. The United States relocated "post offices" by opening up stalls selling stamps inside malls and other commercial enterprises; in 2013, some of the notable local post offices were offered for sale.[445] Moreover, to the extent the encounter is virtual, the site was once called "USPS.gov," as the Postal Service shared its ".gov" with other government providers—members of the judiciary, legislators, and executive branch officials. But users are instead directed to "USPS. com," whose ending (".com") is shared by many businesses. Thus the identity of the government as the visible conduit for uncensored and subsidized exchanges is diminishing.

Private couriers—DHL, FedEx, and UPS—have entered the market for both domestic and international routes. Part of their success stems from their ability to capitalize on what government investments in and subsidies for postal services produced: addresses, zip codes, routes, and delivery networks, as well as demand for the service. The public and private systems are deeply intertwined; in 2012, one estimate is that FedEx received more than $1.6 billion for transporting U.S. mail.[446] Moreover, unlike the public sector mandate to support universal services for first-class mail, private providers do not have to provide free services to users such as members of the armed services and can cherry-pick which "products" they want to offer, vary prices by customers, and cut services to unprofitable locations.

Like the world of migration, the use of mail services is filled with asymmetries. Some countries are sending and some receiving, and rich and poor do not share equally. The UPU reported more than 660,000 post offices around the world that enabled 368 billion letter items (52 per capita) to be mailed yearly.[447] Almost all of the items mailed (99 percent) move within a single country rather than across borders. Seventy-five percent of international letter exchanges take place in "industrialized countries."[448] Eighty-three percent of the "world population benefits from home mail deliveries."[449] Ninety-five percent has postal services more generally; the 350 million—or 5 percent—estimated to lack postal services are disproportionately (if continents are the relevant unit of measurement) located in Africa. There, about 30 percent lacked services of any kind, as contrasted with about 11 percent in "Arab countries" and 3 percent in "industrialized countries."[450]

Just as national systems are being reassessed, and some dismantled, the UPU's goals are also under scrutiny. Questions abound not only about the facts (How many people living where get what mail or parcels by what service? What electrical systems and computer resources are reliably available for which users?) but also about metrics of measurement and their import. Not surprisingly, there is a "close relationship between postal performance and economic development."[451] A study by the World Bank reported in 2004 that postal services correlate with a country's total economic activity (its Gross Domestic Product per capita),[452] as well as with trust in postal sectors and performance, which also correlates with income.[453]

The World Bank researchers argued maldistribution of resources; they noted disapprovingly that "Maldives has a post office for every 1,500 people, with each office handling an average of only two mail items per day,"[454] as contrasted with 5,500 mail items per day in France, which maintains post offices for every 3,000 people.[455] In the United States (not the World Bank's focus), Connecticut, with a population of more than 3.5 million people, has 302 post offices, or one for about every 12,000 people; South Dakota, with about 830,000 people, has 317 post offices, or about one per 2,629 people.[456]

The questions of course are about the baseline: which places and volume frame the issues; whether the metrics are persons and mail items or whether distance to travel in addition to population is a relevant factor; whether the post offices in Maldives and France or Connecticut and South Dakota provide services other than delivering mail daily; and what would happen were such service stations closed. In many areas, post offices function as banks, providing a repository for savings and a method of transferring money,[457] including what are known in migration parlance as "remittances" sent home via wire transfers, through private commercial entities or the post, with the prices for doing so regulated or not.[458]

In short, debates are under way about the breadth of mandates for services,[459] the extent of subsidies,[460] the declining demand, and the degree to which cross-subsidies are efficient methods to support "access targets."[461] The study by the World Bank recorded skepticism about the aspiration for universal service and identified a "Postal Dilemma"; half of the 700 items per capita per annum travel by way of the U.S. Postal Service, in contrast to 50 percent of all countries "generating less than 10 items" a year.[462] The researchers proposed retreating from the goal of "universal service" to what was termed "universal access"[463]—a system that did not entail everyday delivery, as "neither required, attainable, nor cost effective.[464]

The threats to the migration of people come from illegalization and criminalization inscribing hostility to such movement by receiving countries, and the unwillingness of governments to see themselves as obliged to facilitate border crossing. The challenges facing the movement of objects are not only how to be green and socially responsible but also about whether the political will to subsidize those exchanges can be sustained or is fading. The privatization of the post rests on the view that government must "defray its own expenses" (to borrow from the arguments of Roland Hill, who in 1837 invented direct mail services and the "penny post")[465] rather than have goals beyond profits and management. Of course, many people no longer need state support to be able to communicate with others. Thriving private sector enterprises—Facebook, Google, and FedEx, inter alia—have become famous for providing networks of global impact. But those institutions can choose to give discounts to high-volume users rather than charging citizen/customers uniform fees. Further, private mail carriers rely on government-built routes and have no commitments to subsidize segments of users in sparsely populated areas, while "rural home delivery" remains a mandate for the U.S. Postal Service.

When government postal services collapse, the distributive and communitarian impact of these commercial, political, and personal exchanges is lessened. Further, the government itself loses its identity as the source of services.[466] Those who argue for cutting national subsidies for postal services do not couple those proposals with demands for government support to make the Internet accessible to all, to create community centers, or to provide home visits by state employees to help them connect to others rather than for surveillance. The failure of "postalization" of the telephone and telegraph in the United States had demonstrated that, absent government mandates, universal coverage for those unable to pay is not what commercial enterprises offer.[467] The state, in turn, loses opportunities to show itself (including on the Net, via the .gov appellation) as a source and as a resource that, under constitutions insistent on equality and dignity, is a universal provider of some services.

IV. "Immigration policy shapes the destiny of the Nation"

This quotation comes from Justice Kennedy's 2012 decision in *Arizona v. United States*, with which I opened this discussion. Justice Kennedy appropriately recognized the centrality of the treatment of migrants to U.S. national identity. Yet the choice of the word "destiny" may deflect attention from the role played by agency—the "policy" with which his sentence begins. The purpose of my excavation of the shifts in attitudes, regulations, and practices of the law of the migrant and of the mails is to underscore the alternative "destinies" that are made through acts of political and legal will.

The mix of migration and mail provides three lessons. A first is that governments can radically reshape policies to connect and support each other in cross-border exchanges. Despite the degree to which U.S. law is focused on criminalization and exclusion of migrants, it is possible to imagine a set of commitments to migration that acknowledge it to be an ordinary and lawful activity that, while subject to regulation, has no relationship to the criminal law.

A second lesson from the inquiry into transnational mail practices is that unilateralism is insufficient, for no one country's policy can produce lasting, functional responses to migrants.[468] "Methodological nationalism" pervades immigration studies, obscuring the need to understand the dynamic effects of migration on the communities from which people exit as well as on those to which they go.[469] Reasoning *from* the sovereignty of individual states blocks thinking about the reciprocation entailed in the movement of persons and families from one place to another, the degree to which individuals, families, and economies are multiply affiliated, and the obligations that could flow among receiving and sending countries. Reasoning *with* the sovereign state (as contrasted to a cosmopolitan claim for a global community) opens up possibilities of transnational activities that mirror the growth of new practices permitting dual or multiple citizenships, as well as differentiated levels of attachments (denizenship, postnational membership, and the like)[470] to recognize forms of affiliations beyond a singular concept of citizenship.[471]

Joint action in migration has begun, albeit in self-consciously circumscribed arenas. World War II's displacement of persons prompted adoption of the Refugee Convention. In 1951, the Office of the UN High Commissioner for Refugees (UNHCR) and the International Organization for Migration came into being.[472] At the founding, as the nomenclature suggests, IOM's focus was on refugees, but its concerns have since broadened. The IOM is an intergovernmental (rather than an international) organization; it lacks its own separate identity and authority.

By the late 1990s, and in part in relation to the General Agreement on Tariffs and Trade (GATT), a project styled the New International Regime for Orderly Movement of People (NIROMP) was created to focus attention on "migration management," aiming to shape a regime of "regulated openness" in the movement of people through harmonizing policies.[473] In 2001, the IOM began an annual "International Dialogue on Migration," aiming to advance cooperation,[474] and in 2007 it launched its effort to address "human and orderly migration."[475] Yearly meetings and workshops focus on themes such as human rights and crises, climate change, and sharing responsibilities across borders.

Another set of its initiatives aims to curb "trafficking in persons," in part through international agreements that prohibit and punish forced labor and sexual exploitation and seek to protect children.[476] These efforts are complemented by a UN Special Rapporteur on the Human Rights of Migrants, the UN-based Global Migration Group, and other groups—the International Labor Organization, the Organization for Security and Cooperation in Europe, the International Catholic Migration Commission, as well as regional efforts aiming to shape thicker structures of transnational governance.[477] Further, an international group of students has identified the rights of migrants under international law and created a compendium, the International Migrants Bill of Rights (IMBR), to articulate a human rights framework for migrants and create a globally applicable set of minimum standards for their treatment.[478]

Yet the requisite international commitments and institutions have not yet come into being. Critics see the limits of the IOM[479] as being too entwined with and dependent upon states,[480] as well as lacking its own legal mandate independent of its member states.[481] The result is reinforcing "border management" and normalizing technocratic authority that obscures the political hierarchies at work.[482] No international commitment to emigrate that obliges countries to welcome migrants matches the conventions addressing refugees, trafficking, human rights,[483] and, I would add, the mail.

The IOM's fledgling status and the other multinational institutional arrangements (termed by some "bottom-up" governance)[484] are reminiscent of nineteenth-century efforts related to the mail, when national systems varied greatly and some bilateral and regional treaties predated the 1874 formation of the UPU, which negotiated cultures, economies, and ideologies to describe a "single postal territory." And like the 1874 treaty that created the UPU, Berne is again the site of activity, styled in 2001 by the government of Switzerland, serving as the host of an International Symposium on Migration, for which the IOM was the secretariat.[485]

The linking of the mail systems in many countries illustrates the capacity to develop both national and transnational institutions enabling persons, rights, economies, and other countries to flourish in a global exchange. In the nineteenth century, not all governments had national mail policies, and those that did priced and processed mail differently. Moreover, a transnational commitment to the liberal movement of objects did not exist. Uncensored mail is a legal and political accomplishment that has crossed boundaries, as state and international postal services dealt with differences in pursuit of diverse ambitions. The outcome has been commitments (unevenly realized) to universal services that entail various cross-subsidies producing egalitarian opportunities.

Many countries lack "comprehensive national migration policies" and "government structures to manage migration,"[486] and those that do often use their policies to ward off entrants. Further, while norms of responsiveness to refugees and rights for migrant workers have developed,[487] much of the focus is on "control" and "management." Shared commitments to cooperative facilitation of migration opportunities have not been shaped. In 2014, more than 50,000 children sat at the borders of the United States, met mostly with efforts to limit their entry rather than to understand that sending ten-year-old children alone thousands of miles away was a call for help. Similarly, the people pressing to enter Europe in Calais or on the Italian coast have put themselves in jeopardy in an effort to find a modicum of safety.

In the twenty-first century, borders have become sites of sovereign incompetence. The spectacles of migrants hiding in trucks and on ships, the human disasters of death in transit, and the children seeking shelter undermine the image not only of a government having the power to control its borders but also of a government committed to human dignity. Law has to find ways to embrace refugees seeking protection from crime and hunger just as law came to provide asylum for those seeking protection from assaults based on identity and politics. The questions are not if but how to enable migration; which forms of subsidies are to be provided; and how to fashion responses to the anxiety that even relatively small numbers of people moving across borders undermine communities' security and identity.

Thus the history of the development of both national and international mail offers a third lesson for migration studies—about the utility and fragility of government services and the desirability of obtaining new resources from outside a country's boundaries. Because the U.S. Post Office was understood as a means of forging a national identity, and because the movement of information about commerce and politics was seen as useful, Congress repeatedly funded budget shortfalls to widen the circle of inclusion—of course, also turning the federal government into a source of jobs and patronage. Government subsidies are now challenged as inefficient, and the related new technologies for communications—most recently the telecom industry—have not been subjected to legal obligations that they provide universal service entailing cross-subsidies for less trafficked routes.[488] The saga of the mail thus teaches about the role governments can play in redistribution. Its contemporary wobbling—transnationally—instructs on the vulnerability of state governance, given the global discourse celebratory of deregulation and privatization.

Collaboration among sending and receiving countries on the migration of people remains utopian, and the crafting of a universal postal service is at risk of becoming a remnant of a bygone age. But sovereignty—the capacity of nation-states to be vibrant sources of identity—is at stake. Returning to the terms chosen by Justice Kennedy, what "destinies" await depend upon ongoing political struggles about the vitality of commitments to sovereign provisions of redistributive egalitarian services for migrants and citizens alike.

NOTES

All rights reserved, Judith Resnick. Thanks are due to many, including the NOMOS group inviting me to participate in the conference "Immigration, Emigration, and Migration," held in January 2013; to commentators James Bohman and Jennifer Hochschild, and the volume's editor, Jack Knight; to workshop participants at the Princeton LAPLA seminar and commentator Paul Frymer; at the University of Toronto Legal Theory Workshop; at the American Philosophical Society, and the Yale Law School Faculty Workshop, as well as at the Liman Program's seminar "Borders" and its sixteenth annual colloquium, "Navigating Boundaries: Immigration and Criminal Law"; to Dennis Curtis, David Abraham,

Muneer Ahmad, Rosemary Barkett, Seyla Benhabib, Kristin Collins, Ingrid Eagly, Lucas Guttentag, Clarissa Hessick, Vicki Jackson, Richard John, Karen Knop, Matthias Kumm, Audrey Macklin, Douglass Massey, Allegra McLeod, Margaret McKeown, Hope Metcalf, Jon Michaels, Mark Miller, Nancy Morawetz, Jennifer Nedelsky, Nina Rabin, Cristina Rodríguez, Sia Sanneh, Ayelet Schahar, Reva Siegel, Kim Scheppele, Margo Schlanger, Joanne Scott, Sherine Shebaya, Brian Soucek, Neil Walker, Michael Wishnie, and Patrick Weil; to Yale Librarians Michael VanderHeijden and Sarah Kraus; to Yale student-colleagues Laura Beavers, Caitlin Bellis, Shouvik Bhattacharya, Edwina Clarke, David Chen, Samir Deger-Sen, John Giammatteo, Sergio Giuliano, Matthew Letten, Marianna Mao, Urja Mittal, Heather Richard, Andrew Sternlight, Jonas Wang, Emily Wanger, and Benjamin Woodring; and to Bonnie Posick, for expert editorial assistance. A special debt is owed to Sarah van Walsum, who, before her untimely death in 2014, pioneered cross-border feminist exchanges on migration.

1. See Jose E. Alvarez, *International Organizations as Law-makers* (Chicago: University of Chicago Press, 2005), 18, 25, 48. The postal organization was initially called the General Postal Union, and its founding followed that of the Universal Telegraphic Union, begun in 1865 as a part of a cluster focused on communications, transportation, and commerce, when these new technologies created incentives for what Alvarez termed shared "learning" and standard setting through interstate cooperation. See also George A. Codding Jr. and Anthony M. Rutkowski, *The International Telegraph Union in a Changing World* (London: Artech House, 1982), 24; George Arthur Codding Jr., *The International Telecommunications Union: An Experiment in International Cooperation* (Boston: Brill, 1952); Francis Lyall, *International Communications: The International Telecommunication Union and the Universal Postal Union* (Farnham, UK: Ashgate, 2011). In 1932, the International Telecommunication Union (ITU) merged with the Radio Telegraph Union; as of 2011, the ITU and the UPU were "the oldest international institutions that still operate." Lyall, *International Communications*, 1. Some of the national entities combine the two functions under the (English) abbreviation of PTT (postal, telegraph, and telephone). Relatively few materials in English focus on the Universal Postal Union. Sources relied upon here include Martin Zober, "The Universal Postal Union: A Case Study in International Organization" (PhD diss., University of Pittsburgh, 1949); M. A. K. Menon, "The Universal Postal Union" (PhD diss., New York University, 1963); Young Whan Kihl, "Functionalism in International Organization: With Special Reference to the Cases of the Universal Postal Union and the International Telecommunications Union" (PhD diss., New York University, 1963); Alfred Walter Holt Pilkington, "The United States and the Universal Postal Union" (PhD diss., University

of Chicago, 1937) (all available via PROQuest); see also Laurin Zilliacus, *Mail for the World: From the Courier to the Universal Postal Union* (New York: J. Day Company, 1953).

2. See "Treaty Concerning the Formation of a General Postal Union," October 9, 1874, 19 Stat. 577, as amended by the Universal Postal Union, March 21, 1885, 25 Stat. 1339 (hereinafter Berne UPU Treaty).

3. This chapter thus joins the literature criticizing the current degree to which aliens are outlawed and borders closed. See Joseph H. Carens, *The Ethics of Immigration* (New York: Oxford University Press, 2013); Joseph Carens, "The Case for Amnesty: Time Erodes the State's Right to Deport," *Boston Review*, May/June 2009; Joseph Carens, "Aliens and Citizens: The Case for Open Borders," *Review of Politics* 49 (1987): 251; Seyla Benhabib, *The Rights of Others: Aliens, Residents, and Citizens* (Cambridge: Cambridge University Press, 2004); Ayelet Schahar, *The Birthright Lottery: Citizenship and Global Inequality* (Cambridge, MA: Harvard University Press, 2009); Yasemin Soysal, *The Limits of Citizenship* (Chicago: University of Chicago Press, 1995); James Bohman, "Living with Noncitizens: Migration, Domination, and Human Rights," in Thomas N. Maloney and Kim Korinek, eds., *Migration in the 21st Century* (New York: Routledge, 2011), 9. See also Arash Abizadeh, "Democratic Theory and Border Coercion: No Right to Unilaterally Control Your Own Borders," *Political Theory* 36 (2008): 37; Thomas Christiano, "Immigration, Political Community, and Cosmopolitanism," *San Diego Law Review* 45 (2008): 933; James Hampshire, "Citizenship, Migration, and the Liberal State," *Migration and Citizenship* 1 (2012–13): 37–43; Daniel I. Morales, "Crimes of Migration," *Wake Forest Law Journal* 49 (2014): 1257. Competing accounts focus on the authority of sovereign states, as a matter of democratic and constitutional theory, to exclude. See, e.g., John Finnis, "Nationality, Alienage and Constitutional Principle," *Law Quarterly Review* 123 (2007): 417; Sarah Song, chapter 1, this volume; Michael Blake, "Immigration, Causality, and Complicity," in Sigal R. Ben-Porath and Rogers M. Smith, eds., *Varieties of Sovereignty and Citizenship* (Philadelphia: University of Pennsylvania Press, 2013), 111; David Miller, "Border Regimes and Human Rights," *Legal Ethics of Human Rights* 7 (2013): 1.

4. See, e.g., *El Dridi v. Italy*, Court of Justice of the European Community, C-61/11 (April 28, ECR I-0000, 2011), 2011 (First Chamber); *Velez Loor v. Panama, Inter-American Court of Human Rights*, Preliminary Objections, Merits, Reparations, and Costs, Judgment, Inter-Am. Ct. H.R. (ser. C) No. 132 (Nov. 23, 2010); Case No. 250-2010, Italian Constitutional Court, 2010, July 2010, n. 250-2010, http://www.cortecostituzionale.it. See also Mario Savino, "The Right to Stay as a Fundamental Freedom? The Demise of Automatic Expulsion in Europe," *Transnational Legal Theory*, May 2016, 25.

5. See Seyla Benhabib, *Dignity in Adversity: Human Rights in Troubled Times* (Cambridge: Polity Press, 2011), 101; see generally United Nations, Department of Economic and Social Affairs, *International Migration Report*, 2002, 2 (hereinafter UN International Migration Report 2002).

6. International Organization for Migration, *World Migration Report 2010*, xix, 2010, http://publications.iom.int. An international migrant is generally defined as "any person who changes his or her country of usual residence." United Nations, Statistics Division of the Department of Economic and Social Affairs, *Recommendations on Statistics of International Migration*, 1998, 17, http://unstats.un.org. See generally Seyla Benhabib and Judith Resnik, eds., *Migrations and Mobilities: Citizenship, Borders and Gender* (New York: NYU Press, 2009).

7. United Nations, Department of Economic and Social Affairs, Population Division, *International Migration Report 2015: Highlights* (2016), http://www.un.org.

8. See Alejandro Portes, "Migration and Development: Reconciling Opposite Views," *Ethnic and Racial Studies* 32 (2009): 5. Patterns also vary for high- and low-skilled workers, as well as "irregular migrants." See Alexander Betts, ed., *Global Migration Governance* (Oxford: Oxford University Press, 2011), 33–108. The impact on "those left behind" is explored in Devash Kapur, "Political Effects of International Migration," *Annual Review of Political Science* 17 (2013): 479.

9. As of 2002, the United States received the "largest number of migrants, followed by the Russian Federation . . . and Germany." UN International Migration Report 2002, 2.

10. Pew Hispanic Center, "A Nation of Immigrants: A Portrait of the 40 Million, Including 11 Million Unauthorized," January 29, 2013, 2, www.pewhispanic.org. See UN International Migration Report 2002, 2.

11. See Sarah Song, "The Significance of Territorial Presence and the Rights of Immigrants," in Sarah Fine and Lea Ypi, eds., *Migration in Political Theory* (Oxford: Oxford University Press, 2016), 225–48.

12. *Arizona v. United States*, 132 S. Ct. 2492 (2012).

13. See Pub. L. No. 70-1018, 45 Stat. 1551, enacted March 4, 1929; entry became a misdemeanor, and reentry after deportation or a criminal conviction became a felony.

14. *Hines v. Davidowitz*, 312 U.S. 52, 71 (1941).

15. Chinese Exclusion Act, Act of May 6, 1882, ch. 126, 22 Stat. 56 (1882), at § 1; Geary Act, Act of May 5, 1892, ch. 60, 27 Stat. 25 (1892), § 6, and *Fong Yue Ting v. United States*, 149 U.S. 698 (1893); *Chae Ching Ping v. U.S.*, 130 U.S. 581 (1889). A sourcebook of materials is provided by Martin Gold, in *Forbidden Citizens: Chinese Exclusion and the U.S. Congress* (Alexandria, VA: TheCapital.Net, 2012).

16. See *Korematsu v. United States*, 323 U.S. 215 (1944).

17. George A. Codding Jr., *The Universal Postal Union: Coordinator of the International Mails* (New York: NYU Press, 1964), vii.

18. Universal Postal Union, *Development of Postal Services in 2014*, 4, June 7, 2016, http://www.upu.int; Universal Postal Union, *Postal Statistics 2011: A Summary*, 11, 13–14. The percentage has also declined from 1989, when international mail represented 2 percent of all mail. See James I. Campbell Jr., "Evolution of Terminal Dues and Remail Provision in European and International Postal Law," in Damien Géradin, ed., *The Liberalization of Postal Services in the European Union* (The Hague: Kluwer, 2002), 3, 14, n13.

19. See Judith Resnik, "Globalization(s), Privatization(s), Constitutionalization and Statization: Icons and Experiences of Sovereignty in the 21st Century," *International Journal of Constitutional Law* 11 (2013): 162.

20. See, e.g., Saskia Sassen, *Territory, Authority, Rights: From Medieval to Global Assemblages* (Princeton, NJ: Princeton University Press, 2006).

21. See, e.g., Eric Ip, "Globalization and the Future of the Law of the Sovereign State," *International Journal of Constitutional Law* 8 (2010): 636, 637; Neil Walker, "Beyond Boundary Disputes and Basic Grids: Mapping the Global Disorder of Normative Orders," *International Journal of Constitutional Law* 6 (2008): 373; Daniela Caruso, "Private Law and State-Making in the Age of Globalization," *New York University Journal of International Law and Politics* 39 (2006): 1.

22. See Richard R. John, *Network Nation: Inventing American Telecommunications* (Cambridge, MA: Harvard University Press, 2010), 401. Opposition to efforts to bring the telegraph and telephone businesses under the wing of the U.S. Postal Department included—after New England telephone operators struck—the labor movement. John Steele Gordon was quoted as explaining that the word "postalization" "meant that government should run the telephone system. And there's a reason the word's forgotten." See John Steele Gordon, "Postalization," *American Heritage* 46, no. 6 (October 1995): 16.

23. See, e.g., Jean-Luc Guehenno, *The End of the Nation-State* (Minneapolis: University of Minnesota Press, 1994).

24. See International Organization for Migration, *Policy Briefs*, www.iom.int (accessed August 24, 2014).

25. See International Organization for Migration, Mission, http://www.iom.int (accessed June 9, 2016).

26. See generally Martin Geiger and Antoine Pécoud, "The Politics of International Migration Management," in Martin Geiger and Antoine Pécoud, eds., *The Politics of International Migration Management* (Basingstoke: Palgrave Macmillan, 2010), 1.

27. See, e.g., Nina Glick Schiller, "Migration and Development with Methodological Nationalism: Toward Global Perspectives on Migration," in Pauline Gardiner Barber and Winnie Le, eds., *Migration in the 21st Century: Political Economy and Ethnography* (New York: Routledge, 2012), 55. Schiller argued that global processes use migration to restructure capital in ways that harm local capital markets—"reducing the opportunity for social and economic equality and justice around the world" through reliance on "short-term labor contracts." See also Sara Kalm, "Liberalizing Movement? The Political Rationality of Global Migration Management," in Geiger and Pécoud, *The Politics of International Migration Management*, 21–41.

28. Menon, "The Universal Postal Union," quoting M. Rennet and Paul Jakob Marperger, "The First Advocate of the Universal Postal Union," *Union Postale*, September 1930.

29. Organization for Economic Co-operation and Development, International Migration Outlook 2013, 9, 2013, http://www.oecd-ilibrary. org.

30. Compare Schiller, "Migration and Development," 55, with James F. Hollifield and Tom K. Wong, "The Politics of International Migration: How Can We Bring the State Back In?," in Caroline B. Brettell and James F. Hollifield, eds., *Migration Theory: Talking across Disciplines* (New York: Routledge, 2015), 227–71.

31. For example, electronic communication networks in the United States are not subject to the universal service obligations applied to the postal system. See Susan Crawford, *Captive Audience: The Telecom Industry and Monopoly Power in the New Gilded Age* (New Haven, CT: Yale University Press, 2013).

32. See *Central R.R. Co. of New Jersey v. Jersey City*, 209 U.S. 473, 479 (1908).

33. When to apply law extraterritorially is a question in many legal systems, with different presumptive answers. See Joanne Scott, "Extraterritoriality and the Territorial Extension of EU Law," *American Journal of Comparative Law* 62 (2014): 87.

34. See also Ayelet Shachar, "The Shifting Border of Immigration Regulation," *Stanford Journal of Civil Rights and Civil Liberties* 3 (2007): 165.

35. Mae M. Ngai, "The Strange Career of the Illegal Alien: Immigration Restriction and Deportation Policy in the United States, 1921–1965," *Law and History Review* 21 (2003): 69, 76. Before 1917, the Page Act of 1875, § 5, 18 Stat. 477, had authorized denying entry to those deemed to be criminals or prostitutes ("at no time thereafter shall any alien certified to by the inspecting officer as being of either of the classes whose immigration is forbidden by this section, be allowed to land in the United States").

36. Passport Control Act of May 22, 1918, Pub. L. No. 65-154, 40 Stat. 559. Such provisions have been described as enabling "remote control" over borders. See Aristride R. Zolberg, *A Nation by Design: Immigration Policy in the Fashioning of America* (Cambridge, MA: Harvard University Press, 2006), 110–13. Noncitizens applied in their home countries and demonstrated that they were "admissible," a term used to describe an immigrant who did not fall into the "classes of aliens [to] be excluded from the United States" and in conjunction with the phrase "otherwise inadmissible." See Immigration Act of 1917, § 3, Pub. L. No. 64-301, 39 Stat. 874.

37. See Immigration and Nationality Act, Pub. L. No. 82-414, 66 Stat. 163 (1952) (codified at 8 U.S.C. § 1225(a) (2012)).

38. The act defined the terms "admission" and "admitted" to "mean, with respect to an alien, the lawful entry of the alien into the United States after inspection and authorization by an immigration officer." See 8 U.S.C. § 1101(a)(13)(A) (2012). Stations were installed in those "foreign airports" that were the "last points of departure for the greatest numbers of inadmissible alien passengers." 8 U.S.C. § 1225(a)(1) (2012).

39. Intelligence Reform and Terrorism Prevention Act, § 7210(d), 118 Stat. 3825 (codified at 8 U.S.C. § 1225(a)(4) (2012)). Those seeking to visit must show that they fit within certain categories, such as a short-time tourist who has not previously violated U.S. immigration laws or has applied for and been granted a waiver. Consular officials have the authority to decide to grant or deny a visa and may be subject to limited judicial oversight, focused on whether a decision was "facially legitimate and bona fide." See *Kleindeinst v. Mandel*, 408 U.S. 753 (1972); *Kerry v. Din*, 135 S. Ct. 2128 (2015). Persons seeking permanent residence require an invitation from a citizen, a legal permanent resident (LPR), or an employer, who must specify that a person is an eligible family member or that the Department of Labor has determined that a worker within the United States is not available for the position that the potential immigrant would fill. See generally 8 U.S.C. § 1101 (2012).

40. 8 U.S.C. § 1101(a)(13)(A) (2012).

41. Pub. L. No. 82-414, § 287(a)(3), 66 Stat. 163 (1952), codified at 8 U.S.C. § 1357 (2012), that the power to "board and search for aliens" extended to "any vessel within the territorial waters of the United States and any railway car, aircraft, conveyance, or vehicle, and within a distance of twenty-five miles from any such external boundary to have access to private lands, but not dwellings for the purpose of patrolling the border to prevent the illegal entry of aliens into the United States."

42. Immigration and Naturalization Service, "Field Officers; Powers and Duties," 22 Fed. Reg. 9765, 9808 (Dec. 6, 1957), codified at 8 C.F.R. § 287.1 (2016).

43. Department of Homeland Security, "FY 2013 Budget in Brief," www.dhs.gov, 57 (hereinafter DHS, FY 2013).

44. Ibid., 29–34. For example, "Beyond the Border: A Shared Vision for Perimeter Security and Economic Competiveness Declaration" was signed in February 2011 by President Obama and Prime Minister Harper of Canada. Ibid., 34.

45. *United States v. Ortiz*, 422 U.S. 891, 892–93 (1975).

46. Before 1996, a person found excludable could have been sent to a "secondary inspection," at which he or she would have had the opportunity to petition for a hearing before an immigration judge (employed by the Department of Justice rather than the INS), and that decision was also subject to review by the Board of Immigration Appeals (BIA), as well as by a federal judge. See 8 U.S.C. § 1225 (1994); 8 U.S.C. § 1252(b) (1994). In contrast, the 1996 statute authorized low-level personnel to offer an individual arriving at the border without proper documentation or attempting to enter by "fraud or willful misrepresentation," "expedited removal"—based on an interview in which the alien had an opportunity to make an asylum claim. See 8 U.S.C. § 1225(b)(1)(A)(i). The government was also empowered to remove any alien, "who has not been admitted or paroled into the United States, and who has not affirmatively shown, to the satisfaction of an immigration officer, that the alien has been physically present in the United States continuously for the 2-year period immediately prior to the date of the determination of inadmissibility." 8 U.S.C. § 1225(b)(1)(A)(iii). These provisions initially applied only to aliens arriving at ports of entry and aliens who had entered without inspection, fraudulently, and within two years of their arrest by DHS. 8 U.S.C. § 1225(b)(1)(A)(iii) (1996). In 2002, the agency expanded the expedited removal process to apply to aliens who arrived by sea, who were not paroled, and who had not been present for two years (67 Fed. Reg. 68,924–25 [Nov. 13, 2002]); in 2004, the agency began applying it to all aliens whom DHS encountered within 100 miles of the border, who entered without inspection within fourteen days of the encounter, and who could not prove two weeks of continuous residence. See 69 Fed. Reg. 48,877–81 (Aug. 11, 2004). See generally Alison Sisken and Ruth Ellen Wasem, Cong. Research Serv., RL33109, "Immigration Policy on Expedited Removal of Aliens" (2005).

47. See 8 U.S.C. § 1225 (1996), 8 C.F.R. § 235.3 (1998), 8 C.F.R. § 1235.3 (2004). DHS regulations do provide for review by a supervisory officer. 8 C.F.R. § 235.3(b)(7) (2012).

48. 8 U.S.C. § 1182(a)(9)(A)(i) (2012).

49. These data, as of 2007, were provided by the American Civil Liberties Union, critical of such practices. See ACLU, "Constitution Free Zone—Map," www.aclu.org/constitution-free-zone-map.

50. *Ker v. Illinois*, 119 U.S. 436 (1886); *Frisbie v. Collins*, 342 U.S. 519 (1952). Ker was in Peru, with which the United States had an extradition treaty, but was kidnapped and brought back to the United States. Frisbie was a Michigan prisoner who argued he had been kidnapped in Chicago and brought to Michigan for trial.

51. *Frisbie*, 342 U.S., at 522.

52. 504 U.S. 655 (1992).

53. This nomenclature includes the International Criminal Court (ICC), which hears cases involving individuals prosecuted for crimes against humanity. See Rome Statute of the International Criminal Court, July 17, 1998, 2187 U.N.T.S. 90. Sometimes the phrase "universal jurisdiction" is used to reference efforts by a particular country to exercise authority over individuals seen to have violated such laws, such as actions in the late 1990s by Spain against Augusto Pinochet.

54. See U.S. Const., Art. I, § 8, cl. 10.

55. See "An Act for the Punishment of Certain Crimes against the United States," L. 1790, ch. 9, §§ 25–28; the Alien Torts Act (ATA), first enacted in 1789 and now codified at 28 U.S.C. § 1350 (2012). The scope of the extraterritorial license for both civil and criminal actions predicated on laws-of-nations claims has been contested. See, e.g., *Filartiga v. Pena-Irala*, 630 F.2d 876 (2d Cir. 1980); *Kioebel v. Royal Dutch Petroleum Co.*, 133 S. Ct. 1659 (2013).

56. U.S. Const. amend. XIV, § 1.

57. "Excludable aliens are those who seek admission but have not been granted entry into the United States. Even if physically present in this country, they are legally considered detained at the border. This is known as the 'entry fiction' . . . Deportable aliens, on the other hand, have succeeded in either legally or illegally entering this country. Excludable aliens have fewer rights than do deportable aliens, and those seeking initial admission to this country have the fewest of all." *Garcia-Mir v. Smith*, 766 F.2d 1478, 1483–84 (11th Cir. 1985).

58. See *Yamataya v. Fisher*, 189 U.S. 86, 101 (1903) ("[A]lthough alleged to be illegally here, to be taken into custody and deported without giving him all opportunity to be heard upon the questions involving his right to be and remain in the United States . . . [is an] arbitrary power [which cannot] exist where the principals involved in due process of law are recognized"). Procedural due process constrains the process by which decisions of deportation are made, and substantive due process concerns may limit the length of time a person can be held pending deportation or if having no country to which to return.

59. Prior to 1996, the terms were "exclusion" and "deportation." In 1996, IRA described both activities as "removal." Pub. L. No. 104-208, §

304, 110 Stat. 3009, 3009-589 to 3009-594 (codified at 8 U.S.C. § 1229(a) (2012)).

60. As a 1892 Supreme Court decision explained, putting a Japanese immigrant "in the mission-house as a more suitable place than the steam-ship, pending the decision of the question of her right to land, and keeping her there . . . until final judgment upon the writ of *habeas corpus*, left her in the same position, so far as regarded her right to land in the United States, as if she never had been removed from the steam-ship." See *Ekui v. United States*, 142 U.S. 651, 661 (1892). In 1953, in *Shaughnessy v. United States ex rel. Mezei*, this proposition was applied to a person who had been a legal permanent resident for twenty-five years. 345 U.S. 206, 213 (1953). The Court found that, despite Mezei's long residence in the United States, an absence of 19 months (itself occasioned by difficulty securing a return visa from the consulate in Hungary) made Mezei an "entering," rather than a "returning," alien and therefore had fewer procedural protections. *Mezei*, 345 U.S. at 213. As no other country would accept Mezei, he was "excluded" from the United States and he remained on Ellis Island, where he had landed. See also *U.S. ex rel. Knauff v. Shaughnessy*, 338 U.S. 537, 544 (1950) ("Whatever the procedure authorized by Congress is, it is due process as far as an alien denied entry is concerned."). Both Knauff and Mezei were later released into the United States. See Charles D. Weisselberg, "Exclusion and Detention of Aliens: Lessons from the Lives of Ellen Knauff and Ignatz Mezei," *University of Pennsylvania Law Review* 143 (1994): 933.

61. William G. Belden, "Paradise Lost: The Continuing Plight of the Excludable Mariel Cubans," *Kansas Journal of Law and Public Policy* 5 (1996): 181. A class action prompted some forms of relief for individuals via executive action, asylum, repatriation, and some consideration for "parole" into the country. See *Garcia-Mir v. Smith*, 766 F.3d 1478 (11th Cir. 1985); 8 C.F.R. § 212.12.

62. The law can also move the border to where it finds a person. Pursuant to an executive order issued by President Regan in 1981 and continued by President Bush and then President Clinton, see Presidential Proclamation No. 4865, 46 Fed. Reg. 48,107 (Sept. 29, 1981), the Coast Guard captured Haitian refugees at sea. In 1993, the United States Supreme Court concluded that the Coast Guard action was lawful and could be followed by an insistence on their return to their country of origin or their detention at Guantánamo Bay. See *Sale v. Haitian Centers Council, Inc.*, 509 U.S. 155 (1993).

63. *Rasul v. Bush*, 542 U.S. 466 (2004); see also *Boumediene v. Bush*, 553 U.S. 723 (2008); *Hamdan v. Rumsfeld*, 548 U.S. 557 (2006); *Hamdi v. Rumsfeld*, 542 U.S. 507 (2004). See generally Judith Resnik, "Detention, the War on Terror, and the Federal Courts," *Columbia Law Review* 110 (2010): 579.

64. *Munaf v. Geren*, 553 U.S. 674 (2008); *Al-Maqaleh v. Gates*, 605 F.3d 84 (D.C. Cir. 2010).

65. Huyen Pham, "When Immigration Borders Move," *Florida Law Review* 61 (2009): 1115; Ingrid V. Eagly, "Local Immigration Prosecution: A Study of Arizona before SB 1070," *UCLA Law Review* 58 (2011): 1749.

66. See U.S. Census Bureau, Current Population Survey (CPS), www. census.gov. Statistics are included under the heading "nativity" beneath the "Define Your Table" menu; Elizabeth M. Grieco, Yesenia D. Acosta, G. Patricia de la Cruz, Christine Gambino, Thomas Gryn, Luke J. Laresen, Edward N. Trevelyan and Nathan P. Walters, *The Foreign Born Population in the United States: 2010*, U.S. Census Bureau, 2012.

67. Pew Hispanic Center, "A Nation of Immigrants: A Portrait of the 40 Million, Including 11 Million Unauthorized," 3, January 29, 2013, www. pewhispanic.org; Jeffrey S. Passel and D'Vera Cohn, *Unauthorized Immigration Population: National and State Trends, 2010*, Pew Hispanic Center (2011), http://www.pewhispanic.org; Robert Warren and Jeffrey S. Passel, "A Count of the Uncountable: Estimates of Undocumented Aliens in the 1980 United States Census," Demography 24 (1987): 375.

68. Pew Hispanic Center, *A Nation of Immigrants*, 3.

69. The "DREAMERS" are one example of "migrant counter-conducts"—a term, building on Michel Foucault, proffered to track the public protests against punitive treatment. See Jonathan Xavier Inda and Julie A. Dowling, "Introduction: Governing Migrant Illegality," in Julie A. Dowling and Jonathan Xavier Inda, eds., *Governing Immigration through Crime* (Palo Alto: Stanford University Press, 2013), 23–27.

70. See Daniel Kanstroom, "'Alien' Litigation as Polity-Participation: The Positive Power of a 'Voteless Class of Litigants,'" *William and Mary Bill of Rights Journal* 21 (2012): 399.

71. Douglas S. Massey, "How Arizona Became Ground Zero in the War on Immigrants," in Carissa Hessick and Jack Chin, eds., *Strange Neighbors: The Role of the States in Immigration Enforcement and Policy* (New York: NYU Press, 2014), 40, 59.

72. Gerald Neuman, "The Lost Century of Immigration Law (1776–1875)," *Columbia Law Review* 93 (1993): 1833–38.

73. Both Hiroshi Motomuro and Aristide Zolberg identify the degree to which policies have facilitated immigrants joining the workforce and gaining membership in the polity. See Hiroshi Motomuro, *Americans in Waiting: The Lost Story of Immigration and Citizenship in the United States* (New York: Oxford University Press, 2006); Zolberg, *Nation by Design*, 165–202, 337–432.

74. Katherine Benton-Cohen, "Japanese Immigrants and the Dillingham Commission: Federal Immigration Policy and the American West," in

Jessie Embry and Brian Cannon, eds., *Immigrants in the Far West: Historical Identities and Experiences* (Salt Lake City: University of Utah Press, 2015).

75. Race was central in forming U.S. policies on quotas, which relied on creating a Euro-American "whiteness" that enabled European immigrants to become "American" while excluding Asian and South and Central American migrants. See Mae M. Ngai, "The Architecture of Race in American Immigration Law: A Reexamination of the Immigration Act of 1924," *Journal of American History* 86 (1999): 67.

76. 70 Cong. Rec. 3636 (1929) (statement by John J. O'Connor, Democrat of New York, against the proposed criminalization).

77. Representative Jed Johnson, Democrat from Oklahoma, read Resolution No. 341, calling for investigation of illegal entrance of aliens and arguing that "hordes of undesirable aliens . . . [were] undermining health, integrity, and moral fiber of the forthcoming generations." 70 Cong. Rec. 4907 (1929).

78. Representative John C. Box noted that "beet-sugar manufacturer[s]" and railroads want "cheap subservient labor." 70 Cong. Rec. 3620 (1929).

79. The xenophobia was wide-ranging, as exemplified by commentary by Senator David A. Reed of Pennsylvania, who stated, "We do not want this country filled with Arabs, who have lived always under a patriarchal government, where the common man did not even dare whisper his views of governmental affairs." 70 Cong. Rec. 2805 (1929).

80. 70 Cong. Rec. 4907 (1929).

81. 70 Cong. Rec. 3620 (1929) (statement of William Thomas Fitzgerald of Ohio).

82. See Pub. L. No. 70-1018, § 690, 45 Stat. 1551 (1929).

83. See, e.g., Ingrid V. Eagly, "Prosecuting Immigration," *Northwestern University Law Review* 104 (2010): 1281; Allegra M. McLeod, "The US Criminal-Immigration Convergence and Its Possible Undoing," *American Criminal Law Review* 49 (2012): 105; Juliet P. Stumpf, "States of Confusion: The Rise of State and Local Power over Immigration," *North Carolina Law Review* 86 (2007): 1557; Stephen H. Legomsky, "The New Path of Immigration Law: Asymmetric Incorporation of Criminal Justice Norms," *Washington and Lee Law Review* 64 (2007): 469.

84. For example, unauthorized entry is one offense; speeding away from an entry point is another. See 8 U.S.C. § 1325(a), 18 U.S.C. § 758 (2012). See generally David Sklansky, "Crime, Immigration, and Ad Hoc Instrumentalism," *New Criminal Law Review* 15 (2012): 157.

85. 312 U.S. 52 (1941).

86. See *Arizona v. United States*, 132 S. Ct. 2492 (2012).

87. *Davidowitz v. Hines*, 30 F. Supp. 470, 476 (M.D. Pa. 1939), citing 35 Pa. Stat. Ann. §§ 1801 (West) (1939).

88. Pennsylvania also had laws prohibiting "unnaturalized foreign born residents" from fishing in the state or being "employed upon any public work." *Davidowitz v. Hines*, 30 F. Supp. at 474.

89. 312 U.S. at 59–60.

90. See *Davidowitz v. Hines*, 30 F. Supp. at 474.

91. See Jennifer L. Hochschild and John H. Mollenkopf, "Modeling Immigrant Political Incorporation," in Jennifer L. Hochschild and John H. Mollenkopf, eds., *Bringing Outsiders In: Transatlantic Perspectives on Immigrant Political Incorporation* (Ithaca, NY: Cornell University Press, 2009), 15–30.

92. See 70 Cong. Rec. 3636 (1929) (statement by John J. O'Connor, Representative from New York).

93. A news story reported that Davidowitz was born in Hungary, migrated to the United States in 1904, was naturalized in 1910, and worked as a "special investigator of delinquent inheritance tax cases for the auditor general." See "Alien Rights Registry Law," *Reading Eagle* (Scranton), June 30, 1939. In 1945, he was state chair of the American Labor Party. See "3 Men Held in ALP Court fight," *Baltimore Afro-American*, September 22, 1945, 17. Bernard Davidowitz was represented by Isidor Ostroff, Herman Steerman, and Harold Jethro Budd, as well as by a Scranton firm. Amicus briefs were filed by A. Harry Levitan and others in Philadelphia. The ACLU filed a brief when the case was before the three-judge court. See "Alien Curb Voided in Pennsylvania," *New York Times*, December 1, 1939.

94. *Hines* record, Complaint at para. 12(a). The complaint averred that Bernard Davidowitz was "a resident of the City of Philadelphia, a citizen of the United States, and taxpayer of the State of Pennsylvania." Complaint at para. 3.

95. Complaint at para. 12(b); see also Statement of Jurisdiction, Appellate Brief, *Hines v. Davidowitz*, 312 U.S. 52 (1941), 1940 WL 46487.

96. Mr. Travaglini argued that, as an alien, he was "directly affected by the provisions" of the Pennsylvania law, and that he was "unfairly discriminate[d] against" because of the registration requirement to which he would be subjected. Complaint at para. 12(b)(c).

97. Complaint at para. 12; Brief for the United States, amicus curiae, *Hines v. Davidowitz*, 312 U.S. 52 (1941), 1940 WL 71236 at 3.

98. "Alien Curb Voided in Pennsylvania."

99. *Davidowitz v. Hines*, 30 F. Supp. 470, 473–74 (M.D. Pa., 1939) (three-judge court). The court reasoned that "existing law" would protect Davidowitz, as a citizen, from any annoyances or harassment by police officers. His effort to proceed as a taxpayer was rebuffed with the comment that he had no real complaint about the law as a taxpayer, and that an "an-

ticipated violation of his rights as a citizen" was not a sufficient basis upon which to proceed. Ibid., 474.

100. *Hines*, 30 F. Supp., 476.

101. Ibid.

102. Ibid., 477.

103. Alien Registration Act, Pub. L. No. 670, 54 Stat. 670, 670 (1940).

104. U.S. Government *Hines* amicus brief, 5.

105. The chief sponsor, Howard W. Smith, a Democrat from Virginia (and for whom the act is named), included other provisions that rendered it a notorious abridgment of forms of speech; the Supreme Court eventually limited its reach. See Mark A. Sheft, "The End of the Smith Act Era: A Legal and Historical Analysis of *Scales v. United States*," *American Journal of Legal History* 36 (1992): 164.

106. All registration and fingerprint records were "secret and confidential," available only to "such persons or agencies as may be designated by the Commissioner, with the approval of the Attorney General." Alien Registration Act, § 34, Pub. L. No. 670, 54 Stat. 670, 674 (1940) (codified at 18 U.S.C. § 2385). The statute provided that aliens were to go to the Post Office (or other places identified by the Attorney General); the postmaster was under an obligation to "designate appropriate space" for registration. Alien Registration Act, § 33, Pub. L. No. 670, 54 Stat. 670, 674 (1940).

107. The 1940 legislation made it a misdemeanor willfully to fail to register, refuse to register, file an application with false statements, or fail to notify the Attorney General of a change in address. The maximum penalty for failing to provide notice was a $100 fine and thirty days in jail. The maximum penalty for the other offenses was a $1,000 fine and six months in prison. Alien Registration Act, § 36, Pub. L. No. 670, 54 Stat. 670, 675 (1940).

108. U.S. Government *Hines* amicus brief, 7.

109. Ibid., 25.

110. Ibid., 21.

111. Ibid., 43–44, citing Civil Rights Act of 1870, § 16, 16 Stat. 140, 144 (codified as amended at 42 U.S.C. § 1981(a)). See generally Lucas Guttentag, "The Forgotten Equality Norm in Immigration Preemption: Discrimination, Harassment and the Civil Rights Act of 1870," *Duke Journal of Constitutional Law and Public Policy* 1 (2013): 8.

112. See, e.g., *Arizona v. United States*, 132 S. Ct. at 2502.

113. *Hines*, 312 U.S. at 70.

114. Ibid. Justice Black cited the reaction against the Alien Acts of 1798 and the concern about discrimination against the Chinese in the late nineteenth century. Ibid. As discussed, proposals for registration had been considered, and rejected, by Congress in the 1930s.

115. Ibid., 71.

116. Ibid., 74.

117. Ibid., 65.

118. Ibid., 69.

119. See Kerry Abrams, "Plenary Power Preemption," *Virginia Law Review* 99 (2013): 601, 624.

120. *Hines*, 312 U.S. at 70. The decision noted that "willful failure to register" was a criminal offense. Ibid., 61.

121. Chinese Exclusion Act, Act of May 6, 1882, ch. 126, 22 Stat. 56 (1882), at §1. See *Chae Ching Ping v. U.S.*, 130 U.S. 581 (1889); Martin Gold, *Forbidden Citizens: Chinese Exclusion and the U.S. Congress* TheCapitol.Net (2012).

122. See Geary Act, Act of May 5, 1892, ch. 60, 27 Stat. 25 (1892), §6. Fong Yue Ting v. United States, 149 U.S. 698 (1893) (rejecting petitions for habeas corpus and upholding the plenary power of Congress and its enactment of the Geary Act). Justice Brewer, Field, and Fuller dissented, and part of the argument was that each of the petitioners were "persons" within the meaning of the Fourteenth Amendment and wrongfully deprived of their liberty. Id. at 732-763. See generally Motomura, *Americans in Waiting*.

123. See Douglas Massey, "Pathways to El Norte: Origins, Destinations, and Characteristics of Mexican Migrants to the United States," *International Migration Review* 46 (2012): 3.

124. *Korematsu v. United States*, 323 U.S. 215 (1944); this passage comes from Justice Murphy's dissent at 233.

125. Justice Roberts described the requirement as "imprisonment in a concentration camp, based on his ancestry . . . without evidence or inquiry concerning his loyalty and good disposition toward the United States." Ibid., 226 (Roberts, J., dissenting). Justice Black disputed the "concentration camp" characterization; he objected to the "ugly connotations that term implies." Ibid., 197.

126. Ibid., 242–243 (Jackson, J., dissenting).

127. *Hines*, 312 U.S. at 71 (internal citations omitted).

128. 8 U.S.C. § 1304(e). This requirement came into place in 1952. See Immigration and Nationality Act, § 264, Pub. L. No. 82-414, 66 Stat. 163, 224-25 (1952). What "registration" means is complex; federal provisions did not take the onerous form that state anti-immigrant proponents aimed to install. See Nancy Morawetz and Natasha Fernández-Silber, "Immigration Law and the Myth of Comprehensive Registration," *UC Davis Law Review* 48 (2014): 141. In the 1940s and 1950s, individuals could register at U.S. post offices. See 8 C.F.R. §§ 264.2, 264.3 (1952). Evidence of such registration became a "certificate" that had to be carried or a

person could be subjected to criminal arrest. Soon thereafter, registration became a part of port-of-entry processes. In 1960, the government ended the practice of using registration offices and issuing certificates and deemed various documents to be methods of registering. See 25 Fed. Reg. 7, 180–81 (July 29, 1960). Regulations did not identify what particular documents are required, per the statute, to be carried as "registration" but refer to "prescribed registration forms" and to other materials as constituting "evidence of registration." See 8 C.F.R. § 264.1 (2012). Thus, the government required individuals who entered lawfully to demonstrate evidence of citizenship, and a variety of documents could do so. See 8 C.F.R. § 264(b) (2012) (listing as evidence passports, I-94 forms, which are arrival and departure records, various kind of crewman and other border-crossing cards, employment forms, and notices of proceedings before the immigration authorities). Given that, under the Immigration and Naturalization Act, the requirement to carry registration is arguably triggered only when the agency provides a "certificate of registration," the lack of specificity could provide defenses to prosecution; prosecution is not common under the statute. On the other hand, "papers-please" inquiries r emain as a request issued by law enforcement officers.

129. Immigration Reform and Control Act (IRCA) of 1986, Pub. L. 99-603, 100 Stat. 3359, provided that the employer "must attest, under penalty of perjury and on a form designated or established by the Attorney General by regulation, that it has verified that the individual is not an unauthorized alien by examining proof such as a certificate of United States citizenship, certificate of naturalization, foreign passport, or resident alien card." Ibid., § 101 (b). Sanctions include civil monetary penalties of between $250 and $2,000 for each hiring, recruiting, and referral violation (ibid., at § 101(e) (4)), and criminal penalties of imprisonment for up to six months for a "pattern or practice" of violations (ibid., at § 101(f)).

130. For example, if apprehended by CBP, individuals may need to contact employers, schools, and family members to substantiate the lawfulness of their presence. See also *Families for Freedom v. United States Customs and Border Protection*, 837 F. Supp. 2d 331 (S.D.N.Y. 2011).

131. See *Arizona v. United States*, 132 S. Ct. 2492 (2012). Arizona's Support Our Law Enforcement and Safe Neighborhoods Act, known as S.B. 1070, had aimed to "discourage and deter the unlawful entry and presence of aliens and economic activity by persons unlawfully present in the United States" by "attrition through enforcement." Id. at § 1.

132. See, e.g., *United States v. Alabama*, 691 F.3d 1269 (11th Cir. 2012)

133. See U.S. Customs and Border Protection, *Snapshot: A Summary of CBP Facts and Figures*, 2012, www.cbp.gov; U.S. Immigration and Customs Enforcement, *Overview*, www.ice.gov (accessed December 9, 2012).

134. U.S. Department of Justice, Bureau of Justice Statistics, *Census of State and Local Law Enforcement Agencies*, 2008, http://bjs.ojp.usdoj.gov/content/pub/pdf/cslleao8.pdf.

135. 521 U.S. 898 (1997). See generally Adam B. Cox, "Expressionism in Federalism: A New Defense of the Anti-Commandeering Rule," *Loyola of Los Angeles Law Review* 33 (2000): 1309.

136. See 8 U.S.C. § 1357(g) (setting out requirements for 287(g) agreements). By 2012, ICE had entered into fifty-seven of the section 287(g) agreements with law enforcement officials in twenty-one states. Immigration and Customs Enforcement, "Fact Sheet: Delegation of Immigration Authority," Section 287(g) Immigration and Nationality Act, www.ice.gov/news/library/factsheets/287g.htm (accessed December 9, 2012). After the decision in *Arizona v. United States*, DHS modified its 287(g) program and rescinded some 287(g) agreements then in effect in Arizona. Jeremy Duda, "Homeland Security Revokes 287(g) Agreements in Arizona," June 25, 2012, http://azcapitoltimes.com. Proposals to permit roles for local law enforcement grew out of debates before *Arizona v. United States*. See, e.g., U.S. Senator Jeff Sessions and Cynthia Hayden, "The Growing Role for State and Local Law Enforcement in the Realm of Immigration Law," *Stanford Law and Policy Review* 16 (2005): 323.

137. U.S. Immigration and Customs Enforcement, "Secure Communities," www.ice.gov/secure-communities/ (accessed June 9, 2016).

138. Michael John Garcia and Kate M. Manuel, Congressional Research Service, "Authority of State and Local Police to Enforce Federal Immigration Law," September 10, 2012, www.fas.org (citing U.S. Immigration and Customs Enforcement, "Secure Communities: Activated Jurisdictions," 2012, www.ice.gov.) Under the "activated jurisdictions" system, federal officials could ask for detention for forty-eight hours, and local law enforcement officers then needed to decide whether to do so. As of January 2013, "the biometric information sharing capability of Secure Communities was activated by the U.S. Department of Immigration and Customs Enforcement in 3,181 jurisdictions in 50 states, U.S. territories and Washington D.C." See Mai Thi Nguyen, "When Local Law Enforcement Officers Become Immigration Agents, Communities Suffer," London School of Economics Research Online, 2014, http://eprints.lsc.ac.uk.

139. Thomas J. Gardner and Terry M. Anderson, *Criminal Law* (Stamford, CT: Cengage Learning, 2015), 524. See also Ana Gonzalez-Barrera and Jens Manuel Krogstad, "U.S. Deportations of Immigrants Reach Record High in 2013," Pew Research Center, October 2, 2014, www.pewresearch.org.

140. DHS, FY 13, 28–29.

141. See, e.g., Immigration Policy Center, "Secure Communities," July 11, 2011, https://immigrationforum.org; "The 287(g) Program: A

Flawed and Obsolete Method of Immigration Enforcement," November 2012, www.immigrationpolicy.org.

142. Hiroshi Motomura, "The Discretion That Matters: Federal Immigration Enforcement, State and Local Arrests, and the Civil-Criminal Line," *UCLA Law Review* 58 (2011): 1819, 1842.

143. Ingrid V. Eagly, "Criminal Justice for Noncitizens: An Analysis of Variation in Local Enforcement," *NYU University Law Review* 88 (2013): 1126. Her analyses focused on enforcement efforts in three large counties.

144. Survey research in 237 cities reported that, as of 2005, about half of the police departments had no local policies on immigration; 4 percent had policies protecting unauthorized immigrants in noncriminal situations. Doris Marie Provine, Monica Varsanyi, Paul G. Lewis, and Scott H. Decker, "Growing Tensions between Civil Membership and Enforcement in the Devolution of Immigration Control," in Charis E. Kubrin, Majorie S. Zatz, and Ramiro Martínez Jr., eds., *Punishing Immigrants: Policy, Politics, and Injustice,* (New York: NYU Press, 2012), 42, 51–52. By 2014, several cities (including Philadelphia and Denver) and a few counties in western states had decided to decline to help the federal government with its deportation efforts. See Spencer Amdur, "How Local Governments Are Hacking Immigration Reform," May 13, 2014, www.theatlantic.com; Christopher Lasch, "Federal Immigration Detainers after *Arizona v. United States*," *Loyola of Los Angeles Law Review* 46 (2013): 629, 678–80.

145. In *Galarza v. Szalczyk*, 745 F.3d 634 (3d Cir. 2014), a divided federal appellate court analyzed 8 C.F.R. § 287.7(a), providing that a "detainer serves to advise another law enforcement agency that the Department seeks custody of an alien presently in the custody of that agency, for the purpose of arresting and removing the alien." Another section (287(d)) detailed that the relevant agency "shall maintain custody of the alien for a period not to exceed 48 hours" (excluding weekends) to permit federal authorities to take over that person's detention. The majority held that a "plain reading" rendered these regulations (entitled "requests") voluntary, in part because, were they mandatory, the regulations would "violate the anti-commandeering principles inherent in the Tenth Amendment." Ibid., 636. See generally Christopher Lasch, "Rendition Resistance," *North Carolina Law Review* 92 (2013): 149; Christopher Lasch, "Enforcing the Limits of the Executive's Authority to Issue Immigration Detainers," *William Mitchell Law Review* 35 (2008): 1.

146. See, e.g., 2013 Cal. Stat. 4650 (codified at Cal. Gov't Code §§ 7282–7282.5 (West Supp. 2014); Conn. Gen. Stat. § 54–192(h) (2014); and Eagly, "Criminal Justice for Noncitizens," 1126.

147. Decisions supporting the view that ICE agents needed probable cause to issue an immigration detainer include *Morales v. Chadborne*, 996

F. Supp. 2d 19 (D. R.I. 2014), aff'd, 2015 WL 4385945 (1st Cir. July 17, 2015); *Miranda-Olivares v. Clackamas County*, 2014 WL 1424305 (D. Or. 2014). As litigation unfolded, nine county sheriffs in Oregon announced they would no longer hold people in jail based only on immigration detention requests. See Julia Preston, "Sheriffs Limit Detention of Immigration," *New York Times*, April 18, 2014. In the fall of 2014, the Obama administration changed its policy to a request for notification of release instead of a request for detention.

148. See Department of Homeland Security, "Fixing Our Broken Immigration System through Executive Action—Key Facts," January 5, 2015, www.dhs.gov [http://perma.cc/U5K8-RE3R].

149. See Juliet P. Stumpf, "D(e)volving Discretion: Lessons from the Life and Times of Secure Communities," *American University Law Review* 64 (2015): 1259.

150. Marc R. Rosenblum, "Understanding the Potential Impact of Executive Action on Immigration Enforcement," Migration Policy Institute, July 2015.

151. A federal appellate court upheld the federal district court injunction that prohibited the program from going into effect on the grounds that Texas had the authority to bring the action and the President had overstepped his authority to create the program. See *Texas v. United States*, 809 F.3d 134 (5th Cir. 2016), aff'd by equally divided court, 136 S.Ct. 2271 (2016).

152. Lasch, "Rendition Resistance," 224–31.

153. For example, in 2010, voters in Fremont, Nebraska, adopted an ordinance limiting the hiring of and rentals to "illegal aliens" and "unauthorized aliens" by requiring prospective renters to obtain an "occupancy license" through the city, charged with verifying the status of the renters with the federal government. Landlords, tenants, and employers, as well as individuals, argued the ordinance was both preempted by federal law and in violation of the Fair Housing Act, other civil rights statutes, the Commerce Clause, and the Due Process and Equal Protection Clauses of the Fourteenth Amendments. The Eighth Circuit upheld the rental provision despite a dissent, arguing that federal law preempted the ordinance because it served as a step in the removal process. See *Keller v. City of Fremont*, 719 F.3d 931 (8th Cir. 2013), cert. denied, 134 S. Ct. 2140 (2014). In contrast, other appellate courts have struck similar ordinances. See, e.g., *United States v. Alabama*, 691 F.3d 1269 (11th Cir. 2012), cert. denied 133 S. Ct. 2022 (2012).

154. Justice Kagan, who had been the Solicitor General during earlier phases of the litigation, did not participate. The majority of five included

the opinion's author, Justice Kennedy, joined by Chief Justice Roberts and Justices Ginsburg, Breyer, and Sotomayor. 132 S. Ct. 2492.

155. Lucas Guttentag, "Discrimination, Preemption and Arizona's Immigration Law: A Broader View," *Stanford Law Review Online* 65 (June 18, 2012): 1; see also Lucas Guttentag, "Immigration, Preemption and the Limits of State Power: Reflections on *Arizona v. United States*," *Stanford Journal of Civil Rights and Civil Liberties* 9 (2013): 1.

156. Complaint for Declaratory and Injunctive Relief, *Friendly House v. Whiting*, 2010 WL 2019492 (D. Ariz. 2010). Another source of constitutional rights for migrants could be the First Amendment. See, e.g., Michael J. Wishnie, "Immigrants and the Right to Petition," *NYU Law Review* 78 (2003): 667.

157. Guttentag, "Immigration, Preemption and the Limits of State Power," 8–9 ("the claim that the statute as a whole constituted an impermissible regulation of immigration had virtually disappeared").

158. Solicitor General Verilli's discussion of *Hines*'s "anti-harassment principle" was met by Justice Scalia's comment that the government ought not to be concerned about "harassing them," as "[illegal aliens] . . . have no business being here." Oral Argument Transcript at 47, *Arizona v. United States*, 132 S. Ct. 2492, www.supremecourt.gov.

159. *Arizona v. United States*, 132 S. Ct. at 2507.

160. Ibid., 2510.

161. Ibid.

162. Ibid., 2503 (citing 8 U.S.C. §§ 1304(e) and 3561, and noting that Arizona law did not offer the option of probation).

163. Arizona had created two new state crimes—a new state misdemeanor that the Supreme Court described as applying to aliens failing to "comply with federal alienage registration requirements," and another state misdemeanor for an "unauthorized alien to seek or engage in work in the State." *Arizona v. United States*, 132 S. Ct. at 2497–98; see § 13-1509; § 3-2928(c). In addition (and again as described by the Court), local law enforcement could "arrest without a warrant a person 'the officer has probable cause to believe . . . has committed any public offense that makes the person removable from the United States,'" and, under Section 2(b), officers can conduct stops, detain, or arrest, "to verify the person's immigration status with the Federal Government." *Arizona v. United States*, 132 S. Ct. at 2498; see § 13-3883(A)(5); § 11-1051(B).

The potential that prosecutions for the same offense by both the state and federal governments are lawful is premised on the view—shaped during Prohibition—that the Constitution recognizes a "dual sovereignty" exception to double jeopardy. See *United States v. Lanza*, 260 U.S. 377 (1922).

164. *Arizona v. United States*, 132 S. Ct. at 2498 (citing Ariz. Rev. Stat. Ann. § 13-3883(A)(5)).

165. Ibid., 2505. A distinct question was whether state and local officials have the power to arrest individuals for violation of *federal* immigration laws. See Motomura, "The Discretion That Matters"; Gabriel J. Chin and Marc L. Miller, "The Unconstitutionality of State Regulation of Immigration through Criminal Law," *Duke Law Journal* 61 (2011): 251.

166. Ariz. Rev. Stat. Ann. § 11-1051(B).

167. *Arizona v. United States*, 132 S. Ct. at 2508; § 2(B), codified at Ariz. Rev. Stat. Ann. § 11-1051(L).

168. Ibid., 2509. The Ninth Circuit affirmed the district court grant of a preliminary injunction on First Amendment grounds against provisions of S.B. 1070 that made it "unlawful for a motor vehicle occupant to hire . . . a person for work at another location from a stopped car." See *Valle del Sol v. Whiting*, 709 F. 3d 808 (9th Cir. 2013). See also *Valle del Sol v. Whiting*, 732 F.3d 1006 (9th Cir. 2013). In the spring of 2014, the parties settled parts of what remained; the federal government agreed to drop its lawsuit against Section 2(B) requiring police officers to check the immigration status of anyone they arrest or detain and to stop anyone upon reasonable suspicion of being undocumented; Arizona agreed to stop enforcing the portion of Section 5 codified at § 13-2929, which criminalized transporting, concealing, or harboring an undocumented person or inducing undocumented persons to come to Arizona. Thereafter, the district court held preempted Arizona's provision permitting a police officer to stop a driver of a motor vehicle upon reasonable suspicion of transporting undocumented persons. See *United States v. Arizona*, CV-10-01412-PHX-SRB (D. Ariz. Nov. 7, 2014). The permanent injunction on aspects of S.B. 1070 followed in September 2015.

169. *Arizona v. United States*, 132 S. Ct. at 2506.

170. Ibid., 2509 (citing *Illinois v. Caballes*, 543 U.S. 405, 407 (2005)).

171. *United States v. South Carolina*, 906 F. Supp. 2d. 463, 471n4 (D. S.C. 2012) (noting that if, as the state asserted, it took an "average of 81 minutes" to do an immigration check, that interval would "raise constitutional concerns"), aff'd, 720 F.3d 518 (4th Cir. 2013). South Carolina had also created crimes—held preempted—of "knowingly or recklessly participat[ing] in the transporting or sheltering of persons in furtherance of an unlawfully present person's entry . . . or to avoid detection." Ibid., 467. See also *Ga. Latino Alliance for Human Rights v. Georgia*, 691 F.3d 1250, 1269 (11th Cir. 2012) (finding preemption of Georgia's provisions criminalizing certain interactions with "illegal aliens").

172. The dissents took different positions. Even as they agreed with the majority upholding Arizona's "papers-please" provision, they disagreed

about Arizona's freedom to do more. In Justice Scalia's view, the vagaries of federal discretionary enforcement created neither a prosecutorial nor a foreign-affairs implied preemption and, therefore, Arizona was "*entitled to have 'its own immigration policy.'*" *Arizona v. United States*, 132 S. Ct. at 2516 (Scalia, J., dissenting) (emphasis in the original). His argument relied on five premises: that Arizona is its own sovereign; that the "core of state sovereignty" is border control; that federal authority over migration is also predicated upon border control as an "inherent attribute of sovereignty"; that state regulation could only be excluded if directly prohibited by a "valid federal law" or in conflict with a "federal regulation"; and that neither the legislation nor the "Executive's policy choice of lax federal enforcement" precludes Arizona from exercising its "sovereign power to protect its borders more rigorously." Ibid., 2514–17. Justice Scalia argued that, as a result of the Court's ruling, "[t]housands of Arizona's estimated 400,000 illegal immigrants . . . are now assured immunity from enforcement, and will be able to compete openly with Arizona citizens for employment." Ibid., 2522.

Justice Thomas, who objected to the concept of implying preemption in the absence of an express congressional direction or of a direct conflict, would have upheld all of Arizona's law; he explained that his "simple reason" was that, in his view, the state and federal regimes were not in conflict. 132 S. Ct. at 2522 (Thomas, J., dissenting). He argued that the majority's use of "implied preemption" was "inconsistent with the Constitution because it invites courts to engage in freewheeling speculation about congressional purpose that roams well beyond statutory text." Ibid., 2524. Justice Alito concurred that *Hines* precluded state registration statutes but found congruence between other aspects of the state and federal systems. That the state made it a crime to seek employment while the federal government imposed sanctions on employers was not, in his view, the kind of conflict that preempted state law. *Hines* foreclosed "Arizona's attempt . . . to impose additional, state-law penalties for violation of the federal registration scheme." 132 S. Ct. at 2525 (Alito, J., dissenting). Further, he agreed that Section 2(B) could stand (and then took the government to task for its "attack" on the provision). Ibid., 2527. Justice Alito differed with the majority, which had concluded that the additional criminal sanctions imposed were preempted. Absent a "clear and manifest" intent by Congress, the state was free to exercise its police powers to authorize warrantless arrests and to criminalize unlawfully present migrants' efforts to seek employment. Ibid., 2530–35.

173. The expansion of that doctrine can be found in earlier decisions. See, e.g., *American Insurance Co. v. Garamendi*, 539 U.S. 396 (2003); *Crosby v. National Foreign Trade Council*, 530 U.S. 363 (2010). I have raised concerns

166 JUDITH RESNIK

about the displacement of state law without a clear mandate from Congress. See Judith Resnik, "Foreign as Domestic Affairs: Rethinking Horizontal Federalism and Foreign Affairs Preemption in Light of Translocal Internationalism," *Emory Law Journal* 57 (2007): 31. Moreover, despite the formal statement of the "plenary power of Congress," the executive has extensive authority. See Adam B. Cox and Cristina M. Rodríguez, "The President and Immigration Law," *Yale Law Journal* 119 (2009): 458.

174. Abrams, "Plenary Power Preemption," 626–35.

175. *Arizona v. United States*, 132 S. Ct. at 2506–7.

176. Ibid., 2506.

177. See Cal. Stats. 1891, c. 140, pp. 185 et seq; Conn., Gen. Stats. (1930), § 6042; Fla., Acts of 1917, ch. 7394, § 1, Comp. Gen. Laws (1927), § 2078; Iowa, Code (1939), § 503; La., Acts 1917 (E. S.) No. 20; Gen. Stats. (Dart, 1939), Tit. 3, § 282; Maine, Rev. Stats. (1930), ch. 34, § 3; Mass. Ann, Laws (Supp.), c 51, §§ 4, 7; Mich. Stats. Ann., §§ 18.41–18.57, Laws 1931, Act 241; Mont. Rev. Codes (1935), § 3040; New Hampshire, Acts 1917, ch. 173, Pub. Laws (1926); New York, L. 1917, ch. 159; Executive Law, Sec. 10; North Carolina, Acts 1927, ch. 185; Code (1939), § 193 (a)–(h); South Carolina, Act of June 1940, § 9; South Dakota, Sess. Laws 1935, c. 16, § 1; Utah Rev. Stats. (1933), § 75-28-6. Some of these provisions were held to violate federal law. See, e.g., *Arrowsmith v. Voorhies*, 55 F.2d 310, 312 (E.D. Mich. 1931) (striking down Michigan's alien registration law because it sought to "usurp the power of government, exclusively vested by the Constitution in Congress, over the control of aliens and immigration"); *Ex parte Ah Cue*, 101 Cal. 197 (1894) (invalidating California's law, which applied specifically to Chinese immigrants, on the grounds that it was preempted by federal law that regulated Chinese immigration).

178. Morawetz and Fernández-Silber, "Immigration Law," 143–55. See also, e.g., H.R. 7379, 76th Cong. (1939); S. 1364, 75th Cong. (1937); H.R. 10669, 72nd Cong. (1932); H.R. 20936, 64th Cong. (1917).

179. See, e.g., Tom I. Romera, "A War to Keep Alien Labor Out of Colorado: The Mexican Menace, Local and State Anti-immigration Initiatives and the Historical Origins of the New Jim Crow," in Hessick and Chin, *Strange Neighbors*, 63, 73–74, 83–87.

180. Mary Fan, "Post-racial Proxies: Resurgent State and Local Anti-'Alien' Laws and Unity-Rebuilding Frames for Antidiscrimination Values," *Cardozo Law Review* 32 (2011): 905; Erika Lee, "The Chinese Exclusion Example: Race, Immigration, and American Gatekeeping, 1882–1924," *Journal of American Ethnic History* 21 (2002): 36; Judith Resnik, "Law's Migration," *Yale Law Journal* 115 (2006): 1564, 1599–600 (discussing state barriers to landownership and licenses for U.S. citizen children of aliens, such as *Oyama v. State of California*, 332 U.S. 633 (1948)).

181. See *Hines v. Davidowitz*, 312 U.S. 52, 71n31 (1941) (citing H.R. 9101 and H.R. 9147, 71st Cong. (1930)).

182. S. 1364, § 4, 75th Cong. (1937).

183. Ibid., § 3.

184. See *Deportation of Aliens: Hearing on S. 1363, S. 1364, S. 1365 and S. 1366 Before a Subcomm. of the S. Comm. on Immigration*, 75th Cong. (1937) at 23 (testimony of John B. Trevor, president of American Coalition). In contrast, opponents of such legislation argued it was anti-American. Ibid., at 75 (testimony of John Thomas Taylor of the American Legion) (stating that singling out aliens was not "what we want in this country. I believe it would be an entering wedge for universal registration or the system they have in Europe, where a man cannot move from one town to another without reporting to the police. I do not believe we want that in America"). Ibid., at 83 (testimony of Cecilia Razovsky Davidson of the National Council of Jewish Women) (discussing "certain fundamental American principles on which I think no American should compromise. I think some of the provisions of these bills are un-American").

185. President Truman, Veto of Bill to Revise the Laws Relating to Immigration, Naturalization, and Nationality (June 25, 1952) (objecting to the "cruelty of carrying over into this year the isolationist limitations of our 1924 law"). The Senate overrode the veto 57 to 26, and the House by a vote of 278 to 112.

186. The Immigration and Nationality Act of 1952 left in place the 1940 federal obligation that aliens register and inform the government of any change in address, and that registration and fingerprint information were confidential. Immigration and Nationality Act, §§ 264–66, Pub. L. No. 414, 66 Stat. 163, 224–25 (1952) (codified at 8 U.S.C. § 1304). The punishment for failing to notify the Attorney General of a change of address included deportation, regardless of whether the alien was convicted or punished for the crime, unless the Attorney General could be convinced that the violation was "reasonably excusable or was not willful." Ibid., § 266(c). The 1952 legislation added the requirement that every alien over the age of eighteen carry or have in his or her possession a "certificate of alien registration" or "an alien registration receipt card" at "all times." Ibid., § 264(e). As discussed earlier, federal regulations no longer create a mechanism for registration per se, and a variety of documents are deemed to be evidence of registration. Morawetz and Fernández-Silber, "Immigration Law."

187. Internal Security Act, Pub. Law No. 831, 64 Stat. 993 (1950).

188. See generally Michael Belknap, *Cold War Political Justice: The Smith Act, the Communist Part, and American Civil Liberties* (Westport, CT.: Greenwood Press, 1977).

189. Note, "State Control of Subversion: A Problem in Federalism," *Harvard Law Review* 66 (1952): 327.

190. Immigration and Nationality Act, § 212(a), Pub. L. No. 414, 66 Stat. 163, 225 (1952) (codified at 8 U.S.C. § 1304). See generally Cheryl Lynne Shanks, *Immigration and the Politics of American Sovereignty, 1890–1990* (Ann Arbor: University of Michigan Press, 2001), 96–145. Shanks argued that this legislation (known as the McCarran-Walter Act) represented a "new way of thinking about sovereignty," in that the United States lost control over the movement of resources and goods through the growing interdependence of trade but aimed to increase its authority over persons through a citizen/alien division.

191. See Walter Gellhorn, ed., *The States and Subversion* (Ithaca, NY: Cornell University Press, 1952).

192. "State Control of Subversion," 327 (citations omitted).

193. Ibid., n. 8 (citing Pa. Stat. Ann. Tit. 62, § 2509 (Supp. 1951)).

194 Jennifer Hochschild, chapter 6, this volume.

195. See Douglas S. Massey, "How Arizona Became Ground Zero," in Carissa Hessick and Jack Chin, eds., *Strange Neighbors: The Role of the States in Immigration Enforcement and Policy* (New York: NYU Press, 2014), 40–45; see also Douglas S. Massey, "America's Immigration Policy Fiasco: Learning from Past Mistakes," *Daedalus* 142, no. 3 (Summer 2013): 5. An analysis of the administration and contradictions in the program is provided by Kitty Calavita, *Inside the State: The Bracero Program, Immigration, and the I.N.S.* (New York: Routledge, Chapman, and Hall, 1992). As she saw it, the program formulated as a "wartime emergency measure" turned the U.S. and Mexican governments into providers of "farm labor." Ibid., 46.

196. Massey, "How Arizona Became Ground Zero," 41.

197. Calavita, *Inside the State*, 31. Her data counted more than 800,000 people entering through the Bracero Accord and INS apprehensions of more than "two million undocumented workers, the vast majority of whom were Mexican." Ibid., 32.

198. Massey, "How Arizona Became Ground Zero," 41. Calavita argued that Bracero Accord policies were a conduit for information to Mexico about work opportunities in the United States, and also inspired some not to wait for the program but to enter without permission. Calavita, *Inside the State*, 32. The four extensions of the law governing the program entailed "little debate" in part because they were routed through the Agriculture Committees of the Congress rather than through the Education and Labor Committees. Ibid., 45. Further, the program did not prevent "Operation Wetback"—deporting undocumented aliens as part of the Cold War hostilities toward immigrants. Ibid., 54–46. Moreover, those who came through the Bracero Program were a "captive" labor force, caught in a narrow channel of permissible employment that some exited. Ibid., 74–82. After the program's end, the limited budget of INS enabled un-

documented workers to remain to staff agriculture needs. Ibid., 162–64. Calavita attributed the program's demise to disputes between the Labor Department and INS and to disagreements among members of Congress.

199. Immigration and Nationality Act, Pub. L. No. 89-236, 79 Stat. 911 (1965); Massey, "How Arizona Became Ground Zero," 41–42.

200. Massey, "How Arizona Became Ground Zero," 42. The Hart-Cellar Act did not apply the quota system to "special immigrants," a term that encompassed immigrants from "independent nations" in the Western Hemisphere. The Hart-Celler Act of 1965, Pub. L. 89-236, 79 Stat. 911–12. In 1976, Congress added amendments so that the quotas applied to the Western Hemisphere. See Pub. L. 94-571, 90 Stat 2703.

201. Massey, "How Arizona Became Ground Zero," 43.

202. Ibid., 44.

203. Ibid., 43.

204. Under IRCA, some 1.1 million people gained legal status through the Seasonal Agricultural Workers (SAW) program, and another 1.6 million came within a more general legalization program. See Donald Kerwin, "More Than IRCA: US Legalization Programs and the Current Policy Debate," Migration Policy Institute, Policy Brief, December 2010.

205. Nicholas P. De Genova, "Migrant 'Illegality' and Deportability in Everyday Life," *Annual Review of Anthropology* 31 (2002): 419, 420. In Switzerland, individual municipalities (cantons) decide whether foreign residents seeking citizenship are granted naturalization rights or rejected. One analysis found that country of origin was a key variable to acceptance. See Jens Hainmueller and Dominik Hangarner, "Who Gets a Swiss Passport? A Natural Experiment in Immigrant Discrimination," *American Political Science Review* 107 (2013): 159–87.

206. In 1952, Congress had made it unlawful to "harbor" an unlawful alien. New obligations flowed from the 1986 legislation. See Immigration Reform and Control Act of 1986, § 101, Pub. L. No. 99-603, 100 Stat. 3359, 3360.

207. Some twelve states had "some kind of employer sanction laws." Hiroshi Motomura, "Immigration Outside the Law," *Columbia Law Review* 108 (2008): 2037, 2051, 67. See also *De Canas v. Bica*, 424 U.S. 351 (1976) (holding that California's employment sanction law for employment of undocumented migrants was not preempted).

208. See 8 U.S.C. § 1373(b); 8 U.S.C. § 1324(a)(1)(A) (2012); 8 C.F.R. § 274a.2(b) (2012). See generally David Bacon and Bill Ong Hing, "The Rise and Fall of Employer Sanctions," *Fordham Urban Law Journal* 38 (2010): 77. This provision prevented local governments from withholding "information" from other governments, state or federal. See Cristina M. Rodríguez, "The Significance of the Local in Immigration Regulation,"

Michigan Law Review 106 (2008): 601. Aliens who work without permission may be ineligible for status adjustment to become legal permanent residents and may be "removed" for unauthorized work. 8 U.S.C. § 1227(a) (2012); 8 C.F.R. 217.4 (2012). Individuals obtaining employment through fraud could be criminally sanctioned. 18 U.S.C. § 1546(b) (2012).

209. Melissa Bailey, "ICE Fines Gourmet Heaven," November 16, 2012, www.newhavenindependent.org. In 2011, the Supreme Court upheld Arizona's creation of additional sanctions on employers of undocumented immigrants, including the possibility of losing a license to do business. See *Chamber of Commerce of the U.S. v. Whiting*, 563 U.S. 582 (2011).

210. Massey, "How Arizona Became Ground Zero," 48.

211. Ibid., 45–46.

212. Ibid., 55–56.

213. Ibid., 49. The enormous dislocation of deportation is detailed in Daniel Kanstroom, *Aftermath: Deportation Law and the New American Diaspora* (Oxford: Oxford University Press, 2012).

214. Massey, "How Arizona Became Ground Zero," 56. Thus "sixty percent of all unauthorized migrants in the United States today come from Mexico," followed by small percentages (under 5 percent) from other countries in Latin America and then from Asia. Ibid., 40.

215. Ibid., 56; the three states were California, Illinois, and Texas.

216. Ibid., 56–57.

217. See vol. 4 of the *Journal of the American Temperance Union* 140 (1840).

218. Thomas G. Pullen Jr., "Why the Proposed Maryland Constitution Was Not Approved," *William and Mary Law Review* 10 (1968): 378, 385.

219. *National Wildlife Federation v. Goldschmidt*, 677 F. 2d 259 (2d Cir. 1982).

220. Another acronym deployed was FAIR, standing for Federation for American Immigration Reform, promoting state legislation such as that of Arizona's S.B. 1070 and proposals to amend the Fourteenth Amendment's birthright citizenship provision. See Krysten Sinema, "The Evolution of Anti-immigration Legislation in Arizona," in Kubrin, Zatz, and Martínez, *Punishing Immigrants*, 62, 65, 76; see also Judith Resnik, "Constructing the 'Foreign': American Law's Relationship to Non-domestic Sources," in Mads Andenas and Duncan Fairgrieve, eds., *Courts and Comparative Law* (Oxford: Oxford University Press, 2015), 437.

221. Proposing to restrict access to "the benefits of public social services" to citizens and "aliens lawfully admitted to the United States," the campaign aimed to divide those living inside from those seeking to migrate to California. See Robin Dale Jacobson, *The New Nativism: Proposition 187 and the Debate over Immigration* (Minneapolis: University of Minnesota Press, 2008), xiii–xx.

222. Prop. 187 defined qualified individuals as citizens, legal permanent residents, and aliens "lawfully admitted for a temporary period of time" and restricted noneligible immigrants from health care (other than emergency care, as mandated by federal law) and education. Prop. 187 barred all except those deemed eligible from enrolling in public primary and secondary schools and in postsecondary institutions. The provisions on school enrollment contravened *Plyler v. Doe*, 457 U.S. 202 (1982), holding such prohibitions unconstitutional.

223. *League of United Latin American Citizens v. Wilson*, 997 F. Supp. 1244 (C.D. Calif. 1997).

224. Personal Responsibility and Work Opportunity Reconciliation Act of 1996 (PRWORA), Pub. L. No. 104-193, 110 Stat. 2105, codified at 8 U.S.C. §§ 1611–46, applied to both state and federal public benefits.

225. Under the prior program, Aid to Families with Dependent Children (AFDC), benefits had been available if either a citizen or a child who was a legal permanent resident was a part of the relevant household. See Steven Page and Mary Larner, "Introduction to the AFDC Program," *Future of Children* 7 (Spring 1997): 21. PRWORA restricted access for "federal public benefits" (defined as "any grant, contract, loan, professional license, or commercial license provided by an agency of the United States or by appropriated funds of the United States; and any retirement, welfare, health, disability, public or assisted housing, postsecondary education, food assistance, unemployment benefit, or any other similar benefit for which payments or assistance are provided to an individual, household, or family eligibility unit by an agency of the United States or by appropriated funds of the United States") to enumerated "qualified aliens" (including legal permanent residents and those given asylum). See 8 U.S.C. § 1641. The statute also licensed states to restrict access further: a "State is authorized to determine the eligibility for any State public benefits of an alien who is a qualified alien . . . a nonimmigrant under the Immigration and Nationality Act . . . or an alien who is paroled into the United States under section 212(d)(5) of such Act . . . for less than one year." See 8 U.S.C. § 1622 (also exempting certain refugees and veteran legal permanent residents [LPRs] from any bars to state benefits). Further, the act denied Supplemental Security Income and food stamps to all aliens, with exceptions (again, for certain refugees, veterans, LPRs, and LPRs who had worked more than forty qualifying quarters). Also exempted were emergency services, including immunizations and "[p]rograms, services, or assistance (such as soup kitchens, crisis counseling and intervention, and short-term shelter) specified by the Attorney General." Ibid., § 1641 PRWORA, at § 402. In 1997, Congress amended the provisions to exempt blind and disabled LPRs. Pub. L. No. 105-33, § 5301, 111 Stat. 251

(1997) (codified at 8 U.S.C. § 1612(a)(2)(F) (2012)). Further exceptions have since been added. See SSI Extension for Elderly and Disabled Refugees Act, Pub. L. No. 110-328, 122 Stat. 3567 (2008) (adding exceptions for victims of human trafficking).

226. See generally Susan F. Martin, *A Nation of Immigrants* (New York: Cambridge University Press, 2010), 265–68.

227. Aliens subject to expedited removal were to be in mandatory detention. IIRIRA, § 302(a). Congress also required the Attorney General of the United States to take "into custody" aliens who had committed certain crimes or terrorist activities. Ibid. § 303(a), P.L. 104-208, 110 Stat. 3009-585.

228. Pub. L. No. 104-132, 110 Stat. 1214. AEDPA also closed internal doors by imposing barriers to individuals who were prisoners inside the United States and who sought to challenge either their convictions or the conditions of their confinement.

229. 8 USC § 1227(a)(2)(A)(i). See generally Nancy Morawetz, "Understanding the Impact of the 1996 Deportation Laws and the Limited Scope of Proposed Reforms," *Harvard Law Review* 113 (2000): 1936. A body of Supreme Court case law interpreted what felonies are "aggravated" and what crimes involve "moral turpitude." See, e.g., *Torres v. Lynch*, 136 S. Ct. 1619 (2016); *Moncrieffe v. Holder*, 133 S. Ct. 1678 (2013). Critiques of the administrative adjudication system are plentiful. See, e.g., American Bar Association, "Reforming the Immigration System: Proposals to Promote Independence, Fairness, Efficiency, and Professionalism in the Adjudication of Removal Cases," 2010, at ES 11–12, www.americanbar.org.

230. See generally Michael Welch, "Panic, Risk, and Control: Conceptualizing Threats in a Post-9/11 Society," in Kubrin, Zatz, and Martínez, *Punishing Immigrants*, 17–41.

231. See the Homeland Security Act (HSA) of 2002, Pub. L. No. 107-296, 116 Stat. 2135 (creating the Department of Homeland Security). One branch of DHS continues to use the word "service," U.S. Citizenship and Immigration Services.

232. Pub. L. No. 107-296, § 411, 116 Stat. 2135, 2178 (2002); see also U.S. Customs and Border Protection, "Timeline," www.cbp.gov (accessed June 10, 2016).

233. Zolberg, *Nation by Design*, 264–67. A decade earlier, forty personnel had done so. Ibid., 266.

234. See Department of Homeland Security, "Fiscal Year 2011 Budget in Brief," 2012, 17, www.dhs.gov; Department of Homeland Security, "Fiscal Year 2006 Budget in Brief," 2007, www.dhs.gov; *We Are CBP!*, *Careers*, www.cbp.gov (accessed June 10, 2016). CBP employed about 45,000 officers, specialists, or agents.

235. DHS, FY 2013, 13–14.

236. Ibid., 84.

237. U.S. Customs and Border Protection, *Snapshot: A Summary of CBP Facts and Figures,* 2012, http://cbp.gov. The CBP also reported that to do so, its agents used 26,875 vehicles, 269 aircraft, 228 watercraft, 334 horses, and 1,576 dogs. Ibid.

238. Data about these practices were required to be produced in *Families for Freedom v. US Customs and Border Protection,* 797 F. Supp. 2d 375 (S.D.N.Y. 2011).

239. See United and Strengthening America by Providing Appropriate Tools Required to Intercept and Obstruct Terrorism (USA PATRIOT ACT) of 2001, Pub. L. No. 107-56, 115 Stat. 272. The act was reauthorized by the USA PATRIOT Improvement and Reauthorization Act of 2005, Pub. L. No. 109-177; USA PATRIOT Act Additional Reauthorization Amendments Act of 2006, Pub. L. No. 109-178; and the PATRIOT Sunsets Extension Act of 2011, Pub. L. No. 112-14. See generally Daniel Kanstroom, "Criminalizing the Undocumented: Ironic Boundaries of the Post–September 11th 'Pale of Law,'" *North Carolina Journal of International Law and Commercial Regulation* 29 (2004): 639. Kanstroom's referent is to a phrase from Hannah Arendt's book, *The Origins of Totalitarianism* that stateless migrants were beyond the "pale of law."

240. *Clapper v. Amnesty USA,* 133 S. Ct. 1138 (2013).

241. *Klayman v. Obama,* 957 F. Supp. 2d 1 (D. D.C. 2013)

242. See generally Stella Burch Elias, "Comprehensive Immigration Reform(s): Immigration Regulation beyond Our Border," *Yale Journal of International Law* 39 (2014): 14–17 (surveying variations both within the United States and in Germany, Australia, and Canada that produce various forms of "immigration federalism"); Monica W. Varsanyi, ed., *Taking Local Control: Immigration Policy Activism in U.S. Cities and States* (Stanford, CA: Stanford University Press, 2010); Rodríguez, "The Significance of the Local"; Hiroshi Motomura, "The Rights of Others: Legal Claims and Immigration Outside the Law," *Duke Law Journal* 59 (2010): 1723.

243. See Pablo A. Mitnik and Jessica Halpern-Finnerty, "Immigration and Local Governments: Inclusionary Local Policies in the Era of State Rescaling," in Varsanyi, *Taking Local Control,* 50, 56–62.

244. As of 2007, ten states provided in-state resident tuition rates to students without documentation. Rodríguez, "The Significance of the Local," 605. By 2013, the number had risen to fourteen. Variables affecting whether states and municipalities were pro-immigrant included shifts in population as well as the mobilization of migrant communities. See Justin Peter Steil and Ion Bogdan Vasi, "The New Immigration Contestation: Social Movements and Local Immigration Policy Making in the United

States, 2000–2011," *American Journal of Sociology* 119 (2014): 1104. Another empirical analysis identified "partisan opportunities and political entrepreneurship," linking federal and state decision making through political party structure, at the center of restrictive legislation. See Pratheepan Gulasekaram and S. Karthick Ramakrishnan, "Immigration Federalism: A Reappraisal," *NYU Law Review* 88 (2013): 2074, 2116.

245. City of New Haven, "Community Services Administration, New Haven's Elm City Resident Card: My City, My Card," www.cityofnewhaven. com (accessed December 11, 2012).

246. *In re Garcia*, 58 Cal. 4th 440, 447 (2014), was decided on January 2, 2014, one day after the California legislation, authorizing admission, came into effect. See Cal. Bus. and Prof. Code § 6064 (b) (West). The California Supreme Court held that the statute met the restrictions that Congress had imposed on undocumented immigrants obtaining professional licenses. See 8 U.S.C. § 1621 (d), which permits states to provide benefits for which an alien would "otherwise be ineligible under [8 U.S.C. § 1621(a) (2012)]" if done "through the enactment of a State law after August 22, 1996, which affirmatively provides for such eligibility." The Florida Supreme Court declined to admit an undocumented immigrant in light of the lack of a legislative provision akin to that in California. See *Florida Bd. of Bar Examiners re Question as to Whether Undocumented Immigrants Are Eligible for Admission to the Florida Bar*, 134 So. 3d 432 (Fla. 2014).

247. See S. Karthick Ramakrishnan and Allan Colbern, "The 'California Package' of Immigration Integration and the Evolving Nature of State Citizenship," *Policy Matters* 6 (2015): 1.

248. Kris W. Kobach, "Reinforcing the Rule of Law: What States Can and Should Do to Reduce Illegal Immigration," *Georgetown Immigration Law Journal* 22 (2008): 459.

249. National Conference of State Legislatures, Immigration Policy Project, "2013 Immigration Report," at 2, www.ncsl.org (hereinafter NCSL 2013 Immigration Report).

250. National Conference of State Legislatures, Immigration Policy Project, "2012 Immigration-Related Laws and Resolutions in the States (January 1–June 30, 2012)," 2012, 1, www.ncsl.org.

251. Ibid., 1.

252. NCSL 2013 Immigration Report: 1.

253. See, e.g., *United States v. Alabama*, 691 F.3d 1269 (11th Cir. 2012) (holding that Alabama's provisions creating crimes based on immigration status were preempted, but investigation into status was not precluded); *Ga. Latino Alliance for Human Rights v. Georgia*, 691 F.3d 1250, 1269 (11th Cir. 2012) (holding that Georgia's new crimes for aliens were preempt-

ed). See also *Villas at Parkside Partners v. City of Famers Branch Texas*, 726 F. 3d 524 (5th Cir. 2013) (holding as preempted a local ordinance imposing penalties on rentals to those "not lawfully present"); *Buquer v. City of Indianapolis, City of Franklin, Johnson County*, 797 F. Supp. 2d 905 (S.D. Ind. 2011) (granting a preliminary injunction against the Indiana statute authorizing arrests for a new state infraction of offering or accepting consular identification cards).

254. In 2005, federal law barred undocumented immigrants from receiving driver's licenses that functioned as federal identification. See REAL ID Act of 2005, Pub. L. No. 109-13, 119 Stat. 231, § 202(c)(2)(B); Maria Pabon Lopez, "More Than a License to Drive: State Restrictions on the Use of Driver's Licenses by Noncitizens," *Southern Illinois University Law Journal* 29 (2005): 91.

255. See Homeland Security—Foreign Nationals—Reports, 2012 Alabama Laws Act 2012-491 (H.B. 658), amending the 2011 enactment. H.B. 56 redefined a "business transaction" as a "public records transaction," which "means applying for or renewing a motor vehicle license plate, applying for or renewing a driver's license or nondriver identification card, or applying for or renewing a business license, applying for or renewing a commercial license, or applying for or renewing a professional license" (modifying §31-13-29 of the Code of Alabama 1975). The Eleventh Circuit rejected a "pre-enforcement" challenge to these provisions. See *United States v. Alabama*, 691 F.3d 1269, 1297–301 (11th Cir. 2012). Texas, South Carolina, and Montana granted licenses to persons present on nonimmigrant visas that expire at the end of the visas' duration. Tex. Transp. Code Ann. § 521.271 (West); S.C. Code Ann. § 56-1-40; Mont. Code Ann. § 61-5-111. Louisiana, Alabama, Mississippi, and Pennsylvania required that noncitizens' licenses be marked differently than those of citizens. La. Rev. Stat. Ann. § 32:412; Ala. Code § 32-6-10.1; Miss. Code. Ann. § 63-1-35 (West); 75 Pa. Cons. Stat. Ann. § 1510 (West).

256. In 2012, the secretary of DHS issued a memorandum instructing that "certain young people who were brought to the country as children and know only this country as home" be permitted to stay without fearing deportation. The initiative, known as the Deferred Action for Childhood Arrivals (DACA) program, applied to immigrants who entered before they were sixteen and were under thirty-one as of 2012 and met other criteria. See 8 U.S.C. § 1182(a)(9)B)(ii); 8 C.F.R. § 214.14(d)(3). In 2014, the secretary proposed a new Deferred Action for Parents of Americans and Lawful Permanent Residents (DAPA) program, aiming to provide relief for three years from deportation and authorizing work if a person had been in the country for five years and was a parent of a U.S. citizen or legal permanent resident.

257. Executive Order 2012-02, Re-affirming Intent of Arizona Law in Response to the Federal Government's Deferred Action Program (August 15, 2012).

258. In 2014, a federal appellate court granted a preliminary injunction on the grounds that the order likely violated the Equal Protection Clause; by distinguishing DACA migrants from other categories of migrants who also lacked formal legal status, the Governor's Executive Order lacked a rational basis. See *Arizona Dream Act Coalition v. Brewer*, 757 F. 3d 1053 (9th Cir. 2014), cert. denied sub nom. *Brewer v. Arizona Dream Act Coalition*, 135 S. Ct. 889 (2014). In 2016, the court affirmed the permanent injunction and, while noting the likelihood of the Equal Protection Clause violation, rested on preemption to avoid the constitutional question. See *Arizona Dream Act Coalition v. Brewer*, 818 F.3d 901 (9th Cir. 2016).

259. See Rob Schofield, "Not So Pretty in Pink," *North Carolina Policy Watch Weekly Briefing*, March 6, 2013, www.ncpolicywatch.com. North Carolina then announced that it would not include the pink stripe on the licenses but would mark them "NO LAWFUL STATUS." Michael Hennessey, "Licenses for DACA Qualifiers: Pink Stripe to Be Removed," March 22, 2013, www.wcti12.com.

260. Zolberg, *Nation by Design*, 303–11.

261. Judith Resnik, Joshua Civin, and Joseph Frueh, "Ratifying Kyoto at the Local Level: Sovereigntism, Federalism, and Translocal Organizations of Governmental Actors (TOGAs)," *Arizona Law Review* 50 (2008): 709.

262. One study focused on local groups' impact found that local political opportunities were "highly significant" for the enactment of pro-immigrant policies but not for anti-immigrant policies, which were most significantly affected by a community's changing demographics framed as "threats." Steil and Vasi, "New Immigration Contestation," 1143.

263. State Legislators for Legal Immigration, "Policy Positions," www. statelegislatorsforlegalimmigration.com (accessed December 11, 2012).

264. State Legislators for Legal Immigration, "Participating States," www.statelegislatorsforlegalimmigration.com (accessed December 11, 2012). SLLI filed an amicus brief on behalf of Arizona in *U.S. v. Arizona*, and it recorded its opposition to the Deferred Action for Childhood Arrivals initiative. See State Legislators for Legal Immigration, "In the News," www.statelegislatorsforlegalimmigration.com (accessed December 11, 2012).

265. See Elise Foley, "Redefining Birthright Citizenship One State at a Time," October 20, 2010, http://washingtonindependent.com; Julia Preston, "State Lawmakers Outline Plans to End Birthright Citizenship, Drawing Outcry," January 5, 2011, www.nytimes.com. Senators Rand Paul (R-

KY) and David Vitter (R-LA) introduced legislation to eliminate birthright citizenship by defining "a person born in the United States" to require that they have "parents, one of whom is a citizen or national of the United States; an alien lawfully admitted for permanent residence in the United States whose residence is in the United States; or an alien performing active service in the armed forces," and apply that provision to persons born after such an act's enactment. Birthright Citizenship Act of 2011, S. 723, 112th Cong.

266. National League of Cities, "Influence Federal Policy, Fix the Nation's Broken Immigration System: Request of Congress," http://www.nlc.org (accessed June 10, 2016); National League of Cities, "Arizona Immigration Law Creates Climate of Fear and an Undue Financial Burden for Cities," April 25, 2012, www.nlc.org.

267. USCM, press release, "The U.S. Conference of Mayors Reacts to the Supreme Court's Arizona Immigration Decision," June 25, 2012, http://usmayors.org; USCM, Comprehensive Immigration Reform as a Means to Strengthen Our Economy, Global Competitiveness, and Security, resolution adopted June 2012, http://usmayors.org; USCM, A National New Americans Initiative to Promote U.S. Citizenship at the Federal, State, Municipal, and Community Level, resolution adopted June 2012, http://usmayors.org.

268. Gregory Minchak, "NLC Files Amicus Brief in Arizona Immigration Law Supreme Court Case, Stresses Immigration as a Federal Responsibility," National League of Cities, April 30, 2012, www.nlc.org.

269. Huyen Pham and Pham Hoang Van, "Measuring the Climate for Immigrants: A State-by-State Analysis," in Hessick and Chin, *Strange Neighbors*, 21. Pham and Van looked at state and local laws. In another study, the authors sought to measure the economic effects of anti-immigrant local ordinances and identified a small drop in employment in such localities, which they interpreted as evidence that workers changed jobs but did not leave the area. See Huyen Pham and Pham Hoang Van, "The Economic Impact of Local Immigration Regulation: An Empirical Analysis," *Cardozo Law Review* 32 (2010): 485.

270. Pham and Van, "Measuring the Climate," 30–31.

271. Illinois and California were at the top by some margin, followed by Connecticut, Minnesota, Washington, New Mexico, Maryland, Pennsylvania, and Iowa. The distinction of being the most negative went to Arizona, again by some measure, followed by Missouri, Virginia, South Carolina, Utah, Oklahoma, Georgia, Colorado, Arkansas, Tennessee, Texas, Alabama, and Florida—a mix of the Old South and the border states. Ibid., 31. The gap between positive and negative on the metric created was about 100 points.

272. Ibid.

273. Phoenix's population grew from 983,403 in 1990 to 1,321,045 in 2000, and to 1,445,656 in 2010. U.S. Census Bureau, Population Change and Distribution 1990 to 2000," April 2001, https://www.census.gov/prod/2001pubs/c2kbr01-2.pdf; U.S. Census Bureau, "State and County QuickFacts: Phoenix (city), Arizona," http://quickfacts.census.gov (accessed December 10, 2012). See also Massey, "Pathways to El Norte," 3–4.

274. See Maryland Highway Safety Act of 2013, 2013 Maryland Laws Ch. 309 (S.B. 715), codified at Md. Code Ann., Transp. § 16–122 (West). These provisions repealed a 2009 law aimed at preventing undocumented migrants from obtaining or renewing driver's licenses.

275. See *Texas v. United States*, Civ. No. B-14-254 (S.D. Tex. filed February 16, 2015), stay of preliminary injunction denied, 787 F.3d 733 (5th Cir. 2015), injunction affirmed, 809 F.3d 134 (5th Cir. 2015), cert. granted, 136 S. Ct. 906 (2016).

276. The terminology prompted an exchange when the California Supreme Court ruled in *In re Garcia*, 58 Cal. 4th 440, 447 (2014), to admit Mr. Garcia to the bar. Chief Justice Tani Cantile-Sakauye described Mr. Garcia as an "undocumented immigrant." Ibid., 446. Her colleague Justice Ming Chin concurred but argued that California law termed a person of his status an "unlawful alien." Ibid., 467. She replied that her choice followed that of Justice Sonia Sotomayor (ibid., 466n1), who had used the phrase in her first opinion on the U.S. Supreme Court—in *Mohawk Industries v. Carpenter*, 558 U.S. 100, 103 (2009).

277. See, e.g., Joseph H. Carens, "The Rights of Irregular Migrants," *Ethics and International Affairs* 22 (2008): 163. In 2006, the Council of Europe called for the use of the terms "irregular migrant" or "migrant without paper" in lieu of the "illegal migrant." Recommendation 1755 (2006) Parliamentary Assembly, discussed in Elspeth Guild, "Criminalisation of Migration in Europe: Human Rights Implications," Commissioner of Human Rights, Issue Paper (2016), 8–9. See also Catherine Dauvernge, *Making People Illegal: What Globalization Means for Migration and Law* (Cambridge: Cambridge University Press, 2009).

278. For example, a publication on Europe's development of "its Area of Freedom, Security and Justice" used the term "illegal migration," even while calling for respect for individual dignity. See Guild, "Criminalisation of Migration," 27–28. Likewise, the 2008/115 Directive for standards on returning individuals deployed the language of "illegally staying third-country nationals," as well as the authority to impose "coercive measures" (not exceeding "reasonable force") for those who resist removal. Directive 2008/115, Art. 8(4); Guild, "Criminalisation of Migration," 34. In 2016, a report prepared for Europe's Commissioner for Human Rights reiterated

concerns about the use of stigmatizing language. See *Criminalisation of Migration in Europe: Human Rights Implications* (Commissioner for Human Rights, Issue Paper prepared by Elspeth Guild, 2016), https://wcd.coe.int.

279. See Gerald L. Neuman, "Aliens as Outlaws: Government Services, Proposition 187, and the Structure of Equal Protection Doctrine," *UCLA Law Review* 42 (1995): 1425.

280. *Takahashi v. Fish and Game Comm'n*, 334 U.S. 410 (1948) (holding that a California statute prohibiting aliens who were not eligible for citizenship from obtaining commercial fishing licenses violated the Fourteenth Amendment); *Namba v. McCourt*, 204 P.2d 569 (Or. 1949) (invalidating alien land restrictions); *Sei Fujii v. State*, 38 Cal. 2d 718, 722 (Cal. 1952) (invalidating alien land restrictions as violating the Fourteenth Amendment).

281. *Graham v. Richardson*, 403 U.S. 365, 372 (1971).

282. See *Plyler v. Doe*, 457 U.S. 202, 207 (1982); see also Linda Greenhouse, "What Would Justice Powell Do? The 'Alien Children' Case and the Meaning of Equal Protection," *Constitutional Commentary* 25 (2008): 29.

283. See, e.g., *Miller v. Albright*, 523 U.S. 420 (1998); *Nguyen v. I.N.S.*, 533 U.S. 53 (2001); *Flores-Villar v. United States*, 564 U.S. 210 (2011) (per curiam), aff'd by an equally divided court, 536 F.3d 990 (9th Cir. 2008). The issue is, as of this writing, pending again. See *Lynch v. Morales-Santana*, 804 F.3d 520 (2d Cir. 2015), cert. granted, 136 S.Ct. 2545 (2016). See generally Kristin A. Collins, "Illegitimate Borders: Jus Sanguinis Citizenship and the Legal Construction of Family, Race, and Nation," *Yale Law Journal* 123 (2014): 2134.

284. *Mathews v. Diaz*, 426 U.S. 67, 83 (1976).

285. Ibid., 81. The German Constitutional Court took a different approach, insisting that benefits be provided based on need, and not on migration status. See *Hartz IV Decision*, BVerfG [Federal Constitutional Court of Germany], 1 BvL 1/09, February 9, 2010, http://www.bverfg.de.

286. See *Graham v. Richardson*, 403 U.S. 365 (1971) (striking down Arizona's and Pennsylvania's rules limiting welfare benefits either to U.S. citizens or to resident aliens who had satisfied a residency requirement). For most of the Court, *Graham* rested on equal protection. Federal supremacy also played a role; because Congress had created a "comprehensive plan for the regulation of immigration and naturalization," which had taken indigence into account, it had occupied the field. Ibid., 377.

287. *Foley v. Connelie*, 435 U.S. 291, 295–96 (1978). In 1976, the Supreme Court explained it would approach federal discrimination differ-

ently because although the "concept of equal justice under law is served by the Fifth Amendment's guarantee of due process, as well as by the Equal Protection Clause of the Fourteenth Amendment," and although "both Amendments require the same type of analysis," "the two protections are not always coextensive." *Hampton v. Mow Sun Wong*, 426 U.S. 88, 100 (1976). Thus, as Brian Soucek has analyzed, the approach results in noncongruence, which is to say that federal discrimination can be tolerated when state discrimination would not. See Brian Soucek, "The Return of Noncongruent Equal Protection," *Fordham Law Review* 83 (2014): 155, 158.

288. *In re Griffiths*, 413 U.S. 717 (1973).

289. *Takahashi v. Fish and Game Comm'n*, 334 U.S. 410 (1948).

290. *Sugarman v. Dougall*, 413 U.S. 634 (1973).

291. *Foley v. Connelie*, 435 U.S. 291, 296 (1978).

292. *Ambach v. Norwick*, 441 U.S. 68, 74 (1979).New York changed its regulations in 2016 to permit certification without regard to citizenship status.

293. Ibid.

294. Ibid., 81, 88 (Blackmun, J., dissenting, joined by Justices Brennan, Marshall, and Stevens).

295. *Arizona Dream Act Coalition v. Brewer*, 757 F. 3d 1054 (9th Cir. 2014), cert. denied sub nom. *Brewer v. Arizona Dream Act Coalition*, 135 S. Ct. 889 (2014). As noted, in 2016, when affirming the lower court entry of a permanent injunction, the Ninth Circuit discussed the likelihood of the Equal Protection Clause violation but avoided deciding the constitutional question by resting its holding on federal preemption. See *Arizona Dream Act Coalition v. Brewer*, 818 F.3d 901 (9th Cir. 2016).

296. In *Toll v. Moreno*, the Court had struck Maryland's denial of in-state tuition to aliens on preemption grounds. 458 U.S. 1 (1982). The 1996 IIRIRA limited state authority to provide tuition benefits to nonqualified aliens on the basis of residency "unless a citizen or national of the United States is eligible for such a benefit . . . without regard to whether the citizen or national is such a resident." Ibid., § 1623. Given these parameters, the states that provide in-state tuition to undocumented students typically do so for those students who have graduated from a state high school as well for citizens and LPRs without regard to their state residency. See National Immigration Law Center, *Basic Facts about In-State Tuition for Undocumented Immigrant Students*, www.nilc.org (accessed June 5, 2016).

297. 426 U.S. 88 (1976).

298. Ibid., 103 (if and when "the Federal Government asserts an overriding national interest as justification for a discriminatory rule which would violate the Equal Protection Clause if adopted by a State, due process requires that there be a legitimate basis for presuming that the rule was actually intended to serve that interest").

299. Ibid., 116.

300. U.S. Const. art. I, § 8, cl. 4.

301. As Harold Koh put it decades ago, relying on preemption "subordinates fourteenth amendment equal protection doctrine governing discrimination against resident aliens to the vagaries of federal immigration policy." Harold Hongju Koh, "Equality with a Human Face: Justice Blackmun and the Equal Protection of Aliens," *Hamline Law Review* 8 (1985): 51, 98.

302. Michael J. Perry, "Modern Equal Protection: A Conceptualization and Appraisal," *Columbia Law Review* 79 (1979): 1023, 1062.

303. Walter A. Ewing, Daniel E. Martínez, and Rubén G. Rumbaut, "The Criminalization of Immigration in the United States," American Immigration Council Special Report, 2015.

304. Nicola Lacey, *The Prisoner's Dilemma: Political Economy and Punishment in Contemporary Democracies* (Cambridge: Cambridge University Press, 2008).

305. See, e.g., *Al-Kateb v. Godwin*, 2004, 219 C.L.R. 562 (Aust.); *Re Woolley; Ex parte Applicants M276/2003 by their next friend GS* [2004] HCA 49 (October 7, 2004).

306. *United States ex rel Klonis v. Davis*, 13 F.2d 630, 630 (2d Cir. 1926). The Second Circuit affirmed the district court's holding that the judge's recommendation against deportation was time barred; Judge Hand wrote to underscore that a pardon remained an option. Ibid. In a 1913 opinion, Oliver Wendell Holmes provided an alternative view, that deportation was "simply a refusal by the Government to harbor persons whom it does not want." *Bugajewitz v. Adams*, 228 U.S. 585, 591 (1913).

307. The Passport Act of 1918 permitted the executive branch to regulate entry and exit, and President Woodrow Wilson relied upon the President's war powers to make entry without a passport punishable by criminal sanctions. Lower federal courts rejected that approach, in part by reading the subsequent Immigration Act of 1921, which did not include criminal sanctions, as a basis for not permitting such penalties without express authorization. See *Flora v. Rustad*, 8 F.2d 335 (8th Cir. 1925); *Johnson v. Keating ex. rel. Tarantino*, 17 F.2d 50, 54 (1st Cir. 1926). In 1924, counterfeiting immigration documents became a crime. See Eagly, "Prosecuting Immigration," 1296–97. See also Doug Keller, "Re-thinking Illegal Entry and Re-entry," *Loyola University Chicago Law Journal* 44 (2012): 65.

308. Act of March 4, 1929, Pub. L. No. 70-1018, 45 Stat. 1551. Presence alone, without intent and action, is not itself criminal. Eagly, "Prosecuting Immigration," 1343.

309. In terms of civil sanctions, Ngai explained that, due to the rapid rise in deportations, the Immigration Service increased its budget request to $10 million in 1928, up from less than $1 million the prior year. The

service also introduced the policy of "voluntary departure." Those without "proper visas" constituted the largest group expelled, constituting more than half of all deportations, which had risen to nearly 40,000 by 1930. See Ngai, "The Strange Career of the Illegal Alien," 76–77. On criminal sanctioning, see Eagly, "Prosecuting Immigration," 1350–51.

310. See, e.g., *Delgadillo v. Carmichael*, 332 U.S. 388, 391 (1947) (citing *Bridges v. Wixon*, 326 U.S. 135, 147 (1945)); *I.N.S. v. Errico*, 385 U.S. 214, 225 (1966); *Costello v. I.N.S.*, 376 U.S. 120, 128 (1964).

311. Immigration and Customs Enforcement, "Total Removals," www.ice.gov (accessed June 10, 2016). ICE removed 396,906 individuals in FY 2011 and, as of August 25, had removed 366,292 during FY 2012. The displacement and suffering for those for whom "home is exile" is captured by interview research of more than 40 sent "back" to El Salvador from the United States. See M. Kathleen Dingeman-Cerda and Susan Bibler Coutin, "The Ruptures of Return: Deportation's Confounding Effects," in Kubrin, Zatz, and Martínez, *Punishing Immigrants*, 113, 120, 132.

312. National Immigration Forum, "The Math of Immigration Detention: Aug. 2012," 1–3, www.immigrationforum.org. The report estimates that from "1996 to 2006, 65% of immigrants . . . detained and deported were detained after being arrested for non-violent crimes," and that in 2009 and 2010, "over half of all immigrant detainees had no criminal records." Ibid., 4.

313. ICE detained approximately 429,000 people in 2011, an "all-time high." John Simanski and Lesley M. Sapp, "Annual Report, Immigration Enforcement Actions: 2011," DHS: Office of Immigration Statistics, September 2012, www.dhs.gov.

314. Ian Urbina and Catherine Rentz, "Immigrants Held in Solitary Cells, Often for Weeks," *New York Times*, March 23, 2013; Alex Krell, "Immigration Advocates Drop Solitary Confinement Lawsuit against ICE," May 12, 2014, www.thenewstribune.com.

315. U.S. Customs and Border Protection, "Southwest Border Unaccompanied Alien Children," July 2014, www.cpb.gov; Frances Robles, "Fleeing Gangs, Children Head to the U.S. Border," *New York Times*, July 9, 2014. In 2015, a federal judge found that the Department of Homeland Security's detention of female-headed families through a "no-release" policy violated a prior settlement limiting the government's authority to do so. See *Flores v. Johnson*, CV 85-4544 (C.D. Calif., July 24, 2015); aff'd in part, 2016 WL 3670146 (9th Cir. 2016). Challenges to the DHS's procedures for assessing applications to remain for mothers and children are, as of this writing, under way. See *Castro v. U.S. Department of Homeland Security*, Civ. No. 15-6153, 2016 WL 614862 (E.D. Pa, 2016), appeal docketed, No. 16-1339 (3d Cir. Feb. 17, 2016) (declining to provide habeas relief).

316. See Juliet P. Stumpf, "The Crimmigration Crisis: Immigrants, Crime, and Sovereign Power," *American University Law Review* 56 (2006): 367.

317. *Padilla v. Kentucky*, 130 S. Ct. 1473, 1486 (2010). Thereafter, the Court held the ruling was not to be applied retroactively. See *Chaidez v. United States*, 133 S. Ct. 1103 (2013).

318. Edwin Harwood, "Arrest without Warrant: The Legal and Organizational Environment of Immigration Law Enforcement," *UC Davis Law Review* 17 (1984): 505.

319. How accurate that characterization was depends on baselines of evaluation. Ingrid Eagly calculated that immigration prosecutions had, in the 1950s, constituted almost 40 percent of the federal criminal caseload. The number of cases—about 15,000 terminated—dipped in the 1960s, returned to the 15,000 mark in the 1970s, and remained relatively stable until the late 1990s, when it climbed to 25,000 and then by 2007, to almost 80,000 cases. Eagly, "Prosecuting Immigration," 1353, figure 4.

320. Harwood, "Arrest without Warrant," 507.

321. Ibid., 513.

322. Sklansky, "Crime, Immigration, and Ad Hoc Instrumentalism," 166, table 1, Immigration Prosecution 1986–2009. Note that disaggregated Federal data by place and type of offense was also provided, and that illegal entry accounted for the "lion's share" of the surge. Ibid., 167.

323. Eagly, "Prosecuting Immigration," 1281.

324. See Rosenblum, "Understanding the Potential Impact," 5.

325. Marc R. Rosenblum and Doris Meissner, with Claire Bergeon and Faye Hipsman, "The Deportation Dilemma: Reconciling Tough and Human Enforcement," Migration Policy Institute, April 2014, 4. See also TRAC Immigration, "Immigration Prosecutions for 2012," https://trac.syr.edu (accessed December 14, 2012) (counting 91,941 immigration-related prosecutions in 2012).

326. 8 U.S.C. § 1182(a)(2) (2012).

327. 8 U.S.C. § 1229(a)(3) (2012).

328. Sklansky, "Crime, Immigration, and Ad Hoc Instrumentalism," 178, table 9; at 179, table 10 (growth in the impact of criminal removals).

329. Ibid., 179.

330. Rosenblum and Meissner, "The Deportation Dilemma," 1, 9. That report also detailed variation in enforcement policies, over both time and place.

331. American Bar Association, "Reforming the Immigration System"; U.S. Courts, "Judicial Business 2013: District Courts," www.uscourts.gov (accessed June 10, 2016) (noting that civil filings in district courts were 420 per judge).

332. See, e.g., Jaya Ramji-Nogales, Andrew I. Schoenholtz, and Philip G. Schrag, *Refugee Roulette: Disparities in Asylum Adjudication and Proposals for Reform* (New York: NYU Press, 2009); Hon. Robert A. Katzmann, "Deepening the Legal Profession's Pro Bono Commitment to the Immigrant Poor," *Fordham Law Review* 78 (2009): 453; Jennifer L. Colyer, Sarah French Russell, Robert E. Juceam, and Lewis J. Liman, "The Representational and Counseling Needs of the Immigrant Poor," *Fordham Law Review* 461 (2009): 461, 462.

333. See National Immigration Forum, "The Math of Immigration Detention," 1–2. The range represents some of the complexity of calculating per diem costs.

334. As of 2011, ICE rented bed space in 220 state and local jails. National Immigration Forum, "The Math of Immigration Detention," 4.

335. See Resnik, "Globalizations(s), Privatizations(s)," 162, 183.

336. National Immigration Forum, "The Math of Immigration Detention," 5–6. In 2011, Corrections Corporation of American (CAA) provided fourteen ICE-contracted facilities and 14,556 beds and received $173 billion. The GEO Group provided another 7,182 beds and receives $1.6 billion annually. GEO Group owns another company that is the "sole provider" to ICE of alternatives to incarceration, Ibid., 5–7, and which provides monitoring and case management. As of 2012, some 23,000-plus enrolled, some with "technology only." Ibid., 8.

337. See Karen Manges Douglas and Rogelio Sáenz, "The Criminalization of Immigrants and the Immigration-Industrial Complex," *Daedalus* 142 (Summer 2013): 199. Under DHS appropriations for 2012, Congress provided that DHS "shall maintain a level of not less than 34,000 detention beds." See Consolidated Appropriations Act, 2012, P.L. 112-74, 125 Stat. 786, 980. See also Associated Press, "Immigrants Prove Big Business for Prison Companies," August 2, 2012, http://usatoday30.usatoday.com; Sharon Dolovich, "State Punishment and Private Prisons," *Duke Law Journal* 55 (2005): 437, 523–32.

338. The GEO Group, Inc., 2011 "Annual Report," 2, March 1, 2012, https://materials.proxyvote.com at 2–3. The DHS 2013 budget called for more access to counsel, visitation, and health care, and fewer long-distance detention transfers, but not a reduction in detention itself. DHS, FY 2013, 16.

339. See, e.g., Finnis, "Nationality, Alienage and Constitutional Principle."

340. See McLeod, "The US Criminal-Immigration Convergence" (cataloging the kinds of harms imposed and describing whether the categorization as a crime does more or less harm to the polity and those prosecuted).

341. The arguments from liberal theory and the rebuttal of a communitarian critique are provided in Carens, "Aliens and Citizens," as well as in *The Ethics of Immigration*. In that volume, Carens offers an analysis that distinguishes rights he categorizes as "human rights" (including the right to work) from "social and administrative rights," as he maps what kinds of distinctions can be drawn between what he terms "irregular" migrants and long-term residents as well as citizens (*Ethics of Immigration*, 129–47). He also explores the morality of regulations of exclusion and inclusion of immigrants who are not refugees.

342. See, e.g., Keller, "Re-thinking Illegal Entry and Re-entry," 65 (arguing that 72,000 federal immigration-related prosecutions yearly, a cost in excess of a billion dollars annually, misdirected federal law enforcement funds and "that such a volume of prosecutions" was ineffective as a deterrent to migrants); Giovanni Matrobuoni and Paola Pinotti, "Legal Status and Criminal Activity of Immigration," Upjohn Institute Working Paper (2014), 14–212 (finding that legalization reduces recidivism in Europe). Another effort is to identify the rights and interests at stake in immigration law to seek policy reform. See Kit Johnson, "Theories of Immigration Law," *Arizona State Law Journal* 46 (2014): 1211.

343. 384 U.S. 436 (1966).

344. 372 U.S. 335 (1963).

345. See Carol Steiker, "Gideon's Problematic Promise," *Daedalus* 143, no. 3 (Summer 2014): 51–61.

346. Some argue for a constitutional right to counsel; see Christopher N. Lasch, "'Crimmigration' and the Right to Counsel at the Border Between Civil and Criminal Proceedings," *Iowa Law Review* 99 (2014): 2131. Statutory initiatives also aim to provide counsel for some migrants. See, e.g., "Accessing Justice II: A Model for Providing Counsel to New York Immigrants in Removal Proceedings," New York Immigrant Representation Study Report, 2012 (providing data that the presence of a lawyer had a dramatic impact on the likelihood of successful outcomes for the migrant). Further, subsets of migrants, such as those with cognitive disabilities, have been accorded counsel as a matter of statutory right, in part under the Americans with Disabilities Act. See *Franco-Gonzalez v. Holder*, 767 F. Supp. 2d 1034 (C.D. Cal. 2010), aff'd. See also *J.E.F.M. v. Holder*, Civ. Compl. No. (W.D. Washington, July 12, 2014) (seeking right to counsel for children as a matter of due process and under the Immigration and Nationality Act's obligation to provide a "reasonable opportunity" of the evidence).

347. In *Zadvydas v. Davis*, 533 U.S. 678 (2001), the Court interpreted the statutory provision as including a presumption of a six-month limit to detention when an alien had entered unlawfully and was removable

but had no country to which to be returned; the Court noted that con-stitutional questions would arise were the statute read to permit unlim-ited detention. See also *Demore v. Kim,* 538 U.S. 510 (2003). The Court concluded that a ninety-day detention, without an option for bail, during removal proceedings, was constitutionally permissible. In 2005, the Court held that the statute at issue in *Zadvydas* could not be interpreted to per-mit the indefinite detention of an excludable alien. *Clark v. Martinez,* 543 U.S. 371 (2005). The circuits have split as to whether the government may indefinitely detain an alien found to pose a danger to the community and who has completed his or her prison sentence and cannot be deported.

348. See Joint Report of Migration and Refugee Services/U.S. Confer-ence of Catholic Bishops and the Center for Migration Studies, "Unlock-ing Human Dignity: A Plan to Transform the U.S. Immigrant Detention System," 2015; César Cuauhtémoc Garcia Hernández, "Immigration De-tention as Punishment," *UCLA Law Review* 61 (2014): 1346; César Cuauh-témoc Garcia Hernández, "Invisible Spaces and Invisible Lives in Immi-gration Detention," *Howard Law Review* 57 (2014): 869.

349. Eagly, "Prosecuting Immigration," 1239–43.

350. Ibid., 1288.

351. *Padilla v. Kentucky,* 130 S. Ct. 1473 (2010).

352. Ewing, Martínez, and Rumbaut, "The Criminalization of Immi-gration," 3.

353. DHS, FY 2013, 15.

354. See Mary Bosworth, *Inside Immigration Detention* (Oxford: Oxford University Press, 2014); Mary Bosworth and Sarah Turnbull, "Immigration Detention, Punishment, and the Criminalization of Migration," in S. Pick-ering and J. Hamm, eds., *The Routledge Handbook of Crime and International Migration* (New York: Routledge, 2014), 382–96; Stephanie J. Silverman, "Internment in the United Kingdom during the Twentieth Century and Its Links to the Evolution of Immigration Detention," *International Journal of Criminology and Sociology* 3 (2014): 168; Alison Mountz, Kate Codding-ton, R. Tina Catania, and Jenna M. Loyd, "Conceptualizing Detention: Mobility, Containment, Bordering, and Exclusion," *Progress in Human Geography* 37 (2012): 522–41; Jane Andrew and Dave Eden, "Offshoring and Outsourcing the 'Unauthorized': The Annual Reports of an Anxious State," *Policy and Society* 30 (2011): 221.

355. Guild, "Criminalisation of Migration," 39, 42, 43. This report, com-missioned by the Commissioner for Human Rights of the EU, recommend-ed that no one be subjected to detention of any kind based only on being nonnational, and that social rights ought not be tied to migrant status.

356. Other analyses look at the impact of immigrant law on federal rules of pleading and government liability standards. See, e.g., Juliet P.

Stumpf, "The Implausible Alien: Iqbal and the Influence of Immigration Law," *Lewis and Clark Law Review* 14 (2010): 231; Gregory C. Sisk and Michael Heise, "Muslims and Religious Liberty in the Era of 9/11: Empirical Evidence from the Federal Courts," *Iowa Law Review* 98 (2012): 231.

357. *United States v. Cotterman*, 709 F.3d 952 (9th Cir. 2013 en banc) (quoting *United States v. Ramsey*, 431 U.S. 606, 621 (1977)). *Cotterman* held that invasive searches required some justification; "reasonableness remains the touchstone for a warrantless search. Even at the border, we have rejected an 'anything goes' approach." Ibid., 957 (citation omitted).

358. *United States v. Verdugo-Urquidez*, 494 U.S. 259, 265 (1990)

359. Ibid., 271. Indeed, being in one's home enhances expectations of privacy. See *Florida v. Jardines*, 133 S. Ct. 1409 (2013).

360. *Verdugo-Urquidez*, 449 U.S. at 265. Further, Justice Kennedy's concurrence, providing the fifth vote, did not focus on that rationale but stressed the pragmatic problems with requiring warrants outside the United States. Ibid., 278 (Kennedy, J., concurring).

361. A plurality in *INS v. Lopez-Mendoza*, 468 U.S. 1032, 1050–51 (1984), concluded that "egregious violations of the Fourth Amendment" could require exclusion of evidence in civil removal/deportation proceedings. The dissenting justices argued that the Fourth Amendment ought to apply generally (Brennan, White, Marshall, & Stevens, JJ., dissenting). See also *Oliva-Ramos v. Attorney General*, 694 F.3d 259 (3d Cir. 2012).

362. The Supreme Court upheld a border patrol relying on "apparent Mexican ancestry" to select some motorists for additional inspections. See *United States v. Martinez-Fuertes*, 428 U.S. 543 (1976). The parameters of constitutional protections are not settled, and the Fourth Amendment may continue to provide some protections, as exemplified by the reference to it in *Arizona v. United States*, 132 S. Ct. at 2509. See also *Melendres v. Arpaio*, 695 F.3d 990 (9th Cir. 2012) (granting an injunction prohibiting a local sheriff from detaining individuals based solely on suspicion of "unlawful" presence).

363. See, e.g., Alfredo Mirande, "Is There a Mexican Exception to the Fourth Amendment?," *Florida Law Review* 55 (2003): 365. See also Christopher Slobogin, "The Poverty Exception to the Fourth Amendment," *Florida Law Review* 55 (2003): 391, 401. William Stuntz, in "The Distribution of Fourth Amendment Privacy," *George Washington Law Review* 67 (1999): 1265, argued that class was a central variable, and his remedial proposal was to relax protections of privacy of the more well-to-do.

364. Linda Gordon, *Pitied but Not Entitled: Single Mothers and the History of Welfare, 1890–1935* (New York: Free Press, 1994).

365. Recipients and their lawyers sought to buffer against those intrusions through a variety of means, such as seeking to require "fair hear-

ings" as a predicate to benefit terminations and through ending certain conditions (such as having to seek child support payments from absent parents) on receipt of benefits. See, e.g., *Goldberg v. Kelly,* 397 U.S. 254 (1970).

366. 400 U.S. 309 (1971).

367. *Wyman,* 400 U.S. at 317.

368. Ibid., 318–19. Justice Blackmun wrote the decision; Justice Douglas and Justice Marshall authored separate dissents. The majority discussed that "Mrs. James" had repeatedly failed to "cooperate" and commented on her "evasiveness." 400 US at 322n9.

369. This discussion draws on that provided by Jordan C. Budd, "A Fourth Amendment for the Poor Alone: Subconstitutional Status and the Myth of the Inviolate Home," *Indiana Law Journal* 85, (2010): 355, 375.

370. Ibid., 381–383 (citing the record in *Sanchez v. County of San Diego,* 464 F.3d 916 (9th Cir. 2006)).

371. *Sanchez v. County of San Diego,* 464 F.3d 916 (9th Cir. 2006), and 483 F.3d 965, 968 (denial of reh'g en banc); *S.L. v. Whitburn,* 67 F.3d 1299 (7th Cir. 1995); *Smith v. Los Angeles County Board of Supervisors,* 128 Cal. Rptr. 2d. 700 (Cal. Ct. App. 2002).

372. Budd, "A Fourth Amendment for the Poor," 395. Florida's plan to subject all applicants for federal welfare benefits to "suspicion-less drug testing" was enjoined. See *Lebron v. Wilkins,* 820 F. Supp. 2d 1273 (M.D. Fla. 2011), aff'd sub nom; *Lebron v. Sec'y, Florida Dept. of Children and Families,* 710 F.3d 1202 (11th Cir. 2013). As the Eleventh Circuit explained the doctrine, the government bears the burden of demonstrating the "special need" for drug testing, and permissible groups to be searched are "closely guarded" categories, such as "children entrusted to the public school system's care and tutelage" and "employees engaged in inherently dangerous jobs."

373. *Griffin v. Wisconsin,* 483 U.S. 868 (1987).

374. See *Ligon v. City of New York,* 925 F. Supp. 2d 478 (S.D.N.Y. 2013) (issuing a preliminary injunction on behalf of a class of African American and Latino residents of New York City challenging stops in privately owned buildings in the Bronx); *Floyd v. City of New York,* 283 F.R.D. 153 (S.D.N.Y. 2012) (certifying class of black men challenging NYPD's "stop and frisk" policy); *Ligon v. City of New York,* 736 F.3d 118 (2d Cir. 2013) vacated in part, 743 F.3d 362 (2d Cir. 2014). See also Creating Law Enforcement Accountability and Responsibility (CLEAR) Project, "Mapping Muslims: NYPD Spying and Its Impact on American Muslims," 2013, www.law.cuny.edu.

375. *Vernonia School District 47J v. Acton,* 515 U.S. 646 (1995); *Board of Education v. Earls,* 536 U.S. 822 (2002).

376. *Sanchez v. County of San Diego*, 464 F.3d 916, 941n12 (9th Cir. 2006) (Fisher, J., dissenting).

377. *Hudson v. Palmer*, 468 U.S. 522, 524–26 (1984).

378. *Atwater v. Lago Vista*, 532 U.S. 318 (2011).

379. *Florence v. Board of Chosen Freeholders of the County of Burlington*, 132 S. Ct. 1510, 1514–15 (2012).

380. Ibid., 1522. Justice Kennedy wrote for the Court; Justices Roberts and Alito concurred to underscore the limits of the holding, that it applied to a person who, while arrested for a traffic violation, was also the subject of an outstanding warrant. Justice Breyer, joined by Justices Ginsburg, Sotomayor, and Kagan, dissented. In a few arenas, the Court has constrained Fourth Amendment searches. See, e.g., *Riley v. California*, 134 S. Ct. 2473 (2014) (holding that police may not, without a warrant, search cell phones of those arrested); *Florida v. Jardines*, 133 S. Ct. 1409 (2013) (limiting dogs entering yards without warrants).

381. DHS, FY 2013, 29.

382. Massey, "How Arizona Became Ground Zero,"

383. The Taxis family were the couriers who provided services around Europe in the Renaissance and thereafter and later services to German states. See Codding, *The Universal Postal Union*, 14–15.

384. Ibid., 15.

385. Menon, "The Universal Postal Union," 4.

386. For example, France had land routes, England had sea routes, and Austria and Prussia were in competition with each other until they entered into a union in 1850. Ibid., 13.

387. S. D. Sargent, "International Aspects of Postal Service," *Journal of the Institute of Transport* 26 (1956): 271, 278. The United Kingdom provided its "first ocean contract . . . with Mr. Samuel Cunard in 1839 for the conveyance of the American mails" with a subsidy of 55,000 pounds a year. Ibid.

388. Sargent, "International Aspects," 278. Some contracts specified routes and hours for stops, with "48 hours grace" allowed given the likelihood of monsoons near the Shanghai coast. Ibid.

389. Codding, *The Universal Postal Union*, 19.

390. Ibid., 18.

391. Ibid., 16–18. Six routes, and six prices, existed for sending letters from the United States to Australia. Menon, "The Universal Postal Union," 14.

392. Sargent, "International Aspects," 271. He described the system as a "troublesome business for the sender and a complicated and expensive business for the administration." Ibid.

393. The twenty-two were Austria, Belgium, Denmark, Egypt, France, Germany, Great Britain, Greece, Hungary, Italy, Luxembourg, the Nether-

lands, Norway, Portugal, Romania, Russia, Serbia, Spain, Sweden, Switzerland, Turkey, and the United States. Menon, "The Universal Postal Union," 9.

394. Codding, *The Universal Postal Union*, 25.

395. Sargent, "International Aspects," 272. Variation has since been introduced as the assumption that countries would receive and send in roughly the same amounts did not prove true, and thus regulated fees took variations into account.

396. Ibid. Every three years, each of the countries within the UPU accounted for the costs of mail during four consecutive weeks and then calculated payment for transit, Ibid., 278. Article IX specified that members kept all of the revenue collected through postage rates. Under Article X, members paid states providing transit to the final destination a fee based on the total weight of mail sent to or through that country. Berne UPU Treaty, Art. IX, X.

397. Berne UPU Treaty, Art. X.

398. Leonard Woolf, *International Government: Two Reports by L. S. Woolf prepared for the Fabian Research Department, together with a Project by a Fabian Committee for a Supernational Authority That Will Prevent War*, in Part II at 127–128 (1916).

399. David Vincent, "The Progress of Literacy," *Victorian Studies* 45 (2003): 405, 406.

400. Woolf, *International Government*, 128–129.

401. Vincent, "The Progress of Literacy," 406.

402. Article Fifteen established the international bureau. Article Sixteen set up a system of arbitration to govern any disputes over the treaty between members. Berne UPU Treaty, Art. XV, XVI.

403. Berne UPU Treaty, Art. XVIII.

404. Vincent, "The Progress of Literacy," 420.

405. Woolf, *International Government*, 125.

406. Narratives of the organization's origins identify "founding fathers" from the United States, Germany, Austria, and Prussia—and include the German economist J. von Herrfeldt, who in 1841 advocated for international, organization and Montgomery Blair, Postmaster General of the United States during the Civil War. Codding, *The Universal Postal Union*, 18–20; see also Montgomery Blair, "Report of the Postmaster-General of the United States," H.R. Doc. No. 1, pt. 4 (1862): 165–68.

407. Vincent, "The Progress of Literacy," 406 (quoting the Union Postale, 1875).

408. Universal Postal Union, "Letter Post Manual," A.5, 2013, www.upu.int.

409. Individuals do not have rights under the treaty, and one of its rules is that savings are not to be "passed on to the individual user." Codding, *The Universal Postal Union*, 78.

410. A domestic question in the United States is which part of government has authority to work with the UPU. In 1792, Congress gave the Postmaster General autonomy in "mak[ing] arrangements with the postmasters in any foreign country for the reciprocal receipt and delivery of letters and packets, through the post office" without the approval of the Senate. Act of Feb. 20, 1792, ch. 7 § 26, 1 Stat. 232, 239. Some scholars rely on this provision to identify postal treaties as one of the "limited circumstances" in which the President can enter into a "treaty" without the approval of the Senate. Oona A. Hathaway, "Presidential Power over International Law: Restoring the Balance," *Yale Law Journal* 119 (2009): 140, 171–72; see also Oona A. Hathaway, "Treaties' End: The Past, Present, and Future of International Lawmaking in the United States," *Yale Law Journal* 117 (2008): 1236, 1267–68, 1289 (discussing postal agreements as one of the early and enduring examples of international law made through congressional-executive agreements as opposed to treaties). In 1998, authority over the negotiation of international postal conventions was transferred to the Secretary of State, who represents the United States at meetings of the UPU. See Omnibus Consolidated and Emergency Supplemental Appropriations Act, Pub. L. No. 105-277, 112 Stat. 2681 (1998) (codified as amended at 39 U.S.C. § 407 (2012)); Department of State, U.S. Strategic Plan for the UPU from 2009 to 2012, 2008, www.state.gov.

411. See Benjamin Akzin, "Membership in the Universal Postal Union," *American Journal of International Law* 27 (1933): 649, 657–58. By 1878, some colonies were grouped together and given one vote for the set. Ibid., 665–73.

412. Codding, *The Universal Postal Union*, 84. After 1966, the requirement of two-thirds approval was extended only to non-UN members seeking to join the UPU. See Lyall, *International Communications*, 268–69.

413. An example of a country-to-country barrier was Israel's to permit delivery to Palestine rather than routing through Jordan. See David E. Miller, "Palestinian Authority Threatens to Block International Mail," April 21, 2011, www.jpost.com.

414. Initially, East Germany, North Korea, and North Vietnam, all under communist regimes, were denied membership in the UN and the specialized agencies of the UN, including the UPU. See Joungwon Alexander Kim and Carolyn Campbell Kim, "The Divided Nations in the International System," *World Politics* 25 (1973): 479, 479. Thereafter, and often concurrent with joining the UN, these states became members. East Germany joined in 1973. See "The Universal Postal Union," *Yearbook of the United Nations* (New York: United Nations, 1976), 951. North Korea became a member in 1974; see James E. Hoare, *Historical Dictionary of the Democratic People's Republic of Korea* (Lanham, MD: Scarecrow Press, 2012), 92. North

Vietnam joined the Union as the Socialist Republic of Vietnam in 1976 after the conclusion of the Vietnam War and the unification of the country. See Konrad G. Bühler, *State Secession and Membership in International Organizations: Legal Theories versus Political Pragmatism* (The Hague: Kluwer Law International, 2001), 89–90.

415. Universal Postal Union, "Doha Postal Strategy 2013–2016: The Global Roadmap for Postal Services" (Berne: International Bureau of the Postal Union, 2012), 14, www.upu.int.

416. Codding, *The Universal Postal Union*, 40.

417. Vincent, "The Progress of Literacy," 425 (also noting that the pictures served as advertisements of the idea of travel "for pleasure").

418. Codding, *The Universal Postal Union*, 60.

419. Sargent, "International Aspects," 272, 281. Air transport was abandoned for a time during World War II.

420. Ibid., 275; see also Codding, *The Universal Postal Union*, 218–27.

421. Codding, *The Universal Postal Union*, 194.

422. European Convention for the Protection of Human Rights and Fundamental Freedoms, Art. 8(1), Nov. 4, 1950, 213 U.N.T.S. 222, 230.

423. International Covenant on Civil and Political Rights, Art. 17, Dec. 16, 1966, S. Exec. Doc. E, 95-2, 999 U.N.T.S. 171, 177. A parallel can be found in Article 16 of the Convention on the Rights of the Child, September 2, 1990, 1577 U.N.T.S. 3, 49 ("No child shall be subjected to arbitrary or unlawful interference with his or her privacy, family, or correspondence. . . .")

424. *Cotlet v. Romania*, App. No. 38565/97, 2003 Eur. Ct. H.R., http://hudoc.echr.coe.int (authoritative decision in French); see also Registrar's Press Release, http://hudoc.echr.coe.int ("the Court found that the authorities had not discharged their positive obligation to supply the applicant with writing materials for his correspondence with the Court").

425. *Narinen v. Finland*, App. No. 45027/98, 2004 Eur. Ct. H.R., http://hudoc.echr.coe.int; *Klass v. Germany*, App. No. 5029/71, 1978 Eur. Ct. H.R., http://hudoc.echr.coe.int.

426. Its plenary meeting can provide revisions to postal conventions, applying to all members, sometimes before they have acceded to the revisions. Alvarez, *International Organizations*, 336. Members need to propose reservations to the plenary meetings, and this system permits, "at least in theory," that the UPU plenary body decides whether reservations are compatible with the treaty's purpose. Ibid.

427. Universal Postal Union, "Doha Postal Strategy 2013–2016," 5.

428. Ibid., 43.

429. Ibid., 20, 39. Thus "special support" from the UPU to "developing countries" was needed. See Farah Abdallah and Yuliya Shakurova, "Mea-

suring Postal E-Services Development: A Global Perspective," Executive Summary, Universal Postal Union, 2012; Universal Postal Union, "ICTs, New Services and Transformation of the Post," 2010.

430. Richard Hooper, Dame Deirdre Hutton, and Ian R. Smith, "Modernise or Decline: Policies to Improve the Universal Postal Service in the UK," 2008, 6, www.gov.uk. The Labour government proposed privatization in 2009 but withdrew in light of widespread opposition and the apparent lack of a credible bidder. See Patrick Wintour and Tim Webb, "Peter Mandelson Abandons Plan for Part Privatisation of Royal Mail," July 1, 2009, www.guardian.co.uk. Until 2011, Parliament had by statute prohibited transfer of government shares to any private entity.

431. Royal Mail Holdings was the umbrella for four wholly owned subsidiaries: Royal Mail (letters), Parcelforce Worldwide (parcels), Post Office Ltd. (counters), and General Logistics Systems (an international logistics company). See Postal Services Act 2000, c.26 part 65–67, 2000, www.legislation.gov.uk (this act was amended but not in the sections cited; it was last amended in 2011 by the act cited next); Postal Services Act 2011, c.5, § 17–22, www.legislation.gov.uk. This act was also amended but not in the sections cited in 2012.

432. Brian Groom, "UK's Royal Mail Set to Be Privatized in 2013," March 26, 2012, http://www.cnbc.com/id/46852987. Under the 2011 legislation, the government retained the discretion to keep its shares, to sell them at a pace it desired, and to sell shares to employees as well as private individuals and entities. Moreover, the act mandated that, in the event that the government's shareholding drops to zero, at least 10 percent of the company's shares must be held by Royal Mail employees under an "employee share scheme." Postal Services Act 2011, § 3.

433. Postal Services Act 2011, § 29–43. The 2011 act vested regulatory and rule-making authority with the Office of Communications (OFCOM), an independent regulator and competition authority for all UK communications industries. The 2000 Postal Services Act had created a licensing regime, which required private postal operators to apply to the government for a limited number of licenses. See Postal Services Act 2000. The 2011 legislation substituted this licensing regime with general authorization for private companies to provide private postal services, subject to OFCOM's regulatory framework. Postal Services Act 2011, § 28. The initial regulations promulgated by OFCOM were similar in substance to the conditions that were previously required for the granting of a license and include, among others, conditions relating to the timeliness of delivery, the integrity of mail, and the assumption of liability. See OFCOM, "Review of Regulatory Conditions: Postal Regulation," December 13, 2011, http://stakeholders.ofcom.org.uk. Under the new law, which came into effect in

October 2011, any private company may provide postal services in compliance with OFCOM regulations, and OFCOM must designate at least one provider as a Universal Service Provider (USP). Ibid., § 35. The Royal Mail was the only company to have received USP designation, but OFCOM retained the discretion to designate other USPs, which were subject to considerably greater regulation than other providers with respect to pricing and geographic access. Ibid., §§ 36–39. In return, the government was to assess periodically the "fairness" of these heightened obligations, and subsidize the USP if compliance with the relevant regulations placed an unfair burden upon them. Ibid., 44–46.

434. Roy Mayall, "If You Don't Like the 60p Stamp, Wait till You See Royal Mail Privatisation," March 28, 2012, http://www.theguardian.com.

435. See Lois Craig, *A Federal Presence: Architecture, Politics, and Symbols in U.S. Government Building* (Cambridge, MA: MIT Press, 1984).

436. David Henkin, *The Postal Age: The Emergence of Modern Communication in Nineteenth-Century America* (Chicago: University of Chicago Press, 2006), 170.

437. Summerfield detailed that before the 1860s, "special delivery" was part of the "luxury services," provided by laws authorizing local postmasters to hire individuals paid on a fee-for-service basis. Arthur E. Summerfield, *U.S. Mails: The Story of the United States Postal Service* (New York: Holt, Rinehart, and Winston, 1960), 76. In the 1860s, "free city carrier services" were provided in sixty-five cities, and by the end of the 1950s, almost 150,000 carriers, costing some $750 million in salaries, provided such services. Ibid., 77.

438. "The Ambassador of Uncle Sam to the American home" is the phrase that Congressman Clyde Kelly attributed to Postmaster General Hays. Clyde Kelly, *United States Postal Policy* (New York: D. Appleton, 1931), 109. In 2013, Canada announced a plan that would, over five years, end home delivery of mail in cities. See Canadian Post, "Five-Point Action Plan: Ready for the Future," December 2013.

439. Richard R. John, "History of Universal Service and the Postal Monopoly," George Mason University School of Public Policy, Appendix D (December 2008), 46–48, www.journalism.columbia.edu; see also Postal Accountability and Enhancement Act of 2006, Pub. L. No. 109-435, 120 Stat. 3198.

440. While the 1970 act sought to have the Postal Service cover its own costs, the act limited the options for new markets and imposed obligations both to workers and to individualized, universal delivery, limiting potential profitability. See generally Sharon M. Oster, "The Postal Service as a Public Enterprise," in J. Gregory Sidak, ed., *Governing the Postal Service* (Washington, DC: American Enterprise Institute, 1994). In 2013, the

Postal Service requested unsuccessfully that it be permitted to cut back to five-day-a-week delivery and that it be permitted to offer new services, such as transporting beer and wine. See Rob Nixon, "Trying to Stem Losses, Post Office Seeks to End Saturday Letter Delivery," February 6, 2013, www.nytimes.com. See also Ron Nixon, "Postal Service Reports Loss of $15 Billion," *New York Times*, November 15, 2012.

441. General Accountability Office, "U.S. Postal Service: Action Needed to Address Unfunded Benefit Liabilities," Statement of Frank Todisco, Chief Actuary Applied Research and Methods, Before the Subcomm. on Federal Workforce, U.S. Postal Service and the Census of the H. Comm. on Oversight and Government Reforms, 113th Cong. (GAO-14-398T 2014), http://www.gao.gov/assets/670/661637.pdf. See also Nixon, "Postal Service Reports Loss." Included was the expense of more than $11 billion to be paid into "its future retiree health benefits fund." Further, the volume of mail declined by 5 percent, down from 168.3 billion pieces to 159.9 billion pieces, and operating revenues likewise declined slightly, down from $65.7 billion to $65.2 billion.

442. *United States Postal Serv. v. Flamingo Indus. (USA), Ltd.*, 540 U.S. 736, 746 (2004).

443. Nye Stevens, Cong. Research Serv., RL31069, "Postal Service Financial Problems and Stakeholder Proposals," 2002, i, 11. Private telecommunications companies played some role in preventing the postal service from entering the electronic mail service market. See Ryan N. Ellis, "The Premature Death of Electronic Mail: The United States Postal Service E-Com Program, 1978–1985," *International Journal of Communications* 7 (2013): 7.

444. "Restoring the Financial Stability of the U.S. Postal Service: What Needs to Be Done?," *Hearing Before the Subcomm. Fed. Workforce, Postal Service, and the District of Columbia*, 111th Cong. (March 25, 2009) (testimony of Dale Goff, Pres., Nat'l Ass'n of Postmasters of the U.S.), www.gpo.gov.

445. Kevin R. Kosar, Cong. Research Serv., R41950, The U.S. Postal Service: Common Questions about Post Office Closures (2012), 4; Robin Pogrebin, "Post Office Buildings with Character, and Maybe a Sale Price," *NewYork Times*, March 8, 2013, A1.

446. Mark Solomon, "USPS's air contract brought FedEx $1.6 billion in fiscal 2012, internal documents show, see www.dcvelocity.com. (Feb. 15, 2013). See also U.S. Postal Service, 2012 Form 10-K, 3, http://about.usps.com; Federal Express, 2012 Form 10-K, 2013, https://about.usps.com.

447. Universal Postal Union, "Development of Postal Services in 2011," 2012, 2, http://www.upu.int.

448. Ibid., 14. Global revenue from postal services was 197 billion SDR. Ibid., 9 (SDR stands for Special Drawing Rights, an international reserve asset created by the International Monetary Fund in 1996 and pegged to

the value of the U.S. dollar, yen, euro, and pound sterling). See International Monetary Fund, "Special Drawing Rights (SDRs)," March 25, 2014, www.imf.org.

449. Universal Postal Union, "Development of Postal Services in 2011," 2. The UPU reported that 96.9 percent of people living in industrialized countries have home delivery, 3.1 percent collect mail from a postal establishment, and 0 percent lack postal services. Ibid., 2. In Africa, 21.1 percent of the population have home delivery, 49.2 percent have to travel to a postal establishment, and 29.7 percent lack postal services altogether. Variation in staffing levels was also evident. In Africa, there was one postal worker for every 14,786 people—compared with 403 people in industrialized countries. Ibid., 5. As for volume, 2.3 letters were posted per year, per person in Africa, while 304.2 letters are posted per person in industrialized countries. Ibid., 15.

450. "Arab countries" appears to include North Africa and the Middle East.

451. Charles Kenny, "What Drives Postal Performance?," in Pierre Guislain, ed., *The Postal Sector in Developing and Transition Countries: Contributions to a Reform Agenda* (Washington, DC: The World Bank Group, 2004), 16, 17. He described the goal as creating a strong postal network on various quality measures but also measured performance in a "narrow way" that did not include "delivery of government and financial services." Ibid., 25.

452. "Introduction," in Guislain, *The Postal Sector in Developing Countries*. If a country had under $1,000 of income per person, then fewer than one letter per year per capita would be delivered, whereas if income was above $5,000, some 100 letters per capita would be delivered.

453. Kenny, "What Drives Postal Performance?," 23. The data had various limitations, and privatization took varied forms, with some more regulated than others. Ibid., 25.

454. Pierre Guislain and Graeme Lee, "Reinventing the Post Office," in Guislain, *The Postal Sector in Developing Countries*, 5.

455. Ibid.

456. These numbers are based in part on U.S. Government Accountability Office Report, *Contract Postal Units: Analysis of Location, Service, and Financial Characteristics*, November 2012, Appendix II, 32–33, GAO-13-41.

457. See The World Bank, "The Role of Postal Networks in Expanding Access to Financial Services: Africa Region (2004–2005)," http://siteresources.worldbank.org (arguing for investments in postal networks to achieve greater coverage for postal financial services in Africa); see also Guislain and Lee, "Reinventing the Post Office," 12–14. A proposal for the use of post offices as banks in the United States has been put forth

by Senator Elizabeth Warren and relates to the White Paper "Providing Non-bank Financial Services for the Underserved," Office of the Inspector General, U.S. Post Office, January 27, 2014, No. RARC-WP-14-007.

458. See Ezra Rosser, "Immigrant Remittances," *Connecticut Law Review* 41 (2008): 1. He cited the figure of "$50 billion" sent home by U.S. Latin immigrants. Ibid., 8. Another commentator calculated that remittances were just under 30 percent of the GDP of Nicaragua in 2004. Jose N. Uribe, "Impacts of Remittances from the United States on Recipient Latin American Economies," *Georgetown Public Policy Review* 11 (2005): 33. On a per person basis, "Latino migrants in the United States sent on average $4,000 per month to relatives." Laura L. Norris, "The Revolving Door of Emigration: The Economic Influences of Remittances in Developing Countries," *Northwestern Journal of International Law and Business* 31 (2011): 479, 481. As Kim Barry explained, those funds were a form of "external citizenship," in which persons can support polities and households from afar. See Kim Barry, "Home and Away: The Construction of Citizenship in an Emigration Context," *NYU Law Review* 81 (2006): 11. Regulation of private provider charges is an area of concern. See Consumer Financial Protection Bureau, "Report on Remittance Transfers," July 20, 2011, http://files.consumerfinance.gov.

459. Kenny, "What Drives Postal Performance?," 32–34.

460. Duncan Campbell-Smith, *Masters of the Post: The Authorized History of the Royal Mail* (London: Allen Lane, 2011), 711, chart 9, provided the real (inflation-adjusted) cost of a standard letter since 1840 and showed that while the cost declined in the 1960s, the costs in the 1840s and 2000 were comparable. Further, he reported that the government made no income on the service. Ibid., 677.

461. Kenny, "What Drives Postal Performance?," 36–37. Kenny argued that overtaxing one set of users reduced their opportunities to have options through competition, yet he also argued that postal services may be a "natural monopoly" and, without regulation, competitors will die off. Ibid., 34–35.

462. Guislain and Lee, "Reinventing the Post Office," 5.

463. Boutheina Guermazi and Isabelle Segni, "Postal Policy and Regulatory Reform in Developing Countries," in Guislain, *The Postal Sector in Developing Countries*, 42.

464. Pierre Guislain, "Conclusion," in Guislain, *The Postal Sector in Developing Countries*, 72.

465. Quoted, by Ronald H. Coase, "The British Post Office and the Messenger Companies," *Journal of Law and Economics* 4 (1961): 12, 63.

466. For further discussion, see Resnik, "Globalizations(s), Privatizations(s)."

467. John, *Network Nation*, 340.

468. I therefore am also skeptical of modeling the problem as a contract between migrants and receiving states. Instead, I suggest building models of transnational state cooperation. Cf. Adam B. Cox and Eric A. Posner, "The Rights of Migrants: An Optimal Contract Framework," *NYU Law Review* 84 (2009): 1403.

469. Schiller, "Migration and Development," 32.

470. See Devesh Kapur, "The Political Impact of International Migration on Sending Countries," Social Science Research Council, 2008, http://essays.ssrc.org.

471. Alternative forms of citizenship are coming into practice. Within less than a decade, "three of the world's largest emigration countries"— India, the Philippines, and Mexico—amended their laws to permit dual citizenship. Anupam Chander, "Homeward Bound," *NYU Law Review* 81 (2006): 60, 69–70. Brazil, Colombia, Costa Rica, and several other countries do so as well. Ibid., 69. Barry, "Home and Away," spoke of how such "external" citizens function, through the flow of funds (remittances) as well as political participation in some polities. While Turkey, Mexico, and Taiwan permitted emigrant citizens to vote only if they returned, the Dominican Republic and the Philippines permitted those abroad to vote in elections. "Home and Away," 51–52. Chander, commenting on that paper, noted that the diaspora is a complex world, in which some individuals seek to remain connected and others avoid such affiliations. Some countries aim to support "bonding" from afar. For example, the Philippines (where "one out of every eleven Filipinos lives abroad") "train[ed] people to be emigrants," complete with "exit lessons and a handbook." Chander, "Homeward Bound," 68. Further, in 2002, Colombia created a congressional seat to represent citizen expatriates, and Mexico organized an advisory council through elections by expatriates to its north. Ibid., 71.

Thus, various proposals advocate multiple, disaggregated, fragmented, and varying degrees of citizenship. See, e.g., Diego Acosta Arcarazo, "Civic Citizenship Reintroduced? The Long-Range Residence Directive as a Postnational Form of Membership," *European Law Journal* 21 (2015): 200–219; Linda Bosniak, *The Citizen and the Alien: Dilemmas in Contemporary Membership* (Princeton, NJ: Princeton University Press, 2006); T. Alexander Aleinikoff, *Semblances of Sovereignty: The Constitution, the State, and American Citizenship* (Cambridge, MA: Harvard University Press, 2002), 147–50 (discussing degrees of relatedness to more than one place, entity, tribe, and nation, and suggesting the term "denizens" to denote the wider range of persons to whom governments may owe particular obligations); T. Alexander Aleinikoff, "Between Principles and Politics: U.S. Citizenship Policy," in T. Alexander Aleinikoff and Douglas Klusmeyer, eds., *From Migrants to Citizens: Membership in a Changing World* (Washington, DC: Carnegie Endowment for International Peace. 2000), 119, 162–68; Peter J. Spiro, "Book Review, *The Impossibility of Citizenship Semblances of Sovereignty: The Constitution, the State, and American Citizenship,* by T. Alexander Aleinikoff," *Michigan Law Review* 101 (2003): 1492; Peter J. Spiro, "Political Rights and Dual Nationality," in David A. Martin and Kay Hailbronner, eds., *Rights and Duties of Dual Nationals* (The Hague: Kluwer Law International, 2003), 135.

472. The IOM describes itself as the only organization formed by member states that is dedicated to migration. In 1951, it consisted of sixteen states and was called the Provisional Intergovermental Committee for the Movement of Migrants from Europe (PICMME). As the time and name suggest, the focus was on assisting Western Europeans displaced by World War II. In 1952, the organization was renamed the International Committee for European Migration (ICEM), and then, in 1980, the Intergovernmental Committee for Migration (ICM) until 1989 when, with 67 state members, it became the International Organization for Migration. See Jerome Elie, "The Historical Roots of Cooperation between the UN High Commissioner for Refugees and the Internal Organization for Migration," *Global Governance* 16 (2010): 345. The IOM grew from 1998 to 2010 from 67 to 125 state members, and its budget increased from about US$242 million to more than US$750 million—a very small sum given the scope of the issues. See Christiane Kaptsch and Philip Martin, "Low-Skilled Labour Migration," in Betts, *Global Migration Governance,* 34, 42–43.

In 2012, the IOM had 149 member states, with additional states holding observer status. See www.iom.int. Located in Geneva, as of 2010 the IOM employed some 7,000 people in some 420 locations around the world. See Klaas Dykmann, Sofie Havn Poulsen, and Lise Anderson, "The International Organization for Migration," in Betts, *Global Migration Governance,* 6–27. This essay was concerned about the lack of transnational migration governance, in that no transnational legal regime—no treaty like the Refugee Convention—governed other forms of migration. Further, the IOM has limited institutional structures and resources—relying in part on working with the UNHCR. Ibid., 16–17. More than 95 percent of the funds came from contributions, as dues for state members were small. Further, the essay criticized the IOM charter as self-consciously not "normative." Ibid., 31 (quoting IOM staff). Whether the IOM could interpret its mandate more broadly is a possibility, given that "migrant" remains undefined. See Richard Perruchoud, "Persons Falling under the Mandate of the International Organization for Migration (IOM) and to Whom the Organization May Provide Migration Services," *International Journal of Refugee Law* 4 (1992): 205, 208.

473. See Geiger and Pécoud, "The Politics of International Migration Management," 2–3.

474. Marianne Ducasse-Rogier, *The International Organization for Migration, 1951–2001* (New York: International Organization for Migration, 2001).

475. See IOM, "International Dialogue on Migration: Infosheet," www.iom.int, and Irena Omelaniuk, "Global Migration Institutions and Processes," in Brian Opeskin, Richard Perruchoud, and Jillyanne Redpath-Cross, eds., *Foundations of International Migration Law* (Cambridge: Cambridge University Press, 2012), 336, 342. Omelaniuk termed the 2007 resolution a "landmark."

476. See Roos de Ruiter, "The International Organization for Migration: Facilitator or Single Player? A Research Project Investigating the Effectiveness of the International Organization for Migration, Mission Romania, in Counter-trafficking Policy, with Respect to the Accession to the European Union in 2007" (master's thesis, Erasmus University Rotterdam, 2006). See, e.g., the Protocol to Prevent, Suppress and Punish Trafficking in Persons, Especially Women and Children, Supplementing the United Nations Convention against Transnational Organized Crime, November 15, 2000, S. Treaty Doc. No. 108-16, 30 I.L.M 335 (entered into force December 25, 2003), www.unodc.org. See also the Protocol against the Smuggling of Migrants by Land, Sea and Air, entered into force January 24, 2004.

477. See Omelaniuk, "Global Migration Institutions and Processes," 339–40, 356–59.

478. See Vincent Chetail, "The Human Rights of Migrant in General International Law: From Minimum Standards to Fundamental Rights," *Georgetown Immigration Law Journal* 28 (2014): 225; Georgetown University Law Center, International Migration Bill of Rights Initiative, "The International Migrants Bill of Rights," Student Series, Paper 7 (2010): 9–104.

479. See Dykmann, Poulsen, and Anderson, "The International Organization for Migration," 6–27.

480. See, e.g., Ishan Ashutosh and Alison Mountz, "Migration Management for the Benefit of Whom? Interrogating the Work of the International Organization for Migration," *Citizenship Studies* 15 (2011): 21.

481. Franck Düvell, "Irregular Migration," in Betts, *Global Migration Governance*, 78, 91–92.

482. Rutvica Andrijasevic and William Walters, "The International Organization for Migration and the International Government of Borders," *Space and Society* 10 (2010): 977; Human Rights Watch, "The International Organization for Migration (IOM) and Human Rights Protections in the

Field: Current Concerns" (submitted at IOM Governing Council Meeting, 86th Sess., November 18–21, 2003).

483. Efforts by other groups on migration—such as the UN's Global Migration Group—have been termed "ineffective, paralyzed by competition and territorialism." Omelaniuk, "Global Migration Institutions and Processes," 356.

484. See Alexander Betts, "Introduction," in Betts, *Global Migration Governance*, 2.

485. Omelaniuk, "Global Migration Institutions and Processes," 358–59. In 2002, Michael Doyle had recommended the development of international institutional structures; the result was the creation of the Global Commission on International Migration (GCIM), which ran from 2003 to 2005; in 2008, the Global Forum on Migration and Development came into being to hold annual meetings. Betts, "Introduction," 2.

486. Omelaniuk, "Global Migration Institutions and Processes," 363.

487. See International Convention on the Protection of the Rights of All Migrant Workers and Members of their Families, December 18, 1990, 2220 U.N.T.S. 3.

488. One critic described the Federal Communications Commission as having "adopted the cable companies' business plan as the country's goal," permitting "asymmetric access" that does not permit "every American to do business from home." Crawford, *Captive Audience*, 262.

5

CITIZENS AND PERSONS

JAMES BOHMAN

Writing in the period after the two world wars, Arendt called the massive number of refugees "the most symptomatic group in contemporary politics."[1] Displaced or expelled from their states of origin and unwelcome everywhere, such groups were a symptom of a fundamental conflict of the post war era between national sovereignty on the one hand and the rights of individual persons on the other. Their fate was not merely due to the lack the rights of citizens, but also, to use a locution of Hannah Arendt, the lack of the "right to have rights," the legality afforded by having membership in a political community.[2] Arendt argues that this problem cannot be solved by some form of transnational citizenship or even the appeal to national sovereignty, since these solutions merely reveal the same problem at a higher level. In lacking the "right to have rights," as "the only human right," they are deprived of standing as such, even in the community of one's birth. We become aware of the right to have rights, she argues, when millions of people emerge who have lost and could not regain these rights because of the new global situation."[3] What was true then of refugees is now true of migrants, who are clearly among those who lack not only such rights but the standing to have rights in our global situation.

It could be argued that the problem of refugees has to some degree been resolved. Indeed, under the current circumstances of politics, refugees are still with us, but they may not any longer exemplify "the most symptomatic group in contemporary politics."

Even while many conflicts around the enforcement of human rights remain, there are now a variety of functioning human rights institutions, such as regional human rights courts and the International Criminal Court. Not only that, there are now effective international treaties and formal organizations concerned with issues related to refugees and stateless persons, including the Geneva Convention related to the Status of Refugees and the UN High Commissioner for Refugees. Given the expansion of international law since the postwar period, states are no longer the only institutions that can address, however imperfectly, the claims of persecuted persons. However, the persons who are symptomatic of the present era are not so much "stateless" as they are denied access to basic protections usually provided by political membership in a state, in terms of which people can live without fear and domination at home and abroad.

Given pervasive vulnerability that results from current forms of rightlessness, people are not persecuted as much as denied entrance, and if they have entered, they lack the legal status and documents of citizenship necessary to live without fear. To assume that their predicament would simply be made better if they became citizens is to deny a now pervasive fact of modern polities: citizens now live out their lives with many noncitizens in their midst, many of whom are illegally present within the borders of the state and thus have no legal status to protect them. The massive migrations of people due to war, famine, and the lack of opportunity leave migrants in the double bind of being dominated both at home and abroad. As Resnik shows us, the circumstances of politics make it likely that many states have become dominators, practicing what Michael Walzer calls "the oldest form of domination," the domination of noncitizens by citizens. These circumstances of politics raise the question of whether democracies that practice this form of domination are in fact democracies.

While ever-increasing numbers of people live much of their lives far from their places of birth, the potential for domination is hardly new. The Greeks invited metics, who despite being noncitizens were integral to their economic life. The legal status of denizenship has also been widely recognized in Europe and often entailed many enforceable rights, claims, and protections for noncitizens. The revoking of citizenship and nationality of citizens by states has in fact become an international crime. Nonetheless, it is a mistake to say, given the many thousands and perhaps millions of people who cross borders daily, the legality of which in international law should afford them protection and standing. Thus, it is false to say, as Seyla Benhabib argues, that international law has successfully decriminalized the migratory movement of persons from the South to the North. It is equally true that such illegal persons cannot even appeal to any "universal status of personhood," since they have no status at all. As Arendt noted for refugees at the end of World War II, it is only retrospectively in those cases of criminal prosecutions of migrants that they are in fact finally recognized as legal persons.

Given the scope of contemporary migrations, the complaint of domination of noncitizens by citizens has become more prevalent, precisely because of the difficult circumstances under which many migrants live who lack the legal and civil statuses necessary for a secure and free human life. To have statuses, as Hegel remarks, is to be somebody; those who lack such statuses are nobodies, persons whose existence is not even to be counted. Crimes against them such as forced labor are rarely enforced, since to make a complaint would open migrants to deportation. As persons without legal or civil status, such persons are often subjected to coercive labor practices, imprisonment, and other mistreatment that we might consider forms of modern slavery. John Bowe has shown the many ways in which American agribusiness simply takes it for granted that existing labor laws and standards will not apply to illegal aliens. This private form of domination is then reinforced often by employer and by police violence and threats against those who are at risk of deportation for lack of legal status. The threat of criminalization and illegalization worsen the lives of the undocumented who lack protective statuses.[4]

While states are not the only sources of domination, their domination is significant given their role in controlling borders and restricting access to the benefits of citizenship within states. Patterns of internal migration within developing states produce similar kinds of displacement and illegality that have produced a similar rise in the movement of persons toward the cities when persons have lost their entitlements and statuses at home in their community of origin. In India, for example, millions have migrated internally from rural areas to cities, in which they illegally occupy public lands, such as railway rights-of-way or public parks. Partha Chatterjee estimates that currently millions of Indians "live in illegal squatter settlements, make illegal use of water and electricity, and other criminal acts."[5] In doing so, they lose their status as citizens, if they ever had it at all. Thus, both internal and external migrants live without the security afforded by citizenship; states are in fact implicated in the system of domination that has been created by those who wish to protect communities and states from international migration. For those who live within states without status, the very conditions of life are subject to ongoing negotiation in a complex modus vivendi, often punctuated by violence and the threat of imprisonment, physical abuse, expulsion, deportation, and resettlement by political authorities. Because of the internal character of this migration, there is very little that is said internationally about the prominent role of the criminalization and illegalization of internal migrants in many societies.

The illegality of most migrants has become a pervasive fact even in the liberal democracies, whose policies require increasing illegalization and criminalization of immigration. Nonetheless, there are possible alternatives, and Resnik and others have explored in their work the role of the Universal Postal Union as a kind of utopian moment that promises the possibility of the flow of persons across borders, where the liberty of exchange of persons and not only parcels might be achieved. This kind of exchange of persons requires that each and every one of us bears the stamp of universal standing. As universal, such a conception cannot be statist, but rather more naturally leads to a distinctly transnational form of authority over the exchange of persons, allowing for inclusive and universal freedom of movement across borders, without the cost of incurring the current risk of what I call "living without freedom." Such a legally enforceable alternative would necessarily decouple various rights from one's nationality or lack of nationality, and thus opens up universal possibilities. But does the utopian model of the postal service adequately capture current possibilities for ending a growing system of domination built around the criminalization and illegalization of migrants? On my view, this system of domination has been furthered by the "full scale militarization" of borders,[6] the primary purpose of which is to create a bright line between citizens and noncitizens. This line between alien and citizens does not justify the forms of subordination imposed on all noncitizens, as when migrants do not have the legal protections of the Fourth Amendment. When subject to the domination of citizens, it is precisely these rightless persons who are symptomatic of the injustice of current immigration regimes.

Given that states are now committed to enlarging their current systems of domination over migrants, I would like to offer an alternative to the role of the utopian ideal of the universal postal service that Resnik advances. Despite her discussion of globalization and privatization as linked phenomena, privatization and globalization are analytically distinct processes. Since states lead the way in promoting illegalization and privatization, the current circumstances of politics suggest that agreements among states will not necessarily reduce domination nationally or internationally. Given the role of the normative role of the Universal Postal Union as a kind of utopia for the global movement of persons, globalization promotes rather than undermines the universal claims that make the postal union a transnational rather than statist entity. Even so, the Universal Postal Union, which served as a utopian ideal for Westphalian states, is no longer the appropriate model. Under current conditions, the internationalization of many forms of authority hardly seems to place in jeopardy by the redistributive aspects of the postal service, ever reliant on states for implementation. Indeed, much more thorough legal innovations and institutions are necessary if states are no longer to rely on systems for the domination of migrants. Here entities such as the European Union have already established the ideal of freedom of movement of persons and economic goods across Europe. Thus, the most effective models here are based not on sovereign states but on such universal arrangements found in emerging kinds of political units such as the European Union. As larger political orders such as the European Union emerge, shared juridical norms and democratic practices of deliberation will make it more likely that migrants will be able to address the dominating tendencies of current practices. Apart from such innovative ways of organizing universal aspects of political life, we are left with sovereigns who do not distribute their authority in the requisitely democratic way given the increasing scale and interdependence of modern societies. It also seems likely that states organized within these larger regional and transnational institutions will generate legal innovations and institutions to organize the movement of persons. This emphasis on larger political units is one approach to border construction, marked by the shift from a focus on the authority of government to the authority of individuals who live inside the territories of the United States.

Such a transnational approach, it seems to me, is both universal in scope and democratic in form. Despite the sometimes draconian and arbitrary measures taken by states to regulate the movement of peoples, it seems likely that when such policies are put under democratic and legal scrutiny in entities such as the European Union, it should become clear that the regulation of people as we understand it is realized thorough systematic forms of domination of purportedly illegal persons. Furthermore, states have now come to see themselves in different terms. In Canada, for example, citizens have come to see themselves as composed of distinct peoples rather than as a fictive unity defined by "We, the People." Here it seems to me that what is needed are better understandings of diverse democratic forms, in which the democratic ideal is applied to diverse peoples and at all levels, from the local to the national to the international.

Although the exact scope of any of these conceptions is a matter of debate, for my purposes all that it is necessary is the importance of the democratic ideal, since it is able to apply at many different levels, from the local to the national to the transnational. Given the new circumstances of politics, new transnational forms of self-rule are needed. Rousseau thought that a robust democracy could not have more than a few thousand citizens; yet today India has more than a billion people. At the same time, the worldwide demand for equal and effective political rights and emerging innovative forms of democracy make it possible to expand democracy as part of the solution, as it will be in the case of treating migrants justly. The standard way in which domination has been justified historically is that legal regimes permit domination abroad while denying any scope for systematic domination at home. But in the case of migration, the treatment of migrants at home transparently undermines democratic practices.

NOTES

1. Hannah Arendt, *Origins of Totalitarianism* (New York: Harcourt Brace, 1997), 277.

2. Ibid., 302.

3. Ibid., 249.

4. John Bowe, *Nobodies: American Slave Labor and the Dark Side of the Global Economy* (New York: Random House, 2007).

5. Partha Chatterjee, *The Politics of the Governed* (New York: Columbia University Press, 2004), 40.

6. Judith Resnik, chapter 4, this volume, citing Douglas S. Massey, "How Arizona Became Ground Zero in the War on Immigrants," in Carissa Hessick and Jack Chin, eds., *Strange Neighbors: The Role of the States in Immigration Enforcement and Policy* (New York: NYU Press, 2014), 55–56.

6

COMMENTARY ON "BORDERING BY LAW" BY JUDITH RESNIK

JENNIFER L. HOCHSCHILD

Two-thirds of the way through her fascinating chapter, Judith Resnik lays her normative cards on the table:

> Another possibility—at the core of my discussion—is that migration ought not to be seen as wrong in either sense [as a "crime, constituted by the willful failure to respect the sovereignty of a polity," or as a "civil tort of trespass"], even if it can be subjected to regulation based on the concerns for the well-being of migrants and of the receiving community. "Legalization" is typically used in reference to changing the status of those present in the country, but its deeper purchase would be to override the idea that border crossing without permission is illicit.[1]

Resnik is, in short, a proponent of almost open borders and almost complete "amnesty" for unauthorized immigrants, as am I. That puts us in the company of a handful of excellent scholars who take the idea of open borders seriously,[2] a few advocacy groups or websites,[3] and almost no citizens of developed, Western countries. Being in a tiny minority does not make us wrong, of course; at various historical moments, few people thought that the earth traveled around the sun, the earth was round, slavery was unjustifiable, or women were morally and mentally equal to men. But it

209

does tend to put us on the defensive and make us overemphasize state failures and undervalue state accomplishments. That, at any rate, is what I will argue here.

"Bordering by Law" has three major themes. First, the United States is strongly and increasingly criminalizing immigration and stigmatizing immigrants, to the detriment of everyone. Second, the United States is engaging in more and more harmful surveillance of migrants as well as citizens. Third, the history of the Universal Postal Union provides a model for how to overcome nationalist solipsism, as well as a warning that the virtues of public governance are threatened by privatized services. This commentary focuses mostly on the first theme, which also takes up the bulk of Resnik's chapter. I disagree to some extent with her characterization of the trajectory of policies surrounding immigration and immigrants, and I aim to substitute a more complicated and multifaceted characterization. I engage only briefly with her second theme, with which I mostly agree. Her final theme provokes several larger questions, which I explore but do not try to answer. My overall message, perhaps not surprising from a political scientist, is that we need more political analysis to fully understand the United States' ambivalent treatment of migration and migrants.

I. "Legalizing, Illegalizing, and Criminalizing Migration"

Resnik argues that the United States has fallen off from its high point of recognizing noncitizen migrants' civil rights, which came in the 1941 Supreme Court decision of *Hines v. Davidowitz* (312 U.S. 52, 71). She refers to the case at many points in the chapter and devotes several pages to its exposition. *Hines* is indeed inspiring, holding that Pennsylvania's system of registration for migrants who had not declared the intention of becoming American citizens was "a departure from our traditional policy of not treating aliens as a thing apart." *Hines* also held that Congress was the appropriate forum for "protect[ing] the personal liberties of law-abiding aliens" while leaving them "'free from the possibility of inquisitorial practices and police surveillance that might not only affect our international relations but might also generate the very disloyalty which the law was intended to guard against.'"[4] In short, as Resnik puts it, "The U.S. Supreme Court spoke about protecting human liberty in general terms . . . [and] rejected making public stigmatization a facet of the government-alien relationship."[5]

Since 1941, in Resnik's telling, there has been a slow but steady downhill slide in the protection of immigrants' rights and a corresponding increase in the "criminalization of migration."[6] She describes and criticizes the recent hardening of the U.S.-Mexico border, the expansion of locations that count as legal borders and thus permit heightened control of individuals' movement, the rise of state laws hostile to migrants, the Court's retreat from concern about immigrants' rights to the more bloodless assertion of federal preemption in migration law, the use of local law enforcement agencies to oversee and harass migrants, increasing deportation of noncitizen migrants, laws requiring employer sanctions for hiring unauthorized workers, and other ways of stigmatizing and criminalizing immigrants. It is a daunting and depressing litany—and since finishing her chapter, Resnik could now add maltreatment of undocumented children fleeing to the United States from violence in their home countries.

And yet this litany seems to me incomplete—and even misleading in the sense that it leaves out the other side of the picture. One can make a plausible case that the United States is among the most liberal polities with regard to immigration and naturalization, that its policies and practices have improved over the past century, and that our recent history shows substantial efforts to incorporate even undocumented migrants. That case by itself would also be exaggerated—as much in the flattering or optimistic direction as Resnik's case is exaggerated in the critical or pessimistic direction. The crucial question is how and why the United States and its various elements engage in such a contradictory mix of policies and practices that include, permit, stigmatize, and exclude people who make extraordinary efforts to live within our borders.

Birthright Citizenship: Resnik does not discuss this rule, perhaps because it has not changed over the twentieth and twenty-first centuries, but it seems a crucial starting point for any analysis of policies with regard to migration and migrants. The United States is one of only two large, wealthy polities (the other is Canada) to offer straightforward birthright citizenship. Unlike in Canada, birthright citizenship in the United States is constitutionally protected: "All persons born or naturalized in the United States, and subject to the jurisdiction thereof, are citizens of the United States and of the state wherein they reside."[7] Constitutional inertia matters, since other large Western states, including Australia, Ireland, India, New Zealand, and the United Kingdom, have rescinded laws of birthright citizenship in recent decades.[8]

Birthright citizenship is highly consequential for unauthorized immigrants and their families. As of 2012, about 11.3 million unauthorized adult immigrants lived in the United States. About 4.5 million children were born in the United States into families with least one unauthorized immigrant parent.[9] Thus at least 9 million people live in mixed-status families in the United States. Their situations are complex and can be difficult.[10] But the fact of birthright citizenship protects our country from the severe political, economic, social, and cultural problems attendant on having second- and third-generation "foreigners" as in many European states.

More generally, as of 2014, 15.4 million American citizen children have at least one foreign-born parent, some but not all of whom are naturalized citizens.[11] Although too many remain subject to the sorts of harassment that Resnik describes, those children at least have the full legal standing of American citizens. This again contrasts favorably with children in many European countries.[12]

Relatively Open Immigration Laws: Given the vituperation in recent immigration debates and in Donald Trump's 2016 campaign for the Republican presidential nomination, it seems perverse to describe the United States' immigration policies as open in any way. But they are, relative to those of many comparable countries and to our own history for much of the twentieth century. I address that history later; here, I consider some international comparisons. The United States is tied for tenth among thirty-one countries with regard to family reunification policies, according to the well-respected Migrant Integration Policy Index (MIPEX).[13] That is hardly stellar, but it is not disgraceful. Well-off Western states with less favorable family reunification policies include the Netherlands, the United Kingdom, Germany, and France; Canada, Spain, and Sweden have been more generous with regard to family reunion; it remains to be seen if their policies survive the pressures of an annual influx of a million or more desperate would-be refugees into Western Europe from Middle Eastern nations at war.

The United States is also relatively generous in permitting poor and poorly educated people to enter the country legally. There is no complete or fully compelling database that compares immigration policies across nations,[14] but the extensive literature comparing particular subsets of countries usually depicts the United States as among the more open to newcomers from around the world.[15] The most recent and systematic comparison of immigration policies includes eleven major European Union immigration destinations, although not the United States. It shows that nine of the eleven states have selective policies and/or point-based systems that give preferential admission to those with considerable education and professional skills.[16] So do Canada and Japan. The United States' looser criteria for legal entry have the effect of enabling low-skilled and poorly educated individuals to enter the United States with comparative ease.

Exclusion: Birthright citizenship and relatively easy entry for legal migrants, of course, are of little benefit to migrants if they are forced to leave the United States against their will. Resnik is eloquent and persuasive on the subject of the increase in deportations over the past decade; I neither can nor have any desire to provide counterarguments to her critique of the rising number of "removals" during the Obama administration. Some deportations are justified on the grounds that their objects are criminals whose behavior is genuinely dangerous, but the evidence suggests that these are only a small portion of those "removed." The best that can be said, in my view, is that (in the words of an opponent of this policy) "immigration enforcement in the interior has slowed significantly in the last few years. ICE is arresting and removing noticeably fewer illegal aliens from the interior now than was the case five years ago, and even two years ago. Its focus has shifted away from interior enforcement in favor of processing aliens who are apprehended by the Border Patrol."[17]

If this critic is correct, deportations are slowing from their peak of a few years ago; whether that is a genuine trend away from criminalizing migration or a short-term deviation remains to be seen. Nonetheless, given her thesis of increasing criminalization of migrants, it is noteworthy that Resnik does not mention the massive deportations in the mid-1930s of hundreds of thousands (or maybe several million) of Mexicans and Mexican Americans. Some estimates suggest that three-fifths of those "repatriated" were U.S. citizens, and none received due process. It seems to me unlikely that such a massive forced expulsion coordinated by federal, state, and local authorities could take place today; if that conviction is not merely wishful thinking, it suggests some doubts about Resnik's claim that criminalization of migration has done nothing but grow during the last century.

Given her focus on the *Hines* case of 1941 as a high point of legal protection of migrants' rights, it is even more surprising that Resnik gives short shrift to the internment of perhaps 120,000 Japanese and Japanese American citizens very soon thereafter. She notes its occurrence and the fact that three years after *Hines* the Court "infamously" upheld the 1942 military order in *Korematsu v. the United States*. Resnik also observes that like segregation, *Korematsu* "made plain [that] the category of citizen did not provide a safe harbor for all the many persons who fell within that definition."[18] Thus, while the eloquent language in *Hines* indeed warrants strong praise from those seeking to promote immigrants' rights, it was not very effective. As a result, I am not fully persuaded by the claim that the criminalization of immigration and the stigmatization of migrants have increased in the United States since the mid-twentieth century.

Inclusion: The trajectories of policies and practices with regard to inclusion are no more unidirectional than those of exclusion. Resnik's portrayals of the invention of the "illegal alien" during the twentieth century, and of the impact of that new category on individuals and polity alike, are compelling and depressing for those of us who share her values. But once again, she does not discuss the contrasting moves during the same decades to open the United States' borders and citizenship rights to those formerly excluded.

That trajectory begins, of course, with a period of extensive exclusion. Resnik describes the 1924 immigration act as "imposing literacy tests for migrants, numerical restrictions, and limits on Asian immigration. The 1924 quota system was aimed, as a member of Congress commented in 1929, 'principally at two peoples, the Italians and the Jews.'"[19] That seems a surprisingly mild description of a law that prohibited any immigration from all of Pacific and Southern Asia, including Japan, China, Korea, India, and a dozen other countries. The law's quotas cut Italian immigration by 90 percent from its peak in 1890, permitted only 1,100 immigrants annually from all of Africa (not including Egypt), and slowed Arab immigration to a trickle. Even setting aside nationality restrictions, in 1933, President Roosevelt's State Department admitted only 23,000 migrants, one-tenth the number admitted annually just before the Great Depression. The law had its intended impact; the foreign-born population in the United States declined from about 14 million residents in 1930 to under 10 million in 1970—or from almost 15 percent of the population in 1900 to less than 5 percent in 1970.

Bars to citizenship paralleled bars to entry, though they began earlier with the denial of naturalization rights to Chinese in the 1870s. The Supreme Court declared subcontinental Indians to be nonwhite in 1923 (*United States v. Bhagat Singh Thind*), thus stripping citizenship from South Asians. Citizenship mattered economically as well as politically and legally; California and eight other states passed laws restricting landownership among "aliens ineligible for citizenship." For good measure, California added a bar on commercial fishing licenses for aliens ineligible for citizenship in 1945. (The Supreme Court upheld California's property laws in 1923 but overturned its fishing law in 1948 with *Torao Takahashi v. Fish and Game Commission* et al.)

In the second half of the twentieth century, these and further exclusions and restrictions were repealed, while others took their place. Chinese were permitted to immigrate in 1943—but only 105 annually. Refugees were admitted in 1948—with provisions that discriminated against Catholics and Jews. The Immigration and Nationality Act of 1952 eliminated race as a bar to immigration or citizenship—but gave each Asian nation an annual quota of 100. The California Supreme Court finally invalidated the state's alien land laws in the same year. The Hart-Celler Act (1965) ended national origin quotas and increased annual ceilings for immigration to several hundred thousand—but also set quotas on Western Hemispheric immigration for the first time, thus inventing "illegal aliens." The Immigration Reform and Control Act of 1986 provided a route to legalization for unauthorized residents of the United States—but also created employer sanctions for hiring the unauthorized. And so on. Neither Resnik's narrative of constriction and criminalization since the high point of *Hines* nor an equal but opposite narrative of steady liberalization and enlightenment is accurate.

Surveillance and Sanctions: A central feature of Resnik's argument about the increasing criminalization of migration is the stream of laws and policies that oversee, constrain, and sometimes punish migrants because of their actual or presumed status as "illegal aliens." Again, the list is long and the descriptions chilling to those of Resnik's and my moral persuasion: state laws criminalizing undocumented status, "border" inspections many miles from any border, Section 287(g) training of local police, Secure Communities' electronic links to local police, more training of local police through the Nationwide Suspicious Activity Reporting (SAR) Initiative, employer sanctions against hiring unauthorized workers, and on and on. But again, this list is a bit misleading.

To begin with, both the 287(g) program and its successor, Secure Communities, have been shut down. Neither was popular with police or elected officials,[20] and neither was widely adopted. For example, the International Association of Chiefs of Police (IACP) did not explicitly oppose 287(g), but it did publish a report exploring all the ways in which taking on immigration enforcement could inhibit local policing. The report set its tone early on: "At the outset, it is important to note that state, tribal and local police are *not required to enforce federal immigration laws.* The federal government and its agencies are the authorities responsible for enforcement of immigration law." It observed that the IACP would be "greatly concerned" if deportable aliens were brought into local enforcement systems; it pointed out that "many executives do not have the resources to tackle this additional federal issue"; and it acidly concluded that "when local police have waded into immigration enforcement, it has often come with disastrous and expensive consequences."[21] The Major Cities Chiefs Association, from the sixty-four largest police departments in the United States and Canada, issued a similar policy statement. It was based on five key concerns with local police enforcing federal immigration law. These concerns are as follows:

1. It ["local police enforcing immigration law"] undermines the trust and cooperation with immigrant communities which are essential elements of community oriented policing.
2. Local agencies do not possess adequate resources to en-

    force these laws in addition to the added responsibility of
    homeland security.
 3. Immigration laws are very complex and the training re-
    quired to understand them significantly detracts from the
    core mission of local police to create safe communities.
 4. Local police do not possess clear authority to enforce the
    civil aspects of these laws. If given the authority, the fed-
    eral government does not have the capacity to handle the
    volume of immigration violations that currently exist.
 5. The lack of clear authority increases the risk of civil liability
    for local police and government.[22]

These are not government actors eager to criminalize migrants or
migration. And after the Government Accountability Office and
the Department of Homeland Security's Office of the Inspector
General piled on with scathing reports about the implementation
of 287(g), Immigration and Customs Enforcement (ICE) put the
program out of its misery in 2012.

Secure Communities was intended to replace 287(g), on the
grounds that its "screening process is more consistent, efficient
and cost-effective in identifying and removing criminal and other
priority aliens," according to the Department of Homeland Security's 2012 budget request. But it proved no more popular among
law enforcement officers and elected officials. Governor Andrew
Cuomo of New York, Governor Deval Patrick of Massachusetts, and
Governor Pat Quinn of Illinois refused their states' participation;
the California state legislature passed a law limiting the reach of
the Secure Communities program. Large-city mayors also resisted
the program. Officials from ICE notified New York and Massachusetts leaders that the program would nonetheless be activated "in
all remaining jurisdictions" in 2012[23]—but in November 2014, the
secretary of Homeland Security announced that "the Secure Communities program, as we know it, will be discontinued." This sorry
history, too, does not provide strong evidence of increasing criminalization of migrants and migration.

What remains, as Resnik points out, is the federal SAR Initiative. In existence across the nation since 2010, this program
focuses not on immigrants per se but on terrorism-related criminal activity. The American Civil Liberties Union has criticized the

growth of "fusion centers" that collect information on "Muslim civil liberties groups, lobbying organizations, peace activists, hip hop bands, a former congresswoman and even the U.S. Treasury Department"; civil liberties groups filed a lawsuit against the program in 2014.[24] The initiative is murky—even its acronym varies on different websites—and it may warrant deep concern as part of Resnik's attention to increasing surveillance of Americans. But it is not specific to immigrants, so it is better analyzed in terms of governmental monitoring of all residents of the United States than in terms of the criminalization of migration.

A more serious threat to most immigrants than SAR is, after three decades of futility, employer sanctions. The Immigration Reform and Control Act (IRCA) of 1986 not only provided a path to legal permanent residence for almost all undocumented immigrants at the time (close to 3 million) but also included a provision mandating government sanctions against employers hiring unauthorized immigrants. Those provisions were carefully balanced in order to induce both liberal and conservative members of Congress to support the bill; the sponsors' political skill is evidenced by passage of the law.

But the provisions' implementation was not so well balanced. The amnesty program was so successful that conservatives have sworn never to be tricked into such a provision again. The employer sanction program, in contrast, "has proven to be highly unreliable" primarily because, as the nonpartisan Migration Policy Institute put it, passage of the IRCA

> sparked a large market for fraudulent green cards and other fake forms of identification. While the law requires employers to check workers' documents, it also undermines their ability to do so. In an effort to prevent discrimination and facilitate the process for legal workers, IRCA established a long list of documents acceptable for proving work authorization. It also prohibited employers from questioning the authenticity of documents that "appear to be genuine" and seem "to relate to the employee." As a result, even good-faith employers seeking to comply with the law are often fooled by fake documents. And bad-faith employers who may know or suspect the prospective employee is in the United States illegally take advantage of the situation. Such employers go through the motions of

reviewing workers' documents to shield themselves from possible prosecution.[25]

For about a decade the federal government did sanction or fine some employers, as figures 6.1 and 6.2 demonstrate. At the peak of activity, fewer than 10,000 employers were investigated and roughly 1,000 fined—a small fraction of the roughly 5 million American firms counted by the Census Bureau in 1990. These data are out of date, and in any case this sort of information does not convey the anguish and disruption of families and communities attendant on even a few dramatic raids such as those in Swift meat-packing plants in midwestern states in 2006, and a garment factory in New Bedford, Massachusetts, in 2007. But even if newer analyses show a rise in employer sanctions after 2004, the pattern would be a zigzag—up in 1990, down in 2000, arguably up in 2010—rather than a steadily increasing criminalization of migration. So the question of why the United States has such mixed, even contradictory, responses to immigration remains.

The federal government has developed a new technology of surveillance in response to IRCA's employer sanction failure. E-Verify enables employers to check on the immigration status of new employees by seeking to match their identity data on mandatory I-9 forms with information in federal databases. According to the U.S. Citizenship and Immigration Services website, more than 600,000 employers subscribe to the service, and the system has verified that almost 99 percent of the 30 million cases submitted to it are confirmed to be people authorized to work. Roughly a fifth of the "initial system mismatches" are false positives, authorizing the employee to work after an appeal and reanalysis; roughly 1 percent of workers "are not found work authorized." About half of the states, many with small numbers of undocumented migrants, require use of E-Verify by some employers, ranging from all (four states) to only state agencies or contractors. Conversely, California and Illinois—in which about three-tenths of immigrants to the United States live—restrict or prohibit the mandating or use of E-Verify.[26]

E-Verify's eventual reach is hard to predict; given that the Census Bureau reports almost 6 million firms in the United States (other sources list up to 30 million businesses), it has not yet reached a

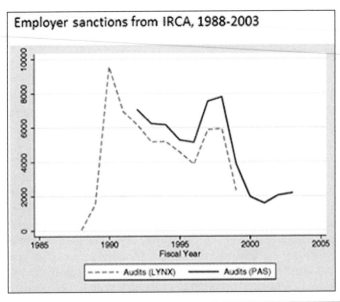

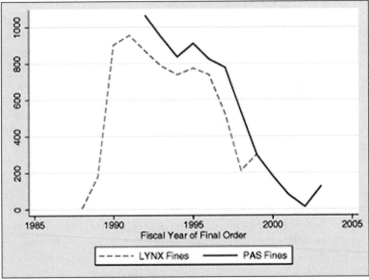

FIGURES 6.1 AND 6.2. EMPLOYER SANCTIONS AND FINES FROM EMPLOYER SANCTIONS, AS A RESULT OF IRCA. SOURCE: PETER BROWNELL, "THE DECLINING ENFORCEMENT OF EMPLOYER SANCTIONS," 2005, HTTP://WWW. MIGRATIONPOLICY.ORG.

critical mass. And because close to half of U.S. employees work for small businesses that are often exempted even in states with E-Verify mandates, it is unlikely ever to cover all employees. Furthermore, political actors ranging from President Obama through the American Civil Liberties Union, some members of Congress in both major parties, Tea Party groups, and business and agricultural interests oppose expansion or mandating of E-Verify as it now stands.

But the system can probably be modified to satisfy some concerns, and unless California and a few other states with large immigrant populations continue to restrict the use of E-Verify, employment of unauthorized immigrants may become more difficult. E-Verify might develop into a powerful and ubiquitous system of workplace surveillance and oversight, with dire consequences for at least some unauthorized immigrants.

"Various and Sometimes Conflicting Agendas Crisscross the States": As Resnik makes clear, living in the United States, or any country, without legal status can be devastating economically, socially, emotionally, and physically, as well as providing a person no right to participate in governance. It is a sobering statement about deprivation in the rest of the world that so many people have striven so hard to place themselves and their families in this unpalatable situation.[27]

Government at various levels can affect the circumstances and prospects of the undocumented. Progressives tend to look to the federal government for protection of rights and mitigation of ills; those of us who imprinted on the 1960s civil rights movement and its successors find it hard to see states and localities as other than impediments to rights and social benefits. And indeed, as Resnik points out, much state action is harmful to migrants or non-Anglo citizens. California's Proposition 187, Arizona's S.B. 1070, and similar state laws authorized punitive—perhaps even hysterical—actions against migrants and people who look like migrants, whereas the federal executive and judicial branches rolled back most of their worst provisions. One can join Resnik in wishing that the Court had relied on migrants' rights rather than federal preemption in rejecting most of S.B. 1070, but in this politically volatile arena, I'll cheerfully take a win regardless of its official justification.

States and localities have taken other punitive or simply mean actions against migrants, people who look like migrants, or unauthorized migrants. Five states copied S.B. 1070. Cities and states have promulgated laws or ordinances to prohibit renting to the undocumented or giving them in-state tuition rates for higher education, to curtail their employment, and to otherwise make their lives even more difficult than they already are.[28] *Mother Jones* magazine counted 164 new laws restricting immigrants or immigration in some way emerging from state legislative sessions in 2010–11, out of a total of 226 immigration-related laws that year.[29]

But as the difference between 226 and 164 implies, states and localities have also passed laws to help migrants and the undocumented. The raw number of laws on either side may be uninformative; some supportive state laws are more important and far-reaching than the often symbolic hostile measures beloved of state legislators. Twenty, including states with a disproportionate share of undocumented immigrants such as California, Florida, Illinois, New York, and Texas, have state DREAM Acts or university system rules that allow undocumented students to qualify for in-state tuition rates. (Four prohibit in-state tuition for the undocumented.) Five offer state financial assistance to university students. Twelve, again including heavily immigrant-receiving states such as California, Colorado, New Mexico, and Illinois (but not Texas or New York), give all immigrants access to driver's licenses. Although federal laws exclude undocumented immigrants from federally funded public health programs such as Medicare or Medicaid, a few states or localities (e.g., Illinois, New York State, San Francisco) cover some or all uninsured children. In about half of the states, pregnant women and children who have been granted deferred action on their immigration status are eligible for publicly supported health care.[30] Some municipalities (Wikipedia identifies thirty-one in the United States; other websites include 100 or more) call themselves sanctuary cities, on the grounds that they take active steps to incorporate the undocumented or prohibit the use of municipal resources to enforce punitive federal immigration laws. They include some of the largest cities or cities with large populations of undocumented migrants—New York, Los Angeles, Chicago, Houston, Washington, DC, San Francisco, San Diego, Minneapolis, and Denver, among others.[31] In short, as

one pair of scholars concludes about "the new immigration federalism," there was "a shifting tide in 2012: pro-integration activists
gain the upper hand."[32]

Researchers have struggled to explain the pattern—or, indeed,
to determine whether there is a pattern—of state and local exclusion and incorporation.[33] Many laws and ordinances in both directions cannot be explained systematically, in that they result from
the successful activity of a more or less randomly located policy
entrepreneur or advocacy group. Idiosyncratic innovation is a
common pattern in state and local policy making, and in that way
immigration law is politics as usual.

Nonetheless, immigration law does have a distinctive feature,
best described as the intersection of demographic change, ideol-
ogy, and partisan incentives. Examining repeated Field Poll surveys, Shaun Bowler and his colleagues found that "racially charged
ballot propositions sponsored by the Republican party during the
1990s in California reversed the trend among Latinos and Anglos
toward identifying as Republican, ceteris paribus, by shifting party
attachments toward the Democratic party."[34] That is, although
Proposition 187 (denying public services to unauthorized immigrants) passed in 1994, as did Proposition 209 (prohibiting affirmative action) in 1996 and Proposition 227 (limiting bilingual
education programs) in 1998, a liberal backlash then ensued. Both
Anglo and Latino voters became more Democratic after 1998.[35]
At the same time, Latino immigrants became naturalized citizens
at higher rates, and more Latino citizens registered and voted.
Republicans have won almost no statewide elections in California since 2000. As Bowler, Nicholson, and Segura conclude, "The
use of these three ballot propositions by the California GOP to
improve their electoral fortunes was unsuccessful in the long run
and, in fact, constituted a significant political error. . . . Our results
raise serious questions about the long-term efficacy of racially divi-
sive strategies for electoral gain."[36]

Although California is unusual in its share of both legal and
unauthorized immigrants, the phenomenon of an anti-anti-
immigrant backlash is not unique to that state. Arizona state
senator Russell Pearce, the sponsor of S.B. 1070, lost in a recall
election in 2011, partly though not only because of his leadership
on that law. He lost to a conservative Republican, but Democrats

interpreted the decision as a victory for "mainstream over extremism."[37] Obviously, not all Republicans fear a liberal or Democratic counterattack, since states and localities continue to pass anti-immigrant laws and ordinances. But it may be reassuring to people who share Resnik's and my values that "partisanship, not Spanish, explain[s] municipal ordinances affecting undocumented immigrants."[38]

DACA and DAPA: Although no legislation has passed Congress since the harsh Enhanced Border Security Act (2002) and the Real ID Act (2005), the federal government has not been totally silent on migration and migrants. Apart from the largely successful legal challenges to S.B. 1070 and its replicas, the most consequential recent actions have been President Obama's two executive orders, Deferred Action for Childhood Arrivals (DACA; 2012) and Deferred Action for Parental Accountability (DAPA; 2014).

DACA provides administrative relief from deportation for three years (originally two years), renewable, for young undocumented adults who meet various criteria. If an applicant is approved, he or she may obtain a work permit and Social Security number and may travel outside the United States; the successful applicant is also, by definition, a low priority for deportation should DACA not be renewed. The successful applicant may be able to get a driver's license in every state and in-state tuition benefits, but not federally funded health benefits.[39] As of March 2015, almost half of the 1.6 million young adults who met the criteria for DACA had applied for deportation relief for two years; among initial applicants, more than 80 percent of recipients had applied for renewal.[40] The Citizenship and Immigration Services agency approves roughly nine-tenths of applications; after hesitating when the executive order was first promulgated, the Migration Policy Institute now describes DACA as "provid[ing] life-altering benefits to so many."[41]

DAPA is the parallel program for undocumented parents of U.S. citizens or lawful permanent residents. It has many of the same eligibility criteria as DACA and will presumably provide similar benefits if implemented. (As of this writing, a court order has suspended implementation; the Supreme Court will rule on its legality in June 2016.). Up to 4 million unauthorized immigrants may be eligible for DAPA, but if DACA is a good indicator, the number of applicants will be considerably lower at least in the first few years.

DACA and DAPA, while infuriating some of Obama's oppo-nents, disappointed a few of his supporters by not reaching far enough.[42] Conversely, proponents worry that the new policies are not secure due to the threat of a negative Supreme Court ruling, hostile legislation, or new executive orders. Presumably if the next president is a Democrat, DACA and DAPA will remain in effect. I make no prediction if the next president is a Republican; much would depend on whether the new presence of several million semilegal college students and adult employees has become a routine feature of the social and economic landscape or provides an attractive political target. The Republicans' political calcula-tions, that is, depend partly on public opinion and partly on other incentives—which opens up several larger questions inspired by "Bordering by Law."

II. SOME LARGER ISSUES

Resnik's thesis of the increasing criminalization of migration and stigmatization of migrants since the nation's high point of *Hines v. Davidowitz* captures a large part of the migration landscape. E-Verify might become an effective surveillance method for the undocumented, or migrants, or people who look like migrants, or even all employees. The militarization of the border in the American Southwest is ludicrous, expensive, and offensive. Tom Tancredo no longer serves in Congress, and "America's Tough-est Sheriff," Joe Arpaio, has been largely defanged—but they will probably be replaced. People can still be stopped along the border and well inland because they look Mexican. Immigrants, especially the undocumented, are often thought to be criminals, and many "are becoming the targets of criminal and antiterrorist policies."[43] "Removal" has reached unprecedented levels.

Nonetheless, other features of the migration landscape are more encouraging to supporters of expanded migration and immi-grants' rights. Birthright citizenship conveys a powerful constitu-tional right almost unique among large states. Massive programs of race-based deportation and internment of American citizens are, in my view, no longer politically possible. A quarter century after *Hines*, would-be migrants from all countries attained the legal right to move to and become citizens of the United States. Most policies for drawing local governments or employers into surveillance and sanctioning have failed and been abandoned, whereas the 1986 amnesty program was a clear success. Advocacy groups are well developed, and in many states and localities with large numbers or proportions of migrants, voters support pro-immigrant measures. MIPEX rates the United States as the best of its thirty-one countries (tied with Canada) on antidiscrimination policy.[44]

In short, the United States' laws, policies, and practices with regard to immigration and migrants are dramatically inconsistent over time, across space, through levels of government, and by types of actors. Some policies and practices contradict others; some states, localities, and federal actions go in opposite directions from others; trend lines for quotas, sanctions, and other policies show sharp inflections, even zigzags. In my view, no single thesis is justified—whether of criminalization and stigmatization or of validation and incorporation. If that summary is correct, it opens three large questions, to which I have no answers.

Public Opinion on Immigration and Immigrants: Resnik does not address the nature or role of public opinion in criminalizing migration and stigmatizing migrants. That is not surprising in a chapter focusing on judicial decisions and laws or regulations. But as a political scientist, I find public opinion to be important politically and normatively. It points to a puzzle: Americans have consistently and strongly opposed increasing immigration since they were first asked in 1965, while levels of immigration have risen steadily since then. Why?

Figure 6.3 shows all national public opinion polls asking if immigration to the United States should be increased, decreased, or kept at the same level. Responses bounce around a little, but they show four things clearly. First, the proportion of Americans who want to keep immigration levels the same has largely remained between 30 and 40 percent since 1965, regardless of the actual rate of increase when the question was asked. That probably reflects ignorance of immigration levels more than a considered judgment. Second, except in a few polls, more Americans want levels of immigration to decrease than to remain the same. In fifteen of the thirty-nine items, furthermore, a majority of respondents said "decrease" despite having four answer options (that proportion is higher if one looks only at respondents who give a substantive answer). Third, over most of the period, considerably fewer than 20 percent want immigration to increase. That is hardly a ringing public endorsement of federal law and actual practice. Finally, the proportion saying "increase" has risen since the mid-1990s; one would need a more complete analysis to determine if that reflects changing views among white and black Americans, or a larger share of survey respondents who are themselves immigrants or the children of immigrants, or both. Immigration is not the only policy in which public opinion is consistently out of line with federal legislation; gun control and free trade are other examples. But the discrepancy does require us to ask why a policy with such clear potential electoral costs persists.[45] Scholars have examined this issue; answers generally revolve around the impact of groups ranging from business and agricultural interests to ethnic and racial advocacy organizations.[46] The answer may also have to do with the fact that Americans are totally inconsistent in their views of immigrants themselves. When asked in surveys, they associate migrants, especially the undocumented, with criminality,[47] higher taxes, and unemployment of American workers. But in response to other queries, "by a margin of 57% to 35%, more say immigrants today strengthen rather than burden the country; by a similar 59% to 35% margin, most believe that the growing number of newcomers strengthens society rather than threatens traditions."[48] Americans oppose unauthorized entry—but in January 2016, 64 percent of registered voters favored "setting up a system for them [illegal immigrants] to become legal residents."[49] Anywhere from 43 percent to 72 percent support the DACA and DAPA executive orders, depending on how the question is worded.[50]

These survey results raise several issues. One is empirical. Citizens' views do not themselves create systems of criminalization and stigmatization, or of validation and incorporation, but they arguably matter to politicians' calculations. How, when, and to what effect? Does public opinion help to explain the zigzag in policies and practices, and the mixed pattern of success and failure? Do members of the public even have views that are clear and consistent enough to call an opinion?[51] Or is public opinion more a consequence than a cause of policy development?

A second issue stemming from the survey results is normative. Most scholars start from the premise that in a democratic state,

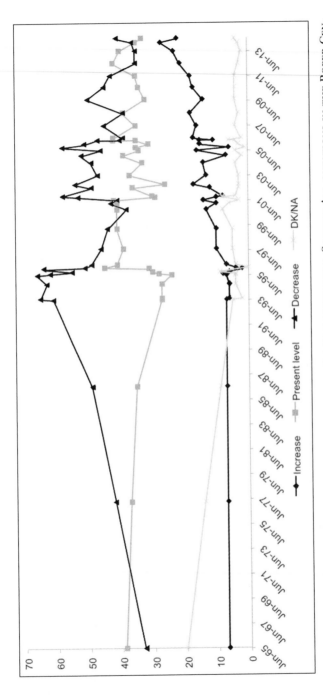

FIGURE 6.3. AMERICAN PUBLIC OPINION ON DESIRABLE LEVELS OF IMMIGRATION. SOURCE: ALL QUESTIONS IN THE ROPER CENTER FOR PUBLIC OPINION'S iPOLL ASKING, "IN YOUR VIEW, SHOULD IMMIGRATION BE KEPT AT ITS PRESENT LEVEL, INCREASED, OR DECREASED?" (OR VERY SIMILAR WORDING). THIRTY ITEMS ARE FROM GALLUP POLLS; SIX ARE FROM CBS NEWS, NEW YORK TIMES, OR CBS NEWS/NEW YORK TIMES POLLS; AND THE REMAINING FIVE ARE FROM OTHER SOURCES. ALMOST ALL ARE TELEPHONE POLLS OF A NATIONAL U.S. ADULT SAMPLE; A FEW ARE OF REGISTERED VOTERS, BUT THE RESPONSES DO NOT DIFFER MATERIALLY. THE MOST RECENT POLLS (INCLUDED IN THE GRAPH BUT NOT INDICATED ON THE x-AXIS) ARE FROM MARCH AND JUNE 2015.

policy ought roughly but genuinely to follow the contours of public opinion, especially when that opinion is consistent over a long period of time. But in this case (and some others)[52] liberal sentiments about democratic control conflict with liberal sentiments about the right to migrate and the rights of migrants. Under what conditions should illiberal public opinion take priority over liberal rights—and if the answer is never, what justifies the claim (which is Resnik's and my view) that outsiders' rights should predominate rather than insiders' preferences? "Bordering by Law" does not explicitly ask such questions, but its rich evidence and argumentation invite them.

Tipping Points: Politicians must balance three demographic phenomena in determining how to respond to public preferences and migrants' needs or rights. First, an increase in hate crimes or hostility to immigrants is more closely associated with a rising share of the disfavored group in the salient population than with the groups absolute numbers or the proportion of the population.[53] Flows matter more politically than stocks, to use the demographers' terms. Second, however, an older research tradition shows that an in-group is especially threatened when the out-group's share of the population is high. As V. O. Key put it, "The hard core of the political South—and the backbone of southern political unity—is made up of those counties and sections of the southern states in which Negroes constitute a substantial proportion of the population. In these areas a real problem of politics, broadly considered, is the maintenance of control by a white minority."[54] Third and finally, if the out-group has a growing set of political resources, such as votes and organizational capacity, a formerly hostile political party may decide at some point that its competitive electoral advantage lies in bringing the out-group into the party rather than fighting to keep its members out of politics. That is the tipping point.

We see all three phenomena at work in the recent politics around Arizona's S.B. 1070, as revealed in one very astute newspaper article.[55] First, flows more than stocks explained the bill's passage:

> The biggest reason of all is that the illegal flow of people across the border is seen as a more acute problem, and a more dangerous

one, in Arizona [compared with the other border states]. In the 1990s, the U.S. government added fences, stadium lights and more agents to the border in Southern California and Texas, forcing a shift in the flow of illegal immigrants that has turned Arizona into the single biggest gateway for people sneaking into the country from Mexico. . . . Arizona's population of illegal immigrants has increased fivefold since 1990, to around 500,000.

Second, high proportions of immigrants can generate a politics of hostility: "California and Texas were forced to deal with illegal immigration decades ago. Both states saw surges in the 1980s because of Mexico's shaky economy and the civil wars that wracked Central America." The result in California was the three propositions in the 1990s—Propositions 187, 209, and 227—widely perceived to be hostile to nonwhites and newcomers. They all passed with strong Anglo support and non-Anglo opposition. The result in Texas has been disproportionately Republican control of the state government since the mid-1990s.

Third, although some states followed Arizona's lead, the new law found little support in border states. The states that had earlier passed hostile propositions or elected hostile candidates had passed the political tipping point by 2010:

California, New Mexico and Texas have long-established, politically powerful Hispanic communities. . . . Many who entered illegally became voters under a 1986 federal law that granted amnesty to 2.7 million people. That political clout is evident today. . . . Los Angeles became the nation's largest city to boycott Arizona over the law, when the City Council voted 13–1 for sanctions that could include canceling $8 million in contracts. The New Mexico Legislature is 44 percent Hispanic, followed by California at 23 percent, Texas at 20 percent and Arizona at 16 percent.

As a result, even a former aide to Texas's Republican governor Rick Perry claimed that "Hispanics and people of Spanish or Hispanic descent have lived among us since the beginning of time. We've all sort of shared this state together and the dream of what it means to be a Texan." Governor Perry himself, a Tea Party conservative, agreed that such a law "would not be the right direction for

Texas," as did California's Republican governor Arnold Schwarzenegger, who said that a law like S.B. 1070 is "not something that we will do here in California."

Obviously, neither the United States as a whole nor many of its governmental units have reached this political tipping point. Perhaps many never will; a lot of Republicans can plausibly calculate that the constituents relevant to their election will continue to be driven by fear of rising numbers or overall high proportions rather than by the judgment that it is time to bring the camel inside the tent. But Resnik's attention to the change over time in treatment of migrants usefully points us to the fascinating analytic question of when, how, and why changing demography generates a changed political destiny, in one or another direction—or perhaps in one, then the opposite, direction.

Political and Normative Lessons from the UPU: My last set of observations builds from Resnik's fable of the Universal Postal Union (UPU). As someone who wrote a long report on the U.S. post office in third grade (which my teacher said was one of the best reports she had ever read!), I was primed to concur that it provides an illuminating comparison to immigration policy. As Resnik says, the creation of an open borders policy and program for the mail from a previously closed and incompatible set of state-specific rules shows that an apparently fixed national and international regime can be changed. One could extend the analogy through parallel analyses of the creation of international monetary and transportation systems, multinational corporations, international drug control and policing programs, the Internet, and other elements of what we glibly call globalization. All of these open international channels provoke two questions.

What political incentives led state leaders to work hard enough to overcome the inevitable psychological, organizational, and legal impediments to opening their borders to mail, money, police, executives, information, or trains and planes? Each case saw opposition, within as well as outside the ruling political party or coalition. As Resnik points out, the "political and bureaucratic systems of Europe and North America" were "initially mistrustful"—after all, some went to war with one another a few years or decades after creating the UPU. They must have had compelling motives to overcome their mistrust and maintain their connections, beyond the fact that it made substantive sense to do so. After all, it makes at least as much sense to permit workers who want jobs to move to countries that have jobs available as it does to send letters across a tense border,[56] but to my knowledge no state has a policy of open borders regardless of its ominously growing dependency ratio. Further attention to the strategies and tactics for establishing and maintaining the UPU would deepen the analogy and make it even more useful.

Finally, Resnik's chapter points us also to the opposite question: How are we to understand and respond to the deep normative differences between the movement of people and the movement of things or ideas? All states seek to protect their borders against "too many" or the "wrong kind" of migrants, and all states at least initially mistrust those they let in even if they want them. It is not clear to me whether weakening state power, for example, by giving noncitizen migrants the same political and social rights as citizens, would in the long run encourage or discourage the free movement of individuals and families to where they think they will best flourish. That is a question to which I hope Resnik next turns her formidable passion, intellect, and knowledge. In the meantime, we can be grateful for what she has already given us to ponder.

NOTES

1. Judith Resnik, chapter 4, this volume.

2. Joseph Carens, *The Ethics of Immigration* (New York: Oxford University Press, 2013); Ayelet Schachar, *The Birthright Lottery: Citizenship and Global Inequality* (Cambridge, MA: Harvard University Press, 2009); Christopher Wellman and Phillip Cole, *Debating the Ethics of Immigration: Is There a Right to Exclude?* (New York: Oxford University Press, 2011).

3. See, for example, "Welcome to Open Borders!," March 16, 2012, http://openborders.info/.

4. These three quotations are from the decision, as quoted by Resnik, chapter 4.

5. Resnik, chapter 4.

6. Resnik, chapter 4.

7. U.S. Const. amend. XIV.

8. According to the Migration Integration Policy Index 2015 (see text in the next section), the United States is eleventh out of thirty-eight Western nations with regard to immigrants' access to nationality. Portugal

and Sweden have the highest scores (86 and 73, respectively); the United States is scored 61; and the lowest-scoring nations are Estonia and Latvia at 18 and 17. "Access to Nationality," www.mipex.eu.

9. Jens Krogstad and Jeffrey Passel, "5 Facts about Illegal Immigration in the U.S." (Washington, DC: Pew Research Center, 2015), www.pewresearch.org; Philip Bump, "How Many American Children Are 'Birthright' Citizens Born to Illegal Immigrants?," August 20, 2015, www.washingtonpost.com. See also Paul Taylor, Mark Hugo Lopez, Jeffrey Passel, and Seth Motel, *Unauthorized Immigrants: Length of Residency, Patterns of Parenthood* (Washington, DC: Pew Hispanic Center, 2011), www.pewhispanic.org.

10. Wendy Zimmermann and Michael Fix, "Immigration and Welfare Reforms in the United States through the Lens of Mixed-Status Families," in Steve Cohen, Beth Humphries, and Ed Mynott, eds., *From Immigration Controls to Welfare Controls* (New York: Routledge, 2014), 59–80.

11. Jie Zong and Jeanne Batalova, "Frequently Requested Statistics on Immigrants and Immigration in the United States," Migration Policy, 2016, www.migrationpolicy.org.

12. Jennifer Hochschild and Colin Brown, "Searching (with Minimal Success) for Links between Immigration and Imprisonment," in Sandra Bucerius and Michael Tonry, eds., *The Oxford Handbook of Ethnicity, Crime, and Immigration* (New York: Oxford University Press, 2014), 663–707.

13. The United States scores 66; the highest-ranking nation is Spain at 90, and the lowest is the United Kingdom at 33. "Family Reunion," www.mipex.eu.

14. One is coming; see Justin Gest, Anna Boucher, Suzanna Challen, Brian Burgoon, Eiko Thielemann, Michel Beine, Patrick McGovern, Mary Crock, Hillel Rapoport, and Michael Hiscox, "Measuring and Comparing Immigration Policies Globally: Challenges and Solutions," *Global Policy* 5 (2014): 261–74.

15. Jennifer Hochschild and John Mollenkopf, eds., *Bringing Outsiders In: Transatlantic Perspectives on Immigrant Political Incorporation* (Ithaca, NY: Cornell University Press, 2009); Christian Joppke, *Selecting by Origin: Ethnic Migration in the Liberal State* (Cambridge, MA: Harvard University Press, 2005).

16. See table 20 in European Parliament, Directorate-General for Internal Policies, "The Integration of Migrants and Its Effects on the Labour Market," 2011, www.europarl.europa.eu.

17. Jessica Vaughan, "Deportation Numbers Unwrapped: Raw Statistics Reveal the Real Story of ICE Enforcement in Decline," 2013, http://cis.org.

18. Resnik, chapter 4.

19. Resnik, chapter 4.

20. Monica Varsanyi, Paul Lewis, Doris Provine, and Scott Decker, "A Multilayered Jurisdictional Patchwork: Immigration Federalism in the United States," *Law and Policy* 34 (2012): 138–58.

21. International Association of Chiefs of Police, "Enforcing Immigration Law: The Role of State, Tribal and Local Law Enforcement," n.d., www.theiacp.org (emphasis in original).

22. Major Cities Chiefs Association, "Immigration Policy," 2013, www.majorcitieschiefs.com.

23. Julia Preston, "Despite Opposition, Immigration Agency to Expand Fingerprint Program," *New York Times*, May 11, 2012.

24. ACLU, "Fusion Center Encourages Improper Investigations of Lobbying Groups and Anti-war Activists," 2009, www.aclu.org; Sari Horwitz, "Government Counterterrorism Program Targeted in Lawsuit by Civil Liberties Groups," *Washington Post*, July 10, 2014.

25. Marc Rosenblum and Lang Hoyt, "The Basics of E-Verify, the U.S. Employer Verification System," July 13, 2011, www.migrationpolicy.org.

26. Verified Person, "I-9 Verification and E-Verify Frequently Asked Questions, 2013, www.verifiedperson.com.

27. According to the Gallup Organization, about 630 million adults around the world would like to migrate to another country. About a quarter—145 million—would like to move to the United States. See Gallup Organization, "OECD Report Profiles the World's 630 Million Potential Migrants," 2012, www.gallup.com.

28. For examples beyond those that Resnik describes, see High & Hazel Darling Law Library, "Arizona and National Immigration Crisis," 2014, http://libguides.law.ucla.edu.

29. Mother Jones State Immigration Law Database, n.d., https://docs.google.com.

30. A patchwork of other laws and policies provides emergency health care, but the system is clearly inadequate. See Michael Gusmano, "Undocumented Immigrants in the United States: U.S. Health Policy and Access to Care," October 3, 2012, www.undocumentedpatients.org.

31. The concept is hopelessly vague; as of September 2014, a website opposing sanctuary cities listed 175 municipalities and three states, some of which contested inclusion on the list (www.ojjpac.org).

32. The first quotation is the title of the book; the second is the title of chapter 5. Pratheepan Gulasekaram and S. Karthick Ramakrishnan, *The New Immigration Federalism* (New York: Cambridge University Press, 2015).

33. Monica Varsanyi, ed., *Taking Local Control: Immigration Policy Activism in U.S. Cities and States* (Stanford, CA: Stanford University Press, 2010); Kyle Walker and Helga Leitner, "The Variegated Landscape of Local Immigration Policies in the United States," *Urban Geography* 32 (2011): 156–78.

34. Shaun Bowler, Stephen Nicholson, and Gary Segura, "Earthquakes and Aftershocks: Race, Direct Democracy, and Partisan Change," *American Journal of Political Science* 50 (2006): 146.

35. Black voters became statistically significantly more Republican in these analyses, perhaps, the authors suggest, because of small and unrepresentative sample sizes in each survey.

36. Bowler, Nicholson, and Segura, "Earthquakes and Aftershocks," 156, 146.

37. Rachel Weiner, "Arizona Recall: Why Russell Pearce Lost," *Washington Post.* November 9, 2011.

38. S. Karthick Ramakrishnan and Tom Wong, "Partisanship, Not Spanish: Explaining Municipal Ordinances Affecting Undocumented Immigrants," in Varsanyi, *Taking Local Control,* 73–96.

39. For a useful FAQ, see National Immigration Law Center, "The Obama Administration's DAPA and Expanded DACA Programs," 2015, www.nilc.org.

40. About 425,000 more young adults are potentially eligible but were not in school or lacked a high school diploma at the time of the study; another 473,000 will be eligible once they reach age fifteen. DACA was expanded to three years in November 2014, but the new rules have not yet been implemented due to unresolved legal challenges.

41. Migration Policy Institute, "MPI: As DACA's Third Anniversary Nears, Vast Majority of Beneficiaries Eligible to Apply for Renewal Have Done So" (Washington, DC: Migration Policy Institute, 2015).

42. E.g., Michael Oleaga, "Immigration Reform News Update: LGBT Organizations 'Deeply Disappointed' with Inaction from Executive Action—What You Need to Know," December 5, 2014, www.latinpost.com.

43. Jessica Simes and Mary Waters, "The Politics of Immigration and Crime," in Bucerius and Tonry, *Oxford Handbook of Ethnicity, Crime and Immigration,* 458; see also other chapters in that volume.

44. Canada is scored at 92, and the United States at 90 (out of a possible 100); Japan and Iceland are at the opposite end of the scale with scores of 22 and 5, respectively (www.mipex.eu).

45. Figure 6.3 also invites an analysis of why Americans, who are mostly descended from either voluntary or involuntary immigrants, are so skeptical of or even hostile to immigration. There are, of course, many answers, the best of which was stated by Stephen Colbert in his congressional testimony: "Because my great grandfather did not travel across four thousand miles of the Atlantic Ocean to see this country overrun by immigrants." See "Stephen Colbert's Congress Routine Fell Flat," *Huffington Post,* September 24, 2010, www.examiner.com. As of this writing (May 2016), Don-

ald Trump is the likely Republican nominee for president; were he to win, he might try to move U.S. immigration policy closer to the preferences of the modal American.

46. For a brief literature review of the "liberal paradox" in the European context, see Hochschild and Brown, "Searching (with Minimal Success) for Links between Immigration and Imprisonment."

47. Simes and Waters, "The Politics of Immigration and Crime."

48. Pew Research Center, "Beyond Red vs. Blue: The Political Typology," 2014, www.people-press.org.

49. The other option was "deporting as many as possible" (Fox News Poll, January 18–21, 2016). The fact that this was a Fox News poll suggests that support for legalization was not exaggerated by any house effect. For similar results, see CBS News/New York Times Poll, January 7–10, 2016; CBS News/New York Times Poll, October 21–25, 2015; Fox News, December 7–9, 2014.

50. 43 percent: Fox News, December 7–9, 2014; 72 percent: Public Religion Research Institute, November 25–30, 2014.

51. John Zaller, *The Nature and Origins of Mass Opinion* (New York: Cambridge University Press, 1992).

52. See Jennifer Hochschild, *The New American Dilemma: Liberal Democracy and School Desegregation* (New Haven, CT: Yale University Press, 1984).

53. Daniel Hopkins, "Politicized Places: Explaining Where and When Immigrants Provoke Local Opposition," *American Political Science Review* 104 (2010): 40–60; Donald Green, Dara Strolovitch, and Janelle Wong, "Defended Neighborhoods, Integration, and Racially-Motivated Crime," *American Journal of Sociology* 104 (1998): 372–403; Walker and Leitner, "Variegated Landscape."

54. V. O. Key, *Southern Politics in State and Nation* (Nashville: University of Tennessee Press, 1984 [1949]).

55. The following quotations are from Elliot Spagat, "Border States Shun Arizona's Immigration Law," U.S. News on NBCNews.com, May 13, 2010.

56. Lant Pritchett, *Let Their People Come: Breaking the Gridlock on Global Labor Mobility* (Washington, DC: Brookings Institution Press, 2006).

PART III

IMMIGRATION AND LEGITIMATE INTERNATIONAL INSTITUTIONS

7

DEMOCRACY, MIGRATION, AND INTERNATIONAL INSTITUTIONS

THOMAS CHRISTIANO

The normative evaluation of rules governing migration is beset with controversy. Some advocate for open borders or nearly open borders, others argue for the permissibility of closed borders, and there are many additional positions between these extremes. My own views tend toward much greater border openness than what we see today, but I want to ask a different question, of a sort that will be familiar to democratic theorists. My question will be not what the right answer to the question of the appropriate level of openness to migrants each society ought to have. I will focus on the questions, who has the legitimate authority to decide how open societies ought to be, and what are the limits on that authority? And I will limit my discussion even further, approaching the subject of migration from a broadly cosmopolitan and democratic angle. I would like to think about the prospects of fairly working out reasonable international rules for migration within the context of a system of state consent that satisfies certain democratic principles.

In this chapter, I will defend two main theses. First, I will argue that there is a source of legitimate authority in migration decisions. But the ultimate source of legitimate authority on these issues lies primarily in international society, which is a society of states that represent their citizens reasonably well and fairly negotiate with one another concerning the terms of migration. Representative states have a share in that legitimate authority, but they must share decision making over the management of migration with other states in international society. Second, though I favor much more extensive openness to migration than currently exists, I will argue that societies do have legitimate interests in shaping and perhaps sometimes constraining the process of migration. Societies may shape and constrain migration in good faith negotiations with other societies. I will explain and argue for these theses within a cosmopolitan framework, which I take for granted here. I will not be able to address the important issues concerning the nature of the conditions societies may impose on migrants as conditions of entrance. This will require a full treatment on its own, though I hope the reflections in this chapter can provide some guidance.

First, I will discuss how the issue of legitimate authority relates to the issue of migration and question some prominent and initially attractive views on migration. Second, I will introduce the idea of international political society and show how it can possess legitimate authority and how it relates to contemporary political societies. Third, I will lay out the basic interests that migrants and receiving political societies have that ground their rights to a say in the process of managing migration. And I will try to show when the interests of migrants are bases for authority-limiting principles and when they are to be taken into account with the other interests societies have. Fourth, I will distinguish the arguments I make from prominent collective self-determination arguments.

Democratic considerations bear on issues of migration in at least four different ways. The first is on the question, who decides who gets to migrate and who doesn't? This first question is about who has the authority to make decisions on these issues. The second question concerns the limits of the authority of the group of persons. What issues are of such a grave and obvious moral significance that no democratic assembly or decision process has complete authority on the issue? Are there questions of migration which are such that a democratic assembly, however constituted, cannot have authority to make certain decisions? The third issue concerns the maintenance of the conditions under which democratic institutions and the legal rights and duties that make them possible can be reasonably stable. Regarding migration, we might think that there are certain migration policies that are inconsistent with the long-run stability and proper functioning of democratic institutions. The fourth issue I have in mind concerns the conditions under which it is possible to make progress toward a more just and more democratic world. In this chapter, I will focus on the first and second questions, though I will make use of answers to the other two in helping to answer the first two questions.

I. Justification, Authority, and Its Limits

The first and the second questions are the fundamental questions about the authority of the political system regulating migration. In particular we may ask, do people have a right to a say over whether borders should be open or not or to some extent, and if so, which people? To address this, we need to distinguish questions of legitimate authority from questions of justification. The answer to the question of legitimate authority on some set of issues determines who has a right to decide the issues, particularly when there is disagreement or conflict of interest on what is the best thing to do. The question of justification is concerned with determining what the best policy is. When we address some political question, we often are primarily concerned with the issue of justification. We try to figure out what the best policy is. But political societies are marked by a great deal of disagreement and conflict of interest, and so irresolvable disagreements about what is justified on some difficult issue are to be expected. In this kind of context, supposing we need some kind of collectively binding decision, we have to figure out how to make such a decision when there is disagreement about it. The function of political authority is to make decisions in the context of disagreement. The function of legitimacy is to be able to make decisions in a morally satisfactory way despite the fact that people disagree with the content of the decision and disagree on which particular decisions are justified. A group of persons can have legitimate authority to decide some issue and then decide it in a way that is not justified but that people nevertheless have duties to go along with. These duties are content-independent in the sense that they are binding on the subjects as a consequence of the source of the duties and not the content (even if the decision is not justified). John Stuart Mill brings out this distinction in his discussion of freedom of trade. Mill argues that the society has legitimate authority to regulate trade among persons within it. He thinks that such regulation would normally be foolish, since he thinks that free trade among persons benefits everyone, but he does think the society has a right to regulate it. This distinguishes the question of justification and the question of legitimate authority.[1]

There are two initial questions of authority, then: (1) Who has the right to create and enforce these duties and under what circumstances? In the case of migration the two distinct elements of this question come out. Who, if anyone, has the right to create and enforce duties on persons who wish to cross a border? Who, if anyone, has the right to stop some people from crossing a border, and who has the right to impose conditions on crossing the border? The second question is: (2) What are the limits of this authority? Can it be that no one can have the right to stop people or impose conditions?

The answer to the first question in some developing parts of international law regarding migration appears to be states have the right to determine who is permitted to cross the border into their territories and who is not so permitted and on what terms.[2] At the same time, limits on the conditions that may be imposed on migrant workers are asserted in the major documents on migrant workers. And this right on the part of the state to determine admissions appears to be the position of a number of contemporary political philosophers as well, though the issue is not always framed as an issue of authority. These philosophers argue, on the basis of principles of collective self-determination, that the community in question has a right to determine who is to become a member and who is not to become a member. Each society has the authority to close its borders to persons. That doesn't mean that it will or even that it is always justified in doing so. But it does have the right to do so. In this sense the state has the authority to do this unilaterally even though it may be acting wrongly. Some who hold these views also think that there are limits to this authority of the state, which limits protect the interests of refugees in escaping life-threatening situations.[3]

In contrast, some have argued that democratic norms do not give receiving societies a right to determine unilaterally who gets admitted. One might think that democratic norms imply that potential migrants ought to have a say in border policies for any number of reasons: the interests of migrants and the sending societies ought to be taken into account in border policy, since their interests are at stake; the potential migrants are coerced by the prohibition from entering the new society; the potential migrants have duties imposed upon them not to enter the new society.[4] To the extent that we think that democratic decision making is a key basis of the legitimacy of authority, the argument seems to imply that societies, whether democratic or not, do not have the authority unilaterally to decide on admissions policies.

This could be thought of as an argument for open borders, but I will argue that a third option ought to be considered. I will lay out a distinct version of this democratic argument, and then I will argue for a kind of international extension of democratic norms through the process of fair negotiation among states that represent their peoples. I will argue that a group of political societies fairly negotiating with one another constitutes a society in which the members of the negotiating societies now have a say in the agreements that are made. We can then ask whether an international society, in which fair negotiation is taking place among representative states, can have the authority to determine whether borders can be closed to some extent and to choose that extent. And I will argue that such a society does give potential migrants a say in the construction of borders.

The answer to the "Who gets to decide?" question can be: the receiving society, no one, or international society.

But there is another aspect to the question of authority. Someone might say that, because of the nature of the right of freedom of movement, no authority can legitimately restrict this freedom except perhaps in superficial ways. The basic idea behind this is that the freedom of movement across borders is such a basic right that it may not be abridged by democratic states or even the fair negotiations among democratic states. In this respect the freedom of movement to cross borders is thought to be a right with the same or a similar status as the rights to freedom of expression, freedom of association, or freedom of conscience in democratic societies. The right involves an *authority-limiting principle*.

This right is distinct from the kinds of rights that come under the authority of democracy to regulate and curtail. Freedom of contract and freedom of property tend to be rights that the society has some authority to regulate in significant part, say, by establishing minimum wage requirements, safe working conditions, protection of unions, and so forth. Also, we usually think that democracies have authority to determine what a reasonable distribution of income and wealth might be for the society, and we think that regulation and tax and transfer are legitimate means to achieve the proper distribution. Democracies can have this authority even when we think there is a right answer as to what ought to be done and there is a significant chance that the democratic society will make the wrong choice. Indeed, citizens within democracies argue for policies and principles on the grounds that these are the right answers to the question of how society ought to be organized. Acting in this way is quite compatible with thinking that it is the democratic assembly as a whole that has legitimate authority to answer these questions. Hence we must distinguish between authority-limiting principles such as freedom of conscience and *authority-compatible principles* such as a particular realization of the rights of property. This distinction is more a matter of degree than I have suggested. Democratic societies are not allowed to do just anything with the private property of citizens, and they have some authority to limit some of the conditions under which the highly protected rights of association and expression are exercised. Nevertheless, though there is a spectrum here, the spectrum has clear extremes. Freedom of movement might be thought of as an authority-limiting principle on the view I am considering here.[5]

Just to be clear, let us observe that once we see the distinction between what one has authority to do and what one is justified in doing, we can see that it is possible that there is no disagreement between Carens's position understood as saying that open borders are justified and the self-determination principle, which says that a society has the authority to exclude others. Collective self-determination is a principle of political authority that gives a right to exclude even though exclusion may not be defensible morally speaking. The only possible limitation here is if the freedom of movement is an authority-limiting principle. In the absence of an authority-limiting principle of freedom of movement, a defender of the right of self-determining societies to exclude could very well think that it would be more just to open borders than not, but that the society has the right to choose this even if it chooses wrongly.

I do not mean to say that Carens's position is merely about justification or that the self-determination views are merely about legitimate authority either. But we can see that once we have made the distinction between authority and justification, it is not clear what the nature of the disagreement is.

II. International Society as a Political Society: Its Authority and Limits

I would like to defend a more complex approach to the question of the authority to limit migration and the limits of this authority. I argue that international society, suitably constituted, has the authority to decide on many questions of migration. In some areas that authority is very tightly constrained, but in other areas of migration, international society has the authority to make decisions with a significant amount of discretion. Some decisions about admissions may be mostly beyond the authority of international society, such as the case of genuine refugees. Here there is simply a duty to admit refugees or to make sure they are admitted somewhere safe and decent, and this is a kind of authority-limiting principle. In the case of migration of high-skilled persons seeking high-paying jobs, the freedom of movement is not an authority-limiting principle. In the case of low-skilled but not desperate people seeking improvements in their economic position, international society has authority to make decisions about the openness of borders, but the authority is more tightly constrained than that which applies to high-skilled persons. This is a kind of intermediate point on the continuous spectrum from authority-limiting principles to principles in which authority has some discretion.

At the same time, the authority is held not by particular societies but by international society. So particular societies do not have a simple right of unilateral veto as the political self-determination theorists would have it; only international society can have that. Particular societies have rights to participate as equals in the process of formulating and negotiating arrangements among societies about borders.

The position I am defending needs some conceptual elaboration and rational motivation. The first point to notice is that international society has legitimate authority over the question of borders and not particular societies. And the idea is that democratic norms can extend to international society by means of application of principles of fair negotiation among representative states. The second point to note is that though decisions are made through negotiation, the participating states do not have a simple veto over proposals for migration.

Let me start to get at both of these ideas through a comparison with another part of international law. In international environmental law, when a society, because of its industrial or other productive activities, sends pollution into another society, the polluting society has a duty to negotiate in good faith with those societies that are harmed by the pollution. The polluting society cannot simply refuse to negotiate or to make an agreement. It must attempt to find a solution to the pollution problem with the other society.[6] This, of course, need not necessarily involve stopping the pollution. There may be other mutually beneficial and fair ways to deal with the problem. For instance, the society can finance some kind of compensation to the other society out of the benefits it receives from the polluting activity. If the polluting activity is highly productive, this could benefit the other society more than merely stopping the activity that produces the pollution. Or the affected society can help in limiting the cost of pollution control. The societies must work something out that is reasonably equitable among them.[7]

I want to say that this requirement is a requirement of legitimacy. A society that permits a great deal of pollution to damage another society and refuses to negotiate in good faith with that other society to the end of producing an agreement that is equitable is engaged in an illegitimate exercise of power over that other society. It is in effect deciding on a distribution of benefits and burdens between itself and that other society without giving that society any kind of voice in the decision. It is unilaterally making decisions for both societies with respect to a set of issues. Negotiation in good faith is a way of giving a say to that other society in a way that is necessary to legitimacy.[8]

This is an instance of international society having legitimate authority where individual societies do not have legitimate authority, though each shares in the legitimate authority of international society, and of course each society also has the authority to carry out the decision of international society. Societies are not permitted to act unilaterally in these contexts when they can act in concert with those affected other societies. And when they do act to negotiate with other societies, they must negotiate fairly, and they must negotiate with a commitment to solve the problem fairly at least by their lights. They may not simply back out of negotiations in the hopes of not having to bear a fair share of the burdens of their activities. Again, such actions would constitute illegitimate exercises of power over the other societies. And I think that such illegitimate exercises of power by societies can be grounds for permissible coercion and sanctioning against the violating society. We can see here the two features I described, namely, the need for decision making by international society and the impermissibility of a simple veto on the part of any particular member. This, of course, implies a significant limitation on the sovereignty of each state.[9]

Now I want to articulate the idea of the authority of international society in the migration case. When two societies are adjacent to or near each other and one society has a large number of very poor people while the other has a demand for workers in positions that are relatively very productive, the potential receiving society has some kind of duty to work something out with the sending society to permit workers to migrate. The potential receiving society has a duty to enter into an agreement fairly negotiated with the potential sending society that enables people to move from the sending society to the receiving society. Here, too, the two features arise with the consequent limitation on sovereignty of each state.

What are the bases of this thesis? The foundation of this thesis is in the conception of the international system that I will argue for here. The conception that I sketch here is meant to give a broadly democratic and cosmopolitan account of legitimate international decision making that remains moored to the state system. The international system might initially be thought to be a system of voluntary association between states, much like a system of contracts and voluntary association within domestic societies. The distinctive feature of this kind of system is that the associative actions of the participants are normally thought to be optional. It is up to the discretion of the parties whether they associate with one another.

In domestic societies, activities of voluntary association are regulated by states that attempt to ensure that certain kinds of morally important aims are pursued such as the maintenance of security, a reasonable distribution of income, the absence of exploitation, and so on. States have authority to regulate and tax and in some cases direct these activities in the society. While states do this, individuals usually pursue their own interests within the framework established by the state. This establishes a kind of moral division of labor between state and individual in the pursuit of morally important aims such as justice, security, and economic prosperity. Individuals pursue their own interests and partial concerns in the activities of voluntary association and contract, while the state makes sure that these pursuits are regulated and taxed in such a way as to produce the common good, justice, and security for the society as a whole.

What I want to say here is that while the international system looks initially like a system of voluntary association and contract (however exploitative), in fact much of the international system is quite different from such a regime. The first thing to observe is that the members of the international system take themselves correctly to be under moral duties to pursue certain morally mandatory aims such as the avoidance of environmental catastrophe, the alleviation of severe global poverty, the protection of persons against large-scale human rights violations, and the creation of a decent system of international trade in addition to the establishment of international peace and security. They are not always very good at pursuing these aims, but they assert them continually in many of the main international documents such as the UN Charter, the UN Millennium Declaration, the basic treaty of the GATT/WTO, the Montreal Protocol for the Protection of the Ozone, and the UN Framework Convention on Climate Change. There are of course many other treaties and conventions announcing the moral necessity of pursuing various aims, but these suffice for the moment.

Societies are bound to pursue those aims in concert. It is hard to see how an international system could be legitimate without making good faith efforts to alleviate severe global poverty, avoid environmental catastrophe, protect people from widespread human rights violations, and assure some kind of international peace and security. These are, I think, minimum requirements for the international system as we know it. The international political system must pursue these aims if it is to show itself to be concerned with the fundamental interests of all persons within that system. No political system of any sort can be legitimate without its realizing in a publicly clear way that it is concerned with the interests of all persons within the system. This does not imply, of course, that the international community must succeed; there is too much uncertainty about these matters to guarantee that.

Second, states correctly acknowledge that the pursuit of these mandatory aims requires the cooperation of states in the form of treaties, agreements, and international institutions. States cannot solve these problems by themselves; cooperation is necessary. Hence, we see efforts to design treaties advancing these mandatory aims. Third, unlike individuals in domestic societies, states cannot leave the pursuit of these mandatory aims up to some higher-level entity like a global state. In international society, states must solve these problems through cooperation with other states. Hence, many of the most important activities of treaty making are in pursuit of mandatory aims. There is no division of labor in the international system analogous to that between individual and state in domestic society. This means that the activity of treaty making, while appearing to be a bit like the activity of contract making, is quite different from the normal activity of contract making in domestic societies. Treaty making often does not display the same optionality as contract making. States are subject to severe criticism for failing to negotiate in good faith on matters of climate change or international trade. They can be subject to sanctions for failing to do their fair share in the pursuit of mandatory aims such as in the case of some international environmental law or nuclear nonproliferation. Hence the mandatory aims establish a requirement for common action in international society that is pursued by means of treaties and agreements.

That common action must be pursued in accordance with broadly democratic norms that give persons a say in the pursuit of common action. For a number of reasons, states do and ought to have latitude in deciding what kinds of treaties to participate in and to what extent. The first reason is grounded in the pursuit of mandatory aims. There is a great deal of uncertainty as to how best to pursue the mandatory aims, and states need to experiment with different ways to do this. This can be by diverse regional associations or even by competing global associations. Second, societies have diverse interests that need to be taken into account when common action is chosen and states are the main mechanisms of accountability of power to persons in the international system. As a consequence, state consent is a way of accommodating the fundamental diversity of interests, disagreement, and fallibility among persons in the international system that is much like the assignment of equal votes to citizens in a democratic society. Hence, state consent is still a basic principle of international law. Of course, for a system of state consent to realize democratic norms, it is essential that the states represent their peoples and that negotiation among states be fair.

I want to comment very briefly here on how the diversity of interests and the reality of disagreement among persons are grounds for a right to a say in determining common international action. The right to a say is guaranteed by the qualified requirement of state consent by representative states to fairly negotiated agreements. The right is established on the grounds that such a right is necessary to realizing in a public way the principle that the international system treats the interests of all persons as equals in the process of collective decision making. It is the analogue in the international system of the right to participate as an equal in collective decision making in domestic societies. They are both necessary guarantees that the society is publicly treating persons as equals in collective decision making in the context of disagreement, diversity of interests, and uncertainty about the best policy.

But the latitude accorded states, strictly speaking, can only encompass reasonable disagreements in how to pursue the aims. States may not just refuse to negotiate or cooperate. The desire to free ride or engage in self-defeating pursuit of a favored coordination point or even irrational rejection (i.e., in opposition to a strong scientific consensus) are not acceptable reasons for refusal to join a treaty that pursues morally mandatory aims. And some kind of pressure from other states is permissible to get states to act in good faith in these contexts. On the other hand, when states refuse to consent to a treaty on reasonable grounds and propose some alternative and feasible form of cooperation, their refusal is permissible.

It is in this sense that the international system presents a distinctive kind of political system. Unlike the state, it is decentralized in terms of enforcement, and its basic legislative powers are founded in the consent of states. But, unlike the usual context of voluntary association, the demand for common action in pursuit of mandatory aims requires all states to negotiate in good faith with other states to form effective agreements and treaties. And it creates a justification for pressure on noncooperating states. Fair agreement making among representative states is what makes such a political system accord with democratic norms and thus confers democratic legitimacy on international law.[10]

Now I want to say that unilateral and unreasonable action by a state in a context in which there is a demand for common action in pursuit of a mandatory aim is a kind of illegitimate exercise of power by the unilateral agent, at least in the case in which the unilateral agent is disrupting the pursuit of common action. The basic reason for this is that when there is a demand for common action, persons, and consequently states as their representatives, have a right to a say in how the common activity is structured. That right is founded in the diversity of interests, pervasive disagreement, and fallibility among persons and the interests persons have in having a say over common action in these circumstances. Unilateral action violates that right by disrupting or disabling the common action, and it seems to disrupt the common action by asserting the interest of the unilateral agent. In this respect, unilateral action when there is a need for common action is very much like a refusal to negotiate in good faith when one society pollutes another. Just as the other society has some right to a say in how the pollution problem is solved, so societies have a right to a say in determining common action, and that right is violated when societies act unilaterally (assuming that this unilateral action is what is disrupting or diminishing the common action). Again, this conclusion has to be qualified by the idea that states may refuse consent if they do so on the basis of reasonable disagreement. Here too we can see the two features that international society has authority over the pursuit of mandatory aims and that states do not have a simple right of veto.

There is thus a significant limitation on the sovereignty of states in this system.

III. International Society and Migration

There are two mandatory aims that are especially relevant to the question of migration. The first is the requirement that refugees are able to relocate; the second is the requirement that severe global poverty be alleviated. Hence, there is a demand for common action regarding migration. I will also argue that each society has morally legitimate interests in having a say over its border policies. I want to say that the bases of the thesis that international society has authority over issues of migration consist in the need for common action established by the mandatory aims. The interests of potential migrants in freedom of movement, the interests of the sending society in development, and the interests in the receiving and sending societies in having their states carry out their core responsibilities regarding the society are the grounds on which the different states must have a say through fair negotiation. Here I will lay out these legitimate interests.

A. The Interests of Migrants

The interests of migrants and the interests of the receiving society vary in urgency and importance. There are interests of such great importance, such as those of political and economic refugees, that they are the basis of essentially authority-limiting principles. Those who seek to escape a society out of a well-founded fear of persecution or a well-founded fear of the most basic human needs not being met must be permitted to enter some society, if not always the one they want to enter.[11] No political system, whether domestic or international, that disables such persons from successfully fleeing life-threatening circumstances is validly exercising its authority.

Here international society has an authority to figure out how to relocate refugees into societies that can afford them a decent mode of living. It cannot merely leave refugees in the life-threatening circumstances they are in, nor can it require them to live in refugee camps that are manifestly inadequate for living a decent life.

Another very highly urgent set of interests are the interests in family reunification.

There are other less urgent interests that are nevertheless very important. These are connected with the desire to escape severe, though not life-threatening, poverty. We have already observed that states and international society see themselves correctly as pursuing the morally mandatory aim of the reduction of severe global poverty. All societies, I have argued, are morally required to cooperate in attempting to reduce severe poverty.

Agreements on migration are ways, by no means the only ones though perhaps currently the most reliable, by which societies can help reduce severe poverty. There are two ways in which this happens. One, a migrant can lift herself out of severe poverty by working in a wealthy society and to some degree lift her family out as well. The wages of low-skilled migrants from sub-Saharan Africa to Europe, from Central America to the United States, and those who migrate from the Caribbean and Mexico to the United States and Canada go up by significant factors of between two and seven. This is a very substantial improvement. Two, low-skilled migration does, in a variety of ways, make some modest contribution to the growth of developing societies. This happens when migrants return to the sending societies with new capital as well as new skills and education. It also happens through remittances that migrants transfer to the sending society.[12] We do not know how much greater the gains would be were migration a lot freer than it now is, but there may well be significantly great gains to be had.[13]

I want to argue that, in light of the difficulties in helping societies emerge from poverty, societies do not have discretion simply to demure in this particular way of reducing poverty. They have a duty to cooperate with others to do this. And this means that they have duties to negotiate in good faith to figure out how to move workers from the poorer societies to the wealthier ones at least as one among a number of different ways of alleviating poverty. This implies that each society has a say in how it organizes the process of migration, but it does not have a simple veto. Only international society has this veto, and particular political societies participate in international society as equals through the process of fair negotiation in good faith.

To be clear, refugees have rights to be relocated in the international system. I do not think that the pressing interests of very poor people in migrating rise to the level of rights. Societies have duties to figure out how to allow very poor people to migrate and must do so, but they retain some discretion regarding the number of such people to be moved.

There are also interests that are not by themselves as pressing as the interests in escaping severe poverty, but they are interests nevertheless. These are the interests of those who want to improve their situations from good to better. They create reasons for all states to allow people to enter in order to improve their economic situation. And they involve reasons of economic efficiency to permit people to move around so that they may put their abilities to the most productive use.

B. The Interests of Societies

I have said that states ought to negotiate with one another to devise reasonable border policies, and the bases that I have mentioned so far are the interests of potential migrants. If these were the only interests at stake, it would be hard to see why there would be any good reason for restricting the movement of people across borders. But I think societies have legitimate interests from a cosmopolitan standpoint to manage and sometimes restrict migration. I will lay these out here.

The basic structure of my argument that societies have legitimate interests in having a say in managing and sometimes limiting migration comes down to the following premises. First, the abilities of states to carry out their core responsibilities in societies are important values in the international system from a cosmopolitan point of view. Second, the abilities to carry out these core responsibilities are potentially threatened by unwise migration policies. Third, we ought to accord respect to a society's judgment about to how best to protect the exercise of these core responsibilities. From these premises I want to defend the thesis that societies have a right to participate in fashioning migration policies in negotiation with other societies in light of their judgments about how best to maintain their abilities to carry out their core responsibilities in a democratically accountable way.

I want to defend a further thesis which asserts that the appropriate balance between the considerations of moral integrity and the morally mandatory aim of alleviating severe global poverty is not a generally defined balance that can be stated in terms of general principles. The comparison of moral weight between these two concerns cannot be made out in a general way. Here, too, there is room for societies to judge by their own lights how to balance these considerations in the formation of their migration policies.

There are interests that the members of receiving states have that may play a legitimate role in determining their negotiations. Any moderately just society has interests in its state being able to continue to perform its core responsibilities. These responsibilities include the maintenance of security and a context in which the basic rights of the citizens are protected. They also include the state's responsibility to ensure justice within the society. By justice I mean the basic rights of citizenship, including rights of free expression, association, conscience, and privacy, as well as the right to participate as equals in politics. I also include rights to due process of law and a fair trial. And I include the concerns for ensuring a basic minimum of services in satisfying basic needs and distributive justice. I also include in this the responsibility to ensure a reasonably stable working and living environment, which includes limiting unemployment and ensuring broad-based economic growth. All these activities are to be carried out in a way that makes the power accountable to people in society. We might call the society's interests in the state carrying out its core responsibilities in a democratically accountable way the *interests in the moral integrity of the political society.*

These core responsibilities are to be carried out within the jurisdiction of the state. Each society also has responsibilities with regard to the international community as well, which include cooperation in pursuit of morally mandatory aims such as international peace and security, basic human rights, the avoidance of environmental disaster, the elimination of severe poverty, and the creation and maintenance of a decent system of international trade. And I want to argue that each state also has the responsibility to contribute to the creation of powerful and accountable international political institutions.

I offer three arguments for why the state's ability to carry out its core responsibilities is a legitimate interest that ought to be protected within the international system despite the fact that the contemporary political society is only an arbitrary assemblage of persons over an arbitrarily defined piece of territory. The arguments are the division of labor argument, the institutionalist argument, and the cosmopolitan argument.

C. The Division of Labor Argument

As I mentioned at the outset of this chapter, I am proceeding on the assumption that the state is the principal mechanism in the modern world that establishes the accountability of power to persons. And it is the principal mechanism by which the activities I described as the core responsibilities of states are carried out. If states' capacities to make power accountable to people and to fulfill their core responsibilities are undermined, there are no other institutional mechanisms in place to do these things, and we cannot expect global institutional mechanisms that perform these functions to arise for a long time.

On the view that I am elaborating here, the world is divided more or less arbitrarily into states. What I mean by this is that there is no fundamental moral reason why the world is divided into states, and there are no fundamental moral reasons why the world is divided into the states it is divided into. The division of the world into the states that exist is mostly a matter of historical accident and convenience. To be sure, shared nationality, language, and history can sometimes facilitate the cohesion of a state, as can shared religion, and sometimes the absence of these can undermine a particular state's capacity to function. But they are not necessary to the cohesion of states, as we see successfully functioning multinational and multilinguistic states.

Yet despite this arbitrariness of origin and boundary, many of the political societies within these initially arbitrary borders have developed highly integrated legal systems with integrated economic and social arrangements. States have arisen to establish justice and protect the basic needs of persons within limited areas. Within those limited areas, states have developed legal systems, civil society, elaborate bureaucratic apparatuses for administering justice, educational systems, systems of redistribution of wealth and income, and systems that make these institutions accountable to those who are subjected to them. These institutions have developed over a number of centuries and have been moderately successful in establishing justice and prosperity for large numbers of people. Though borders arose more or less arbitrarily, they now separate fairly well-defined units and help define the spheres in which those units operate. Without those borders, states would have a hard time operating because of the indefiniteness of their charges. Particular borders do not have any fundamental justification; they are simply the borders within which states can carry out their responsibilities in some reasonably efficient way. But the borders do characterize the units within which the core responsibilities are fulfilled. And states have some interest in protecting the borders to the extent that such protection is necessary for them to carry out their core responsibilities.

From an international perspective, the way to think about this situation is that it is a kind of division of labor in which the world is divided into units that are capable of establishing justice in each unit. What this means is that aside from the states that pursue justice and the common good for their societies, there is no other entity that is presently, and for the medium-term future, capable of carrying out the tasks states carry out. On a cosmopolitan view, justice ultimately must relate all persons in a single framework, but it would be extraordinarily premature to suggest that we should wish away the state as it is currently constituted in order to achieve cosmopolitan justice.

I think we must hope and press for more cosmopolitan political institutions in the long term, within which states will become less powerful federal units. But for the time being this is what we have. And if cosmopolitan political institutions are to arise, they will probably and hopefully arise through the activities of states acting to create them, since that will ensure that the process of creating those institutions will be somewhat accountable to those who will be subject to them.

The division of labor is desirable despite the deplorable fact that many of the units in the division of labor are not functioning properly. Many of the world's political societies have states that do not function well. Many are corrupt, authoritarian states that have arisen partly as a consequence of the imperial activities of European states from the sixteenth to the early twentieth centuries. Many fail to establish much in the way of justice or prosperity for their subjects. But this does not imply that the reasonably successful functioning states that do continue to exist ought not to carry out their core responsibilities in a democratically accountable way. It implies that a significant part of the help that successful societies can give to the less successful for the time being is to help establish better states.

My argument is meant to be grounded in a cosmopolitan idea. The idea is that the division of labor is important from a cosmopolitan point of view, and all persons have some duty to do their part in the section of the division of labor in which they find themselves. This need not be an overriding duty generally, but it does constitute an important consideration in how to organize the society one lives in. And so it makes sense that this is a consideration that needs to be taken into account in deciding who may come into the society and who may not (if, of course, this makes a difference to the capacity of a state to fulfill its core responsibilities).

D. The Institutionalist Argument

The second argument for the interest in the moral integrity of political societies is that many political societies have developed reasonably successful institutions for establishing justice and advancing the common good in a democratically accountable way. This is a difficult and fragile achievement. That they are at least reasonably successful is a reason for wanting to maintain them. Partly they are good in themselves as is suggested by the division of labor argument, and partly they serve as models for the creation of international political institutions. It is as models of good institutions and as sources of experience and learning from institution building that I emphasize here. There are two aspects of this success that are worth bringing out. First, the successful states have managed to bring about a great deal of economic growth and in a reasonably egalitarian way. They have succeeded in realizing a great deal of moral, religious, and political pluralism in their midst. And they have succeeded in realizing a significant degree of economic and political equality while also bringing about prosperity. We do not know what other kinds of institutions can bring these results about, though we have some ideas about what kinds of institutions do not bring about this kind of well-being. These institutions are worth preserving on their own and because they can help us shape better cosmopolitan institutions.

There is a second dimension to this institutionalist argument. Many modern democratic states have managed to realize a kind of minimal egalitarian justice in the democratic processes of political decision making, in the protection of basic liberal rights and rights to a basic economic minimum. They have made it possible for people to come to see themselves as being publicly treated as equals in some basic sense. This sense of a community of equals is an important achievement, morally speaking. It is imperfect and incomplete, but nevertheless it is also quite a real accomplishment, and it deserves to be accorded respect.

In the long run, what we want is for all the people of the world to be able to have the sense that they are publicly treated as equals. We are very far from that, but it is important that the institutional arrangements of many contemporary states are capable of establishing this kind of sense of public equality among millions of people. Again, we do not know what other kinds of institutions can do that, and we know which ones cannot, so we want to preserve those institutions that are in place that are actually capable of creating a community of persons who can think of themselves as equals. We can hope that we can learn from these institutions how to create more inclusive institutions in the long run.

E. *The Cosmopolitan Argument*

The third argument for the interest in the moral integrity of political societies is that modern democratic states hold the possibility of creating cosmopolitan political institutions in the long run. Democratic states have so far been responsible for the creation of international institutions at the regional level and at the global level. My sense is that democratic states are essentially necessary for the development of international institutions and ultimately for more cosmopolitan institutions. Democratic states have shown themselves uniquely capable of building nonimperial and nonexploitative international institutions such as the European Union, the United Nations, and the many important trade agreements that have been set up. And they tend to be the most willing to comply with those institutions. Furthermore, democratic states have the propensity to try to work out their disagreements peacefully with each other, as we see in the democratic peace argument.[14] To the extent that the full cosmopolitan norms of justice and democracy can be realized only by the creation of cosmopolitan political institutions, we have reason to think that we need to preserve the integrity of contemporary democratic states and their abilities to carry out their core functions.

These three arguments are essentially cosmopolitan arguments and they have an essentially impersonal character. They tell us that we must value the proper functioning of democratic states and that this valuation derives from their abilities to bring about some modicum of justice and prosperity for their members, to realize public equality among their members, and to provide a platform from which international and eventually cosmopolitan institutions can be constructed. They give everyone a reason to think that they are valuable. But I also describe these concerns as the legitimate interests of societies because each society has the job of making sure that its integrity is maintained, and each society is the principal beneficiary of that integrity.

These arguments can establish derivative special responsibilities on the part of members to take care of these institutions and the members of the institutions. The institutions can survive and flourish in a democratic way only to the extent that those who live under them are devoted to their proper functioning. This is a general feature of the division of labor. Even though the justification of the division of labor may be impersonal, the institutions work only to the extent that the members perform the limited roles assigned to them. In this case, those limited roles are the application of the rules of the institutions to the members. In this sense, the preservation of the institutions requires that persons who are members have special duties to the other members of the institution.[15] Of course this is qualified by the need to pursue the mandatory aims of international society.

F. Migration and Democracy

The second premise in the argument for the relevance of the interest in the moral integrity of political societies to the issue of migration is to state that some kinds of migration policies may be detrimental to the functioning of modern democratic states.

My discussion of these issues must have a conditional character, since I am not an expert in this area. But many have argued that a very large influx of migrants from another country could under certain circumstances undermine democratic institutions because they could undermine the kind of trust among citizens that is necessary to a well-functioning democracy. I do not mean to be referring to lack of trust based in xenophobia and racism. These would be illegitimate grounds of distrust and thus could not be the basis of a legitimate interest of the society in managing its borders, though a prudent politician must take these too into account in the making of policy. My concern here is with a concern that is not tainted by illegitimate sentiments of racism or xenophobia. The idea is that the influx of a very large number of migrants who speak a different language and who derive from societies with very different political traditions may innocently use political power in such a way as to arouse the distrust of citizens already present. The already present citizens themselves may come to distrust the large numbers of newcomers in a way that is innocent of xenophobia, racism, or religious intolerance. They may come to distrust the new arrivals because they do not grasp the norms on which the new arrivals base their actions.

Democratic societies depend on mutual trust among citizens because they depend on citizens being willing to accept the decisions of majorities even when they themselves are not in the majority. Being willing to accept the decision of a majority depends in part on the thought that one will find oneself in the majority now and again. It also depends on the thought that the majority is acting in good faith. But if one finds that one is outvoted by a majority that includes a significant section of the population that one does not understand very well, one may lack both of these assurances. One may fear the new majority is simply advancing its own interests or even being simply hostile, and one may wonder if it is willing to relinquish power. A lack of trust may undermine the pursuit of policies that would be normal in most democratic states such as policies of redistribution or the funding of public goods.[16] In other words, it may damage the functioning of democracy as well as the fulfillment of the core responsibilities of modern states.

These problems can be exacerbated by the fact that migration may have distributive effects on the society. Low-skilled migrants make a significant contribution to the societies they enter. But, first, standard economic models predict that they will lower wages and employment among native low-skilled workers. And many economists think that they do tend to exercise a downward pressure on the wages and employment of the worst-off workers in the receiving societies. This is an area of much controversy, with many arguing that low-skilled migrants do not depress wages or employment of native workers. Much depends on assumptions concerning the substitutability of migrants for native workers.[17] And there is presumably significant variation among societies and the parts of societies on this score. There is, however, significant agreement on the thesis that new migrants lower the wages of previous immigrants.

Second, low-skilled migrants tend to increase the overall crime rate a bit, though they do not commit as much crime as native-born low-skilled persons. And, third, low-skilled migrants tend to be a net fiscal burden on the state because they tend to use the institutions of the welfare state more than others do.[18] Of course, none of this need be attributed to bad qualities in the migrants. They exhibit similar features to low-skilled native workers in the domestic societies. But all these effects are mostly imposed on the worst-off members of the receiving society. Their wages may decline, and the quality of provisions of the welfare state (mostly in public education and public health) may decline a bit. And they tend to live in neighborhoods with the worst off. Of course, prices also decline a bit, but this benefit is distributed more evenly throughout the society.

These observations do not imply that migrants must make the worst off even worse off, but they do imply that only a concerted effort on the part of the state can rectify these effects. Presumably, low-skilled migrants make a net overall contribution to the society, and so the benefits that are conferred on most people can conceivably be redistributed to the worst off so that they receive a net benefit or are at least not worse off. But this requires that the state make a significant effort to tax and transfer the gains from migration. All this poses a challenge to a democratic state's capacity to carry out its core responsibility of distributive justice. Moreover, the preceding discussion is not meant to imply that there is nothing a society can do to limit the effects of migration on social trust; it is meant to suggest that any society will face a significant challenge here.

What we see here is that *modest* migration of low-skilled workers into a wealthy society may present significant challenges to the state's ability to ensure that the basic interests in material well-being and security of the worst-off members of its own society are not significantly undermined. We do not know entirely what the effects of *large-scale* migration might be were borders significantly more open than they are now. Very large-scale migration may well put more strain on the state's ability to maintain its welfare system as well as the well-being of the worst off more generally. At the same time, it may impose a significant strain on the kind of trust necessary to sustain significant policies for the public good and redistribution. Disagreement and uncertainty are likely to be prominent here, and so this is an area in which democratic decision making will play a significant role.

Let us briefly reflect on some of the dilemmas states may face. To limit the downward pressure on wages, the state could require that migrant workers receive the same wages as other native workers by establishing requirements on employers. Or it could require that migrant workers join unions that collectively bargain for wages.[19] These are both ways of trying to limit the downward pressure on wages for domestic workers. But these policies would have a cost as well. The consequence of policies of this sort in societies in which labor is mostly sold on an open market would be that the demand for migrant workers would be lower, and so fewer developing world workers would be able to benefit from work in developed societies. Presumably the demand for migrant workers is partly based on the fact that they receive lower wages on average.

Another possible cost would be that such policies would help generate a market for irregular migrants. Irregular migration is a clear challenge to the state's ability to carry out its core responsibilities toward the society. Irregular migrants are often exploited, cheated, and abused when they have little recourse to help from the state. They also find themselves unable to call on the basic services of the state such as public health care and housing (fortunately, most societies require that children be educated regardless of their immigration status).

To limit the fiscal deficit, the state could also withhold various welfare benefits from recent migrants such as public education for their children or public assistance for health care, nutrition, and housing. This would seem a rather odd measure when we consider that the best reason for admitting migrants is to alleviate severe poverty. Allowing persons to go homeless or without food or without health care in the case of illness would seem to be inconsistent with the basic aim of helping people out of poverty. And stopping a person's children from going to school seems similarly problematic, and it is no doubt harmful to a society to have a significant group of children who are unable to go to school.

An increasingly used method has been the creation of bilateral agreements that allow for workers from a developing country to migrate temporarily to a developed country for the purpose of working in a specific industry for a specific period. This kind of agreement lessens the downward pressure on the wages of the worst off because it is flexible and directs workers to areas where there are genuine labor shortages. It also lessens the strain on the welfare state. But it is also in the interests of the developing country, since the workers do return to their homeland with more income and skills. In return for the receiving country increasing the number of temporary workers, the sending country does much of the work screening migrants (thus limiting the contribution to crime) and making sure the migrants return at the end of the specified period. This latter provision also lessens the extent of irregular migration.[20]

So we can see that large-scale migration may pose a threat to democratic institutions generally and to their abilities to carry out their core responsibilities. Hence, the society needs to figure out how to integrate a significant migrant population, and it needs to figure out how large that population can be before the difficulties for democratic institutions become intractable. In any case, significant migration poses challenges to the state's ability to make good on its core responsibilities to limiting inequality and insecurity. The state faces significant dilemmas in trying to fulfill its core responsibilities to its citizens and fulfilling its duties to help the global poor through migration.

I do not want to argue that these interests of societies always override the interests of migrants in being able to enter a country.

But they are legitimate considerations that receiving states may take into account when they negotiate with sending states about who to let in, how many to let in, and the conditions of admission. And the considerations become comparatively weightier as the interests in migration are weaker.

The last premise in the argument is that societies should have a say (though not usually a simple veto) in the process of migration is that the difficulties stated here are usually best thought through by the society that must face them. A democratic society should be better suited to make such judgments than others.

IV. FREEDOM OF MOVEMENT AS AN AUTHORITY-LIMITING PRINCIPLE

It remains to determine whether the freedom of movement is an authority-limiting principle or an authority-compatible principle. Carens notes that the freedom of movement is a principle that is highly prized within domestic societies. He says that it is and should be thought of as outrageous when societies limit the freedom of movement of their citizens. This is not completely true. States limit movement on public lands such as national parks and public institutions. These restrictions are presumably present for the purpose of protecting the parks and for protecting the state's ability to carry out its responsibilities. Nor is it quite enough to establish that the freedom of movement is an authority-limiting principle within a domestic society. Democratic societies can do some things that are outrageous but that are nevertheless compatible with their having authority to do them. But let us suppose that it is an authority-limiting principle in the case of domestic society. Does that imply that it must be an authority-limiting principle for international society? Certainly this does not follow in any straightforward sense.

First, even garden-variety authority-limiting rights are not authority-limiting in all contexts. For example, freedom of association is an authority-limiting principle in some contexts but not all. The fact that freedom of association in the case of religious association or intimate association is an authority-limiting principle does not imply that freedom of association in economic association is authority-limiting. These principles have greater or lesser weight and thereby greater potential for limiting authority depending on the nature of the interests that they protect. I want to say the same is true for freedom of movement. When the freedom of movement protects really fundamental interests such as the interest in survival (in the case of refugees) or the interest in family reunification, then it has significant potential to limit authority. This may also hold if the freedom of movement is necessary to protect basic rights such as freedom of expression and association and conscience. When the interest involved is the interest in escaping severe poverty, I think this has a lesser though still significant authority-limiting potential. When the interest is merely improving one's economic position from a good one to a better one, this is a significant interest, but it does not have the kind of weight that is necessary to authority-limiting principles.

Now I have argued that each society has interests in its state's being able to carry out its core responsibilities. No one else is in a position to make sure that the kinds of political goods states provide are provided. These interests are ones established by the division of labor in the world. I want to argue that the interests in a state being able to carry out its core responsibilities are ones that a society has a legitimate interest in taking into account when it negotiates with other societies about migration between them. These interests can be balanced against the interests in freedom of movement of many migrants, particularly those who are simply seeking to improve their situations over good ones. These interests ought to be considered in determining the modalities of migration in the case of migrants seeking to escape severe poverty. But these interests can only have minor significance when we are talking about persons seeking to escape serious threats to their lives and physical integrity or seeking to rejoin their families.

So to the question whether freedom of movement is an authority-limiting principle, there is no completely general answer. We must consider the nature of the interests of the persons whose movement is in question, and we must consider the nature of the societal interests in limiting movement. Ultimately, the extent of authority over movement must be a function of these two considerations. I want to say that the extent of proper authority comes in degrees, since these different considerations come in degrees as well. So given the interests of societies in managing migration and the interests of individuals in migrating, I want to argue that international society has the least authority to determine the freedom of movement of refugees. To be sure, the limitation on authority from refugees is a limitation on the authority of international society. States do not have an unqualified requirement to take in refugees. The requirement on international society is to make sure that all refugees have decent places to go to and that these refugees can return home once the threats to their basic needs have subsided. This requirement need not be fulfilled by the state that neighbors the threatening state.

International society has more discretion with regard to the movement of persons escaping severe poverty. Here the interest of international society in enabling its participating states to carry out their core responsibilities gives it some discretion in determining how many people are able to move from one society to another to work. This discretion is exercised through each negotiating state being able to take its legitimate interests into account in negotiating agreements for managing migration. This may mean that in some cases persons will not be able to move to escape severe poverty, at least not when and where they want to.

I have also said that international society and the states that make it up have authority to determine whether to let people into societies who seek to improve their economic situations from good to better. These tend to be high-skilled migrants. In the case of high-skilled migrants, states tend to want to have more of them. There is a demand for their labor, they are not a net financial burden on the state, and to the extent that they do diminish the wages of domestic competitors, this can be seen as a benefit as well because the competitors are already well-to-do. Many have argued that the employment of high-skilled migrants tends to lessen inequality of income in the society. The influx of high-skilled migrants usually brings an increase in the productivity of high-skilled labor and an increase in the productivity of the society.

V. The Right of Exit

Is the right to exit one's society an authority-limiting principle? I want to say that the basic analysis that helps us think about the authority to limit entry should also help us think about the authority to limit exit. The importance of exit increases with the importance of the interests that are at stake, as does the importance of entry. And the authority to limit exit can vary in similar ways. The right of exit of a refugee is an authority-limiting principle. The right of exit of an impoverished person has great weight in limiting the authority of a developing society to stop a person from leaving. The interest in family reunification is also an authority-limiting principle. The interest in improving one's job from good to better is not as strong a consideration. However, there are some considerations that increase the weight of the considerations that limit the authority to block exit. First, if we think of exit from a society, the limitation on the right of exit is a far greater limitation than a limitation against entering a particular society. One is confined to a place if one does not have a right of exit, while one is not confined to a particular place if one doesn't have a right to enter a particular country. Furthermore, the activity of exit retains a powerful expressive component and can be an exercise of power against a particular state if it is in protest against a state in which one has lived. Finally, I think that exit of migrants to developed societies is usually a benefit to the developing society, so it is hard to see that it will be justified to limit exit. Still, there are some circumstances where I can see that a limit to exit may be defensible. For example, temporary worker agreements involve some kind of limit to exit insofar as they usually stipulate that the sending country must take the migrant back and the developing country plays a significant role in enforcing these requirements. This implies that the sending country is imposing some limit on exit.

VI. International Agreements

We do see agreements on migration between states. The most striking one is the set of agreements that make up the Schengen Convention in the European Union (EU), but there are other regional agreements that have these qualities.[21] This agreement has essentially eliminated barriers to entry for the purpose of work between many states in the EU. It did not end up producing a huge amount of migration because the member states of the EU are relatively prosperous, and in the cases of societies that were not as prosperous, the wealthier states financed development in the poorer states for a number of years before the borders were open.

There are a number of bilateral agreements among states, some of which have been relatively successful in managing migration. These usually are temporary worker agreements. They can be mutually beneficial even among states where one is primarily a receiving state and the other a sending state. An example is the set of bilateral arrangements between Canada and Jamaica on temporary low-skilled migration from Jamaica to Canada. Here, Canada admits a number of migrants on a temporary basis from Jamaica, and Jamaica makes sure that the migrants eventually come home. This makes a significant amount of migration possible, with the beneficial effects on the development of Jamaica, and also cuts down on the number of irregular migrants in Canada.[22]

VII. THE NONAGREEMENT POINT

I want to make one last set of observations about the conception of the legitimate authority of international society over migration. What happens when there is no agreement? I have already said that when states fail to enter agreements on unreasonable grounds, they may be subjected to pressure from other states to get them to enter agreements that are already established. The only way that a state may permissibly refuse entry is if it has a reasonable argument that there is a better way to pursue the mandatory aims. The normative nonagreement point for states is that they must be genuinely seeking to improve the pursuit of the relevant mandatory aims.

But what is the non-agreement point for individuals, for example, of migrants who are being kept out of a country? Here my remarks have to be somewhat tentative. I have argued that a state that unreasonably refuses to enter into agreements with other states to allow potential migrants to move is illegitimately exercising power with regard to borders and thus with regard to the potential migrants who wish to cross those borders. As a consequence, the relevant border rules that remain in place are illegitimate exercises of power on the part of international society and on the part of the relevant state. In the case of refugees, who have a right to enter a society different from their own, the illegitimate exercise of power is particularly heinous. In this case, in my view, other things being equal, the legal prohibition on entry of refugees establishes no moral duty on the part of refugees to obey. The non-agreement point is open borders for these persons. They may cross, and they may not be sent back. The receiving state may work out agreements with other potential receiving states to share the burden of taking care of refugees.

For those fleeing severe poverty who are prohibited unreasonably from entering, as a result of the failure of the receiving state to make reasonable arrangements, the situation is murkier. The rules of the border are in some way illegitimately made, and this constitutes a kind of illegitimate exercise of power over them. But the migrants in this category do not have a right to cross. So to an extent, many migrants are, morally speaking, permitted to cross the border. But they also have duties to regularize their situations. And the receiving state also has some permission to limit the number of such persons, so it may permissibly return some of them. Furthermore, the migrants have a duty of justice to uphold just or at least legitimate institutions in the receiving society. But the duties and rights are unclear in this kind of case. I think this captures some of the ambivalence developed societies experience when they encounter significant irregular migration.

VIII. THE WAY FORWARD?

I want briefly to address the question whether the suggestion I am making here is a plausible way forward for the international system. Or is it merely pie in the sky? In my view, it is a plausible way forward in the sense that in general everyone can benefit from the migration of workers. The reason people benefit from migration of workers is because most migration occurs only when there is a demand for work in the receiving society. Migration in this sense is mutually beneficial if and when exchange of labor for wages is beneficial. Of course, in the context we are talking about, the mutual benefit actually serves a fundamental moral purpose, which is to help lift people out of poverty.

But there is a second reason for international society to exercise authority over issues of migration. And that is that the alternative to a more open and managed system of migration is irregular migration as we see in Europe, the United States, Canada, Australia, and other societies. Irregular migration is a more serious threat to the core responsibilities of states. The United States is constantly trying to figure out how to regularize irregular migrants. Irregular migration poses a variety of problems to any receiving society, and an effort to manage migration on a larger scale is a way to attempt to solve these problems. This is why more bilateral agreements are arising between societies to manage migration between them. Each participating society has an interest in pursuing these agreements.

So I want to say that the way of thinking about migration that I am proposing aligns the interests of societies with the acknowledged duties societies have to solve problems of poverty and refugees.

IX. Comparison with Noncosmopolitan Views

Now I want briefly to contrast my account of the interests of societies in participating in deciding what kind of and how much migration to permit with some recent noncosmopolitan reasons. Some have argued that societies may limit migration on the grounds that the citizens have the freedom to associate with whomever they wish, and so if they wish to exclude some persons, they may do so.[23] I think this argument has a little bit of weight, but not much. The reason is that the consideration of freedom of association varies in significance with the nature of the association that is under consideration. We tend to take intimate association and association for the purpose of pursuit of a particular conception of the good life and association for the sake of pressuring political institutions to be very weighty kinds of association that ought to be protected from a great deal of intrusion. On the other hand, we take ordinary economic association to be important, but we also impose severe constraints on who one may exclude and who one may not exclude. The association at the basis of the political society seems to me to be even weaker in many respects than that connected with economic association, since the association is with strangers and is normally anonymous. Furthermore, it is a form of association that is regulated more heavily than others by norms of impartiality and equality. In respect to anonymity and impartiality, this kind of association is fundamentally different from even economic association, which permits association on the basis of mutual advantage and thus permits a great deal of partiality, though we accept significant regulation of this kind of association. I just don't see how this kind of association can be the basis of much of a claim to be able to exclude people.

My argument is also distinct from those who argue that *fundamentally* we have special duties towards fellow citizens and weaker duties to foreigners. There is some sense in which we do have greater duties toward fellow citizens than toward noncitizens, but this is not a fundamental moral idea. It is the result of the desirable division of labor that we find ourselves in in the modern world. We take care of our fellow citizens primarily because this is the way the world is divided up. Who else will take care of them if we don't?

I agree with David Miller that nationality has played an important role in many circumstances in ensuring the willingness of citizens to look out for each other's interests and sacrifice for fellow citizens. But I am not convinced that it is a basis for special political duties owed to fellow citizens. The norms of impartiality and equality within political societies imply that special duties to co-nationals are not primarily political duties and thus ought not fundamentally to shape what we owe to fellow citizens or fellow human beings.[24] But this is far too brief a discussion; my main purpose here is to distinguish my approach from the approaches that argue for special duties as fundamental to explaining societies' rights to limit migration.

X. Conclusion

I have argued that international society is authoritative with regard to many questions of migration, though there are some limits to its authority. This means that societies must negotiate in good faith for multilateral agreements to take in refugees, and wealthy countries must negotiate with poor countries to define equitable terms of migration for very poor migrants. I take it as a requirement on societies that they negotiate in good faith to create these terms.

There are a number of important issues that I have not addressed. First, I have not said much about the conditions under which migrants should be admitted. What kinds of rights should they be guaranteed? I hope that what I have said provides some indication of how best to think about this question, but space does not permit dealing with this question here. Second, I have not said much about the interests of the sending country and what it may do with regard to migrants. I am assuming primarily that migration from poor sending countries can be a development benefit for them if the arrangements are properly designed. But this question needs to be answered more systematically. This reflects a preoccupation among receiving societies with the conditions of reception. Finally, I have not said much about the strategic structure of international negotiation about migration, or how it can be fair. These are essential issues here, but they must remain for another essay.

Notes

I would like to thank Andrew Williams, Leif Wenar, Carol Gould, Houston Smit, Eleanor Brown, and audiences at Singapore National University, the University of Pavia, the University of Rijeka, and the North American Society for Social Philosophy for helpful discussion of previous drafts of this chapter.

1. See John Stuart Mill, *On Liberty* (Buffalo, NY: Prometheus Books, 1986 [1859]), 107. A. John Simmons is the thinker most responsible for reviving this distinction in contemporary thought. See Simmons, "Justification and Legitimacy," in his *Justification and Legitimacy: Essays on Rights and Obligations* (Cambridge: Cambridge University Press, 2001), 122–57.

2. See Article 79 of the International Convention on the Protection of the Rights of All Migrant Workers and Members of Their Families, in *UN Treaty Series*, no. 39481, and *International Labor Organization Multilateral Framework on Labor Migration: Nonbinding Principles and Guidelines for a Rights-Based Approach to Labor Migration* (Geneva: International Labor Organization, 2006), 11, for statements of the rights of states to determine their admissions policies.

3. The locus classicus of this argument is Michael Walzer, *Spheres of Justice: A Defense of Pluralism and Equality* (New York: Basic Books, 1983), chap. 2. Other defenses include David Miller, *National Responsibility and Global Justice* (Oxford: Oxford University Press, 2007), chap. 8, and Andrew Altman and Christopher Wellman, *A Liberal Theory of International Justice* (Oxford: Oxford University Press, 2009), chap. 8.

4. See Arash Abizadeh, "Democratic Theory and Border Coercion: No Right to Unilaterally Control Your Own Borders," *Political Theory* 36

(2008): 37–65. See the exchange on this paper between David Miller, "Why Immigration Controls Are Not Coercive: A Reply to Arash Abizadeh," *Political Theory* 38 (2010): 111–20, and Abizadeh, "Democratic Legitimacy and State Coercion: A Reply to David Miller," *Political Theory* 38 (2010): 121–30.

5. Joseph Carens, *The Ethics of Immigration* (Oxford: Oxford University Press, 2013), chap. 11, is ambiguous on whether he is speaking of authority-limiting or authority-compatible rights: "I want to challenge that view [that every state has the legal and moral right to exercise control over admissions in pursuit of its own national interest and the common good of the members . . .]. I will argue that, in principle, borders should generally be open and people should normally be free to leave their country of origin and settle in another." Ibid., 225. The subsequent discussion does not clear up this ambiguity. And the claim that societies do not have the legal right to exercise control over admissions must be unintended because it is surely false.

6. See Daniel Bodansky, *The Art and Craft of International Environmental Law* (Cambridge, MA: Harvard University Press, 2010), 97, for a discussion of this principle.

7. For examples, see Scott Barrett, *Environment and Statecraft* (Oxford: Oxford University Press, 2005).

8. A fuller account of the conditions must include that (1) the detrimental effect is not reasonably avoidable, and (2) the nature and cause of the damage must be something other than the simple exercise of a protected interest in the other person such as interests in intimate, religious, or political association. Hence, this is not an application of a simple all affected interests principle of the sort criticized by Robert Nozick, *Anarchy, State and Utopia* (New York: Basic Books, 1974), 189. (3) There is no higher-order collective decision-making process that regulates interactions of this sort.

9. I have discussed this principle of legitimacy in international environmental law in my essay "Climate Change and State Consent," in Jeremy Moss, ed., *Climate Change and Justice* (Cambridge: Cambridge University Press, 2015), 17–38.

10. I defend these propositions in more detail in my essay "The Legitimacy of International Institutions," in Andrei Marmor, ed., *The Routledge Companion to the Philosophy of Law* (New York: Routledge, 2010), 380–94.

11. See Andrew Shacknove, "Who Is a Refugee?," *Ethics* 95 (1985): 274–84.

12. See Paul Collier, *Exodus: How Migration Is Changing Our World* (Oxford: Oxford University Press, 2013), for a summary of some of the evidence.

13. See Michael Clemens, "Economics and Emigration: Trillion Dollar Bills on the Sidewalk?," *Journal of Economic Perspectives* 25 (2011): 83–106, for some especially sanguine views about significant increases in migration. See George Borjas, *Heaven's Door: Immigration Policy and the American Economy* (Princeton, NJ: Princeton University Press, 1999), for the thesis that the effects of migration on the American economy are fairly modest.

14. See Beth A. Simmons, "Compliance with International Agreements," *Annual Review of Political Science* 1 (1998): 75, 77, 83–85, for evidence of democratic state compliance. See Jack S. Levy and William R. Thompson, *Causes of War* (Malden, MA: Wiley-Blackwell, 2010), 108, for the statement of a near consensus on the democratic peace.

15. I take this approach to be in line with Robert E. Goodin's view in "What Is So Special about Our Fellow Countrymen?," *Ethics* 98 (1988): 663–86, esp. 678–79.

16. See Robert Putnam, "E Pluribus Unum: Diversity and Community in the Twenty-First Century: The Johan Skytte Prize Lecture," *Scandinavian Political Studies* 30 (2007): 137–74, for a thorough argument to the effect that migration can have this effect to some extent. On Putnam's view, the effect of migration can be to lower trust among all the members of society. See Collier, *Exodus*, for a discussion of these issues. I do not accept Collier's particular recommendations for migration here, but I do accept the idea that the issues of trust raise relevant considerations for a society to take into account. See Ryan Pevnick, "Social Trust and the Ethics of Immigration Policy," *Journal of Political Philosophy* 17 (2009): 146–67, for criticisms of the empirical claims about trust and about the normative implications for immigration policy.

17. See Borjas, *Heaven's Door*, and Tito Boeri and Jan van Ours, *The Economics of Imperfect Labor Markets* (Princeton, NJ: Princeton University Press, 2008), chap. 9, for a discussion of the models and evidence for these claims. See Noel Gaston and Douglas Nelson, "Bridging Trade Theory and Labour Econometrics: The Economics of International Migration," *Journal of Economic Surveys* 27 (2013): 98–139, esp. 100–103, for a critique of the Borjas approach.

18. See Kjetil Storeletten, "Fiscal Implications of Immigration: A Net Present Value Calculation," *Scandinavian Journal of Economics* 105 (September 2003): 487–506. See also Pia Orrenius and Madeline Zavodny, "Economic Effects of Migration: Receiving States," in Marc R. Rosenblum and Daniel J. Tichenore, eds., *The Oxford Handbook of the Politics of International Migration* (Oxford: Oxford University Press, 2012), 105–30, for a review of the economics of migration in receiving countries. See also Arash Abizadeh, Manish Pandey, and Sohrab Abizadeh, "Wage Competition and the Special-Obligations Challenge to More Open Borders," *Politics, Philosophy*

and Economics 14 (2015): 255–69, for the view that only previous immigrants experience diminished wages from new migration.

19. See Martin Ruh, *The Price of Rights: Regulating International Labor Migration* (Princeton, NJ: Princeton University Press, 2013), for a discussion of different societies' responses to the trade-offs here. In particular, Ruh discusses the Swedish migrant worker policy, which requires that migrants be paid what native workers are paid as a result of collective bargaining. Ruh's view is that this has significantly dampened the demand for migrant labor in Sweden. See Ruh, *The Price of Rights*, 102–3, for this discussion.

20. See Alan Sykes, "International Cooperation on Migration: Theory and Practice," *University of Chicago Law Review* 80 (2013): 315–39.

21. Ibid., 332.

22. See Eleanor Marie Lawrence Brown, "Outsourcing Immigration Compliance," *Fordham Law Review* 77 (2009): 2475–535, for an in-depth study of such agreements between Canada and Jamaica and their effects.

23. See Altman and Wellman, *Liberal Theory of International Justice*, chap. 8, and see Bas van der Vossen, "Immigration and Self-Determination," *Politics, Philosophy and Economics* 14 (2015): 270–90, for a different and powerful critique of the Altman-Wellman approach.

24. See also Michael Blake's argument in "Immigration, Jurisdiction, and Exclusion," *Philosophy and Public Affairs* 41 (2013): 103–30, esp. p. 105.

8

REGULATORY PLURALISM AND THE
INTERESTS OF MIGRANTS

CRISTINA M. RODRÍGUEZ

Debates concerning how to manage migration generally prioritize the interests of states. In this chapter, I begin from the premise that the interests of potential and actual migrants in the act of migration itself must also be a central feature of these debates. After briefly justifying this premise, I take off from this cosmopolitan objective to explore whether and how the different institutional arrangements available to regulate the movement of people productively take account of migrants' points of view. If we set our goal as designing a system that reasonably takes account of potential and actual migrants' interests, should regulatory energy and advocacy efforts be directed toward multilateralism, bilateralism, or old-fashioned domestic regulation?[1] As Thomas Christiano underscores in his chapter for this volume, the primary gatekeeper in this domain remains the nation-state. But in the last decade, an academic literature devoted to conceptualizing and promoting global migration governance has emerged, and scholars' and policy entrepreneurs' wide-ranging objectives include facilitating migration through these channels, in some cases with redistributionist goals. In this chapter, I question whether it makes sense to equate the international with the cosmopolitan when it comes to migration. I suggest that institutional dynamics of the nation-state, at least in its democratic form, will better serve the individual migrant's objectives.

As Christiano points out, the cosmopolitan objective faces significant hurdles, most immediately because intending migrants stand outside the territory they seek to enter. The state-centered, democratic decision making that largely occupies the field of migration regulation tends to result in immigration politics and policies that revolve primarily around promoting the interests either of the state or of existing citizens and residents. Migrants as outsiders to a polity have neither vote nor voice with which to influence a state's admissions decisions. One response to the consequences of this regulatory monopoly might be to call for greater international involvement in migration regulation, but agreement over the legitimacy and purposes of migration has proved elusive at the domestic level, not to mention the international one, and systematic forms of transnational migration regulation therefore remain underdeveloped. With the exception of the 1951 Convention Relating to the Status of Refugees and its 1967 Protocol, no true multilateral treaty governing migration exists, and even the varieties of regional and bilateral mechanisms that have emerged in the recent past to address global migration prioritize state or governmental interests, particularly the state interest in control of low-skilled labor migrants who are often "irregular" or "unauthorized."[2] Sending states today have limited control over the decisions of receiving states, not to mention mixed incentives in relation to emigration, which affect their willingness and capacity to promote the interests of migrants as migrants themselves see them.

The prevalence of illegal or irregular migration in fact highlights a powerful preference among receiving and perhaps even sending states for leaving at least some movement to the market and the realm of private transactions, backstopped by ex post enforcement actions—a perverse kind of open borders that might initially serve but then crush migrants' aspirations. Because decision making at the domestic level is decidedly biased, even when and perhaps particularly when democratic, and because the profound asymmetries that exist between sending and receiving states can thwart international agreement, it may be wishful thinking to aspire to a regulatory regime that enables the realization of migrants' preferences without the risks and costs to migrants of irregular movement. Much as Christiano laments, illegal immigration for me hangs like a dark cloud over technocratic and human rights discussions alike.

Yet despite all these reasons to conclude that the cosmopolitan objective amounts to a quixotic goal, social justice movements in defense of migrants' interests, including irregular migrants, percolate and expand at the domestic level and in transnational discourse.[3] They have helped shape regulatory policies and diplomatic initiatives, and arguably have moved public opinion toward greater openness to potential new immigrants and citizens. And so the pessimism justified by the sheer challenge of the cosmopolitan goal need not be paralyzing; nonexploitative migration is both possible and morally desirable, at least to some degree. Various forms of migration regulation, initiated by different actors, can and do coexist, and some integration among the international, regional and bilateral, and domestic will be necessary to channel the movement of people across borders no matter regulation's goal (whether it be control, development, welfare maximization, or pursuit of justice).

But while the transnational nature of migration might suggest that we should turn increasingly to the international sphere, or even invigorate bilateral or regional forms of agreement to harness sending states as proxies for migrants' interests,[4] I argue instead that the most robust channels for advancing migrants' interests still lie within the institutions of the democratic nation-state, which in an increasingly interconnected world can serve cosmopolitan ends, including the interest in giving voice to those who seek to traverse borders in pursuit of their own life plans.[5] Importantly, this observation does not require rejection of internationalism. Instead, it is based on a skepticism about the direction in which internationalist thinking regarding migration has evolved in recent years, coupled with a certain resignation to the powerful logic of sovereignty and a belief in the cosmopolitan potential of democracy.

Before turning to the principal focus of this chapter—the ways in which different regulatory structures either advance or elide the interests of migrants—I pause for a moment to provide some definition of and justification for my starting premise. First, what exactly do I mean by the interests of migrants? Second, why should those interests matter in the formulation of immigration regulation? On the first score, the central question I pose is how to ensure that the desires of would-be migrants to move from one society to another are accounted for in the formulation of migration policy generally and admissions policies specifically. The primary interest I seek to advance is the individual's interest in relocation itself, rather than the protections that ought to be afforded to migrants already on the move or present in receiving societies. Though the extent of the latter will certainly shape the scale, viability, and success of the former, how to capture and channel the interest in movement itself represents a kind of threshold interest that remains underconceptualized and underexplored in scholarly and policy conversations concerned with protecting immigrants' rights.

Following Christiano, I narrow the focus to economic or labor migrants at the low-wage end of the economic spectrum. A broad, albeit imperfect, international consensus exists regarding the interests of refugees and the obligations of states to protect persons with well-founded fears of persecution, and would-be high-skilled and professional migrants, often portrayed in political discourse as the desirable migrants, already benefit from a largely cosmopolitan world order (though movement is far from friction free, to be sure).[6] But the lower-wage economic migrant engenders deep ambivalence bordering on hostility and therefore presents some of the most confounding and pressing regulatory problems of the day. To be sure, states throughout the world (and not just fully developed, wealthy ones) admit large numbers of economic migrants, albeit on very different terms from one another.[7] But the question of how to better address economic migrants' interest in movement becomes salient in the shadow of the problem of illegal or irregular migration, which underscores how the interest in economic migration outstrips the legal opportunities for it.

To identify the core interest as one of movement only begins the conversation, however, because migrants' interests vis-à-vis relocation are neither singular nor stable. Global migration consists of numerous forms of movement by people with varied motivations that change over time as the result of the experience of migration. At a high level of generality, as a 2009 UN Human Development report describes it, movement is the "natural expression of people's desire to choose how and where to lead their lives." To be more specific, we might define the economic migrant's interests as fulfilling his or her life plans as he or she sees them, which entails migrating to pursue economic opportunity on fair terms while maintaining a connection to the home country in order to facilitate the transfer of resources to a family or a community. But the terms migrants might be willing to accept to fulfill their life plans vary, too. At least at the outset, many economic migrants seek only temporary opportunity. And some economic migrants might be quite willing to trade any number of protections (such as freedom from exploitation or mobility rights) for the possibility of temporary employment abroad, on the theory that having fewer legal rights and protections is the price to pay for the opportunity to move in the first place.[8] And yet, even if one would make these trade-offs ex ante, as the experience of migration unfolds, interests may mature into the desire for permanent relocation, including with family, and migrants may begin to demand fair and even equal treatment by seeking social and legal support to better their lot—see migrant-led campaigns in the United States for legalization and a path to citizenship, for example. As a result, the concept of migrants' interests should include not only the initial interest in movement and resource acquisition but also the flexibility to adapt to maturing expectations in light of the experience of migration.

Defining migrants' interests in these ways does not explain why those interests ought to be taken into account when admissions policies are formed. The fact that migration constitutes a feature of the global community suggests that the interests of migration's protagonists are relevant to its regulation, simply as a matter of good public policy. If all relevant factors ought to be considered and somehow incorporated into regulatory decision making, surely the interests of would-be migrants matter to any cost-benefit analysis that might guide admissions, since migrants both experience and produce benefits (as well as costs). This form of argument could take shape as a global utilitarian claim—that maximizing global welfare requires consideration of migrants' interests in relocation, even as welfare maximization might ultimately require restrictions on movement in some contexts.

My starting premise also could be defended with reference to more profound moral intuitions, whether of the distributive or corrective kind. On the most basic level, would-be migrants are individuals with aspirations that ought to matter to any government that seeks to regulate them, particularly given the arbitrariness of the place of one's birth.[9] The happenstance of birth not only can unfairly thwart pursuit of one's life goals but also can prevent the living of a decent life.[10] A global conception of justice thus requires that attention be paid to the interests of those who seek to overcome these inequalities through movement. Of course, the required response could be redistribution rather than facilitation of migration.[11] But labor migration is a persistent phenomenon, even in the face of recession. It often results from complicated historical relationships between sending and receiving societies and policy decisions made by the multiple states and international organizations that constitute the global financial order—decisions that can exacerbate global inequalities.[12] In other words, those states that block migration are in some cases responsible for the conditions that make migration part of an individual's life plan, giving rise to some degree of responsibility on the part of the decision makers in wealthy states to acknowledge those life plans, which include movement.[13]

I do not purport here to settle on any one of these reasons to defend my starting premise. I also stop short of framing this discussion in terms of a right to migrate not because I think such a right cannot be articulated or defended but because to justify this position and explain its implications would distract from the pragmatic purpose of this chapter—to think about the value of different regulatory approaches for advancing my starting premise. I rely instead on the more pedestrian and malleable concept of interests. To say migrants' interests exist, which they undeniably do, does not require justifying them as superior to or in rank order with other interests or rights in play, such as the interests of sending states in retaining their human capital and the interests of receiving states in prioritizing the needs of their own citizens, particularly the least well off among them. In other words, because I want to leave open the possibility of trade-offs, I do not attempt to formulate a comprehensive theory of the migrant's rights to move or to particular forms of treatment, but instead take the interest in migration as a valid one and consider how best to facilitate it, leaving the trade-offs and the difficult normative conclusions for another occasion.

I. MULTILATERALISM AND ITS LIMITS

In theory, a multilateral approach to labor migration could serve the interests of migrants in relocation were it to create a regime of burden sharing that distributed obligations to admit, perhaps based on receiving state responsibility apportioned according to capacity and sending state and migrant need. Such a system might be attractive to states that already confront the pressures associated with labor migration, on both the sending and the receiving side. The existence of a treaty-based obligation to admit, and the perception that participating states would bear the costs of economic migration in a mutually agreed-upon fashion, could result in a greater willingness on the part of receiving states to accept and even integrate economic migrants, especially in light of the benefits of stability and predictability that would accrue from a regularized and internationally coordinated system. Relatedly, as the global governance literature emphasizes, the multilateral mode can help produce state buy-in to a policy, including by expanding the number of participants and thus enhancing the moral weight of any accord reached, as well as by expanding the information and tools available to states to manage economic migration by bringing multiple actors with varied experience and expertise into a common enterprise. Proponents of global migration governance often use the rhetoric of "win-win-win" to describe the advantages of multilateral cooperation. The third victory belongs to migrants themselves as the result of the creation of an international system that enables their movement by having made that movement advantageous to sending and receiving societies alike.[14]

The interests of migrants could be further advanced if the multilateral negotiations were structured to ensure that poorer and sending states had prominent positions at the bargaining table and in oversight of the regime. Because of its international and multiparty character, negotiations of this kind could provide sending states an opportunity to influence the formation and implementation of the regime in a way that serves their interests, which to some degree will include their citizens' interests in migration—or at least a greater opportunity than asymmetrical bilateral negotiations or receiving-state-centered, unilateral decision making would afford. In a multilateral setting, particularly one convened based on a ethos of burden sharing and mutual responsibility, the interests of powerful receiving states may be more tempered or offset by the presence of numerous sending states in the dialogue. In the same vein, a multilateral setting arguably creates the best conditions for encouraging states to transcend, or at least temper, their parochial interests in order to focus on humanitarian or human rights concerns, or on maximizing global as opposed to local welfare—tendencies that would create room for consideration of migrants' interests. The emergence of an international commitment to facilitating labor migration might then produce a set of norms that come to be reflected in domestic legal regimes that expand on or augment the international regime, including in ways that serve migrants' interests even more robustly than the international regime itself. The international regime could even facilitate this outcome by leaving important details of implementation to individual states and to informal cooperation among state participants.

And yet, the intuition that international phenomena are most effectively and fairly governed through international decision making has not resulted in international governance of economic migration in a way that resembles the sort of multilateral regime just described.[15] Any theoretical advantages a multilateral, formal, burden-sharing regime negotiated as a matter of international law might offer to migrants have been elusive as a matter of institutional design. The reasons why can be elucidated through a comparison to the one major international regime governing migrant admissions that does exist—the system of refugee protection. The Refugee Convention of 1951 and the domestic asylum regimes it has spawned could be taken as the paradigm case of a reasonably successful treaty-based instance of multilateral migration governance. The Convention itself protects the interests of certain types of migrants—those with a well-founded fear of persecution on account of enumerated grounds—from refoulement, or being returned to harm. It thus protects at least temporary movement under specific conditions. Though the core guarantee of the Convention could be characterized as limited in many ways, the domestic asylum regimes the Convention has inspired have provided more robust opportunities for permanent resettlement. And the Convention has given rise to an international architecture that, while underfunded, carries moral weight in the international community that can translate into policy action.

Of course, criticisms of the Refugee Convention have been legion. Perhaps its most significant flaw is its limited mandate—the definition of refugee excludes large numbers of people who would colloquially be understood as refugees, or as deserving of protection, such as those fleeing natural disasters or civil strife. This particularity reflects its origins as a resolution to post–World War II refugee crises. The Convention also does not require signatories to do much more than decline to send refugees back to persecution—the substantive rights guarantees of the Convention either are not mandatory or are framed in a way that gives states a legitimate way out of acknowledging them. And the Convention has not ensured equal burden sharing among wealthy nations (most refugees flee from one poor state to another geographically proximate poor state). These factors contribute to states' incentives to provide the minimal protection required,[16] as does domestic political resentment, which is especially prevalent in Europe, based on the belief that economic migrants claim to be refugees in order to take advantage of social welfare largesse.[17] Finally, the circumstances of crisis that give rise to refugee flows mean that the demands for protection will often outstrip state capacity, particularly when the state affected by refugee flows is itself poor or unstable.

And still, these problems, though significant, are largely of implementation rather than lack of moral vision, or moral consensus about the obligation to protect the victims of certain calamities and injustices. What is more, domestic legal systems have filled some of the gaps left open by the Refugee Convention and corresponding asylum laws. In the United States, for example, Congress has created the mechanism of Temporary Protected Status, which authorizes the executive branch to permit noncitizens fleeing natural disasters and other emergencies not covered by the asylum regime to remain with legal status and work authorization in the United States, at least temporarily. This status is conferred on groups of foreign nationals and often extends for long periods of time. And though critics have long lamented the absence of a burden-sharing ethos, Peter Schuck, one such critic, recently has highlighted some limited developments over the last fifteen years in precisely that direction.[18] For the purposes of my exposition, what matters most is not whether and how the refugee regime is flawed but that it exists at all. It remains an ongoing subject of reform debate, and informs domestic legal systems, because of a coherent set of international, normative commitments to protection against persecution and atrocity, backed by strong academic and popular agreement that genuine refugees have legitimate moral claims on nation-states not their own.

The thought of a treaty regime for economic migration that resembles the Refugee Convention, not to mention one that embodies an ethos of burden sharing, seems fanciful precisely because of the absence of such moral consensus over the case of the economic migrant. The kind of historically driven, normative commitment to refugee protection that gave rise to the Convention in the years after World War II and still sustains numerous domestic refugee regimes has no parallel when it comes to economic migration. Even the existing treaty that protects migrants' rights (but not the right to migrate) has not been ratified by any of the major receiving states. Whereas the moral claims of refugees have been internalized by legal systems around the world, the idea that economic migrants might also have moral claims has only begun to penetrate the academic community,[19] much less the policy-making world. Scholars and regulators disagree vehemently about the value and purposes of labor migration. In some economics and sociology circles, it amounts to the obvious corollary to free trade and has value because of its tendency to promote growth, enable labor to achieve its highest value use, and maximize welfare in an absolute sense, both within domestic settings and without regard to borders.[20] For libertarians, it represents an expression of individual choice that ought not be constrained. And for proponents of development, it helps stimulate important feedback effects in the form of remittances and other types of social capital, at least insofar as it remains cyclical and temporary. But to social democrats, economic migration can threaten the welfare state and hard-won labor rights within domestic systems by putting downward pressure on wages.[21] In domestic political settings, the arguments made against large-scale migration of poorer workers run a familiar gamut.[22] This absence of consensus helps explain why some scholars who identify and descry the inequalities that result from birth in poor versus wealthy states advocate the redistribution of money and resources, rather than the redistribution of people, as remedies.[23]

More practically, the asymmetrical interests of sending and receiving states are likely to thwart any efforts to promote multilateral forms of agreement to facilitate and apportion economic migration through a burden-sharing regime that imposes on states obligations to admit. The major sending and receiving states whose participation would be crucial to the success of this sort of framework are too differently situated to produce agreement—receiving states have the power and political support to control their admissions policies and acquire the labor they need unilaterally,[24] and sending states as a group are unlikely to be able to offer enough in exchange to convince states to cede this authority to an international regime.[25] In the absence of a moral consensus concerning the right of economic migrants to relocate, destination states will have limited incentive to participate in a regime under which they would cede the control they would otherwise exercise when making admissions decisions. Though wealthy states might have an incentive to enlist the participation of sending states in the control of illegal immigration, or in screening potential workers, such incentives are far more likely to give rise to law enforcement agreements, ad hoc efforts to stop particular flows, and bilateral forms of cooperation over which receiving states retain far more control than a comprehensive regime of regularized immigration,[26] particularly to the extent that wealthy states are actually ambivalent about the undesirability of illegal immigration.

Domestic political obstacles to the negotiation of effective multilateral immigration agreements also abound. They include skepticism of multilateral action prevalent in major countries of immigration like the United States, popular resistance to the cultural change and economic dislocation immigration potentially engenders, and related challenges to the enactment of implementing legislation, all of which beset many efforts to craft international treaties. Admissions decisions in particular implicate control over the shape of the polity, as well as a vast array of bureaucratic and economic policy choices. They may well strike too close to the heart of state sovereignty to ever be realistic subjects of international agreement. For example, the United States and the United

Kingdom both have expressed skepticism concerning international cooperation spearheaded by the International Labor Organization on the grounds that its efforts would hamstring their ability to make admissions decisions based on national priorities.[27] Other international obligations states have assumed, such as a commitment to protecting internationally defined human rights within their territory, or the agreement to abide by the rules of the international trade regime, either require the state to give up little of its regulatory control over its own population or redound to the state's benefit.[28]

Finally, international economic migration might not be well suited to the sort of regime created by the Refugee Convention because the patterns of economic migration reflect geographic imperatives and historical relationships forged in large part through colonial and imperial encounters. Economic migrants move not just to secure jobs but also to join networks of family, friends, and co-nationals—networks responsible for the dissemination of information and cultural capital that make migration feasible and desirable. The extensive Mexican and Filipino migration to the United States is not the product of coincidence, nor is the presence of large numbers of North Africans and Turks in Europe.

All these factors help explain why the multilateral frameworks that have emerged to date to "govern" migration have been ad hoc, informal, and mostly regional; as one scholar frames it, "they constitute a dense tapestry of complex, diverse, and contested institutions," rather than "formal inclusive multilateralism," and generally "do not attempt to establish binding norms but play a role in facilitating bilateral cooperation."[29] What is more, the institutions operate according to "competing discourses," with some prioritizing low-skilled migration and others emphasizing that any migration occur on terms comparable to those that protect local workers.[30] The burgeoning academic literature on these forms of management reaches divergent conclusions on their effectiveness and whether they represent the seeds of an international regulatory regime that resembles the system governing international trade. In T. Alexander Aleinikoff's often-quoted estimation, global migration governance is "all substance and no architecture."[31]

This assessment may be too pessimistic, but it remains the case that the organizations and consortia that do exist do not directly manage migration in the sense of imposing obligations or even recommendations on states to admit certain numbers of economic migrants. Instead, many of the practices and institutions consist of dialogues among states, or networks for information sharing. What is more, the rhetorics of efficiency, rationality, and control structure most of the conversation about how to build these global mechanisms. To be sure, the efficiency and control perspectives might not be mutually exclusive with the interests of migrants. Mechanisms designed with these goals in mind can indirectly advance migrants' interests by making migration easier and safer. By helping to "rationalize" the process of migration, they can help facilitate movement by reducing its costs and helping to persuade states of its value. But thus far, these structures at best represent methods for heightening awareness of migrants' interests and providing ancillary forms of support to migrants. They do not provide obvious points of entry for migrants to press their interests directly with the regulators who control their entry into states of immigration. The regulatory facilitation of migration itself happens largely through domestic laws and bureaucracies, even as institutions beyond the nation-state might constrain and shape the behavior of states.[32]

Implicit in this discussion, and in much of the programmatic global governance literature, is thus the recognition of a tension between the ideal and the possible. Ideally, we would have a functioning world order in which traffic across borders is coordinated, voluntary, rights respecting, and sustainable by virtue of being welfare maximizing in both sending and receiving states and being seen as legitimate by all parties involved. An international architecture to facilitate global labor migration that simultaneously protects the interests of migrants in migration and ensures that migration enhances rather than undermines the fair distribution of resources and opportunities around the globe represents a cosmopolitan dream. The fits and starts of the global migration regime partially serve this objective, even as they suffer from bureaucratic and technocratic ineffectiveness and arguably serve the interests of elites in cheap labor and social control.

But existing internationalism in the immigration domain remains too underdeveloped and powerless to serve the interest of migrants in migration on a large scale, not to mention to adapt to the complexities and shape-shifting quality of those interests. It may be that meaningful international agreement on the purposes of labor migration, the optimal numbers any given state should accept, and the status migrants ought to have within the receiving state will forever be elusive, and that the right to migrate will remain the province of theorists. But whether the problem rests with existing international structures and the reigning moral confusion surrounding the economic migrant, or with the very concept of international regulation of migration, multilateral decision making is far from adequate to the task of advancing the interests of migrants in movement across borders. While these limitations do not mean abandoning the global governance project, they do suggest that regulatory and advocacy efforts are more productively concentrated elsewhere.

II. BILATERALISM AND ITS ASYMMETRIES

At least from the American point of view, bilateral migration accords have been anathema to advocates for immigration reform and migrants' rights, largely because of the sordid legacy of labor exploitation and arbitrary law enforcement of the Bracero Program pursued in the decades following World War II. Mexico's inability to protect the interests of its citizens recruited as guest workers by growers in the Southwest pursuant to U.S.-Mexico accords subsequently entrenched by statute and regulation highlights for critics the destructive asymmetry inherent in bilateral negotiations between sending and receiving states. Whereas in multilateral settings, the bargaining power of the most powerful states can be offset by the presence of middle powers and developing nations working in tandem, bilateral negotiations by definition will be based on asymmetries in power that will enable the wealthier receiving state to exploit its weaker sending-state counterpart. And not only will the interests of the more powerful state dominate the negotiation of the accord, but its implementation will occur largely within the receiving state's jurisdiction. This geographic dimension of the accord will mute the sending state's power to influence implementation, particularly in the absence of the kind of international supervisory mechanisms or pressures that often exist in multilateral relationships. Though the diplomatic establishments of sending states might be able to exert some influence over the sending state in response to egregious abuses, the influence is likely to be limited in time and scope, and migrants themselves will generally be left without an effective proxy to advance their interests in the terms of their migration.

But these sorts of assumptions may be overly shaped by the particularities of the Bracero era and are unlikely to characterize every sending-receiving state relationship. Take, for example, the bilateral U.S.-Mexico relationship today. The development of the Mexican state and economy, along with changed labor and civil rights norms in the United States, have altered the conditions that would govern any sort of bilateral labor accord. Moreover, the U.S.-Mexico relationship is marked as much by interdependence as by power imbalances. Overlapping or common interests between two countries with shared borders and migration networks may well offset even significant economic differentials. Where states face numerous issues of mutual concern, bilateral agreements can be effective mechanisms for joint problem solving, making efforts to bargain more likely than in multilateral settings where common cause will be harder to find. The United States, for example, can trade increased admissions and agreements to protect the interests of Mexican migrants for security guarantees and law enforcement assistance from Mexico.[33] Bilateral agreements also present the strategic advantage of allowing states to retain a much higher degree of control over administration and are far easier to rescind or modify than multilateral, international agreements, giving states more incentives to enter into them.

Of course, even if bilateral negotiations can proceed from a more even playing field than has traditionally been assumed and are far easier to strike than multilateral agreements, it remains to be answered whether the strategic advantages to states of this approach will advance the interests of migrants. From a theoretical point of view, a bilateral approach to regulating migration, assuming conditions of fair dealing, will better capture particular migrants' interests than a multilateral approach because the bilateral engagement will flow from a historically and geographically determined relationship between two nation-states. Indeed, bilateral and regional cooperation have arisen to a degree that multilateral coordination has not because the former emerge from the local dynamics that actually produce migration, give it its demographic and economic features, and thus create incentives for states to address their common concerns.[34]

To be sure, neither state's interest in a bilateral relationship will be congruent with migrants' interests. With respect to some issues, interests at work in receiving states might more closely align with migrants' interests than with the objectives of the sending states; well-off elites in destination states might share migrants' strong interest in migration for jobs, even as the origin state might prefer to retain its human capital. Sometimes the interests of states will diverge altogether from those of migrants. Whereas the United States and Mexico, or Canada and Jamaica, might have mutual interests in cyclical migration (the United States might prefer temporary labor that does not create permanent residents with claims on the public purse, and Mexico might prefer an ongoing flow of remittances from cycling groups of migrants who ultimately remain Mexican and return permanently to Mexico), migrants might develop their own interest in permanent resettlement. Receiving states might also have an incentive to cooperate in programs of migration control to ensure that at least some migration remains permissible and legal, or to win other sorts of financial and technical support from their receiving-state counterpart, thereby thwarting migrants' relocation aspirations.

The fact that state interests will dominate the exchanges in bilateral agreements may be a reason to yearn for the formulation of a "neutral" international norm that transcends these particularities. But as suggested earlier, such norms are neither readily available nor likely to crystallize. More to the point, individual interests are never perfectly reflected in governmental decision making, whether at the domestic or the international level. The degree of congruence between the negotiating sending state and the migrant will depend in large part on the structures of that state (e.g., whether it is democratic, respects individual rights, and seeks to advance the welfare of its citizens). As a largely developed, mostly democratic state, Mexico has formulated an emigration policy that heavily prioritizes protecting the social welfare interests of its citizens abroad, including by establishing networks in the United States to advance those interests.[35] The state has adjusted its own citizenship practices to account for an emigrant form of citizenship, such as by permitting dual citizenship and voting by its out-of-country citizens—moves that acknowledge migrants' desires for long-term residence abroad and even relocation.

Bilateral accords have become increasingly common around the world. As Jennifer Gordon has documented, by 2010 the nations of Latin American had struck 144 bilateral migration agreements, and the Philippines had struck agreements with fourteen countries as part of a development strategy that relies heavily on emigration,[36] though many of these accords involve high-skilled workers generally and health care workers in particular.[37] Canada maintains numerous bilateral agreements to promote temporary labor migration to its agricultural sector from the Caribbean and Mexico,[38] according to which employer demand, not the accords themselves, determines admissions levels. It is an open question the extent to which these agreements serve migrants' interests rather than just development interests. Their temporary nature precludes resettlement or long-term relocation, which can create conditions for exploitation.[39] But these programs' reliance on source countries in the administration of the programs at least enables those countries to serve as advocates for workers and monitor their welfare.[40]

At the turn of this century, the governments of the United States and Mexico had high hopes for negotiating a bilateral agreement that would have expanded the legal channels for entry of low-wage workers to the United States and brought stability and predictability to migration across their shared border. But the advances made by the administrations of George W. Bush and Vicente Fox were derailed by the events of September 11, 2001, and the United States' subsequent shift in foreign policy focus. No realistic effort to reinvigorate such an approach has occurred since, despite the fact that bilateral accords are far easier to strike than legislation is to pass,[41] particularly in a presidentialist system and under divided government. The United States' failure to embrace the bilateral option likely has arisen from the passing of a very particular moment in time coupled with structural features of the American political process.[42] Indeed, all of their advantages notwithstanding, the trouble with the bilateral approach to opening and expanding channels for economic migration to the United States is that efforts to adopt formal accords directed at such objectives will face the same sorts of domestic challenges as multilateral accords, including the general aversion by American politicians and their public to formal international agreements. Moreover, Congress historically has monopolized admissions decisions, marginalizing executive-led immigration solutions. This dynamic has oriented the president and the bureaucracy less toward efforts to strike formal legal agreements and more toward the use of diplomatic and bureaucratic channels to work with foreign governments such as Mexico to address migration and related matters, and law enforcement channels to advance executive policy goals.[43]

But even if the formal accord may not be a consistently viable vehicle for regulating migration, other bilateral channels may be productive, particularly between countries whose relations are already defined by ongoing, informal, and "soft" sorts of interaction and cooperation, such as the United States and Mexico. In other work, I have identified several such frameworks and assessed their relative effectiveness.[44] Diplomatic and information-sharing networks that involve consultation and conferencing among cabinet officials and agency heads in both the United States and Mexico can be effective in building mutual will for joint action and improving policy on either side of the border. For Mexico, informal and diplomatic channels have proved fruitful avenues for influencing U.S. policy on an ad hoc basis. For instance, Mexico and other foreign governments applied effective diplomatic pressure on the Obama administration to address the Arizona law designed to crack down on unauthorized immigrants—pressure that likely informed the administration's ultimate decision to file suit against the state. Further, actual cooperative ventures between administrative officials on both sides of the border give bureaucratic heft to bilateral cooperation. Regional consultation processes also have become valuable sites of information sharing regarding capacity building, as well as priority setting, even as their outputs lack binding effect.[45]

These sorts of transnational interactions need not be entirely between governmental actors, either. Civil society groups help facilitate migration by providing resources to migrants abroad. The so-called Mexican hometown associations, which consist of business groups, labor unions, and churches that sponsor social and development activities, sometimes with funding from the

Mexican government, help materially and psychologically ground the participation of Mexican migrants in the United States, thereby enhancing the viability of migration.[46] Other scholars have cited the potential for transnational social movements to influence government policy and to help create conditions for greater acceptance of economic migrants by ensuring that those migrants will impose fewer costs on members of the receiving society.[47]

On the whole, these forms of cooperation reflect an ethos of burden sharing, even as they serve the particular interests of each state. The question then becomes how to amplify the effects of these interactions to ensure that they serve migrants' interests. As with the mechanisms of global migration governance discussed previously, these forms of transnational activity only indirectly advance the migrant's interest in movement and will most likely serve as complements to rather than substitutes for the primary means of enabling migration—the admissions decisions themselves. But these bilateral forms of support matter to the formation of political will to open channels for migration and should be nurtured.

III. A DOMESTIC COSMOPOLITANISM?

The domestic political process might seem like the least likely means through which to advance the interests of migrants, or any related cosmopolitan objective. As suggested at the outset, bureaucracies and political communities alike harbor strong desires for control over the size and character of the polity and over traffic in and out of a state's territory. Before they move, migrants remain abstractions; as individuals with actual preferences (rather than as ideas constructed by the receiving population), they lack the capacity to influence domestic political processes. Even after migration, when individuals become embedded in domestic settings, migrants lack formal access to the political process because they rarely have the right to vote. As newcomers or outsiders, they also tend to lack informal purchase on the sympathies of existing citizens. In the United States, in particular, advocates for legislative immigration reform confront numerous structural and political hurdles, especially in an era of hyperpartisan polarization. Attempts at immigration reform, therefore, must serve national interests and the interests of existing citizens, especially if the reform is to expand the scope of admissions. And so successful immigration legislation generally prioritizes domestic interests. Though its adoption for self-interested reasons can certainly benefit migrants and expand opportunities for relocation, reform tends to result for reasons other than the fact that it will benefit migrants.[48]

But even if we accept each of these observations as true, together they provide an incomplete picture of domestic decision making. For a variety of reasons, domestic processes provide meaningful channels for migrants' interests. First and foremost, within our democratic processes of government, numerous proxies for migrants' interests carry influence, particularly for migrants from sending states with long-standing ties to the domestic regulator. These proxies include commercial interests, ethnic lobbies, and citizens themselves, who have their own personal interests in both family and labor migration—interests that tend to be self-perpetuating. Sending states might value their migrants primarily for their economic potential. But the noncommercial domestic proxies, in particular, will be more likely to conceptualize and value migrants as individual people, aligning those proxies' positions more closely with migrants' interests than will be the case with sending state bureaucracies, especially to the extent the latter are ambivalent about losing human capital in the wake of permanent resettlement. Not surprisingly, co-ethnics display high levels of support for more migration, though their attitudes do fluctuate over time.[49] Particularly when those groups reach a certain size and consist of enough voters, they will have traction in the domestic political process—a kind of direct influence over decision making that is attenuated at best in the international settings. Even though recent arrivals, who by definition are less likely to be part of the political process, are most likely to support increased migration, politicians with long-term vision will respect their preferences to some degree.

In addition, constitutional and humanitarian norms historically have informed domestic legal processes governing migration. Civil rights principles, for example, have contributed to producing a more expansionist immigration policy in the United States, helping to influence the 1965 elimination of national origin quotas and expansion of admissions opportunities.[50] Moral concerns helped drive the Obama administration's 2012 and 2014 policies to defer removal of certain unauthorized immigrants, including those brought to the United States as children and those who are parents of U.S. citizens and lawful permanent residents. These actions also authorized beneficiaries to work in the United States, making them a type of expansion of economic migration (though as of this writing the 2014 policy applicable to parents remains enjoined by court order). Though not expressly articulated in any policy documents, motivations for the executive actions included the concern that children not be held accountable for the illegal actions of their parents; a belief that children who have come of age in the United States, as well as others with deep ties to the country, should be allowed to remain; and an acceptance of a degree of complicity on the part of the United States in creating circumstances of injustice. In general, the scope of these civil rights or moral norms and how they relate to immigration policy will be context-specific and shaped by a particular domestic society's historical trajectories, as well as by the education of the population.[51] But these very factors likely mean that such norms are more entrenched and reflect greater consensus concerning the value of migration at the domestic level than parallel and more abstract norms at the international level.

To identify these norms does not mean that other, less migrant-regarding factors do not heavily influence domestic migration policy, of course. The mobilization of humanitarian norms has been intertwined with foreign policy objectives, as with refugee admissions from largely communist countries in the Cold War period and legalization programs for nationals of Central American states with whom the United States has been entangled. And humanitarian rhetoric has complemented commercial, partisan, and interest group goals; for example, the Obama administration's deferred action initiative, announced in the summer before the 2012 election, may also have been designed to appeal to particular Democratic constituencies. It therefore becomes difficult to disentangle the extent to which principles as opposed to pragmatics have driven the expansion of immigration and immigrant's rights. What is more, humanitarian principles can themselves contribute to policies and politics that limit migration. Lawmakers terminated the Bracero guest worker program in response to flagrant labor abuses, and civil rights advocates' general skepticism of temporary worker programs has stymied their adoption in recent years—positions that ultimately limit migrants' opportunities for relocation.

But it is precisely this combination of principle and politics that makes the domestic political process, at least in traditionally immigrant-receiving democratic states, a viable vehicle for the advancement of migrants' interests, even as those interests are traded off of others'. Indeed, it is well documented that, in major receiving societies, public opinion generally opposes existing levels of immigration, but admissions policies remain expansionist. Some scholars attribute this phenomenon to the purchase of humanitarian norms such as family unification and civil rights principles that weigh against exclusion, especially of migrants already present despite their legal status,[52] and others to the "porous nature of American institutions" that enable lobbying, as well as the technical difficulties associated with restriction.[53] Whatever its source, the expansionist phenomenon suggests that factors other than popular self-interest help shape domestic immigration policy in a way that serves migrants' interests in relocation.

Finally, as I have suggested already, sending states have considerable influence in the domestic political processes of receiving states, through diplomatic channels and trade and diasporic networks[54]—interdependencies that are especially profound between countries with shared borders or intertwined histories such as the United States and Mexico. These forms of transnationalism can significantly influence domestic political and bureaucratic processes, thus making such democratic processes viable vehicles for advancing migrants' interests, particularly under conditions of significant international integration. The influence of diplomatic and trade networks is probably most pronounced over the administrative and enforcement policy managed by the executive, which will take foreign policy and diplomatic goals into consideration whenever they might be implicated (whereas the legislative processes that are more directly accountable to the domestic electorate will be less consistently focused on foreign affairs). Diplomatically active sending states, as well as their migrants abroad, can shape enforcement judgments—a form of influence that ultimately can serve migrants' interests in remaining in the receiving state. Such lobbying is not necessarily a substitute for the kinds of regional and bilateral consortia discussed earlier, but it may well be more effective by virtue of being more entrenched in the bureaucratic practices of sending and receiving states alike.

More generally, executives historically have been more expansionistic in their approach to immigration than Congresses, in part because of these very foreign affairs imperatives. And as the Obama administration's relief initiatives reflect, in the face of a polarized political climate that exacerbates the already considerable difficulties of achieving legislative reform, the executive sphere can provide a rich site for migrants and their allies to lobby for their interests and, to a lesser extent, the interests of those who have not yet arrived. In other words, domestic institutions actually contain a range of entry points for existing and would-be migrants' claims, even under hostile political conditions.

* * *

Migration may be a global phenomenon, but its logic does not necessarily produce global regulation. Ideally, we would live in a cosmopolitan world order in which traffic across borders is coordinated, voluntary, and rights respecting. But because we are far from a world of frictionless movement and instead face a system where state interests take primacy, it becomes imperative to identify the forms of regulation most likely to take migrants' interests into account and to develop the means of advancing them. Once we shift to the realm of the possible to focus on where migration regulation is most likely to occur, the importance of domestic processes to the protection of migrants' interests becomes inescapable. One implication of the discussion I hope to initiate with this chapter is that advocates for migrants' interests in migration itself should channel their efforts toward the domestic level and the particular constituencies with incentives to advance migrants' interests, as well as toward the diplomatic establishments of sending states. Retaining a primary focus on the domestic level does not mean abandoning the project of global labor migration. But we should put the utility of that project into perspective and think about how it can reinforce the tendencies of democratic states to account for the interests of people outside their formal purview.

NOTES

Thank you to Bruce Ackerman, Owen Fiss, Paul Kahn, James Silk, and participants at the Yale Law School Human Rights Workshop for their insights on an early version of this chapter. I am also very grateful for the excellent research assistance of Christina Koningisor and Yenisey Rodriguez.

1. I cabin the question of whether an open borders regime would be optimal from migrants' standpoint, both for practical reasons—to limit the discussion to the realm of the institutionally viable—and because I believe states and their citizens have interests worth protecting that could be undermined by friction-free migration. As Christiano observes, there is a cost to democratic states being overwhelmed by migration, given that the existence of robust democracies is central to the long-term promotion of cosmopolitanism and global governance; he justifies the right of wealthy democracies to exclude in order to advance the agenda of building international institutions that will be more likely to assist the world's poor. Thomas Christiano, "Immigration, Political Community and Cosmopolitanism," *San Diego Law Review* 45 (2008): 933. Instead, I frame migrants' interests as one relevant, albeit crucial, factor that must inform debates about how to regulate migration. And so, while concerned to think through how best to capture interests easily elided by the governments and structures that channel migration, I do not reject the discourse of migration management altogether.

2. According to one estimate, approximately one-fifth of all migrants in the world, or 40 million people, lack legal status. Frank Duvell, "Irregular Migration," in Alexander Betts, ed., *Global Migration Governance* (Oxford: Oxford University Press, 2011), 78. "Some irregular migration is permanent immigration, some is temporary, and some is for transit. . . . The motives of individuals range from seeking refuge, finding employment, joining family members, and gaining experience to pursuing lifestyles." Ibid., 80.

3. For a discussion of the potential of transnational social movements to advance the interests of unauthorized migrants and a canvassing of the relevant literature, see Jaya Ramji-Nogales, "Undocumented Migrants and the Failures of Universal Individualism," *Vanderbilt Journal of Transnational Law* 47 (2014): 56–60.

4. For a leading and early call for the establishment of an international organization that would harmonize nations' admissions and residency policies, see Jagdish Bhagwati, "Borders beyond Control," *Foreign Affairs* 82 (2003): 98.

5. Christiano himself emphasizes that the existence of robust democracies is central to the long-term promotion of cosmopolitanism. The challenge becomes understanding what facilitates cosmopolitanism in democratic decision making.

6. For a discussion of states' preferences for high-skilled migrants, as well as the controversies associated with such migration, and the obstacles to freedom of movement for this type of migrant, see Alexander Betts and Lucie Cerna, "High-Skilled Labour Migration," in Betts, *Global Migration Governance*, 60.

7. In the United States, though small numbers of visas, whether permanent or temporary, are available for nonprofessional migrants, the system of family-based migration is often characterized as a substitute for admissions of low-wage workers.

8. I have called this the admissions-status trade-off—"a dynamic whereby the acceptance of large numbers of immigrants is accompanied by parsimonious treatment of those same immigrants" that helps explain illegal immigration. Cristina M. Rodríguez, "The Citizenship Paradox in a Transnational Age," *Michigan Law Review* 106 (2008): 1112. See also Christiane Kuptsch and Philip Martin, "Low-Skilled Migration," in Betts, *Global Migration Governance*, 50–54.

9. As Joseph Carens puts it, the question is not whether the state has a right to make a decision regarding immigration and citizenship but whether the decisions the state makes are moral. He argues, "State sovereignty and democratic decision-making are morally constrained." Joseph Carens, *The Ethics of Immigration* (Oxford: Oxford University Press, 2013), 6–7.

10. For a classic argument in defense of open borders based on borders' arbitrariness, see Joseph H. Carens, "Aliens and Citizens: The Case for Open Borders," *Review of Politics* 49 (1987): 251–73. For a developed argument that open borders are morally required based on democratic principles such as freedom, equality of opportunity, and substantive equality, see Carens, *The Ethics of Immigration*, 225–54. In her work, Ayelet Shachar analogizes birthright citizenship to inherited property and critiques the way in which both serve to perpetuate divergent life prospects in a world of unequal states and societies. Ayelet Shachar, *The Birthright Lottery: Citizenship and Global Inequality* (Cambridge, MA: Harvard University Press, 2009).

11. Shachar advocates imposing a levy on wealthy countries whose citizenship is "valuable" in order to redistribute resources as compensations for the asymmetries of birth; she emphasizes that open borders can be only a limited means of remedying global inequalities because of the very few people who would be able to meaningfully pursue betterment through migration. Shachar, *The Birthright Lottery*.

12. Stephen Castles and Nicholas Van Hear identify a growing sedentary bias in development discourse that assumes low-skilled migration should be stopped but accepts that the wealth will be mobile. But they

argue that "the history of human development shows that people have always enhanced their capabilities and livelihoods by moving from poor areas to those offering more opportunities. . . . In other words, strategies to stop migration through development are misguided, because migration is more likely than immobility to lead to better livelihoods." What is more, they argue, contrary to popular assumptions in the same discourse, "development is likely to initially increase emigration rather than to reduce it." Stephen Castles and Nicholas Van Hear, "Root Causes," in Betts, *Global Migration Governance*, 297.

13. This principle borrows from Rogers Smith's idea of "constituted identities," according to which the United States becomes responsible for facilitating noncitizens' status in the country, to the extent U.S. actors have constituted individuals' identities in ways that make a relationship with the United States fundamental to their capacity to live a good life. Rogers M. Smith, "Constitutional Democracies, Coercion, and Obligations to Include," in Jeffrey K. Tulis and Stephen Macedo, eds., *The Limits of Constitutional Democracy* (Princeton, NJ: Princeton University Press, 2010), 280–96. He argues that this principle means that Mexicans are entitled to greater access to the American polity than are nationals of other societies. For an elaboration of the policies this principle might require, see Rogers M. Smith, "Living in a Promiseland? Mexican Immigrants and American Obligations," *Perspectives on Politics* 9 (2011): 545–57.

14. Some scholars have pointed out how this discourse attempts to depoliticize migration governance because it "negates the existence of divergent interests and asymmetries of power and of conflict both within and between countries" by suggesting that policies can be divided into the workable and nonworkable. Martin Geiger and Antoine Pecoud, "The Politics of International Migration Management," in Martin Geiger and Antoine Pecoud, eds., *The Politics of International Migration Management* (New York: Palgrave Macmillan, 2010).

15. Multilateralism, or at least bilateralism, in immigration has been justified on many fronts. In addition to the efficiency case for global governance based on the need to address externalities, equity-based distributive arguments and the impetus to protect the individual rights of citizens and migrants have been characterized as requiring interstate cooperation. Alexander Betts, "Introduction," in Betts, *Global Migration Governance*, 24–28.

16. Peter Schuck has articulated many of these limitations and argued that burden sharing is crucial to transforming the international system into an effective regime of protection. Peter Schuck, "Refugee Burden-Sharing: A Modest Proposal," *Yale Journal of International Law* 22 (1997): 243.

17. For an analysis of the welfare externalities imposed by migration and an argument that restriction is therefore not necessarily inefficient, see Alan O. Sykes, "The Welfare Economics of Immigration Law: A Theoretical Survey with an Analysis of U.S. Policy," in Warren F. Schwartz, ed., *Justice in Immigration* (Cambridge: Cambridge University Press, 1995), 168–79. For an argument that states' concerns with economic migration have led them to "shade" on their obligation to refugees, see Ryan Bubb, Michael Kremer, and David I. Levine, "The Economics of International Refugee Law," *Journal of Legal Studies* 40 (2011): 367.

18. Peter Schuck, "Refugee Burden-Sharing: A Modest Proposal, Fifteen Years Later," John M. Olin Center for Studies in Law, Economics, and Public Policy Research Paper No. 480 (2013), 38–43.

19. In addition to the foundational work of Joseph Carens cited earlier, see also Mathias Risse, *Global Political Philosophy* (London: Palgrave Macmillan, 2012) (arguing that it is unjust for persons with the good fortune of being born in resource-rich countries to exclude others from sharing in the wealth); and Arash Abizadeh, "Democratic Theory and Border Coercion: No Right to Unilaterally Control Your Own Borders," *Political Theory* 36 (2008): 37 (arguing that a state must either allow freedom of movement or involve potential immigrants in the democratic processes that determine border restrictions).

20. Dani Rodrik puts it especially pointedly: "If international policy makers were really interested in maximizing worldwide efficiency, they would spend little of their energies on a new trade round or on the international financial architecture. They would all be busy at work liberalizing immigration restrictions." Dani Rodrik, "Final Remarks," in Tito Boeri, Gordon Hansen, and Barry McCormick, eds., *Immigration Policy and the Welfare System* (Oxford: Oxford University Press, 2002), 314.

21. David Abraham identifies "two hearts that beat inside the liberal breast"—a human rights liberalism, which recognizes all individuals' right to pursue their choices regardless of their place of birth, and communitarian liberalism that prioritizes redistribution and social justice, which is best realized within national contexts and through the formation of solidarity with one's own community. David Abraham, "Doing Justice on Two Fronts: The Liberal Dilemma in Immigration," *Ethnic and Racial Studies* 33 (2009): 968. This tension helps explain the absence of consensus concerning the moral status of the economic migrant among left-leaning liberals and is only compounded by similar sorts of tensions along more conservative points on the political spectrum.

22. Studies of public opinion research highlight the difficulty of pinpointing the true sources of resistance to immigration, in part because of the difficulty of conducting adequate research. For instance, one re-

cent study concludes that economic explanations for opposition to immigration find weak support in the United States, and the concerns about cultural identity are more likely to shape American attitudes. D. Stephen Voss, Jason E. Kehrberg, and Adam M. Butz, "The Structure of Self-Interest(s): Applying Comparative Theory to U.S. Immigration Attitudes," in Gary P. Freeman, Randall Hansen, and David L. Leal, eds., *Immigration and Public Opinion in Liberal Democracies* (New York: Routledge, 2013), 93–95.

23. While this sort of redistributive approach may provide a crucial and perhaps even the best response to global inequalities, it elides the interests individuals have in migration itself, which may change if opportunities to live a meaningful life in one's home country expand, but which are likely to persist for myriad reasons, including the likelihood that income disparities will survive even meaningful reductions in poverty.

24. For elaboration of this point, see Rey Koslowski, "Global Mobility and the Quest for an International Migration Regime," in Joseph Chamie and Luca Dall'Oglio, eds., *International Migration and Development: Continuing the Dialogue: Legal and Policy Perspectives* (New York: Wiley, 2008), 104.

25. Christiane Kuptsch and Philip Martin explain that the "reciprocity principle so central in the international trade regime is absent with international migration," including because the demand for low-skilled workers in wealthy countries is relatively low, and such workers tend to benefit discrete sectors rather than the economy as a whole. Kuptsch and Martin, "Low-Skilled Migration," 46. Alan Sykes calls this the "one-way" problem, whereby workers from one country have an interest in moving to another whose workers have no interest in trading places. Alan O. Sykes, "International Cooperation on Migration: Theory and Practice," *University of Chicago Law Review* 80 (2011): 327–30. "Issue linkage" may provide a solution, he argues, such that the sending state can offer other things in return for admission for its migrants. Ibid., 328. Especially in an international setting, such exchanges will be enormously bureaucratically complex and may have more promise in bilateral settings, as I explore later.

26. For discussion of "return agreements" signed by the EU with seventeen countries in Europe, Asia, and Africa that address comanagement of illegal immigration, as well as information campaigns sponsored by European governments in sending states regarding the dangers of illegal immigration, see Duvell, "Irregular Migration," 83–87.

27. Kuptsch and Martin, "Low-Skilled Migration," 54.

28. For a sharp critique of the idea of a World Migration Organization modeled on the World Trade Organization, on the grounds that migration implicates very different interests and structural relationships between citizens and their states and among states than trade, see Timothy J.

Hatton, "Should We Have a WTO for International Migration?," *Economic Policy* 22 (2007): 342, 373.

29. Betts, "Introduction," 9, 13. For a summary of the leading governance institutions, including one dialogue launched by the United Nations and the Multi-lateral Framework on Labor Migration initiated by the International Labor Organization, see ibid., 12–22, and Kuptsch and Martin, "Low-Skilled Migration," 39–41.

30. Kuptsch and Martin, "Low-Skilled Migration," 45–48.

31. T. Alexander Aleinikoff, "International Legal Norms on Migration: Substance without Architecture," in R. Cholewinski, R. Perruchoud, and E. MacDonald, eds., *International Migration Law: Developing Paradigms and Key Challenges* (The Hague: TMC Asser Press, 2007), 467–79.

32. For an account of global migration governance along these lines, see Betts, "Introduction," 4–7.

33. Jennifer Gordon describes an agreement between Spain and Morocco whereby Morocco monitors and polices unauthorized migrants from other nations in exchange for Spain's admission of Moroccan workers. Jennifer Gordon, "People Are Not Bananas: How Immigration Differs from Trade," *Northwestern Law Review* 104 (2010): 1141n137. For a general argument regarding trade-offs, see Marion Panizzon, "Temporary Movement of Workers and Human Rights Protection: Interfacing the 'Mode 4' of GATS with Non-trade Bilateral Migration Agreements," *Proceedings of the Annual Meeting, American Society of International Law* 131 (2010): 135.

34. For a discussion of this "pragmatic rather than normative" logic in relation to illegal immigration, which "unfolds along the paths of irregular migrants," see Duvell, "Irregular Migration," 99–100.

35. For the leading analysis of Mexico's multifaceted emigration policy, see David Fitzgerald, *A Nation of Emigrants: How Mexico Manages Its Migration* (Berkeley: University of California Press, 2008). For discussion of efforts by the Mexican government and other networks to enhance the welfare of Mexican migrants in the United States, see Cristina M. Rodríguez, "The Transnational Regulation of Migration," *Columbia Law Review Sidebar* 110 (2010): 7–9. I argue that "the civil society networks, in particular, reflect the burden-sharing ethos, demonstrating through actual practice a commitment to treating migration as a binational responsibility requiring transnational mechanisms of governance. The concepts of 'burden sharing' (or mutual obligation) and 'management' (or regulation) thus offer general but sufficiently substantive umbrella ideas under which to develop the mechanisms of bilateralism." Ibid., 9.

36. Gordon, *People Are Not Bananas*, 1126.

37. See Betts and Cerna, "High-Skilled Labour Migration," 64–66.

38. For an analysis of such agreements and their reliance on source labor countries to identify, screen, monitor, and oversee the return of temporary workers, see Eleanor Marie Lawrence Brown, "Outsourcing Immigration Compliance," *Fordham Law Review* 77 (2009): 2475, 2499. In her work, Brown also highlights how cooperation across bureaucracies can streamline or "improve" labor migration by helping receiving societies to select foreign workers who have been screened by their home governments for reliability and by enlisting governments of sending societies to ensure that migrants do not overstay their visas. Such efforts might help expand support for migration in domestic contexts by making it seem more orderly and law-abiding, but they also reflect how migrants' interests can diverge from state interests—the former may tend toward either prolonged or permanent relocation, and the latter may tend toward resource acquisition through cyclical migration without regard to how long any single migrant individual spends abroad.

39. For accounts of worker abuses, some of which arguably stem from structural features of the program, see North-South Institute, "Migrant Workers in Canada: A Review of the Canadian Seasonal Agricultural Workers Program," 2006, 11, www.nsi-ins.ca. Some commentators criticize the move away from permanent migration toward temporary labor migration in Canada as unlikely to provide Canada with a stable labor force and as exclusionary of low-skilled migrants in the interest of preserving a particular vision of the Canadian nation-state. See, for example, Delphine Nakache, "The Canadian Temporary Foreign Worker Program: Regulations, Practices, and Protection Gaps," in Luin Goldring and Patricia Landolt, eds., *Producing and Negotiating Non-citizenship: Precarious Legal Status in Canada* (Toronto: University of Toronto Press, 2013), 71, and Salimah Valiani, "The Shifting Landscape of Contemporary Canadian Immigration Policy: The Rise of Temporary Migration and Employer-Driven Immigration," in Goldring and Landolt, *Producing and Negotiating Non-citizenship*, 55.

40. See Brown, "Outsourcing Immigration Compliance," 2498–99.

41. Gordon, *People Are Not Bananas*, 1142–43.

42. Some scholars cast the "blame" on Mexico, arguing that the negotiation of an accord depends on the sending state's ability to control its borders—an ability Mexico lacks. Pamela K. Starr, "Challenges for a Post-election Mexico: Issues for U.S. Policy," *Law and Business Review* 13 (2007): 799, 816. Whether this limitation is the result of lack of capacity or lack of will, it is also likely to undermine enactment of domestic legislation expanding migration, though a bilateral approach still will be less attractive because its upsides will be less apparent.

43. For a general discussion of these dynamics, see Adam B. Cox and Cristina M. Rodríguez, "The President and Immigration Law," *Yale Law Journal* 119 (2009): 458.

44. Rodriguez, "Transnational Regulation of Migration."

45. Betts, "Introduction," 18–19.

46. Rodriguez, "Transnational Regulation of Migration," 7–8.

47. Jennifer Gordon, for example, advocates the formation of a transnational migrant workers organization and proposes that receiving societies require potential migrants to commit to adhering to certain principles of labor citizenship to ensure that migrant workers do not undermine labor conditions. Jennifer Gordon, "Transnational Labor Citizenship," *Southern California Law Review* 80 (2007): 503–4. Such commitments could result in greater openness to economic migration, though they could also raise its costs and diminish its desirability for employers.

48. I have argued, for example, that the major immigration reforms of 1965 that rid the U.S. Code of national origins quotas stemmed not from any sort of meaningful public deliberation over the purposes of immigration law or the interests of migrants themselves but instead from ethnic lobby pressures, State Department influence, and a significant but amorphous desire on the part of officials to harmonize the immigration law with the ethos of the landmark civil rights acts enacted around the same time. Cristina M. Rodríguez, "Immigration and Civil Rights," *Daedalus* 142 (2013): 232.

49. Voss, Kehrberg, and Butz, "The Structure of Self-Interest(s)," 109–10.

50. Given the tilt of the American system toward family immigration, this expansion does not necessarily reflect an overt consensus regarding economic migrants, but, as noted earlier, family migration in the United States amounts in practice to a form of admission for lower-wage workers.

51. Studies of public opinion suggest that more educated citizens are more likely to value cultural diversity and have the cognitive sophistication to "grapple with a complex world," suggesting that exposure to democratic norms through education builds support for immigration. Voss, Kehrberg, and Butz, "The Structure of Self-Interest(s)," 101.

52. Peter Schuck, *Citizens, Strangers, and In-Betweens: Essays on Immigration and Citizenship* (Boulder, CO: Westview Press, 1998), 93–96.

53. Gary P. Freeman, Randall Hansen, and David L. Leal, "Introduction," in Freeman, Hansen, and Leal, *Immigration and Public Opinion in Liberal Democracies*, 2–3.

54. For discussion of the work of these networks in promoting cooperative efforts to regulation migration, see Philip L. Martin, Susan F. Martin, and Patrick Weil, *Managing Migration: The Promise of Cooperation* (Lanham, MD: Lexington Books, 2006), 232.

INDEX